By the Same Author

EPITOME OF CHORAL TECHNIQUE

THE ART OF THE CHORAL CONDUCTOR

THE CONDUCTOR *RAISES* HIS BATON

SHARPS AND FLATS
IN FIVE DECADES

Sharps and Flats in Five Decades

AN AUTOBIOGRAPHY

BY

WILLIAM J. FINN

FOUNDER OF THE PAULIST CHORISTERS

HARPER & BROTHERS PUBLISHERS

NEW YORK and LONDON

CONTENTS

v

PART TWO

Tuning Before the Prelude

THE writer of an autobiography normally writes only one narrative of his life. Therefore, he has no opportunity for practice, and, since only by practice can one acquire a deft technique in any art, the odds are against him. This is to be an autobiography recounting musical experiences. Therefore, I must be careful to set the right pitch at the outset, and, if fortunate in catching the correct vibration-frequency, I must adhere to it faithfully throughout.

If the pitch were to be too low, the tale would be dull, probably weighted with the heaviness of self-importance, the writer seeming to take himself too seriously. If too high, the thinness of his timbres would make his recitatives and arias too baroque, too facetiously piquant. A well-organized gamut requires good intonation. Silly anecdotes, irrelevant to purpose or plan, break a gamut into the shapelessness of bad intonation. It is easy to make inane tunes even more fribbling.

If the pitch be fluctuating, even a trivial tune cannot be manufactured. There will be no arcs of melody to hold the attention of an audience. There will be few left, after the start, to listen to the fiddle-faddle.

In tuning up for this historiette, I have made several attempts to capture and hold captive the right pitch—the heart of the right pitch. I wonder if I am fortunate in this final effort? I'd rather be *sharp* than *flat*, but I honestly wish to be *natural!*

Sound the A, Mister Oboist!

A Short Prelude on a Ground Bass

CAN you define a *Ground Bass?* Musicians know that it is not a species of fish belonging to the common perch family ground into small particles fit for dusting into a New England chowder. A ground bass, if you pronounce the second word *base,* is a musicial theme used persistently on the lowest line of a composition. It is a clear and ever-recurring melody. The ear is addressed by it at the start, and its constant iteration and reiteration keeps listeners aware of it.

Concertgoers recognize the ground bass as the outstanding feature of a slow three-beat dance named *passacaglia* by the Italians and *chaconne* by the French. Perhaps the most celebrated ground bass in music is the German Bach's Passacaglia and Fugue in C Minor.

Here is the theme of that great composition:

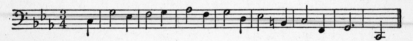

This melodic pattern throbs through the whole one hundred and twenty-four measures of the stately opus. Occasionally the ground bass is transferred to other voice lines, notably in the fugue proper where the higher *rilievos* * convert the broad boldness of the bass melody into italicized acuteness. When a passacaglia or chaconne is finished, the principal impression retained by the listener is of the ground bass.

Is this an odd manner of beginning what you know to be my effort at autobiography? Probably. But it is necessary for me to write this album of reflections and reminiscences over a basic theme. Without a ground bass whose insistence would point to real values, I would be conscious of stupid futility in assembling the material. Just as the notes which I have given above come through the whole composition of John Sebastian Bach, so the ground bass melody of this book must declare itself throughout.

Here is my Ground Bass. It is neither an improvisation nor an adapted motif. It is a fact. A truth. The fundamental truth of an art, an art richer, more colorful, more irresistible than any other medium of aesthetic communication:

* *Rilievos:* the high, medium or low positions of musical phrases.

Music (after religion and racial prepossessions) *is the most powerful spiritual instrumentality by which human beings can be moved.*

This is the theme, then, over which the episodes of my musical life will reveal themselves.

I have been aware of this throbbing theme during my many decades on the podium and the organ bench. There was an impelling urge within me from my mid-teens to discover and to reduce to formulae for general use the elements which impart such spiritual potency to music.

During my boyhood I loathed music! A strange start? Perhaps. But you see, I was a real boy, and in my time, the Boston boys figured that music, crocheting and knitting were of the same ilk. Interest and skill in any of the three suggested a petticoat and hair ribbons.

But I graduated from boyhood and its Arcadian whimseys.

Harry Hansen, distinguished literary critic, reviewing one of my recent volumes,† congratulated me for emphasizing substantial topics in it rather than reminiscences. But this, however, is not to be a technical treatise. Certainly, the chief convictions which have sprung from the Ground Bass over the years will make their appearance, but the *raison d'être* of these pages is different from that of my other efforts at literary communication. This is an over-the-shoulder look at many years of pioneering on the podium; a kaleidoscopic survey of the major musico-psychological experiences and reactions of an organist, choirmaster and orchestra conductor.

Friends, former choristers, professional musicians and educators have urged me to write these reminiscences. Friends of a lifetime usually like to review the whys of one's doings before the public. The former choristers are interested in having the picture of their own picturesque pasts spread out before them. Perhaps some professional practitioners of the art of music expect a confession of Svengali trickery. Probably, in fact most likely, a few pedagogues who have found me a most troublesome person for so long will search the book for discrepancies between what I've written and lectured about, and the procedures which will accidently disclose themselves in these candid memoirs.

There are two tough problems to be met fairly. First, what material to exclude; second, how much of later impressions and convictions to consider as influences at work in my earlier days. I'll try to be conservative, even though the imagination of a musician is not a substantial guarantee of moderation.

These analecta are not a chronological record, but a summary of incidents that marked a long journey to the vales and mountains of Thessaly toward which I early set out, hoping to scale Mount Parnassus, home of the Muses.

† *The Conductor Raises His Baton* (New York: Harper and Bros., 1944).

Probably I was not conscious of going off on a great expedition. But much more than probably, I was subconsciously aware of the start. The itinerary was of course undisclosed. Certainly—how certainly!—I never arrived at the top of Parnassus, but I had many interesting, exciting and enlightening adventures while attempting the ascent. A few times I thought that I was in sight of Delphi or the Castalian Spring on the southern slope. Every once in a while I would catch a refrain from the symphonies on the Mount. Sometimes Apollo and Euterpe were kind, whispering a phrase or two about their mysterious art. Often, and most of the time, they were indifferent to the strainings and strivings of an untrained mountain climber. Very likely I spent too much time on the northern slope! When the wind was blowing down the mountainside in my direction, I could hear Orpheus plucking sweet music from his lute. On such occasions I would be refreshed, encouraged, reassured.

For long periods on end, however, the wind did not blow in my direction. No melody would ride a zephyr down the trails. There were times when good reasoning should have urged me to abandon the journey, retrace my steps and settle down in the ease and security of mediocrity. But Horace's *nulla vestigia retrorsum* (no steps backward) is too sharp a prod to be ignored, and so the journey continued day after day into the long series that made it year after year.

The trip to Parnassus is long and arduous. It is a trip away from superficiality and smugness in unsubstantial achievement. There are many obstacles to surmount within oneself and without. There are many intersections of paths to be studied lest an error in choice send one in the wrong direction. In the many ravines one finds dire aloneness. One shivers frequently with an icy hopelessness. Black nights and foggy days. Feebly marked trails and inviting fissures. Eerie voices. Fears hovering and perils prowling. When the wind blows long in the wrong direction one needs much determination, fortitude and singleness of purpose. Altogether a formidable pilgrimage!

Nevertheless, he who would be a bona fide artist must undertake the journey. If his footprints are not to be found on the trails, they will never mark the parquet of even any small village's Hall of Fame. Obstinately, with the seeming foolhardiness of artistic abandon, he must pursue the course until he reaches the spot as near the hearthstone of the Muses as the full quota of his spiritual, mental, aesthetic and physical resources makes possible. Otherwise his alleged art-product will be shallow sham. His technique will outline only vague silhouettes. Color, beauty, significance will be missing. Validity, vitality, value—of these there will be none.

PART ONE

Chapter I *Some Themes Developed from the Ground Bass*

WHEN I was about sixteen years of age, I started out on the trip to Parnassus. I was not an ordinary chap. By no means! The whole family, including cousins at Albany and Rondout, New York, had tagged me subordinary. I was as highly esteemed in the blood-relative circle as a Republican bee in a Democratic hive.

Before my sixteenth birthday, I had had no slightest hint that I would be interested in music. During the ensuing winter, however, the first notes of the Ground Bass must have sounded clearly enough to awaken some feeble response within me. Before that season music had been a major annoyance. I disliked the sounds which I was obliged to listen to in church, at recitals and at concerts. If music had a cultural value, as aunts and uncles as well as parents were wont to insist, then I was all for chucking culture. Perhaps the cold, snobbish, modern-ancient Athenian atmosphere of Boston of the 1880's and 90's provided a background and perspective in which everything that savored of culture seemed artificial, overrighteous and puritanical. All the boys in my neighborhood abhorred music, poetry, painting, sermons and lectures, dancing lessons and the long list of other things that we were told were essential to goodness and refinement.

A visiting aunt, who, I feel sure now, had a fairly good soprano voice, would irritate me to nervous discourteousness by her daily chirping of *do mi sol do*'s. The local church choir made even more dread the dreariness of the typical New England Sunday. We were grateful, however, for one feature of that stiff Sunday holiness: the solemn and always-to-be-observed custom of pulling the dark green shades and closing the piano, with the stool pushed under a square instrument or well out of the way to the side of an upright, lest a holy visitor, even if only one's own kin, be shocked by the impression that someone had surreptitiously been manipulating the ivories. It was good to be forbidden to play the piano on Sundays. The Saints knew what unsaintly thoughts were uppermost in our minds on weekdays when the mater or an aunt or a presiding maid

3

would send us to the parlor in turn to whack out scales and Czerny's *Five-Finger Exercises*. My brother and I developed a delightful feud about practice periods. We deliberately allowed confusion to grow as to our exact times. He was learning to scratch the fiddle and I was learning to tell the white from the black keys on the piano. It wouldn't do for the two of us to assail the quiet of the capital city of the Bay State with our unmodulated rackets at the same time, so both of us skipped many a practice period with the thoroughly valid but hypocritical excuse that each thought the other to have priority on the period.

At church, where the whole family except the pater, who usually had a round of medical calls to make before noon, would gather for the second time each Sunday morning (the children had attended the early Sunday-school Mass and the Queen of the household an even earlier Mass), the booming of the organ at High Mass, the stridor of what I learned later to be reed stops and string diapasons, the stabbing piquancy of piccolos, four-foot flutes and high mixture combinations, the violent impacts of the choir with tortuous and meaningless phrases, and the long drawn-out cadenzas of calliopic sopranos at the ends of *Credo*'s and *Gloria*'s (how I detested Haydn's Sixteenth Mass!)—these and similar experiences were part of the price I must pay for being alive and a BOSTONIAN!

The music lessons and the smell of fish cooking on Fridays were twin bogies. These had to be endured; there was no escaping them. And dressing up in a black broadcloth Eton suit, with high button boots, a derby hat and a walking stick to go to a recital of Chopin's music! The Little Lord Fauntleroy suit and Chopin's Etudes were equally in my disfavor. It would have been pleasant to learn of a great fire in which all pianos had been burned, with the House of Lords thrown in for extra fuel. A real hatred for piano music and the British peerage had developed, for the latter not because of my Irish ancestry but clearly because of the silly Fauntleroy rig. I think, too, that culture made such demands upon us that the "refined" boys wore curls down to the shoulders right up to the preadolescent finish.

Clementini and his Sonatinas, and, after a while, the arithmetical calculations of Bach would reduce me to a state of the most torpid inertia. Every so often my brother and I were required to go to the home of a relative to perform for the household in an effort to attest the cultural purposes of our parents before skeptical aunts and uncles. Probably we did little to clear away their doubts.

Music was an unqualified nuisance, and practically all the boys in the Mount Pleasant district felt as we did: you were a sissy if you liked music, and an ass if you submitted voluntarily to study and practice.

And yet, at sixteen I was aware of a developing aesthetic sense. Little by little I outgrew the distaste of the junior years. I began to be keen about certain phases of the art. The melody of the Ground Bass which was to give direction to my adult life was beginning to disclose itself. More and more notes of the theme were assembling. Of course, there was in me a latent talent for musical expression which the preoccupations and biases of my Bostonian boyhood had suppressed.

There must have been a moment of sudden conversion from the prejudice against music in general which stands out as one of the clearest memories of my childhood. I had been an anti: why had I become a pro? I suppose that the answer is simple. Probably the dislike I felt for music was nurtured deliberately in my conscious mind while I was too young to be guided by any subconscious impressions. The Bostonian proprieties emphasized the summum bonum of acquiring culture. And a boy among boys didn't have the nose to appreciate the aroma of what seemed to be a weed rather than a flower.

I could not disregard the growing sensitiveness to the intimations of music. Much music that I continued to hear still annoyed me, but evidently the Muses had cleared some sound tracks to my subliminal self. I began to be strangely moved by snatches of melody and harmony that I would hear occasionally. The most impressive of these *moments musicales* seem, at this distance, to have been casual. That is to say, they were not connected with any organized or professionally prepared exercise of the art.

A few experiences that gave new orientation to appreciation merit chronicling. One of these had to do with the organ playing at the High Mass which had contributed so much to the Boston Sunday gloom. The organist had begun to improvise between the liturgical canticles and hymns. Perhaps he had been improvising long before I was sensitive enough to take sympathetic cognizance of what was in progress. But about that time, I heard that Archbishop Williams of Boston had stated to a group of Catholic organists that, except during the Consecration at the Mass, an organist should always have his fingers on the keys. Sudden modulations to set compositions were abhorrent to the quiet atmosphere demanded by aesthetics as well as by piety for religious worship. Therefore, the organist was to prepare, by suitable improvised interludes, for the prescribed anthems. At any rate, the organist at the parochial church began to arrest my attention with striking progressions of chords played quietly. These progressions would take hold of my imagination. The absence of splutter and bombast and the gentle movement of delicately fibered triads carried certain vague but quite delightful intimations. Naturally, I couldn't analyze the intimations then, nor have I ever been able to interpret them. They were from the latencies of music, the underneath profoundness of the art, the plinth upon which my Ground Bass has stood so firmly for so long. After High Mass, with these triads fresh in mind, I was wont, at first furtively and shamefacedly, to sneak into the parlor, throw the Boston Sunday shroud off the piano, try to reproduce the chords, memorize them, and join the family at the "Late George Apley" Sunday dinner.

This Sunday dinner of the Finn family in the eighties and nineties was the formal domestic event of the week. It was a rite. A ceremony with a protocol. Throughout the city probably the same ritualistic solemnity was observed. Thoroughly New Englandish. A dash of puritanism in the soup. A garniture of prohibitions decorating the roast. Subdued, desultory and prosy exchange of sentences between the adults. "Little children should be seen but not heard" was exemplified in the strict conventions which made the food tasteless and the whole ceremony vapid. We children were allowed short rations of conversation. And pianissimo. If much pianissimo sibilation was observed by the governor, suspicions would be aroused in his French-trained Celtic mind, and one or more of his progeny would be banished from the dining room. How often I missed the rice pudding or pumpkin pie!

Frequently, the governor's suspicions were justified, for our underbreath murmurs usually bore upon the possibility—not the probability—of avoiding the walk to the maternal grandfather's home, whence, after the usual and thoroughly restrained expressions of delight at beholding us, aunts and uncles would send us across the street to the Church of the Immaculate Conception, administered by the Jesuit Fathers, for Vespers. If the weekly High Mass at the parochial church was a heavy experience, Vespers, with the long Psalms, the *Hymn, Magnificat* and *Anthem,* was a service which would begin to cast its shadow upon us early on the preceding Saturday mornings. We had a tough Sunday! Strictly from the human point of view of strictly human children, oh my, of course! But while aunts and uncles permitted their avuncular and auntish spirits to rest in the sweet repose of a Sunday afternoon coma, Mollie, Willie and Jimmie Finn (sometimes Anna who became a nun) joined Moses in his departure from Egypt across the street. The fifth Psalm was frequently the *In exitu Israel de Aegypto* (When Israel went out of Egypt). While Aunt Massie was accomplishing crescendos and diminuendos with soporific respirations, and Uncle Tom shook dust off the chandeliers with vibrant snores, we were beholding the picture of the river Jordan sending its waters back to its banks to provide a dry crossing for the escaping Jews, imagining the mountains rejoicing as rams and the hills as little lambs, and trying to figure out the truth of

Dominus memor fuit nostri, et benedixit nobis (The Lord was mindful of us and hath blessed us).

When Mr. George Whiting, organist at the Immaculate would play his own harmonizations of the Gregorian psalm tones, each verse being different and therefore unorthodox in the rating of rigorous liturgists, after I had become interested in music, I took keen delight in listening and even regretted that Moses' trip out of Egypt was not longer. I trust that the charitable reader (he or she who really understands the thirteenth chapter of St. Paul's First Epistle to the Corinthians) will not make a snap judgment to the effect that Mr. Whiting's unorthodoxy was what claimed my attention and won my approbation!

I used to listen for an occasional improvisation from Mr. Whiting, but he preferred apparently to adhere to written notation, for he seldom drifted off into the ether of musical clairvoyance. Once in a while, the announcement of Mr. Whiting's Echo Mass would get me permission to attend the High Mass at the Immaculate. This composition assigned some phrases to a semichorus singing behind a screen. The effect was both that of an echo as in the "Echo Song" of Orlando de Lasso, and of a choir of seraphs praying for human beings beyond the stratosphere, as in the *abbellimenti* of Allegri's *Miserere*.

So, you see, already some of the mystical potentialities of music had begun to attract my attention.

The fact that one never knew when the organist would play his dulcet triads in the parochial church or when Mr. Whiting would dress the Psalms in exotic harmonies began to stimulate a degree of expectancy about the Sundays, and I frequently was so intent upon arriving at the Immaculate that I forgot to look in upon the aunts and uncles and to bolster them up with a loving nephew's kiss.

On unlucky days, when neither the parochial organist nor Mr. Whiting obliged with the tidbits, I continued to suffer from the noise developed by the cataract of sharps, flats, fugues and counterpoints which rushed down from the galleries of both churches. In the parish church, my chief resource for whiling away the long *Gloria*'s and *Credo*'s was to study the interior decoration of the church, trying to figure out why the pastor had allowed real woodwork ornamentation and the imitation of this in plaster or merely in paint upon the walls to be distributed at such inexplicable random. At the Immaculate one could find delight in scrutinizing the faces of the angels which decorated the chancel walls. George Santayana, in his recent memoirs,* has given a charming description of

* George Santayana, *The Background of My Life* (New York: Scribners, 1944), pp. 169, 170.

these pictured disembodied seraphs and his reactions to seeing them.

Another experience at about this same time invigorated the growing Ground Bass with quite a crescendo. I began to listen to, and to watch, a venerable gentleman who sang at the Carmelite Monastery the Gregorian proses the *Rorate Coeli Desuper* (Rain down Dew from Heaven) four times during Advent, and the *Attende Domine et Miserere* (Attend, O Lord, and Be merciful) six times during Lent. He was a stately old fellow with enough of the characteristic Boston brusquerie to make us lads a bit careful with him. If we were stealing a smoke (Sweet Caporals!) near the convent gate when he came swinging along twirling his stick, we were hard pressed to avoid a taste of its fiber. Report credited him with having had a notably good lyric tenor voice in his younger days, but the ruthless calendar of years had long since dispossessed him of both younger days and voice. The sounds which emerged from his long-wearied larynx were, by any strict criteria of timbre and quality phonation, on the pain-provoking side. The old arytenoids simply couldn't manage the pitch-tensing required for good intonation. The veteran's Adam's apple did considerable bobbing up and down, and surely the old gentleman's blood pressure registered high when he lunged at the top notes. But he was extraordinarily effective (and not in the satirical interpretation of the phrase!). He was making the sounds elsewhere than in the larynx. That is, after the withered cartileges and worn-out muscles had put together acoustically their maladjusted elements, his mind and soul took over, converting really ugly tones into agencies of aesthetic and spiritual worth.

I don't mean to imply here that correct and good vocalization are not essential to the correct and good performance of music. This was obviously an exceptional instance, one in which the psychological effect of the old man's effort was immediately more discernible and telling than the physical effect. (There is a subtle point involved here. It should interest artists.) I used to be amazed at the disparity of the acoustical and the over-all impressions made by his chanting. This, in a manner of speaking, "gave to think." Out of a voice box whose paneling was warped in some places and cracked in many others emerged a compelling effect. His soul seemed to come through ahead of the notes. One could tell from the changing lights in his eyes. It was impossible *not to know* from the physical reactions of his body to the texts of the two great chants. If, in the days when his voice was sure and supple, his interpretative contributions were as convincing as on these occasions referred to, the effect of his singing must have been moving, indeed.

From this experience, I learned to look for something underneath the mere notes, for latencies hidden in sounds which could be brought to the surface only by processes which transcend technique—and for the key to the code of the Ground Bass.

My first lessons on the pipe organ helped to clarify this new state of mind still further. (Perhaps the zeal of the lady organist who strove quite successful to dress up the banality of the tune of "Holy God We Praise Thy Name" was a factor which influenced me to sign up for these lessons.) The Chopin-Lord Fauntleroy combination had continued to predjudice me against the piano and my father prophesied that my interest in the organ would be short-lived.

The organ teacher, Mr. John Hession of the local church, explained at the outset the general classification of organ stops, their division into families of tonal timbres. Like the orchestra. Of course, at that time, my information about the orchestra was limited to the recognition of differently shaped and constructed instruments, the names of many being unknown, and the quality of their characteristic tones and contribution to the whole unsuspected. At any rate, he instructed: draw these stops and you'll have the effect of the two flutes (those long black tubes into which the player blows while the tubes are held horizontally between the left and right hands!); draw those, and the sounds will be those of violins; over here for small violins such as your brother plays; up here for somewhat larger ones (which were to become my favorite orchestral instruments—the violas); over there for medium-size violins (cellos); and down in that corner for the great violins (bass viols), but you must play the notes to sound these latter with your feet. And so on. He acquainted me with the various controls for oboe, clarinet, English and French horn colors, etc. This revelation of the many tone colors of sound and their easy control opened up a new vista of musical speculation. I had heard these different species of tones, of course, in listening to orchestras and organs but was not interested before in identifying them more specifically than louder or softer, more or less piercing, pleasanter or less pleasant. I think that I knew, at my first organ lesson, what I would seek in music, viz., a control of tone colors, a blend of seemingly opposed timbres, and probably, although I cannot be sure that it crossed my mind at the moment, what the old tenor chap had intimated in his chants.

During ensuing lessons, besides the technical instruction for manipulating the manuals and pedipulating the pedals. Mr. Hession illustrated further the relationships of the tone colors. At my request, he sometimes played the progression of triads which had caught my fancy in church, using combinations of lovely shades and tints: flute with light string—it was more than beautiful, it gave off an essence floating through the vaulted church with a living vibrancy which made you feel lonely when it had gone altogether; flute and oboe, rich, communicative, convincing

as by tonal telepathy; eight-foot flute and *vox celestis* in the tenor range
stirring vague memories and vaguer hopes with its lovely iridescence of
viola-cello unison.

Yes, those first organ lessons brought my awareness of the Ground
Bass almost to its last notes, as though I could hear all save the last two
measures of the Bach Passacaglia theme. These final measures came
through presently and with dazzling clarity.

My mother, a dainty little somebody of exquisite natural graces which
she had pointed up from girlhood by devotion to the Supernatural (she
was always an intransigent Bostonian, too!), chose me as her escort to
the service of Tenebrae at the Holy Cross Cathedral. She said, equivalently, in her most delightfully modulated voice (with its very broad
a's and undulating crescendos to the verb of a sentence and ensuing
diminuendos to the period) : "Willie," (I have forgiven few individuals
who had the temerity to address me by so effeminate a name!) "it will
be a long service, and you will probably suffer ennui to a degree, but the
chants will interest you in some places. It is a liturgical service dating
back to the earliest days of the Church." (I looked up "liturgical" in the
dictionary.) "Please do not squirm in the pew." And then she probably
added, as she often did, since a sense of humor is never more keen than
in a truly spiritual person (even in a Bostonian!) : "And don't look
about, for people will study your face and affect to see a resemblance to
your mother. You cannot imagine how awkward it is for people to remark that you resemble me."

And so, with the procedure "briefed" as the word is now, we set off to
the Cathedral, where archbishop, bishop, chor-bishop, monsignori, reverend doctors, reverend fathers, reverend deacons and subdeacons, sub-
ordinate seminarians, choristers young and old, acolytes, and cute little
window-dressing altar boys assembled for the great Holy Week function. The Cathedral was dark, not only with a low degree of visibility,
but dark with the sepulchral joylessness of Antiphons and Psalms
grunted with hollow resonance by the seminarians; dark with that ponderous obscurity which envelopes loud bass-baritone intonations in the
second Gregorian (hypo-Dorian) mode.

Suddenly I was aroused from a deepening lethargy. I fancied first
that my mother had nudged me into consciousness, but I saw that she
was absorbed in the service and altogether unmindful of her difficult
progeny. Like a ray of light, not glaring, not brilliant, but illuminating
and revealing, through the somber darkness came the intonation of boys'
high soprano voices. I learned later that they were singing the treble line
of a harmonized "Lamentation." The Tenebrae "Lamentations," even

when indifferently rendered, are memorable items in the Church's liturgy. These voices curved upward and downward, topping what seemed to be a beautiful mixture of undervoices, insinuating thoughts that defied easy interpretation. I knew nothing of the appositions of the voice lines of a chorus at that time, and could make no analysis of the combination of timbres which produced so psychic an aura in the Cathedral.

Later, years later, I identified this. The unworldly effect which had arrested my suddenly concentrated attention was due to the seemingly high, floating, volatile quality of the soprano voices over a seemingly well-balanced unit of altos, tenors and basses. I go straight back to that experience in accounting for the tenacity with which I have clung to this fundamental of choral and orchestral efficacy, viz., that the treble line (in the chorus, the sopranos; in the orchestra, the first violins, flutes, oboes, first clarinets, trumpets and first French horns) must be projected out and over the other lines, in the literal sense of *sopra,* which of course means "above," with more of suggestion than of actual dynamic reality. The treble line, when composed of natural harmonics and intoned overtones of the lower parts, should pick up elements from below, and with fleecy floating move about as a cloud which comes into being by drops ascending from beneath.

I must record here, that when I described my reactions to the "Lamentation" to a later teacher of mine, Samuel Brenton Whitney, of the Episcopalian Church of the Advent, Boston, this distinguished organist and master of choristers was interested but amused. He said something like this: "I think I know what you are trying to express, but words cannot convey your impressions. Words are too stiff. I feel something akin to those impressions of yours when I have accidently drawn the right treble stops on the organ, perfectly balanced over the lower timbres, and have opened the swell-box shutters to the exactly effective degree. *But it was the acoustics of your Cathedral that really did the job for you.* The soprano tone of the boys there could never produce an ethereal effect unless the vaulted Gothic roof, the long nave, the transepts and the acute apse had completely made over their tone production."

Some years later, Mr. Whitney and I went several times together to listen to that Cathedral choir. We sat at different spots on different occasions. Reasonably close to the chancel, the sopranos sounded very badly. Far from creating a spiritual aura, they stimulated painful reactions. The boys snarled; they tossed ugly sounds up to the high arches. But when we sat far back in the nave, we caught the disembodied effect which I have described. The arches had metamorphosed their outcries. Mr. Whitney commented at length on two points; first, on the influence of acoustics on the *impressions* which tones can create; second, on the fact that I was heading in the right direction if I was determined to discover the mystical qualities of music.

Apropos of acoustics, it is not a digression (could there be a digression in such a recording as this?) to state that I became interested at once in observing various phenomena of acoustics and therefore I owe much to Mr. Whitney. Regarding his comment about the quest for the spiritual: this came as a confirmation of my own conviction, for at that time the Ground Bass was vibrating *con brio*.

I studied organ and boy-choir training with Mr. Whitney during the period in which I was engaged as organist and choir director of the Mission Church of the Redemptorist Fathers. I shall write of this period in due course. In gratitude to Mr. Whitney I am impelled here to acknowledge his excellent tuition. In the organ field he was a specialist in in Bach's works and passed along the best Bach traditions with simple but thorough pedagogy. In the boy-choir field, he was an out-and-out American-Englishman; that is to say, all of his ideas, approaches and techniques were British-made. Although the development of a better method of training boys than had been in vogue since the Renaissance may be credited to the English cathedral choirmasters of the middle and especially of the late nineteenth century, it cannot be said truly that their scheme was apt for evoking the spiritually aesthetic qualities. Up to a certain point this English Cathedral technique is excellent, being compounded of processes which are based on the related facts of physiology and the physics of sound. But the processes are only remedial or preventive. They do not extend to the building and expanding of positive natural qualities in the boy's voice. Therefore, the aura is missing from the intonations.

The distinctive feature in the singing of the average English Cathedral chorister is its artificiality. The trained English boy *hoots* from his little choir stall. And so, of course, all boys all over the world who are trained after the English fashion hoot or make other kindred hollow sounds. Later on, in the course of these memoirs, I shall have opportunity of referring to this topic in connection with my journeying along the trails to Parnassus. I learned something in England—not something which the English did but what they needed to do. I am sorry that Mr. Whitney had missed this. He was one of America's greatest organists and choirmasters, sharing leading choral distinction with Mr. Messiter of New York, and I know that he would have been happy in discovering what I discovered at a rehearsal one day in London, and worked out in my Chicago choir hall by the trial and error method. It was only after I had left Chicago and operated in New York for some years that I was able to simplify and to put on paper the procedure for eliciting the spiritual intimations from sopranos. Probably, by that time, I had arrived at a spot on Parnassus where fairly often I could hear the duets of Euterpe and Apollo.

To revert to my teen age, the influence of the experiences which I have recounted was paramount in determining my relationship to the art of music.

You can see, from the material in this chapter, that the Ground Bass and the early themes that sprang up from it as inescapable corollaries gave direction to my life. The ups and downs on the trails to Parnassus were full of interest and excitement. Stopped by circumstances here and there, sure enough, but never so thoroughly impeded as to be unable to resume the journey.

Chapter II *The Ground Bass Moves into the Treble for a While*

THE theme of the Bach Passacaglia in C Minor passes from the bass to the treble line in the eighty-ninth measure, returning to the bass in the one hundred and twenty-ninth. With me, the Ground Bass climbed the treble staff much sooner after the start. It seemed to me, without analyzing the premises, that I should focus immediate attention on the *sopra* aspects of choral music. The soprano voices in the Tenebrae "Lamentation" had first caught my interest, and similar soprano voices in the same choir later, while listening with Mr. Whitney, without the purifying help of acoustical improving, had well-nigh threatened me with disillusion. And so I busied myself at once with experimenting. The first experiments of course antedated my acquaintance with Mr. Whitney. Therefore, it would be inaccurate to indicate that my first efforts with sopranos had been colored by the glum grayness which pursued me for some time after going back to the Cathedral with Mr. Whitney. I met Mr. Whitney when I was twenty-one years of age.

My first venture as a choirmaster was in my seventeenth year. One of the curates of the parish church selected me to guide a chorus of untrained boys averaging twelve years of age. The choir carried the heavy title: The Crusaders' Choir of St. Patrick's Church, Roxbury.* Why the alleged singing unit was dubbed thus I never learned. Were the old Crusaders organized into choral units which would chant the Gregorian unisons of the eleventh, the organum and descants of the twelfth and thirteenth centuries, and the multipart, if crude, polyphonies of the fifteenth?

Perhaps my vigorous Crusaders were not supposed to have kinship with the seekers of the Holy Grail. Maybe they were waging a crusade against something of which I was kept in velvety ignorance unless it was directed against the choral art. In retrospect, however, I can perceive adequate reason for the title, for the noise which came from those boys' throats, in the middle register, was not unlike the probable noise of the

* Roxbury is a district in the city of Boston.

clinking and clanking armor plates of the knights when their horses were galloping full speed onward. The piercing shrieks of their voices trying to hurl the top notes down the aisles were as the cries of tortured steeds when foemen's lances found deep targets in their flanks. To undertake to convert these vigorous, valiant and vociferous American Celts into musical instruments, with the signally scant information at my disposal, was rash, indeed. Perhaps in later years I could have prescribed some musical medicament to quiet their undisciplined braying. I am not sure. The memory of it marks it incurable. Then, however, I felt that I had accomplished a feat of which parents, aunts, and uncles, and even second cousins should be proud if I kept the hardy lads in some sort of order (the curate would bob in and out of the room).

That curate was zealous surely, but as surely unoriented. He knew that he wanted the boys to do something that would savor of religious and of Bostonian culture, but he did not know what he wanted. He was no help. In fact, he was quite a pious nuisance. To begin with, he would call me "Willie" in a loud voice and frequently during the so-called practice periods (the word "rehearsals" must not be affronted by use in this connection!). At every repetition of the effeminate vocative, my husky and raucous urchins would intone a fugue of what I shall call, for the polite needs of a book, horse laughs. The name of a juicy little subacid berry could also be used with dramatic effect as a tangy expression of the general idea. This young ecclesiastic, inflamed with ardor for showing the pastor and perhaps the archbishop what he could accomplish with the little gamins, would beat time for the hymn tunes, with a long blackboard pointer, on the floor. With the thick end. And he had no sense of rhythm, unevenly thumping out three thuddy beats when there should have been four, and four when only three were indicated. (I might early have developed facility for conducting the 5/4 movement of Tchaikowsky's Sixth!)

In the midst of my amateurish effort to straighten out a resonant disagreement as to whether F sharp, F natural, E or G should be sung in deference to the composer's intentions, and similar efforts, the monitor-curate would throw a mighty thump at the church floor and cry out: "Willie, what on earth are you bothering about? Don't make the little boys nervous. It sounds very well. God"—in a softer, saintlier tone— "is not annoyed if some boys sing one note and some another. The congregation will not be critical."—And again in the louder more worldly tone—"Get on with it. There's another new hymn to be learned and there are only a few minutes left for practice."

I resigned after six months of futile activity. But that was my start. I had gone down the wrong lane. Spirituality? Aura? Aesthetics?

Soprano tone quality? Evidently I had taken up with the wrong group
of crusaders. Years later, upon hearing the lovely melody in Pierné's
"Children's Crusade," beautifully sung by boys and girls, I went back in
memory to that strange start.

Children three were we,
On our way to meet Jesus.

That was the text of the Pierné refrain. History tells that the children
did not arrive at the Holy Land, many having been drowned in the
Mediterranean and others sold into slavery, but my Roxbury children
crusaders would have forewarned the entire Mohammedan empire of
their march. Their outcries would have spanned the inland sea and
hordes of Moslems would have been ready to massacre the entire company.

Perhaps it was fortunate to have begun in untoward circumstances.
One cannot rightly evaluate the worth of difficulties. It is likely that hard
beginnings are good discipline and that if one continues to strive, having
learned something from the difficulties, these may be recorded among
the best assets of a career. My experience with the Roxbury Knights
taught me definitely what I did not want. It made clear that the raucous,
untrained chest tones of small boys were the ugliest utterances possible
to human beings. Years later, however, I came to the conclusion that the
unnatural, affected and vocally insincere *whoings* and *kooings* of the
choristers trained after the scheme of the English foundation choir
schools might successfully challenge the right of the Roxbury Lancers
to the medal for worthlessness. Probably in the period intervening between the Roxbury experiment and the day in England when I finally
admitted to myself that the British choirboys' muttering of vowels with
lips pursed into vertical ellipses and cheeks sucked in between upper and
lower molars had neither musical nor psychological kinship with the
Ground Bass, I was sensing the fact that properties from the Roxbury
and the Thames extremes could be brought together to serve as a basis
for correct training. Finally, I did work out an alliance for good tone
quality between some features of these widely opposed uglinesses.

After recuperating from the rigors of my winter with the curate and
the Roxbury Stentors, I started off again, the route taking me this time
to a group of adult female sopranos and carelessly termed contraltos.
To record that the group was merely adult and female would be shame-
fully unfair to the long service which many of the grandmothers had
rendered in praising God from choir lofts. These pious songbirds had
twittered on the branches of oak trees since early acorns had sprouted
sufficiently to provide first twigs. There were folios of reminiscences of

the long ago in the notes which these haloed ladies caroled forth. Often, in the fastnesses of afteryears, the echoes of their laryngeal exercise would startle and dismay! My task, as officially explained to me, was to improve the chanting to the extent of having all members of the charming sorority open their books to the same pages, read the music and text right side up, begin together, continue together as far as feasible, and conclude approximately at the same time, within, let us say, the latitude of some seconds.

Since my Ground Bass theme was then up on the soprano staff, I directed my attention to the quality of the intonations of the holy women. That was a mistake of sizable dimensions. I proposed to the mid-Victorian "cantatrices" that at first we devote the major part of practice time to clearing away the most outstanding obstacles to tolerable singing. I probably suggested that the type of warbling to which they had for so many years been inured was minus the properties which could be considered an asset to religion. With the tactlessness of youth and inexperience, I began to raise quite a row in the practice room, and at public services I would glare with undisguised censure on my heavily bonneted old girls. Many of these had been patients of my father who was the senior physician in the district.

They tolerated the revolutionary and ungallant schemes for a fortnight or more and then cut loose at me. They used the imperative mood, while my mood became morosely subjunctive. With mid-Victorian deftness they hurled stinging sentences at me. Not a split infinitive in the lot, the adverb always preceding the preposition in their careful structure of this much-abused part of speech. They threatened me with my father, a menace of no mean might. They knew of the razor strop which the Doctor kept handy for stropping his sons. It was understood throughout the neighborhood that the Doctor liked his boys to have a good edge, and he was an expert at producing edges.

Naturally, I made swift haste to modify my methods. The difficulty of making adequate explanations at home prevented my withdrawing from the post. And so, in a mild, negative fashion, I endeavored to make music from unmusical elements. I had had a bad time with the gamins, but at least I could get square with them after practice periods, and even during these, when the curate wasn't looking, it was comforting to place an accurate wallop in the ribs of a particularly tough egg, or to pull down vigorously the lobe of a sneering urchin's ear. But one couldn't go about settling solid punches in the ribs of pious, middle-aged and venerable females. It simply wasn't done. Lord Chesterfield wouldn't have stood for that, and we were all out, in those days, for dear old Chesterfield. And then there was the razor strop! Scoffing and grimaces were of necessity abandoned. I tried a few ineffective vocalizations, but the raspiness, hoarseness, stridency and general off-pitch character of their imitation of singing had been distinguishing marks of their style long before I rolled out of the cradle. They had built up a musical ethos of their own.

This set-up was obviously hopeless. Apollo and Euterpe, having heard some of the squeaks and squeals, hurried off to hide in a secret den. The Ground Bass had left the treble line and broken itself into fragments that required some pushing together to reassemble itself, just as in the Bach Passacaglia, the theme, leaving the definite locale of the treble, spreads itself through figures and arpeggios from the one hundred and fifth to the one hundred and twenty-ninth measure.

From my experience with the elderly women and the young boys, I learned that it was necessary to find a remedial plan for stripping voices of encumbrances and constrictions before one could reasonably undertake the task of furbishing latent good qualities. I began to ask questions and to read. The average chorus in Boston at the time had a shrill and unlovely soprano tone. The masters couldn't talk clearly about tone quality, for they simply didn't know. I filled ears and notebooks with their platitudes, carried them around for a while and presently dumped them as useless. A dozen years later, I had a similar experience with the publicized masters of polyphonic music. These were theorists in polyphony, but they could not make the written notes sound as music. When questioned, these and the Boston choral directors talked glibly on the periphery of the subjects, but couldn't find a crack through which to penetrate to the center. There is quite a gap between theory and practice which, at an early age, I realized one would have to find a good bridge to cross.

At this juncture, I came upon a remarkable book, *The Boy's Voice,* by the Englishman, John Spencer Curwen. The book was a digest of the opinions and methods of the leading English cathedral choirmasters of the latter half of the nineteenth century. Dr. Curwen had canvassed the field thoroughly, having visited most of the great song schools of the English Cathedrals, talking with the masters and observing them at rehearsals and services. At one time I practically knew this book by memory. The outstanding feature of Dr. Curwen's findings was that the great majority of the leading British choirmasters agreed upon two points of procedure as being indispensable to the preparation of boys for duty as choristers. They could readily have agreed that these two points were applicable as well to female sopranos, and to all types of voices with some modifications.

Then I looked for other books. I found several. The two most important ones were those by Sir George Martin, of St. Paul's Anglican

Cathedral, London, and Dr. George Edward Stubbs, of St. Agnes Chapel, New York City. These authors were in substantial agreement with the views so well epitomized by Dr. Curwen. One Englishman, Dr. Varley Roberts, of Magdalen College, Oxford, published a monograph in which he disagreed with his colleagues, arguing for a system of training which would put more body into the middle register.

But I must not anticipate here. The reading of Dr. Curwen's book left me prepared to deal with boy sopranos to a certain point, if given a free hand under fair circumstances.

Chapter III *Men's Voices Vocalize over the Ground Bass*

AFTER doing my stint with the *choeur des dames,* I went off to college, where, with the Ground Bass still broken into arpeggios, I continued on the circuitous paths to Thessaly. The college was a preparatory seminary for junior candidates for the priesthood. I had arrived a day or two in advance of the returning students and was examining the single-manual pipe organ on the eve of the opening Solemn Mass, when a prefect seminarian, in charge of the choir, noticed me. He asked if I could play the organ? Would I be available for the Solemn Mass? Would I be too nervous, playing an unfamiliar instrument? Could I read Gregorian chant?

Upon receiving affirmative answers to all but the last two questions, he proceeded to instruct me in the Gregorian notation. The book in use was a very thick volume which would not remain open readily at the correct page. The edition of Les Coffres Frères, Paris. The notes were like tiny flyspecks. The clef signs looked like hieroglyphics, faint and faded as though made in the era of Cleopatra. No stately G clef with its fancy serif; no unmistakable F clef marking F on the fourth line of the staff. Little *do* and *fa* clefs, sometimes on one line, sometimes on another; confusing guide notes at the end of each staff; no indication of key or pitch; no hint as to the time value of the notes or the tempo of the melody. But the prefect was a good teacher, clearly underlining the principal points. As soon as he had ascertained that I was facile in the movable *do* system, we made rapid progress.

This movable *do* system had been thoroughly taught throughout the grammar school grades in Boston and, even in our junior days when we disliked music, the boys as well as the girls learned the simple system and acquired and easy skill in translating notation to sounds. We learned to read music as we learned to read English. Progressively. We could parse musical phrases as we could parse English sentences, and conjugate the flat and sharp keys as we conjugated verbs—I have, you have, he has, key of F, one flat (B flat) ; do on F, first space treble clef ; fourth line bass clef; fa on B flat, third line treble clef; first space above the bass clef, etc.

With this background, it was easy to achieve quickly a facility in reading the Gregorian melodies which were all written out in the *do re mi* symbols. The prefect said that each note had practically the same time value, that there were no measures and that the notes proceeded at about the speed of the spoken syllables of words. I was told to supply simple harmonies, and the keys for the proper pitches were written down for me.

I went to the organ for the Mass without much nervousness, and was proceeding with increasing ease for a while until I realized that either I myself, or a group of singers, or the little one-manual organ was contributing an element hitherto unknown to me. Was I reading the notes correctly? It seemed so. Was I depressing the right keys on the manual and pedal board? Yes, as far as I could ascertain. Was I keeping the organ in time with the singers? Apparently. Was the progression of chords according to the accepted norms of harmony? I could detect nothing irregular. Well, what was wrong?

During the interval in which the subdeacon was chanting a long epistle, the prefect assured me that all was going comfortably, and I looked for the first time over the singing group which included all of the student body. I was amazed to discover several boys in knicker-bockers and several gangling youths evidently in the twilight between boyhood and early manhood. These smaller boys and the youths had probably been making the sounds which every once in a while during the *Introit, Kyrie* and *Gloria* had been disconcerting me. During the *Credo,* I nearly lost my place a few times by listening to the strange sounds made by a few sopranos over the adult student body and the stranger splutterings and sirenlike whoops of the twilight lads. Changing voices, I learned afterwards, of course!

But that experience was my introduction to the deadly effect on music of such unprepared, unrefined and unforgivable unison-octave singing, the type which unfortunately and unnecessarily prevails in the majority of junior high schools, junior colleges and preparatory seminaries. Unison-octave singing, unison-octave registration on the organ, and unison-octave playing in the orchestra can be developed into an extraordinarily beautiful agency of musical expression. But changing voices, those which slide up and down octaves out of control, hopping from the low bass clef to the high treble and down, somersaulting through thirds, fourths and fifths when the progression calls only for a semi-tone—to employ these with the inartistic and insouciant freedom noted in our junior institutes is to aim a blow at the art of music at a time when it is sure to do the most damage to the appreciations of growing youths. If the reader is a musician and interested in this technical point, I refer him to a book of mine, *The Conductor Raises His Baton.**

A wag might remark that since I have been citing frequently the position of the theme in Bach's Passacaglia, and since at this period I found myself among the broken arpeggios, I should consistently admit the propriety of the melodic line jumping about on the two clefs. But Bach, my dear banterer, preconceived an orderly plan for the migrations of his notes. A definite continuity is always in progress, but with the adolescent vocal jumpers, there is no prearranged plan. There is no means of foretelling when their voices will vault to the heights or plunge to the depths, when they will remain for a while in one region, or when they will undertake a series of most eccentric gaddings.

To encounter two such unfamiliar subjects as Gregorian chant and the changing boy voice at the same time was a bit on the exciting side. It was easy to make reasonable progress in the chant, for in spite of all the current nonsense about it being difficult, complex rhythmically and esoteric, it is the simplest of the musical art forms, and, when stripped of the confusing terms with which many teachers have obscured it, is easily mastered. But the matter of the changing voice is a challenging one. It is enough here to record that I was studying the subject for fully fifteen years before I was satisfied that I had worked it out satisfactorily. Fifteen years to find out, and only fifteen minutes required on the lecture platform to unfold the technique!

During the two years which I spent at the preparatory seminary, I was in charge of the junior choir, but was allotted insufficient time to do much more than tinker. I think that I did make some experiments with two-part singing, but I can't remember having learned much from the enterprise. The boys were not interested, and the schedule for prayers, classes and studying was rigorous.

During that time, however, I profited from my acquaintance and association with Father John Bannister Tabb, the great poet-priest. He was a well-trained musician. From observing him at the piano after supper in the recreation hall, playing excerpts (sometimes entire acts) from the operas, my interest in the latencies of music grew into a most active curiosity. The Ground Bass had come down from the treble and settled itself firmly once more in the solid notes. Oh, it was to go up again certainly, and have a place of power in the treble line, just as Bach's theme necessarily ascends again to the top line in the driving exposition of the fugue. But now it was down. As the old chanter at the Carmelite Convent had unwittingly turned my mind towards the non-

* (New York: Harper and Bros., 1944), pp. 133 ff.

physical side of music, so Father Tabb, with his most impelling and sometimes almost frenzied interpretation of scenes in the operas (he always epitomized the story before playing), whetted my inquisitiveness about the psychological, emotional and spiritual communicability of music. He would often break out into song. As he played, sometimes the music would paint so vivid a picture in his mind that he was literally forced to sing the texts, and, poor though his voice was, he would practically hypnotize the large group of students who were standing near. Soprano, contralto, tenor and bass arias, recitatives, soliloquies, conversations. He knew them all, could and would play the chief figures of the orchestral score, and undoubtedly made every listener conscious of the emotional experience of whatever character he was portraying. Manrico singing in the tower before dying, Manon pleading with Des Grieux at St. Sulpice, Desdemona praying her "Ave Maria" before Othello smothered her. Elsa, Marguerite, Carmen, Micaela, Lohengrin, Valentine, Faust, Don Jose and the toreador—all came to life in that recreation hall; came to life and told what he or she was experiencing in those make-believe circumstances. Athanael groaning in his difficulty about Thais never groaned with groans so real on any stage, I venture to state, as when interpreted in the thin, reedy voice of Father Tabb.

Frequently when Father Tabb would be passing a room in which a student had a piano practice period, he would stop, listen and fling open the door, shouting to the embarrassed lad, "You have no feeling! The music means nothing to you. Give it up. Go in for algebra or trigonometry. Bah!" Father Tabb was an "intimationist" (do you mind the coined word?) in poetry and in music. He sensed the entente between these two arts, and sought to make potent the latent implications both in his writing and in his music. His sonnets are just fourteen-line arrangements, if you fail to follow his clues to many under ideas. His "Brother Ass and St. Francis" is a silly fancy if you don't catch the inner refrain. Each word and each note is as if in code.

My progress along the route to Parnassus was, during those two years, slow, quiet and not too disturbing. I had begun to read the history of music, and to parallel periods and styles and developments with the contemporary events and points of view outlined in general history. This exercise awakened an interest that was to endure, viz., an interest in music as an expression of the minds and manners proper to different peoples at different times.

During my second year at the preparatory seminary, I was appointed to conduct the classes in Gregorian chant for the lowest form. Twice a week the students were wont to gather in their various class rooms, and

after a few instructions in the chant itself, they would rehearse the
variable parts of the Mass for the following Sunday. But in my class, I
was held to instruction in theory for the first semester. It was incumbent
upon me to instill knowledge about notation, to explain the eight different modal scales, and to teach the psalm tones of the eight modes so that
the beginners' class could sing them by memory. The assignment presented me with excellent opportunity for discovering some salient points
about teaching. I learned almost immediately that I should have to make
deep research into the secrets of good pedagogy if I were ever going to
develop into a teacher of anything. I had been a failure "all bound round
with a woolen string" with the crusading Spearmen and with the tonal
executioners of the "chignon choir," † but these failures were only rehearsals for the grade A flop which my best friends on the campus
agreed I made as a college professor.

The class over which I affected to preside was made up for the most
part of youngsters, but many youths older than myself were included
in the personnel. They disliked plain chant more belligerently than I had
disliked the Fauntleroy editions of Chopin. They made no effort to concentrate on my erudite observations about the place of the square notes
and the funny little diamond-shaped things on lines and spaces. In
magnificent silence they shouted their instinctive antipathy to the *do re
fa sol fa—fa, fa mi do re* of the most lugubrious of the psalm tones.
They brought schoolbooks, storybooks, letters and letter-writing material
into the classroom, and immersed themselves in things of purely personal, non-Gregorian interest as soon as I had mounted the dais and begun the professorial monologue.

After a few weeks of honest but inadequately enlightened endeavor,
I succumbed to the prevailing epidemic of indifference and made a deal
with the students. I pointed out the necessity of giving audible evidence
to the adjacent corridors and to the scrupulous scouts from the head office who might be on patrol duty there that we were at work on the
chants, and that if they would agree to a man to sing a chant lustily
every ten minutes or so, they could well do what they wanted the rest
of the time.

The scheme worked for a few months, our outbursts having been

---

† *"Chignon choir"* was a term of opprobrium used by liturgical purists in my
early days to designate a choir made up of female sopranos instead of liturgically
approved young males. *Chignon,* the French for "hair twisted into a knot at the
nape of the neck," seemed an appropiate epithet to the ultra-rigorists. I sometimes
suspected that one or two exceptionally biassed individuals would have been happy
if the twisted knot of hair could have been slipped around to the front of the
throat, and pulled taut around the breathing apparatus of all female singers, and
the way cleared for a world-wide glorification of boy sopranos.

fortunately timed. But before the end of the term, the President sent for me and told of the report handed in for some successive weeks by the scouts who, at first accidentally and then by carefully arranged strategy, had discovered my disedifying ruse. He told me that if certain members of the faculty had not interceded for me, I would have been dismissed not only from the high office of Sixth Form Plain Chant Professor, but from the college as well. (Some American-born members of the faculty had probably remembered the tedium of their own sessions with the chant.) I was ordered, as a religious penance, to put the class on the strictest schedule, to prepare the unit for a gruelling examination to be conducted by the Dean of the Plain Chant Department, and to remain on the college grounds for the rest of the term when the others went off on prefected hikes. The wound didn't rankle badly, however, and some of the faculty found in the incident a source of amusement, affecting to crouch away from me in recreation as though I had been excommunicated.

What did hurt was at the very end when my lads, thoroughly reformed and decently dismayed at my plight, having passed the testy Dean's examination, singing all the psalm tones by heart including the "Tonus Peregrinus" about which many in the senior class (and some of the teachers) had a comfortable obscurity, the President informed me that the stipend which was to have come to me as a professor had been forfeited. This was a cruel blow, for in fancy I had planned an easy summer to be financed by that stipend. My father, a real leader in the school of conservative parents, would never give his children money. We were brought up to the disconcerting but dramatic refrain that evil communications corrupt good morals, and money in the pockets of youths invites such communications. Of course, our strict parent had considerable on the ball there, as we are so acutely aware in these days when the opposite philosophy is in vogue, but he always pursued his convictions as far as they could lead him, often too far for me, and my only means of going down to Nantasket beach for a swim with my brother and taking on an adequate supply of Boston clam chowder and broiled lobster would be surreptitiously to use the professor's stipend when safe opportunities would present themselves. And so I had a Nantasketless summer.

In general, the two years at the preparatory seminary had sharpened my sense of musical understanding and although I did not have opportunity for regular practice on either piano or organ, I was surer of whatever tricks I had learned before, and the leadership of the junior choir had developed my confidence. I also learned Gregorian chant.

Upon my arrival at the major seminary of the Paulist Fathers at the Catholic University, Washington, the next autumn, the master of students placed me in charge of the choir of seminarians. The choir was accustomed to sing the unison Gregorian chants and some harmonized music as well. This was my introduction to the direction of an adult male choir. I cannot indulge in the type of satirical reminiscence which amused me a few pages back apropos of my venture with the adult females because the vocal endowment of the male group was promising —and besides, I have identified it! (Lord Chesterfield's, Maurice Francis Egan's, or Emily Post's warning about politesse!)

The personnel of the seminarians' choir was made up of tyros and seniors soon to be ordained. There were a few rather extra dry tenor voices, a few baritones who had been willing in preceding seasons valiantly to reach for tenor notes, some bona fide singing baritones, and, I think, two or three basses, the quality of these latter being resonant with masculine dignity if not with the ring of true *basso cantantes*. As usual, a minimum of time was allotted for rehearsals, since the schedule of the essential routine called for busy bell ringing from five o'clock in the morning to ten at night. However, we did manage to arrange a fair amount of practice time, for the young men were well disposed and keyed to the pitch of trying to do well whatever they undertook.

Along toward the first of October, the first assignment of my career to a public service before a congregation representing a cross section of many types of people loomed. How it loomed! And threatened! And cowed! The master of students instructed me to prepare the choir for the laying of the cornerstone of Trinity College, one of the first great institutes for the higher education of women to be opened under Catholic auspices in this country. The Apostolic Delegate was to be there. Visiting bishops, college presidents, clergy and sisters of many communities would assemble. I was told to plan and to produce a program of excellence, of such excellence that not only would the rites and the Pontifical Mass be properly accompanied by music, but that the transcendent ideals which the hierarchy and clergy and sisters had for some decades associated with all Paulist undertakings and participations also would be abundantly exemplified. This was a tough task. It would have been tough for a tanned and cheek-furrowed veteran.

I was nineteen years of age and most of whatever talent the Lord had bestowed upon me was just shaping into the chrysalis stage.

Several difficulties congregated in an unfriendly bloc. There was the problem of lubricating the dry-throated tenors. Even with the broad technique of half a century's acquiring, I find the lyricizing of this type of tenor one of the most enigmatical items on the agenda of a choral director. A dry tenor intones without fluency. One thinks a bit of spraying with eucalyptus oil might ease the functionings of the larynx. He makes sounds that are just sandy sounds in the tenor compass. There is little of what is implied by the word "music" in his throatings. He sounds as an English horn should sound, if it could sound, with the inner sides of the tube coated with talcum powder and one or both of the two reeds split at the tip. How to blow out the talcum and mend the reed?

Even with the tenors made liquid ("liquidated" has a savor of obituary finality!), there was still the problem, more of a *social* than of a *musical* nature, of dissuading the baritones who had been trying to soar with too much tonnage into the tenor range from continuing their uneasy flights. It requires more tact than one can get out of a textbook on metaphysics to persuade a holy man accustomed to sing the tenor parts that God, according to the natural evidence at hand, had destined him for a garden variety of baritone. He would feel unjustly demoted from the dignity of flower to that of a tare. One inured to the more melodious responsibility of tossing off the high notes rebels when told by a junior to descend to the lower rungs of the vocal ladder and to contribute to the less conspicuous serenities of harmony.

Furthermore, I didn't know what I could do to give the impression of solidity to the bass line.

But the job was to be done, and the master of students was known throughout the Paulist community and, in fact, quite generally in church circles as an "or else" man. (I don't remember the "or else" equivalent of that period.) Excuses offered for nonperformance to this excellent, if highly insistent, and bearded gentleman were roared down into unforgivable inanities. What a voice for rebuke he possessed! One of the unique agencies of sound and terror in this epoch! Put a walnut in the right position and his pianissimo sneeze could crack it open.

Well, his manner and his voice and his insistence were effective whips, and although I felt as though I were being "flogged through the fleet," I started to make the right motions and to let him know that I was making them. I was never really afraid of the "old man," though many of my fellow seminarians would tremble as the quivering aspen when his footstep forewarned of approach. I didn't plan to be howled down for a tepid, mediocre performance. He probably understood what was good for the cornerstone service and what was good for me. At any rate, we were tacitly fighting each other to good ends for the ensuing weeks. Occasionally he'd pull his beard or arch an eyebrow when passing the practice room as though to provoke me to greater efforts.

The singing seminarians, too, were conscious of his vigilance. And so we pitched in and turned out what was an amazing performance; amazing, not only because of my lack of information and experience, but because we actually made real music. I seem still to hear an echo of some the effects achieved even at this long distant moment. The Apostolic Delegate sent a note to the student master immediately after the conclusion of the service commending the contribution of the Paulist youths. The rector of the University, and the droll professor of Psychology who always impressed one as being more open to the findings of science than of art, and many noted visitors were voluble in expressions of approval. It seemed that we had achieved a memorable tour de force.

However, lest the singers and especially myself be carried away with the impression that we were the American Sistine Choir, the master of students announced at the seminary dinner table shortly after the service that my leading "chanteurs" and myself would wait on table although out of turn. When I brought the soup plate filled almost to overflowing to the Bearded Voice, he sang out, *"Mr. Finn, take your thumb out of my soup."* The thumb was almost but not quite at the shore-line of the bubbling purée.

I have often adverted to that disciplinary strategy of the old gentleman. Dramatically he had inculcated the wholesome point of view about seeming successes. I owe him much for many good things. This was one of the best. Self-congratulation, excessive elation, satisfaction with one's achievement—how stupid, harmful, disastrous!

Many times in later years, somewhere in the middle ear of my memory, I heard the command, *"Take your thumb out of my soup."* The echo would register when sliding off the organ bench after great Cathedral services in many parts of the world, the musical contribution to the ritual having seemed to be strikingly effective. At New York, Boston, Chicago, San Francisco, Toronto, Paris, London, Lucerne, Rome! When stepping off the podium at Carnegie Hall, the Boston Symphony Hall, the Paris Theatre du Châtelet, the Chicago Orchestra Hall or Auditorium, the great concert arenas of the United States and Canada. When patted on the back by Isadore de Lara at Countess de Briganza's near the Trocadero in the world's gay capital. When acknowledging the plaudits of throngs of people at Balboa Park, San Diego; at stadia in Tacoma, Kansas City, Chicago, Hollywood; at Madison Square for a Liberty Loan drive; in the old, and the new, Madison Square Garden, New York, for religious, charitable, civic and patriotic ends; on Forty-second Street and Fifth Avenue for the home-coming parade of New York's Fighting Sixty-ninth after World War I; at the New York World's Fair. On so many occasions under gala conditions, dignitaries presiding and notables in attendance; in the Throne Room of the Vatican and in the Consistorial Chamber; before the Pope, cardinals, and high ranking prelates. Before several presidents of the United States in the White House; before British vice-royalty, and President Fallières of France with his cabinet, while that funny little Lehvinne, Chief of the Paris Police, annoyed us. When soprano boys would seem to have hypnotized enormous audiences, and the ensemble with or without orchestra had climbed to a high plane of artistic recreation.

Yes, on such tempting occasions and after what even coldly academic newspaper critics had acclaimed to be a *grand succès,* the thought of "putting my thumb in the soup" was a salutary influence. It tended to keep a man open-minded, to keep him from avoiding the miserable mistake of taking on dimensions, of thinking himself large, while knowing in his best self that he was only small, inconsequential and jejune. Smug people usually do slide their thumbs all the way into the soup.

And so perhaps the greatest value which accrued to me from those years in charge of the seminary choir was an understanding of the need to watch my thumb. Spiritually and psychologically this was good understanding.

Certainly, I advanced in technical knowledge and craftsmanship in that era. The Bearded Voice arranged for me to practice on week days on the pipe organ at the University chapel. This entailed missing the siesta, which, for chaps who had emerged from their quasi-monastic pallets at 5 A.M., was almost essential in view of the demands made upon energy and concentration during the late afternoon and evening. Twice a week, an organ professor would bicycle out from the city and instruct me in organ technique, harmony, counterpoint and composition.

I was carrying a heavy schedule. Too heavy, for, in my second year, after the Holy Week services which I had prepared and conducted with the seminarians at a local city church, I was obliged to return to my home in Boston for diagnosis and therapy. I am not implying that the master of students had overworked me with a sort of religious ruthlessness. He had kept me busy, indeed, and this training in keeping busy was to be an asset during ensuing years. But the reverend gentleman was unaware of a physical disability which has handicapped me all through my life. A careless nursemaid had left me, when I was two years old, on a grass bank after a long rain. I developed what is now known as infantile paralysis. The result of this affliction was, mainly, a definite damage to the nervous system. And so I eased out of the seminary for what was intended to be an indefinite period, but which was actually a year. During that time I was to make more progress to Parnassus than in all the preceding years, for in spite of a degree of physical disability I could not permit myself to remain idle. Therefore, I didn't really dally for more than a few weeks. I took on a professional engagement.

My assurance must have been appalling, for although I thought I was keeping my thumb out of the soup, I dashed about here and there where ordinarily intelligent men would agree there was no place for them.

I think I am right in stating that I actually created a position for myself. I opened a door and walked straightaway in. And, having opened, I let myself into an arena where things were bound to happen. Often this arena took on the shape of the Coliseum at old Rome. Lions, leopards and gladiators seemed to stalk my movements day and night. Some of the fangs and blades drew blood.

Chapter IV   *First Efforts to Blend High and Low Voices*

SHORTLY after returning to Boston, I assisted at the Vesper service of the Mission Church, administered by the Redemptorist Fathers. Visitors to Boston en route from New York glimpse this towering church building as they come within the city limits.

There was then a highly esteemed choir of women and men at that church. The organ was the first great electrically operated instrument to be installed in New England. Its twin went into Symphony Hall later. I remember associating the name "bulletin organ" with these two instruments, for by pushing any of several pistons (gadgets which brought into action various combinations of stops) white-faced numbers would register in little holes of a black tablet high on the right side of the keyboard to apprise the player, as by bulletin notices, of the combinations in use. Perhaps I bestowed the nickname myself, for even then I was well into the habit of attaching sobriquets to persons, places and all sorts of things.

My acquaintance with this organ began through my own daring, as reported above. On the evening of my first visit to the celebrated shrine of the Mission Church, I mounted long stairways to the organ loft. The choir was singing unison and harmonized Psalms. The vocal blend was superior to any chorus I had heard in such close proximity. The *In exitu Israel,* a long Psalm which invariably became tedious when sung by the seminarians, and the "Magnificat" were particularly impressive, and the organist operated his bulletin organ with notable ease and musicianly taste.

I was quite stirred by the experience. During the four preceding years I had been only at the producing end, having no opportunities of listening to other producers at work. The next day, bright and early, I went to the rectory adjacent to the Mission Church, calling for the Rector himself. My memory of the reason for calling upon him is vague. Perhaps I merely wished to express my appreciation of the high standard of choral singing which he was sponsoring, or perhaps, not urged by

31

such an urbane consideration, I merely intended to ask permission to examine the organ. (How many selfish motives we disguise!)

Whatever the reason, I was there in front of him. He was the Reverend Father John Frawley, C.SS.R., well known and deservedly beloved throughout the Eastern Province of the Redemptorist Fathers. I remember telling him how well the Vesper service had impressed me.

His reply was as startling to me as my next remark was to both him and myself. He said something like this: "Yes, that choir is without doubt the best choir in Boston, but I don't like it because the sopranos are women. In a great church such as this, and in a parish where hundreds of boys are available, *only a choir of boys and men is fitting,* in consonance with the long traditions of the Church. I would disband the present choir and organize a boys' and men's unit if I could find the right director. *No musicians hereabouts know anything about boys' voices.*"

And here is my rejoinder in substance: "Father, you are mistaken about the latter item. *I* am your man. I have been working on the subject of boy-voice training for several seasons and if you want a choir of boys and men, just appoint me director, and you will have one."

Chortling a bit, he stammered out a few comments, trying withal, as a priest and a Bostonian, to remain polite and inoffensive: "But what can you possibly know about such a choir? I am not interested in a namby-pamby, unskilled group of boys taking the place of our present excellent soprano choir. I want what you'll find in the great European Cathedrals. You probably play the organ like a piano player, and touch the pedals only on the second Tuesdays of the week. However, you have a lot of nerve, young man. You interest me. Return here tomorrow morning."

Upon my arrival the following morning, he summoned two of the Fathers attached to the parish, instructed them to lead me to the choir gallery, put me on the organ bench, turn on the electric motor, and ascertain if I could manage the big instrument and finally bring him my complete dossier. These two kindly Fathers, one a trained musician and the other a better-than-average diletante, en route to the organ loft, knowing that I could not possibly have had experience with the new type of organ, explained some of the main features which differentiated this instrument from the organs almost universally in use. They warned me about its sensitive action—that the slightest brushing of a key would open an electrical contact and produce a sound; that the controls of the shutters which made nuances of crescendo and diminuendo possible were operated by electricity; in brief, that I should abandon the conventional technique of playing old-fashioned tracker organs (with their long stick controls of notes and pipes) and the more recent pneumatic types. By the time we had finished the ascent to the gallery and I was about to display my prodigious mastery of a great art, I had reached the all-time (ante and post) low of my professional career. I could hear the old master of students crying out, not: "Take your thumb out of my soup," but: "Finn, you have spilled the soup all over me."

Through the spilling soup, however, I could locate the position of some favorite stops on each of the three manuals and pedals. So, still challenging the old master of students in my subconsciousness, I stilled his disturbing voice, drew the stops and, with the help of the Holy Ghost, the Blessed Virgin Mary, St. Cecilia, and St. Philip Neri (sponsor of Palestrina), actually made music in the great church. I touched the electrical controls very gently. I didn't attempt any fancy exhibitionism, such as many unwary candidates are wont to do, especially on the pedal board, but the Ground Bass was coming through, clearly and urgently. I heard myself controlling sounds such as I had only dreamed of before. After a few measures I became rapt in a great adventure, and the Fathers were obliged to remind me that they had other duties. Their report to Father Frawley induced him to put aside his misgivings about my youth and relative inexperience, for presently he appointed me to the post. I was worried then, not through fear of the undertaking which would be public and aesthically unpopular, but because I thought that I was depriving the incumbent organist of his position. When assurance came that he was to have taken another post in any event, I threw myself into the task of preparing untrained boys in a three months' period to take over in place of the ladies who not only sang uncommonly well but who had acquired a most extensive repertoire of masses, motets, and settings for various liturgical offices and oratorios.

I was clearly in a position where failure with its accompanying ridicule could bowl me over with leering finality. I signed up for organ lessons with Mr. Whitney immediately. I plunged headlong into an academic review of the principles of chorophony * which I had been studying, and inaugurated daily rehearsals with the boys even though they were on summer holiday from school. Father Frawley said that he wanted the three principal styles of ecclesiastical music exemplified, but that at the outset I could confine myself to the Gregorian chant and modern music, postponing for a while the polyphonic style. He did not realize what a boon this postponement was, for I had given no hint that the Palestrinesque style was a complete mystery to me, the meandering and seemingly unrelated series of notes on the various voice lines looking as musical to me as the graphs in the financial section of the Boston Transcript which purported to indicate the fluctuations of commerce.

* The choral art in all its aspects.

It was necessary to systematize the work at once. First, the boys had to be taught to *sing,* and immediately. The raucous utterances, which were the characteristic sounds made by boys in their throats in those days as well as nowadays, would have to be replaced by a smooth, fluent and mellifluous tone quality. I knew from my reading that this undertaking alone would normally require double the time at my disposal. Mr. Whitney was horrified when I told him in early July that the new choir was to make its debut in September. He insisted on the eight months of preliminary training which all British choirmasters agreed to be essential. When he realized that it was an emergency situation, he went vigorously to work with me, analyzing each successive problem with a view to practical help rather than merely for its theoretical interest.

Each week day found me on the organ bench from 6 A.M. until high noon. There were three early Masses to be accompanied; after these a funeral or wedding to be played, and then practice. If the list of services extended straight through the morning, I would return to the organ for practice in the early afternoon.

A soundless keyboard with pedals had been set up in a room off the gallery, and one could practice without the disconcerting necessity of always listening to notes. A quiet method of practicing has proved itself effective for various reasons in every phase of musical exercise. A chorus must be trained *pianissimo,* otherwise its *mezzo fortes* and *fortes* will never be musical; an orchestra must be deterred from practicing in the loud panels of the diagram of dynamics, lest the constant strain to the performing muscles and to the listening ears impede relaxed contact with notes and aesthetic satisfaction in hearing their own eventual performances. A great violinist told me once that he never practiced on the violin itself during a concert season. He would practice fingering in a basin of lukewarm water and draw an imaginary bow with his right hand. He didn't want to hear the sounds of the pieces he was to play lest the music become stale, and the performance perfunctory.

And so I would work away in the little anteroom, teaching my feet to move independently of my hands and evolving a special pedal technique for the upper pedal board, for one of the effects of the infantile paralysis was to make impossible the normal way of playing the upper pedal notes, viz., by depressing the black notes with the toe and the whites with the heel.

The Ground Bass was inaudible most of the time in those days. The aesthetico-spiritual potentialities of music are discovered ultimately in latent elements. My concern then was very definitely with the patent elements. It was necessary to make over the boys' voices, to teach the youngsters the notes of Masses, Vespers and motets. Before one could go in quest of the intimations of music, one had to produce the architectural props. One had to have the material before one could build a perspective.

And so I applied myself with great energy to the simplest phases of the art, eagerly checking the progress from day to day. Perhaps it is inaccurate to give the impression that all consciousness of my Ground Bass theme had been dimmed out temporarily, for often during that summer, while playing the organ for early Masses, the mysterious, mesmerizing influence of certain stops and combinations of stops on the organ would take control. There were some extraordinarily well-voiced registers of pipes in the Mission Church organ. It was a Hutchings-Votey instrument. That name was a guarantee for the excellence of the instrument. Mr. Ernest M. Skinner, one of the greatest organ builders of this century, was active at that time in the Hutchings-Votey company, and I began an acquaintance with him then that was to ripen into a fine association, with great benefit accruing to me. He was and is an outstanding master of tone quality. More than other organ builders, he seemed to me to sense the difference between mere acoustical timbre and the latencies. Years after those long-gone days at the Mission Church, Mr. Skinner's own company under his direct supervision built an organ for me at the Fifty-ninth Street Church of the Paulist Fathers, New York City. That instrument is an enduring record of my days at the Mission Church. In it are embodied timbres, ratios of pitch and dynamic strength, colors for all kinds of blending and balancing, which I began to think about and for which I began to develop formulae, both in the instrumental and choral fields, when I was organist for the Redemptorist Fathers. I shall always feel grateful to Mr. Skinner, for, although he was probably unaware of it, he intensified my interest in tone quality. It was quite an experience, just a few seasons ago, to see Mr. Skinner at several lectures of a summer course I was conducting at New York. He was listening to my recipes for producing tonal effects in a chorus analagous to those which he produced from ogan pipes.

The boys made rapid progress. After a month or six weeks the men of the former mixed choir assembled for rehearsal. They looked on me with undisguised scorn. One could almost detect the sneers in their tone quality. I was a disturber, a faddist, and worst of all a youthful amateur. The news of the undertaking had been noised throughout the city and veteran musicians wagged their knowing heads with disapproval. The forecast in professional circles was failure. The families and friends of the ousted sopranos and contraltos regarded me as an arrogant interloper. Many of the Fathers attached to the Church and a not inconsiderable portion of the clergy throughout the city expressed themselves eloquently as being out of sympathy with Father Frawley's experiment. I was too busily engaged in working out the details of the venture and in rehearsing the boys, however, to have time to analyze my psychological reactions to the pitter-patter and chitter-chatter of sceptics and scoffers. Probably I dismissed the ridiculing as more good-natured raillery than rancor. God was kind in giving me a disposition which naturally tended to minimize the meanness that one feels one encounters every so often. Throughout my whole life I have been thankful for this natural gift, for I have been able always to eliminate ninety per cent of the bitterness from any situation. But such subjective control does not disprove the objective reality of antagonisms.

In the family circle, apprehensions were seething. Occasionally I would be conscious of furtive attempts to "look me over," to appraise my estate in relation to accepted standards of normality. My father made no attempt to conceal displeasure, disgust and disdain. I think that he was expecting me to surrender after the inevitable and terrific blow the opening Sunday would provide. As a matter of fact, on that opening day, he arrived in the organ gallery just as I was about to begin the processional hymn, and said in a John Drew whisper which caused the unsympathetic tenors and basses to snicker with glee: "Don't forget that our family has had an honorable name in this city for generations. I earnestly hope that you are not going to put a blot on our escutcheon." What I felt like doing to the family escutcheon, I never revealed to anyone, not even clearly to myself.†

Catholic Boston turned out in a representative cross section for the first appearance of the boys' and men's choir. This was the first choir of its kind to be organized in New England to undertake the complete music ritual of the Catholic services. The boys' and men's choir at the Cathedral sang only the Responses, motets, perhaps the variable parts of the Liturgy, and the Tenebrae. We had everything to do—the *Kyries, Glorias, Credos, Introits, Graduales, Psalms,* and *Canticles,* etc.

My recollection of the first appearance is that it was moderately successful. By the standards of later years, the work was probably dreadful. At any rate, my father's fears for the escutcheon were not realized, and I was promoted to a more dignified place before the domestic hearth.

Two School Sisters of Notre Dame, Sister Mary Auxentia being the

† I must underline here the fact that although my father was the "stern parent" and every inch a Bostonian (Irish version of same!), he was devoted to the Church, his family and his profession. He was beloved by a multitude of people, many of whom he treated without a professional fee. He had an arresting personality, and, when relaxed, was much more charming than his offspring. But he was a bending-backward conservative.

senior, took over the prefecting of the choir when school reopened, and I was relieved of the disciplinary phases of the work. Sister Auxentia was a great ally, always encouraging and aiding in straightening out the snarls that would occasionally tangle things. I am sure that she was the best and most valued friend of my youth. During the many decades which have elapsed since that period, I have, perhaps unconsciously, been paying a debt to Sister Auxentia, by trying to share with the Sisters of many Orders whatever I discovered that might be of use to them in their teaching and directing. Later on, in this volume, I plan to tell of my activities with a choir of Sisters recruited from twenty-three religious Orders in Chicago and a similar group in New York. Here I wish to pay tribute to all nuns for their splendid service to the Church, to their local charges, and to the world at large. What a graceful, glorious body is the Sisterhood of the Catholic Church!

Sister Auxentia was one of those sanctified Sisters whose smile was ever a glow of celestial light.

Chapter V *The Theme Appears on the Alto Line*

THE soprano boys of the Mission Church choir made rapid strides, but I was handicapped by ignorance about alto voices. Of course, I thought that as there is a boy-*soprano* voice there must be a corresponding boy-*alto* voice. Mr. Whitney never cleared up this point for me. Perhaps I did not drive him sufficiently hard on the subject. My recollection is that he, as did practically all Episcopalian choirmasters in the larger churches, used that sad and saddening type of voice on the alto line which is one of the destructive elements in English Cathedral choirs. It is called the "male-alto," and is really only an unusable baritone thrown up an octave. It is a falsetto voice—false, indeed, as the tinsel which would pose as gold, spurious as a forged document, untrue as plausible pretense, made out of whole but imitation cloth. I can't remember why I did not immediately make serious inquiry about this vital item in choral technique, for I was having trouble on the alto line.

The structure of the preadolescent boy's throat does not permit the intonation of true alto notes, as do neither the flute or the oboe. You must change the structure of the instruments to create the quality and low range of the alto. You need the larger tubes of the bass flute and the English horn. The boy whose voice has not begun to change is a sort of flute-oboe. His natural compass stops where these instruments stop.

I made the mistake of assigning boys with notably thick timbres in their middle and lower registers to the alto line. They were forcing their throats to function in an area where they did not belong. The resulting tone was without quality; there was only a husky quantity. Therefore, I could not achieve a blend in the ensemble. One boy, a lad with the surname of Twombly, had a true alto voice, as I know now, but his throat was much wider at the base than is normal, a prominently arched chest formation making possible the subglottis resonance characteristic of the true contralto. Later, I had a similar case in Mr. Thomas McGranahan, distinguished tenor now in Hollywood. He came to me as a boy when I organized the Paulist Choristers at Chicago. He sang with a velvety, rich

Mme. Louise Homer and Ernestine Schumann-Heink quality. His was the richest boy voice I have ever heard, but, like young Twombly, the anatomy of his chest was unusual.

I kept struggling with this pseudoalto section and during the preparation of the Easter music, I knew that I was blundering but failing to identify the error. Mr. Whitney bicycled up to the Church one day to listen to a rehearsal of Bruno Oscar Klein's "Haec Dies." I had told him that there was something faulty in our rendition that I could not diagnose. He studied the score, listened to our rendition, asked us to repeat here and there, agreed that something was basically wrong, but admitted that he could not indicate the something. We tried the number at different tempos and in various dynamic panels. I think that we even transposed it up a key and down a key, but to no avail. After Mr. Whitney had coasted off down the hill, Sister Auxentia said, "The sopranos sound well by themselves but when they sing with the altos the combination is unfortunate. Let us do a little experimenting."

We directed the sopranos to sing more softly and the altos more loudly; this was worse. Vice versa, not quite so bad, but not right. Finally we had the sopranos sing at their normal dynamic level, and the altos at piano pianissimo. *Voila!* That was it. We had it! By reducing the hoarse croakings on the alto line, we had removed the obstruction to blend and balance. Presently I dismissed a good fifty per cent of the froggy lads, and we were as well set as any unit could be that had made no provision for a distinctive musical contribution from the alto line. Mr. Whitney later agreed that we had come upon the right solution, calling himself uncomplimentary names for having missed it.

The alto line became thenceforth a subject for much study, speculation and experimenting. The episode described above occurred in 1903, and I was still uncertain as to the right course to pursue with the alto line when I arrived in England in 1908 for my first first-hand examination of the English choral technique. I'll tell in later pages some experiences that gave me at least a sense of direction about this topic.

It was exceedingly fortunate for me that my attention was drawn to this matter of the altos when I was so young, for, in addition to the study of alto voices which it prompted, my interest in the alto line from the composer's point of view (and therefore from the conductor re-creator's as well) grew into an urge which has persisted throughout the years. The alto and tenor lines (cousins-german in both choruses and orchestras) hold my attention always. The bass line must provide the solid plinth, the sopranos must breathe out their fleecy cloud-tones beyond and over the ensemble, but the alto-tenor combination must furnish the mandrel around which the real effects of concerted music rotate.

The alto line in the average chorus is totally inadequate, having neither
personality nor authority. In choirs of boys and men, it is generally as
my alto line was at Boston. In the Episcopalian choirs and others where
the English alto technique is employed, the effect is dolefully counterfeit. Contraband that can never get across the frontier into Thessaly!
In the majority of symphony orchestras, the alto-tenor combination is
rarely worked out either academically or artistically. There are no distinctive instruments of tonal or quantitative adequacy to cope with the
instruments on the other lines.

This lifelong study dates to the Bruno Oscar Klein motet, to Mr.
Whitney's and my own bewilderment—and to Sister Auxentia's suggestion.

Not only does effective choral singing rely tonally on what happens
in the alto-tenor area, but correct interpretation of all contrapuntal music
and especially of a cappella polyphony demands that these two voice
lines, and their synthetic equivalent in the orchestra, be managed with
great understanding and skill.

Well! the last few paragraphs seem to be on the academic side. Most
likely, every once in a while I'll be unable to resist the urge to write
reflections like those above. Please remember that I am trying to write
over a Ground Bass, and that incidents and anecdotes must spring from
that only as the sixteenth notes of Bach's Passacaglia spring from the
theme written out on the first page of this album.

"Father Frawley's experiment" was considered by unbiassed observers to be tolerably successful, but there were no demonstrations
of frenetic enthusiasm to encourage. Much criticism, constructive as
well as destructive, was leveled at our work. I don't see how we could
have escaped some chiding. The venture was unpopular, the congregation was unprepared to appreciate Gregorian chant which comprised a
considerable part of our repertoire, sufficient time had not been allotted
for careful and comprehensive training, and I was a callow youth. But
interest was stimulated locally in the history of church music and church
choirs. Some people even went to the encyclopedias and manuals of
music history to read about boy choirs, a cappella singing and other
kindred points which our new organization had brought to the consciousness of the people.

Gradually the singing became more refined, and after the exodus of
the superfluous pseudo altos, we achieved a passable blend. The a cappella Responses were effectively rendered and, although at that time I
was using the traditional but bald and banal harmonies, it was reported
that visitors came from distant districts merely to listen to these Responses. This was a source of satisfaction to me, for even while very

young I had realized the importance of the answers to the priest's Versicles and directed them with special care. Long years later at the Paulist Church in New York, our Responses, harmonized in the Russian style, attracted wide notice. Even in the Boston days, I would sometimes experience a real thrill when a delicately poised *Et cum spiritu tuo* or a vigorous and animated "Amen" would wing its way through the church, rebound from a far away wall, come back to us, and slip off finally to hide in the spaces of the clerestory.

The Responses and the simpler harmonized numbers of our repertoire grew steadily in spiritual intimations. The Ground Bass thus came through occasionally.

Father Frawley was interested in dressing up the boys and men in cassocks and surplices and placing them in the chancel. To have installed the choir permanently in the chancel would have been an expensive undertaking, for much architectural remodeling was indicated. Furthermore, the great organ in the gallery would not have served well, for even with an extra keyboard near the choir stalls in the chancel, the hiatus between the depression of the keys and the speaking of the pipes at the other end of the church, would have been too great to permit artistically accompanied numbers of involved styles. But for Holy Week, the good Rector wanted the choristers to appear near the altar, attired in ecclesiastical garb, and well rehearsed in the ceremonies of the many processions, etc., which make up the complex ritual of the services. A little reed organ was placed near the altar rail.

One of the lay brothers found the necessary cassocks and surplices and helped to fit the singers. Many of the men rebelled (some of them not at all unreasonably) at being dressed up as clerics, realizing that mates in the congregation would twit them over merry steins and more merry tall glasses in nearby emporiums for the refreshment of wearied tenors and basses. One of these rebels (he was reported to be the undisputed sovereign of chit-chat-in-the-vernacular at the merriest of the emporiums) decided to do something definite about the matter. The men would not refuse to sing, for they were really excellent Catholics and devotedly loyal to Father Frawley. But if the plan of the Rector could be quietly and effectively circumvented, why not? "With due respect to his Reverence, and all that, it's a silly idea. The poor priest must have been working too hard, and probably that young Finn chap got hold of him in a weak moment."

At any rate, the undisputed sovereign sought out a Father who was volubly opposed to the whole set-up of the boys' choir, enlisting his cooperation. The loquacious one probably pointed out to the pious but "anti-Finn and his boys" Father that if the choir made a specially good impression on the congregation in the picturesque ceremonials, it would be harder to persuade the Rector to disband the unit and recall the ladies. Piety sometimes accomplishes strange ends. Flights of enthusiasm for the spiritual do not exclude other flights of fancy and ingenuity. (How sordid it would be for me to risk letting you interpret "ingenuity" as implying "disingenuous contriving!")

The pious Father and the garrulous member worked well together. No lack of hearty teamwork there. No signs of sluggish appreciation of each other's sympathies. No delays. Immediate action! And the cassocks disappeared. Not a robe nor a rag in the lockers!

Fortunately for the Rector's plan, and unfortunately for the purposes of the p.F. and the g.m., I arrived very early on the morning of Palm Sunday. The friendly lay brother was stricken with alarm. He looked as though he felt as other earlier lay brothers of ancient Orders probably felt when the Saracens were announced to be approaching, intent upon razing the monastery and massacring the monks. His full measure of a lay brother's endurance was already used. He was the Sacristan, and Father Rector would naturally hold him to account, perhaps influencing the Father Provincial to remove him to a distant house of the Order. He had been so happy in Boston!

The Rector was scheduled to celebrate the Solemn Mass, and we dared not waken him so early. Our message would not have helped him to start the day in a blithe mood. While the lay brother and I were pondering the situation, a friendly little Irish Father came through the sacristy. He overheard us talking. Looking furtively over his shoulder, he said in a winsome brogue as though to himself and with seeming irrelevance: "Sure, and God knows there was a tirrible commotion up in the triforium on the Gospel side last night. A couple of men were throwing things up from the landing on the stairway. I hope they weren't up to any mischief." It was a matter of seconds only, after hearing those ripples from the Lakes of Killarney, to mount to the Gospel-side triforium and discover the wardrobe piled helter-skelter on the floor. Laboriously we conveyed the robes back to the lockers.

The undisputed sovereign, as soon as he knew of the failure of his unblessed scheme, pleading an attack of laryngitis made himself scarce. The pious Father's face was of a very light green tint, when, on hurrying through the outer sacristy to vest for the Deacon's part in the ceremonies, he beheld us, about a hundred strong, gowned and surpliced as all good Roman Catholic liturgical choristers should be, according to the traditions of Holy Mother Church. I felt sorry for the pious Father. He and the undisputed sovereign must have put much time and backbone into the job the night before. It had been a tough enough chore to fetch them down, so toting them up must have involved major exertion. When he turned around to sing the *Procedamus in pace* at the start of the Palm Sunday procession, he gulped at the sight of the maneuvering choristers and emitted a tuneless wail that sounded like a siren out of order, sighing down in the harbor.

The choir did make a splendid impression. The late Bishop James A. Walsh, founder of the Maryknoll Fathers, then known as Father James, attended the service and was most congratulatory. His only critique was aimed at me personally. "Why did *you* keep singing? I can understand that you might want to start them off right at the beginning of a number, but you should stop as soon as possible. Don't you know that you have a most unpleasant voice?" I made some inquiries pertinent to this point, discovering that there was unanimous agreement with Father James.

The undisputed sovereign put in an appearance on Wednesday night, but he sat with the congregation in a front pew quite close to my position at the altar railing. He was a good "lead" tenor, and I needed him badly for the Rheinberger *Miserere* which, for a new choir, was full of hazards, due not to the difficulty of the notation progressions, but to the arrangement of syllables to notes. We went through a few verses without mishap but at an awkward spot, like the *Libera me de sanguinibus,* the tenors improvised some arabesques which confused the sopranos, and as I was waiting for a few sluggish basses to catch my signal to quit and proceed to the next verse, the rebel tenor focussed upon me the most desiccating leer it has ever been my fate to try to evade.

After Holy Week the choir returned to "civies" and the choir gallery. But the over-all effect of the appearance in the chancel was stimulating and I proposed another scheme to the Rector. It was for a special Vesper service ritual on Pentecost night. The story of the Gabrielis at St. Mark's in Venice in the sixteenth century, and of Antonio Lotti a century and a half later had stirred my imagination since I began to study the history of music. In this great Cathedral, these masters had followed a tradition (perhaps it was established by "Messer Adriano" Willaert) of using three choirs, variously placed, on great feasts. The Mission Church was architecturally so built as to make a triple-choir service effective. It was a feasible plan to divide the main chorus into three units, keeping the larger unit in the west-end gallery and disposing the others respectively in the Gospel and Epistle triforiums. The triforiums (galleries in arcade form extending over the arches of the nave) had ample space to accommodate the semichoruses.

The Rector was enthusiastic about the triple-choir Vespers, and we worked industriously on the preparation. I arranged the "Magnificat" and perhaps the Vesper "Hymn" to be sung as a colloquy between the three groups. Every so often the score called for the three choirs to sing together. The effect at St. Mark's had been described as extraordinarily satisfying, and I remember being much moved myself at the final rehearsal in the Mission Church.

At the appointed time, the members of the triforium groups left the west-end gallery to assemble at their posts. I was in my regular place with the large choir. We began the number, sweeping the melodies and harmonies along to the musical apex of the verse. A dramatic pause was to follow for a few seconds, whereupon the Epistle-side choir was to waft a lovely minor-mode sentence across to the Gospel-side to be returned thence presently in bright major-mode harmony. The pause that followed our opening measures was more than dramatic; it was melodramatic in the most sensational implications of the word. There was no response forthcoming. I waited for a series of eternities. The priests were nearly finished with the incensing of the altar. Presently, in a panic, I played the Epistle-side's part and gave a "gathering note" * signal to the Gospel-side to contribute their part. No response from the Gospel-side. The congregation which had been especially urged to attend the "Echo Vespers" strained in vain for any echoes. There were none. People turned around in the pews to gaze curiously at the group in the west-end gallery. Finally I went madly into a series of improvisations to substitute for the missing verses. In France some years later, I found the improvisations on the organ instead of the singing of the alternate texts an approved custom. Our Mission Church "Echo Vespers" was a disagreeable experience. Two thousand people were chagrined, and I crawled down the hill and homeward on my hands and knees.

Whether the sovereign had been at work again, I never learned, but some crafty, disturbing, sleight-of-hand artist had sneaked up to the triforium doors and securely locked them. These had been open a few minutes before the service began. And so I was not able to bring to the Bostonians a reproduction of the mystic effects achieved at St. Mark's.

During that season I had a little foretaste of work on the road. It was only a sip-taste but it had the tang of the experiences which were to add up to an enormous total in later years. Two Paulist Fathers were conducting a mission in Abington, a town some miles away. They prevailed upon me to bring a group of my boys to sing at one of the services. It was quite an adventure. For days the boys were excited. Parents of boys who were not chosen for the group complained to the Rector and to me. Sister Auxentia looked the boys over carefully, before we set out, examining necks and pinning back some ears. Clean shirts and collars,

---

* A "gathering note" signal is the playing of the initial soprano note preceded by a short note a semitone below.

neatly tied cravats and boots glittering with the blue-blackness of a homemade shine. We took a railroad train. Perhaps this was the first time for some of the lads to board a train. In those days train riding was regarded a momentous event. Boys who had been on trains were considered a bit on the uppish side socially, and almost the equals of boys whose families had received telegrams. And we were to have luncheon in a real downtown restaurant near the railroad station.

We had a one hundred per cent railroad ride. It was on the Old Colony Road, now a division of the New York, New Haven & Hartford. Cinders came through the open windows, lodging carefully or carelessly in the eyes of some of the boys. Good Old Colony cinders than which none better could be found except perhaps on the Erie, famed in satire and limericks. And the most turbid, clinging variety of soot that soft coal could produce adhered to the napes of treblish necks. An old chap dressed to look a half century younger in the uniform of a *Union News'* "butcher" selling candy, Sweet Caporal cigarettes, and the *Police Gazette!* The baggage master throwing our wardrobe trunk off at the station, and the baggage "smasher" on the platform looking it over as though it were a Jordan Marsh container consigned to some rich dowager of the locality with a mania for buying dresses in bulk.

I don't recall many parents having gone to the Boston depot to see their sonnies off. But there must have been a few, for in those days it was a custom rarely transgressed to see off departing kinsfolk, no matter how short the journey on a train. Whenever it was necessary for some member of my family to travel to far off points like Worcester or Providence, both of these foreign citadels being approximately forty miles from Boston, several of us went to the depot to bid him farewell. It was a sort of holiday. It gave us a sense of importance to wave a relative onto a train. And if the relative were so extravagant as to purchase a ticket for a seat in the Pullman Palace Car, we were thrilled with an awe that challenged even a Bostonian's vocabulary.

Once we were depressed into the lowest depths of gloom when my father was required to travel to New York, that city which to a Bostonian was the most formidable of all the alien metropolises here or in Europe. He was obliged to make the fantastically long journey by night, and he booked a berth on the Ghost Train which left Boston at midnight on the old New York and New England Railroad. The leaving time was too late for the ladies and the young fry to see him off. We were being cheated of a thoroughly first-class adventure. But we stayed up beyond our normal bedtime. Uncles and aunts came. There was much whispering, and esoteric gestures indicated the weighted importance of the night. My father shone in a pool of glamor even though the gas-lighting facilities couldn't work up so much of thaumaturgical wonder as the lights of today. He was a man of distinction; he stood out among thousands; he was a hero, for he was going to a strange, forbidding city—and on a night train.

About an hour and a half before train time, the Doctor was wrapped into muffler and great coat, tears were shed by mother, aunts and children, a few globules coursing down the cheeks of the Doctor as well. A Clarence (a four-wheel enclosed horse-drawn vehicle) pulled up at the curb, and in solemn silence an uncle escorted the Doctor to the Clarence, entered the carriage with him, and off they went to the mysterious shed where night trains would make up and start adventurous journeys. Oh, for Aladdin's lamp!

There wasn't this degree of the dramatic about the Mission Church choir boys starting off for Abington, fully twenty-five miles away, but the event made history for the local families.

We didn't have much to sing. The program went reasonably well. All simple music, of course. But I had been heralded from the local pulpit as a "boy wonder." I was a modern edition of Mozart, of Haydn, even perchance of Beethoven. Just wait until I put my fingers on that organ! The little instrument would rebuild itself. It would come to life and hypnotize all listeners. The choir would then confirm the impression made in the prelude by the young Mozart-Finn. No music ever before offered in the county had equalled what we were to provide. The voices of the boys would bring echoes of the choirs of the seraphim into the church. All Abington had better turn out! And a good percentage of the proud town's population did turn out, unfortunately!

We had been melodramatically overadvertised. We couldn't without miraculous intervention, by any stretching out of natural resources, meet the expectations of the Abingtonians. No miracle occurred.

What a dreadful experience to be overadvertised! To have big words used about you when you know that you have a tiny product! This happened many times in afteryears, but the Abington episode gave me my first shock. During the performance at the church, one could sense the disappointment and chagrin of Abington's best. Silk had been advertised, denim delivered. From the front of the church, from the roof, from the floor, from all through the nave, from both transepts, and from the sacristy, where specially invited clergy were listening, emanated a miasma of surprise and disapprobation. A sham outfit, indeed! And to add ignominy by indirect method (this is an effective one!) a young lassie, who was the church organist, slid onto the organ bench when I had finished and played circles around me, doing things with the little box of whistles which I could not hope to do on any organ for another decade of years.

The Ground Bass didn't have much of a chance at Abington. But the expedition gave the boys a feeling of being professional, and for weeks they strutted around the Roxbury Crossing district with superior mien and disdainful manner.

Altogether, my activities at the Mission Church and the intensive study of organ, choral technique, harmony and other allied subjects, made the year 1902–1903 most fruitful. Some of the older organists of Boston used to make fun of my juvenile efforts, and a few of the clergy were unsympathetic with that strange, censorious and inexplicably opinionated disparagement which some ecclesiastics have copyrighted as their own. But I netted great profit. Even from the carping critics. Ideals were no longer in silhouette. The need for study and experimenting was made crystal clear. The art of the choral conductor had begun to present itself in an orderly sequence of subjects. Zeal for the advancement of the true content of music as an accessory to divine worship was intensified.

And so my year away from the seminary was equivalently a year spent in the novitiate of the Memories of Monastic Music. A boon and benediction!

Chapter VI *The Ground Bass Worries about the Treble*

WHILE the undertaking at the Mission Church was somehow shaping up, I listened to symphony and oratorio concerts whenever possible and managed to become fairly well acquainted with the standard operas. We had our own distinguished Symphony Orchestra in Boston, of course, the Apollo Club, and the Handel and Haydn Oratorio Society, but we depended upon New York for the more elaborate performances of opera. The stock company at the Castle Square Theatre provided opportunity for becoming acquainted with the best known Italian operas.

But there was something awry with the performances of the choral groups and the orchestra. I had no trouble in analyzing my dissatisfaction with the singing societies, at least from the tonal point of view. The singers on the various choral lines did not utter pleasant sounds. Their vocalization was unbeautiful. Therefore, there could be no blend. From the interpretative angle, I was in no position to judge of their inadequacies or errors, for sensitiveness to the proprieties of interpretation comes only after years of study and experience. I knew clearly, on the whole, that I was working in the opposite direction from that pursued by the choral maestros of Boston. This meant, of course, that I was pitting my reactions to the Ground Bass against the choral approaches of the profession in general, for if conditions were below an aesthetic standard in the "Athens of America," could they, by any satirical caprice of the wheel of fortune, be better elsewhere? It was quite a shock to find myself discovering serious faults in the choral singing conducted by the most widely acclaimed directors of the era. Perhaps I was frightened by the aloneness of my situation. Maybe a little frightened, but not very much. The singing was unforgivably bad. I had set myself to produce a better, the real, the attainable and the historical standard of concerted vocalism. So why be afraid? (That's a good question for the imperturbability of youth!)

But as to the performances of the Boston Symphony Orchestra which made me uneasy, fretful and altogether dissatisfied, I was at sea, tossed around in billowy confusion, seeking in vain for a diagnosis of the discontent. There was some disruptive element disfiguring the musical offerings of America's principal symphony orchestra. The same disruptive element still mars the performances of that orchestra and the many orchestras which I have heard and conducted. It was beyond my ken at that time to understand the symptoms. The personnel of the players of the Boston Symphony, as of other virtuoso orchestras, was and is made up of the world's greatest instrumentalists. The Boston string choir was acclaimed for its tone quality and unisonous playing, under the concert-mastership of Franz Kneisel, who later became my friend and valued counselor. There were great conductors, too. Haenschel, Gericke, Nikisch, Paur.

I fancy that at that time I charged myself with lack of appreciation of instrumental music; that, being committed to the choral aspects of the art, I had little sympathy with mechanical media of musical communication. If this were the case, I was mistaken, for it was not long before I realized that all my thinking about the external phases of music was in terms of orchestral color. I developed a passion for orchestration. Following from afar the example of Sir Edward Elgar, I taught myself orchestration, practically as well as theoretically. I played and still play the organ more orchestrally than in the Cathedral mode. When I face a chorus, I see and hear an orchestra and vice versa. My choruses must play and my orchestras sing.

No, it was not aversion for orchestral music that affected my appreciation of the Boston Symphony Orchestra, Boston's most highly publicized cultural asset. It was an imperfection in the performance of a unit that needs perfect balance before its performance can be convincing; a defect in the acoustical compensatings and interpretative readings of even those world renowned conductors—an imperfection and defect that fought the essential meaning of the Ground Bass. It is a long time ago, now, since I identified the source of the shortcomings. *There was no balance between the higher and the lower instruments.* To me this defect, which persists today in many celebrated orchestras, is the bane of concerted instrumentalism.

The soprano instruments, with their acute timbres sounding in registers where the acoustical vibrations are most rapid, overplay the milder alto-tenor combinations, at the same time offering a dare to the bass instruments, frequently accepted, to equal their output. This lack of balance, disturbing chiefly when the dynamic level is mezzo forte forte, denies a chance for expression to the inner parts. It is in the inner parts that one finds the soul of music.

Interpretatively, conductors are wont to stress this defect by according prominence to the top line even when this is only the octave duplication of a melody or figure on a lower line. For example, the haunting melody, which is familiar to many of you readers, from the first movement of Tschaikowsky's Sixth Symphony (Pathétique) makes its initial appearance with first violins over cellos. Listen to any of several recordings. The violins in the upper octave so overplay the cellos below as to smother completely the rich low cello timbre which is meant to plumb the depth of the melody. At the repetition of the melody, after the moderate mosso, the score calls for a distribution of the melody in three positions.

The first violins play in the ether, the second violins in a medium range, and the plaintive violas in the lowest of the positions. The mezzo forte symbol is given for the three parts. But listen to live performances and to the recordings. What do you hear? Are you conscious at all of what the composer was trying to communicate from his much-plagued soul, and which the viola, by its tonal character and its low position, is the best fitted to communicate? Are you even primarily aware of the second violins' singing? Is not your attention drawn forcibly away from the violas and seconds by the shrill fiddling of the first violins?

There has been too much treble in orchestras and choruses since the mystic blend and balance of the Renaissance surrendered to the more physical insistences of following eras. What had stimulated my interest in music was precisely that mystical element which the choruses and orchestras of the current century ignore. Any and all exercise of the art which does not promote this element has scant appeal for me. I don't mean that fine, bold, popular tunes fail to bring pleasure or to stimulate emotions; that a military march sturdily played, even with the top woodwinds and brasses screaming a bit, doesn't arouse enthusiasm; or that a great dramatic climax cannot be achieved when the trebles are signally poignant. What I mean is this: *music—serious, gay, religious or secular —which is not a synthesis of carefully adjusted acoustical properties, of compensating differentials of tone colors, and of thoroughly co-ordinated contributions of harmony is not music in its ultimate sense.*

Such reflections suggest an aspect of music which invites extensive consideration, but which is obviously beyond the scope of this book to undertake. Well! there's the reason, probably, why the Boston Symphony Orchestra did not give me the thrill all good Bostonians were supposed to receive from its playing. And then, also, there was quite a lot of uninteresting music played. Rusty iron. Some of it labeled as coming from the forge of master smithies. And the aura of the sacrosanct which Boston's dowagers threw around the concerts! The old Music Hall and later, Symphony Hall, were Sanctuaries of Aestheticism, where the vergers, beadles, sacristans and even the parsons were appointed by descendants of Brewster and Bradford and other Puritan or Pilgrim sires who would probably have pronounced the *bass* in Ground Bass with a flat fishy *a*. Much hushing. Much tiptoeing when it was necessary to move about. Bach on the program was to be reverenced as a new revelation from on high. Oh! yes, the bustled custodians of Bostoniana guarded their concert halls as concernedly as the Mormons guard their temple at Salt Lake City.

Probably a score of years had passed from the time of my experiences as a postadolescent listener to the symphony concerts to the date when I was sure of what had been wrong with orchestral playing. But when I was sure, it was with a sureness that was a one-color certainty. No thin stripes of pinkish doubt tinting the assurance!

But it is still difficult to persuade musicians that in "too much treble" one finds "too much trouble." Veteran violinists, flutists, oboists, clarinetists and trumpeters shake shaggy (sometimes bald) heads in disdainful dissent when a conductor insists that these players reduce their top fortes to mezzo fortes and their fortissimos to fortes minus. Many seem to be loath to relinquish sovereignty to the lower instruments. The treble furious scrapers and blowers are as reluctant to accept the principle of acoustical balance as entire orchestras and choruses are averse to adjusting their accents and slack beats to the needs of metrical patterns, or to the addressing of new phrases with the indirect attack rather than by inartistic collisions with them, which makes their impacts another source of faulty performance.

Even the popular bands are proving the principle discussed to be right, for unless you like your music "hot" as the bobby-soxers and the adults who still wear bobby-sox on their brain cells, you must be offended and disgusted with the screeching of fiddles and the altitudinous blasting of trumpets. One day in a Far Western town, I encountered the maestro of one of these hot bands. He greeted me with effusion. "I read a book of yours recently. Put it there"—extending a hand. "It's about time someone called the conductors to account." I listened to the maestro's performance—Ah! the futility of scribbling!

Even with the Paulist Choristers in New York, years after my Boston experiences, I had difficulty in inculcating a sense of treble-bass and alto-tenor balance. Boy sopranos were ever eager to see the comet tails of their high notes trailing through the clouds. One of my most exhausting and scarcely interrupted efforts was to reduce the superfluous quantity of tone in the soprano parts.

I trust that the conductors of great orchestras will not condemn me too savagely for having been candid. The more they consider the validity of the Ground Bass over which this album of memoirs is emerging, the more keenly will they realize that the fundamental need of effective concerted music (after good tone quality, of course) is a proper balance between thin and thick tones, between piercing and dull timbres, between soaring phrases and plunges into the depths. Before one may reasonably essay the conveying of a psychological message or the portrayal of a picture through the medium of choral or orchestral music, he must have perfected a well-balanced and blended instrument for the communication. Above all, he must have learned to discern perfect balance.

Chapter VII   *A Few Arpeggios*

A DELIGHTFUL old priest from the south finished reading the manuscript of these reminiscences up to this point. His comments were that I didn't seem to have had much fun as a boy or as a youth, and that it wasn't clear how one who had loathed music as a boy suddenly was seen on the conductor's podium, intent upon developing definite ideals in one of the most difficult fields of musicianship.

Probably the narrative has been lacking the continuity which would correlate episodes.

As a matter of fact, many of the boys with whom I grew up in Boston were restricted to a scant measure of fun. There was little room for easy going standards of juvenile conduct in the old New England discipline. In my home, the armorial bearings seemed to egg the children to observe Irish-Catholic-Puritan patterns of conduct. I never had a birthday party. If one were unfortunate enough to bat a baseball through a pane of glass in the Manor House of the Finns, one would pay with at least three square inches of tergal epidermis.

Nor were pranks and jolly capering approved at the preparatory semin-seminary. The "smile of dissipation" was condemned by the French code which guided the holy Fathers in training their youthful charges. Much grinning and laughing were indications of a proneness to vulgarity, and my sense of humor was, therefore, anaesthetized. I was always aware, however, of the lamentably comical (do you mind the paradox?) set-up in Boston and at the seminary near Baltimore. When I told all this to my friendly critic, he remarked that I had come out of ether well enough, in fact, just a bit too well!

As to the comment of the friendly critic about my having suddenly come out into the open as a "gesturing" musician, I admit the difficulty of recounting steps probably taken in the dark. At the moment when a boys steps across the line from childhood to adolescence, new impressions begin to assemble. The period of youthful development seems full of the mysterious, as one goes back in memory hoping to find an explanation for many things. A new awareness of life and values is activated by the change over from the boy to the young man. It is clear in my mind that

I held music in low esteem all during my childhood. It is equally clear that from my sixteenth birthday I began to be excitedly interested in some aspects of the art. I commenced to study seriously, to practice diligently and to go through all the movements prescribed for progress in the exercise of any art form. But my growth was chiefly an inner development. My power of understanding of musical facts increased. By the time I was twenty years of age I was conscious of an orientation which I could explain to neither masters nor student colleagues. The Ground Bass, although not identified at the time, had become the paramount influence. Although this book is entitled *Sharps and Flats in Five Decades,* it is true that these symbols were of less consequence that the implications which they were employed to communicate.

Why should Little Lord Fauntelroy suddenly shed his prejudices and leap onto a podium? I must have been in an unconscious process of preparation for the determining reaction of my life, when the boy sopranos of the Boston Cathedral awakened interest by their singing of the Tenebrae "Lamentation." Transcendentalism was in the air one breathed in Boston. I mean that Ralph Waldo Emersonism blended easily with the east winds that swept in from the Grand Banks. This in turn means that there was in the atmosphere of New England a breath of intuitionism which would quicken perception of truths behind and under all external manifestations. At any rate, I am sure that my apprehension of the basic truths of music began early to be stimulated as much, if not more, by a sort of aesthetic clairvoyance than by written or oral instruction. This is probably a vague explanation of the processes by which I grew quickly from a state of dislike to a state of warriorlike zeal for music. The Ground Bass established itself as my basic theme, while I was still adolescent. This forced me to undertake the trip to Mount Parnassus. This kept me single-minded. It explains my groping for technics and formulae. The Ground Bass nurtured whatever talent God had bestowed upon me.

But if there was not much fun, in the ordinary sense of the word, during the years of my boyhood and youth, there were certainly some amusing episodes to season the seriousness of my undertakings. A few gay sixteenth notes rippled down the gamut during the years which afforded me the proximate preparation for my life's major enterprise—the founding and conducting of the Paulist Choristers. While at the Mission Church, I hewed close to the line, devoting myself to phases of musical practice which seemed of first import. I did little in the field of secular music, having few contacts with the popular musicians of concert hall or theatre.

My one effort at accompanying a lady recitalist is worth recording. She was a beautiful young thing, gifted (or burdened?) with a most seductive contralto voice. She could produce tones that would shear the locks of the most phlegmatic Samson. When she made a crescendo on a low B flat, even modern air conditioning could not have kept an auditorium cool. The Rector of the Mission Church asked me to substitute for her accompanist at short notice. I was timid about undertaking the task. I had never appeared in such a role. The young charmer was to sing for one of the fraternities at a theater near Harvard College. What I didn't know about accompanying beautiful young damsels in the German *lieder* would have filled many unwritten books. Furthermore, I was obliged to hire a "claw-hammer" suit, as full evening clothes for gentlemen were called in those days.

I went across the Charles River to Cambridge full of misgivings. The hypnotic young edition of the famous contralto Scalchi was uneasy, too. Could I play all those involved accompaniments? I was to be in the pit, instead of on stage where a rapport could be more easily established between vocalist and accompanist. And she, yielding to a movement sponsored by the Dowagers of Symphony Hall to promote the singing of foreign language songs in English, had promised to sing a song of Brahms in the Bostonian argot of English. She failed to provide herself with a book of words. Halfway through the Brahms piece, which she had never sung in English before, she forgot the text. Down in the pit, I was concentrating on getting all the flats and sharps and naturals into the allocation designated by the great Johannes. The cute little contralto Circe had ceased "liedering." I found myself soloing, so I withdrew my graceful hands from the keyboard. The silence grew louder. The soundlessness became a din. Pretty Siren did a little "stage business," shifting from one sandaled foot to the other, peering down wistfully into the pit, and sending her extravagantly successful eyebrows into a Gothic arch, her Lake Louise blue orbs rolling in simulated terror.

I looked quickly at the text, discovering at once that I and not she was under the heel of the predicament. I whispered the forgotten words. The whisper failed to register. Then with some sibilation I breathed them across the footlights. She couldn't translate the hiss. Then storm clouds gathered over Lake Louise. The chagrin of embarrassed femininity blew down into the pit as a windstorm from the lakes in the clouds above Lake Louise. The ghost of the histrionic Scalchi materialized in the fair contralto's subconscious, and she stepped forward, hurling a loud command to me to read the next few sentences of the song clearly and slowly. I felt as though I was the one who had forgotten the words. A bad spot for a seminarian on a leave of absence! Not a good spot for the organist of the Mission Church! But facing the inevitable with all the fortitude expected from a New Englander, I rose, and articulated the text distinctly and with stentorian resonance: "Sweetheart, I love thee. I adore thee. I pine for thee. The stars behold me languishing, while the cold moon mocks."

The gentlemen of the Harvard fraternity felt life leaping through them with great pressure. They broke out into unanimous and vociferous approval of my choice in ladies, guffawing with that special sort of satirical merriment which seemed indigenous to Harvard Square. But with broad *a*'s (even the chaps from the prairie states had taken on these wide vowel sounds), the elite of America's college students proceeded to develop the thought that the piano pounder in the pit was totally unfit to be in such apposition to so very, very beautiful a lady; that the football players of the fraternity were much more worthy of regard; that even the bespectacled junior who had a copy of the *Iliad* with him in the balcony had clearer title to the position usurped by the tame accompanist. The lady dashed off the stage in rubicund confusion, while I escaped through the passage from the pit to the stage entrance. Of course, in one way, perhaps in a big way, I was the hit of the show. Probably never before or afterwards did a Brahms song evoke so much enthusiasm from a Harvard audience.

But a little of that spelled too much in my book, and I could find no semblance of excuse to study the art of accompanying dazzlingly gorgeous female recitalists. This would require some experimenting in prompting them without making declarations of love. Church music, the boy's voice, Gregorian chant and Eros! Better let the last go!

At about this time, I had the privilege and pleasure of studying a vocal score under the baton of Signor Augusto Rotoli. This distinguished maestro embodied the principles and methods of choral singing as accepted and practiced during the late nineteenth century. It was interesting and enlightening to observe one of Italy's greatest conductors in action. I knew from the first rehearsal that he was not urged by the Ground Bass of this book. But he was a master of the more mechanical phases of chorophony, such as attack, release, synchronous movement and good phrasing. Like other Italian conductors, he could hypnotize a chorus into great bursts of song. He had an eagle eye. He was the nineteenth-century choral Toscanini. A great man for surface effects. For the public this sort of greatness suffices, as the history of conducting attests.

I have since thought that singing under another's baton is an invaluable aid to a young conductor. Probably many choral conductors have profited by the experience. But my experience had been only on the podium. I didn't know how a conductor's gestures looked to the performers. I learned, among other things, that it is easier for a conductor to indicate the right moment for entrance than it is for choristers to follow the indication. And in the matter of variations of pace and quantity, I ascertained that the gentleman on the podium is often more vague than he fancies. This experience under Rotoli improved my own conducting, for I watched him carefully and eagerly. He was kind enough to discuss certain points about which I queried him, but he would look at me with great interrogation marks flecking his eyes when I mentioned such things as tone color, economy in quantity, and conservatism in *fermatas*. Neither Signor Rotoli nor his brilliant orchestral organist, Mr. Walter Kuber, was interested in the sequence of stresses and slacks which I was beginning to appreciate as the most influential factors in determining rhythm. But there was only one well-known musician of my acquaintance, Mr. James McLaughlin, sometime supervisor of music in the Boston public schools, who was at that time interested in rhythm as distinguished from mere temporal values. And so I did not condemn the great Italian too severely, although I did make note of his indifference to one of the most important agencies of musical expression. Profound study of rhythmical structure and implications of melody had been discontinued shortly after the end of the polyphonic era. It has not yet been resumed by many professional musicians.

During the rehearsals under Signor Rotoli, I must have learned something about putting the movements of an oratorio together, for at about the time of the Abington episode, I rehearsed and conducted a performance of Eliot Trowbridge's *Peace Of Jerusalem*. Also, I took a fancy to Signor Rotoli's arrangement of an old Italian melody, "Alla Trinita Beata," which for many years the Paulist Choristers sang throughout this country and Canada. Pope Pius X liked the number very much, and laughed heartily at the Chicago-American pronunciation of the Italian text.

Apropos of this Italian piece, I must confess that unwittingly I treated it badly. Concert audiences were accustomed to demand an encore whenever we offered the motet, and so instead of putting it through once, I developed the habit of presenting it three times, each time with a different reading, the third reading being an extravagant overemphasis of the bass part. Such trifling distorted the contours of the delicate little motet. My only excuse for this violent misrepresentation is that no teacher had ever discussed with me the inviolability of the melody of a song written originally for unison performance. Some professional critics, indeed, professed to find a high degree of artistry in our performances!

I wrote earlier in these pages that I would tell of Some Fountain Pens I Have Met. The "Alla Trinita Beata" was programmed for performance at the debut concert of the Paulist Choristers (then a Chicago unit) concert at Carnegie Hall, New York. Through a mistake of the librarian, however, the copies of this piece were sent through to Baltimore, and a substitution was necessarily made in New York. Our announced debut in the great Metropolis had failed to win favor among the professional musicians of that city, for we were Midwesterners, an advance notice of inferiority. In spite of the announcement that an a cappella number from Humphrey Stewart's "Nativity" would be offered in place of the "Alla Trinita Beata," we were taken to task by a leading critic for our performance of the latter. If this critic had not been so overwhelmingly unfriendly, I would have concluded that he couldn't understand our English, which probably was not in the most approved style of Oxford, Cambridge, or even Harvard, and let it go at that. But there was so much sulphuric acid in his ink that I concluded the scrivener had not been in the Hall. For seasons on end I could see that critic penning his vitriolic comment whenever the Choristers began the little Italian motet.

During my incumbency at the Mission Church, I had splendid opportunity for learning the art of accompanying large congregations. At one of the daily Masses, practically the entire personnel of the large parochial school was accustomed to sing the music of the Mass. One cannot successfully guess at the proper means for keeping a couple of thousand singers in time with themselves and with the organ: one must work out a method by the trial and error plan. After having allowed the children to stray off into a half-dozen tempos on a few occasions, I gradually began to master the technique involved, which was rather simple, indeed. One had to anticipate the beat so that the sound of the organ coming from a distance would synchronize with the intoned notes of the singers, at the same time employing a sturdy organ register for the melody and a combination of lighter stops for the harmony. Later, in Chicago, I learned from a practice promoted by Harrison Wild to establish the rhythm and tempo by beating time with the pedal notes (bunting the pedals). At Notre Dame Cathedral in Paris in 1912, the facility acquired at the Mission Church and later at Chicago, in this connection, made it possible for my choristers and myself to maintain perfect synchronization during a procession which brought the singers the full length of that great Gothic nave away from me, playing in the chancel. And on many occasions in American Cathedrals, it was reassuring to know that singers and organist would be together on the right fraction of the beat.

When I returned to the seminary in 1903, my musical understanding had been enriched by study and experience. My musical purposes had been still further clarified, and the necessity of developing tact in dealing with men, both clerical and lay, had been demonstrated to be of urgent importance. Mr. Francis X. O'Brien, the virtuoso organist of the Gesu in Philadelphia took over my portfolio.

The ensuing scholastic year did not differ in the matter of music from my two years before the Mission Church interlude. I practiced several times a week on the organ at the Divinity Hall Chapel. This was a good instrument for its size, and its limited color range probably emphasized the importance of the color scheme in concerted music by the very absence of the multiple timbres to which I had become accustomed on the great Boston organ.

During the months of classes, it was difficult to hear the Ground Bass. Probably I slid down a snowy slope on Parnassus, for practically all the time I was permitted to devote to music was the afternoon recreation period. While other lads were on the athletic field or walking about in the beautiful Soldiers' Home Park, I found myself perched on the organ bench trying to persuade diapasons, gambas, cornopeans, etc., to merge in a euphony of hypnotic sounds. Sometimes the water motor by which the little instrument was supplied with air refused to operate, and I would waste an afternoon waiting for it to behave. Once, at the end of a practice period, I forgot to disconnect the water motor, and the old French priest in charge of the Chapel made so great a fuss about the forgetfulness that a neurosis about turning off motors and lights attacked me as a leech which I have never been able to throw off. Even to this day, having pushed the proper gadget for stopping a motor, I return, after walking a few paces, to check the situation. It has become a frightful nuisance. The old French priest was a charming man, but an American youth's stupidity intensified the old gentleman's chronic stomach acidity, and I cannot blame him for having been less charming. Probably the neurosis has saved money for rectors and superiors!

And the academic faculty kept me well within the range of visibility. It would not do for me to become better acquainted with Apollo, or even the Greek Pythagoras, than with St. Thomas Aquinas. And so the weekly examiners would cheat a bit, and, ostensibly drawing a name out a box, would put me up for quizzing about twice a month, while my colleagues were unfortunate about once every three months. But all this was good. "Don't permit a young ecclesiastical musician to ride at random along the trails of the Muses. Make him alight often from his mythological horse." That sort of thing! Sound training! The faculty probably reasoned that Hucbald, Guido of Arezzo, Palestrina, Bach and Beethoven might be all right to a limited degree, because several learned historians so attested. But give them a syllogism every time! Plato, Aristotle, St. Augustine to the fore! A fugue was credited with having some inexplicable value, but a thesis in metaphysics, ah! there you had worth, lucid and lasting!

Chapter VIII *A Pope Thinks about the Ground Bass*

IN NOVEMBER, 1903, Pope Pius X initiated his holy effort "to restore all things in Christ," by issuing an encyclical letter on the subject of church music. For some generations the music of public worship had been excessively operatic. By excessively, I mean that it went far beyond the limits of dramatic expression which the Church traditionally had set for Her ceremonies, pageants and religious spectacles. If a parish could bear the expense, the musical program was quite generally ostentatious and frequently outclassed local productions of opera.

Unwittingly, the clergy had permitted the sung portions of the Liturgy to become a travesty. The *Kyrie, Gloria, Credo, Sanctus* and *Agnus Dei* were as the five acts of a garish music drama. Frequently the Masses sung suggested the emotional developments unfolded in a mid-nineteenth century Italian opera. In the *Kyrie,* the female soprano soloist would reveal her animosity towards the contralto. The *Gloria,* act two, would hint of the baritone's jealousy of the tenor (the latter having the inside track with the soprano) while the bass began nefarious plottings. And so on. Choruses would trip gaily through lively movements while the text was imploring the forgiveness of God for the sins of mankind, including those of the choir and the congregation. Often a flourishing cadenza gave the leading lady a showy opportunity for a finale with chorus. The *Benedictus* not infrequently resounded through churches, after the solemn moment of the *Consecration,* as a mocking serenade by Mephistofeles. There were anguished love laments, seductive "Ave Maria's" and Soldiers' Chorus "Tantum Ergo's." The priest at the Altar would often be obliged to delay the progress of the Holy Sacrifice while the music intimated that the contralto and baritone were arranging a rendezvous in the moonlight. The music was not only unchurchly, unspiritual, unbecoming; it was grotesque. Tosca and Manon in the west-end choir loft, Carmens habanera-ing to the pews, and Elsa dueting with Lohengrin while a corpse was being conducted up the aisle for a Solemn Requiem Mass.

In parishes where the budget would not permit vying with La Scala or Covent Garden, one would hear silly ballads adjusted (sometimes with monkey wrenches, hammers or crowbars) to Latin texts. "Alice, Where Art Thou?" "Drink To Me Only With Thine Eyes" and "Maman, Maman, dites-moi" were the masquerades for the hymns of St. Thomas and St. Bernard. The drinking songs of central European college students were the raucous vehicles for praises to the Blessed Virgin. And so the Pope said equivalently: "Send the opera troupes back to the theatres. Let them do their ogling and swooning on the stage. Prevent Romeo from serenading the priest in the pulpit. Dispatch him to Juliet's balcony. Mail the ballads to the troubadors. Sing the music of the Church." The publication of this official document caused consternation among the so-called church musicians. Gregorian chant? Ugh! Boy sopranos? Palestrina? No modern musician knows anything about these things! Etc.

The editor of the *Ecclesiastical Review*, a publication with a large circulation among priests in this country, asked me to undertake a series of articles in which the major points of the papal letter would be discussed with a view to passing on to organists, through the clergy, the practical information needed to effect the reforms. It was a bold thing for me to have accepted the commission. With the collaboration, however, of Francis X. O'Brien, my successor at the Mission Church, and George Herbert Wells, organist of the Jesuit church in Georgetown, D.C., I published what seemed at the time to be a passable series of articles on the subject. There was enough interest in the series to prompt the editor to publish it as a booklet, *The Dolphin Manual of Church Music*. (At this writing, I am pleased to record that the masterpiece is out of print.) Anent this *Dolphin Manual of Church Music*, I quote here from a brochure of mine written for the reverend Sisters.*

"At the behest of the great Catholic publishing house which was to bring out the book, I called on a leading Prelate of the Church to request that he write a foreword. He was pious and learned and gracious. But he was less informed about choral-music and particularly about teaching choirs than he fancied. He said something like this to me: 'Certainly, I'll be happy to write an introduction for your book, but why are you publishing a book? What is there to write about? You musicians make too much fuss about what is after all a very simple matter. I myself could train a choir in two weeks to sing the Gregorian Chant beautifully and much modern music as well.' But piety, learning and graciousness cannot repair the *couacs* in boys' throats, impart fluency of intonation to thick voices, or appose dynamic-ratios so carefully as to make of

* *Ten Letters About The Child-Voice* (Chicago: Fitzsimon, 1944).

choir-singing an aesthetico-spiritual asset to public worship. The Prelate was a charming old gentleman and is probably now enchanted by the lovely music of angels. But he would have made a poor choirmaster! It occurs to me that the old gentleman's point of view has found too many adherents. 'Why make such a job of a simple thing like teaching a chorus of children to sing? Work on them for a fortnight, and let them *sing, sing, sing!*'

"However, you are not interested in having your choirs *sing, sing, sing!* You are seeking to find that something in choral music which, creating a spiritual aura where it is heard, will be an irresistible influence of religious fervor; more than an influence, for influence is an oblique agency. A real power, direct, strong, and efficacious. No artform can serve religion successfully, if its aesthetic implications and the technique for unfolding them are ignored.

"And so, my dear Sisters, with no disrespect to the dear old Prelate's naivete, I urge you to stress the first undertaking of chorophonic technique; otherwise it will be only *sing, sing, sing.*"

Later on in these pages I plan to review at some length the efforts made by clergy and musicians to comply with the papal decree. I have interpolated this brief chapter here, because the date of the celebrated *Motu Proprio* on church music was only a few months in advance of the date of the founding of the Paulist Choristers.

Chapter IX *Perhaps Chicago Was on the Southern Slope of Mount Parnassus*

IN THE early spring of the year 1904, the Ground Bass began to pound out its theme with intense insistence. I sensed subconsciously that a great undertaking of my life was just beyond a near horizon. Something was about to happen. Something soon did happen. The really important part of my journey up to the Castalian spring on Parnassus began. There was no intimation of how hazardous this portion of the grand tour would be. This I have been ascertaining by bitter-sweet experiences ever since. Here's a contradiction. Sheer cliffs with unsafe footholds, in a prairie state! Mesas with only sand and sagebrush. Deserts without oases. Dinosaurs, brontosaurs, occasional lions and pouncing panthers, not only in the Zoo, but throughout the city. Severe moments. But there were good and great moments, too. Easy, flower-bordered lanes. Fertile areas. Well-watered spaces. Lowing cattle and benign lambs. Kind men and kind women.

Shortly before beginning this part of the great journey, I was assigned to prepare the young ladies of Trinity College, Washington, for the musical portions of the graduation exercises. These exercises were deemed important, for the first class of the college was to receive degrees. The first four years of the college's history had been completed. Prelates and dignitaries were to assist at the functions. The standard of the musical adjuncts had to be high, to bespeak worthily the dignity of the occasion. The chief difficulty confronting me in the fulfillment of this task was to find musical compositions suitable for a choir of young ladies and appropriate to the proceedings. I knew practically nothing about the repertoire available for women's voices. The Sister Superioress suggested a Gregorian Mass, harmonized for three voice lines. In those days, the anomaly of harmonized Gregorian was quite popular. Alexander Guilmant, Theodore Dubois, Sir Edmund Hurley and others had made harmonizations of many Masses for sopranos, altos, tenors and basses. But I was obliged to set to work to make the sort of arrangement which would be right for three female parts. It was quite a job, considering my schedule and the almost weekly examination in theology by the faculty members. The Superioress also wanted a special "Magnificat" composed for the young ladies, and I seemed to be the only one available for that little undertaking.

When the composing was finished, the rehearsals began. Also the fun —fun for the seminarians who twitted me about rehearsing a bevy of blondes, brunettes and redheads. And fun for this same colorful bevy, for the girls delighted in making coy, covert glances at a student for the priesthood, knowing that any young seminarian could easily be teased and embarrassed in such circumstances.

I was a Grade A victim, for many of the lassies were from Boston and well acquainted with my sisters. They planned to have as much fun at my expense as possible, and at every correction, direction or suggestion I would make at rehearsal, blue orbs, grey orbs, brown orbs and orbs speckled with those exclamation points which have created so much history (not only in Paris) would roll around, affecting timidly to glance at me with that languishing, hopeless look of the female who despairs of getting her man. You know what I mean. One doesn't have to be a Bernhardt, an Ethel Barrymore or a Jane Cowl to roll the orbs in that fashion. The talent is universal to the female species. I would ask for better intonation of a phrase, and the eyes would say, "Oh! dear me, whatever shall we do?" A measure would be out of time, and the eyes would roll out a heartbreaking appeal, "Is it altogether hopeless?" Or when I would urge an *animando,* the eyes of all the naiads would seem to glisten with a sparkle of hope, and the orbs of the oreads to tap dance on the hill tops!

That was indeed not a pathetic but a bathetic experience. There was a prefect Sister sitting at the rear of the rehearsal room always, which would make it ungallant for me to tell the nymphs what I thought of their ocular gymnastics. One day toward the end of the rehearsal, the prefect Sister was summoned to an unexpected duty elsewhere. Immediately I hurled the first words of a juicy Philippic at the most histrionic orb-roller, but a girl whom I had known since childhood interrupted, saying: "Don't be stuffy and stupid! We haven't had so much fun in our four years here. Cut out this rehearsal stuff while SHE is downstairs and let us dance."

Well, of course I did let them dance, perpetrating a theatrical hypocrisy of melodramatic quality, for which I have never repented. One of the naiads or oreads, or maybe one of the mermaids from the West Coast, took up sentry position at the head of the long stairway to warn of approaching DISCIPLINE. Then I sat at the piano and played waltz-time hymns in waltz tempo, the best being "Mother Dear O Pray for Me." If this melody is played in the tenor range and the atempause * is employed, the hymn tune makes the "Blue Danube" and the "Merry Widow" seem like elegies. Quite a merry waltz tune. Johann Strauss would have liked it for the "Vienna Woods." A few of the girls kept singing vowel sounds (not the hymn text!) so that the dear Sisters below would believe them to be rehearsing. They danced to most of the three-four tunes in the old *Christian Brothers' Hymn Book*. Maybe I gave them an occasional two-four.

I have never atoned adequately to the Art of Hymnody! The girls did not roll the orbs after that, and I'm not sure that I didn't suffer a sense of real loss. Well, that's water over the dam and the oreads as well as the naiads and West Coast mermaids went along with the water. So there!

The conferring of degrees was accomplished with fitting dignity, the singers giving an excellent account of themselves. The senior of the class did the actual conducting, and to her went my rehearsal baton as a souvenir. The presentation of the baton on that occasion established a precedent for me. Ever since that time, after important concerts, summer-school courses, etc., it has been my habit to toss the baton to the group, much as a bride throws her bouquet to the waiting bridesmaids. A coy little habit!

One amusing concomitant of the musical performances was a highly animated debate between two university professors as to the source of the music. You recall that it had fallen to my lot to arrange or compose the numbers. One professor, internationally known in the field of empirical psychology, insisted that the music was by Handel, that it had all the traits of that master's style, etc. The other gentleman, learned in mathematics and astronomy, professed astonishment that his distinguished colleague could fail to identify the data which proved the music to be that of the Italian Rossini. Having overheard the discussion, I tried to walk with what I presumed was the gait of the great Handel, and making a poor job of the attempt, I shifted to the likely waddle of the fat composer of William Tell. Suddenly remembering the need of "keeping my thumb out of the soup," I resumed my own carriage which, both in actual step and in musical composition, was quite distinctively lame and lopsided.

At any rate, Handel or Rossini or just plain Finn, I hobbled back to the seminary where my meager luggage was already packed in readiness for my start on the great adventure. For I had been ordered by su-

* The atempause is a slight delay on the third beat of the waltz, practiced by Viennese conductors.

periors to go to Old St. Mary's Church, Chicago, the administration of which the Paulist Fathers had taken over shortly before. I was instructed to organize and train the greatest boys' and men's choir of the Middle West! Those were sweeping and rather unenlightened instructions, considering the great reputation already achieved by the Grace Church Choir of Chicago, under H. B. Roney, with Blatchford Kavanaugh its nationally acclaimed solo boy; and considering as well the excellent work with boys and men which the eminent Clarence Dickinson, later of Brick Church, New York, fame, had inaugurated at St. James' Episcopal Church in the same city.

The Chicago undertaking was to be the beginning of the "new life" for me. I knew that I was going to attempt something way out and beyond what had been attempted with boys and men in this country by any other choirmaster—Roney, Messiter, Whitney, Stubbs or Dickinson. For a few weeks, the seminarians had looked on me as an Alice in Wonderland, for I would chatter almost incoherently to any buttonholed listener about plans, purposes and the assurances that I had of unprecedented undertakings. But *I* knew that I wasn't peering through a looking glass. I knew with certainty that the Chicago trip was an expedition into reality so profound that all I could do was to approach it with humble reverence.

I left Washington for Chicago via New York. When the seminarians gathered to bid me adieu, I must have looked queer, indeed. The superior had given me a suit that had been made for a deacon, but which, being badly cut for the deacon's architectural idiosyncrasies, was deemed admirable for me. The trousers were narrow. Skimpy with the terrible threat of parting seams if one would lean over too quickly. My Apollo-like form was poured into these tubelike trousers with the help of a comrade who kept wondering how I would manage in the Pullman car. The coat was of the severe ecclesiastical style of the day with about a thousand black buttons running up from close to the ground to my Adam's apple. The sleeves were too short, and, like the trousers, clinging like leeches to the limbs. Having already received some of the Minor Orders, I was obliged by the Paulist rule to wear a Roman collar. A kindhearted chap, with more charity than sartorial discernment, insisted upon my wearing his hat, an immense creation in rusty black felt, which completely obscured my intellectual dome and pinned my ears nicely under the hatband. An umbrella chapeau!

It was sundown when I appeared before the assembled seminarians in this extraordinary rig. A wonderful sunset for the boys! I had a glance at myself in the broken mirror of my room just before barging forth, and I admit to having looked like an ecclesiastical scarecrow especially made to frighten gargoyles off the eaves of Cathedrals. I can still hear the roars of satirical laughter with which my comrades made their farewells. It was a very odd-looking chap who was leaving to organize the "greatest boys' and men's choir in the Middle West!" Oh, well, I had begun in a Lord Fauntleroy outfit and if the common stock of the Paulist Fathers' Seminary could furnish me only such gala attire, I shouldn't worry, for in my suitcase was a plain suit which I could don immediately after boarding the train.

I am telling some details of this first trip to Chicago, for they seem to have set the pitch for many of the tunes that were to follow through the years. It was necessary to travel via New York, because at New York I would be given a free pass on a differential (second-class) railroad to the great metropolis of the hinterland. What a train! More than thirty hours between New York and Chicago. An upper berth. The whole history of acrobatism was epitomized in my approach to, possession of and recession from that upper insomnia shelf.

About enough money for a glass of water at dinner and a cigarette for the Pullman porter! No provision for transportation money in Chicago. I was told to walk from the depot. The exercise would be beneficial! How foul the Middle West began to look as the low-geared engine reluctantly pulled us west of Buffalo! How off-key I felt when I saw the flat lands of Indiana, and how unmusical as I caught the first whiffs of that attar of odors which has made Chicago famous—the effluvium of the stockyards.

Having remembered, just before arriving at a dismal railroad depot, that there was a very strict priest in charge of Old St. Mary's, I made myself up again into a clerical scarecrow, and disembarked from the train with unco-ordinated ecclesiasticism bursting from every seam. (Some of the seams had already begun to experiment with the verb literally.)

An Irish police officer directed me to the church—to the wrong church. There were and still are two Catholic churches in the downtown near-loop district of Chicago, Old St. Mary's and St. Peter's, the latter a national church for Germans. I couldn't blame the Irish police officer for being confused. My appearance would have bewildered the most astute son of the Emerald Isle. It was evident that I was an ecclesiastic of some sort. The collar and the thousand-button coat attested that much. But I did not resemble a Catholic, an Episcopalian, a Lutheran or any of the non-conformist ministers. My attire was a synthesis of orthodoxy and heterodoxy. The officer may have thought that I was about to start a new religious cult of my own.

At any rate, in the great heat of the late afternoon, with the southwest wind telling its virile story of the slaughterhouses, and the soot of the differential railroad still clinging closely to my attire, I arrived at the German church. A lay brother of the Franciscan Order answered the doorbell. My conformation must have startled him, for he beat out a drum figure on the floor with his sandals that would have intrigued Pat Gilmore, the old bandmaster. A sort of flamparadiddle. When I asked if this were the Paulist Church, he, having gargled a bit in Bavarian, came out into quasi-English with a direction which landed me in the Illinois Central Station. Some kindly soul there set the wild looking "man of God" right, and the collar, thousand-button coat and canopy hat eventually arrived at Wabash Avenue and Eldridge Court which was to be the site of my operations for many years.

The strict priest (I used to confuse "cross" with "strict"), for whose benefit I had redonned the amorphous drapery, opened the door. He looked me over carefully before permitting entrance. He wasn't taking any chances on allowing a State Street hobo dressed up in discarded clerical clothing to enter the portals of the rectory. When he was convinced that most likely I was the Mr. Finn expected, he showed me to a room, told me of the supper hour, and then advised me to shed the ermine and tiara. This gentleman was a saintly old priest, but it was generally believed in the Paulist Community that God had left out both imagination and its derivative, the sense of humor, when He was throwing the Father's personality together. But the Father had sense of humor enough to realize that with the deacon's coat and the extraordinary helmet I would be no asset at Eldridge Court. I asked him if I might lay aside the Roman collar as well, since I was not a priest, but he insisted that I wear it, perhaps as a protection in Chicago, which, an old devotee of the Church presently assured me, was "a den of iniquity."

Well! There's the tale about my arrival at Chicago where I was to organize the Paulist Choristers and underline some of the great principles of choral technique.

The gentlemen of the household gave me a complete picture of the set-up immediately. The outstanding facts were that there was no money, that the equipment was scant and inadequate, that there were no parishioners, the majority of Sunday worshippers coming from nearby hotels, and that therefore there were no boys in the vicinity who might be potential choristers. I may add another outstanding fact which I noticed the first evening—the air was heavy with the most grimy dirt. One look around would convince anyone who was not attempting the ascent of Parnassus that the idea of producing translucent, disembodied, spiritually sparkling tonalities in this neighborhood was Utopian and vain. I admit candidly that the prospects were far from heartening. An announcement heralding my coming had been made from the pulpit on the preceding Sundays and boys were requested to appear for audition on the evening of my arrival.

Immediately after supper, it was suggested that I repair to the organ gallery to play the Benediction service. Upon inquiry as to who would sing the service, he gave further evidence of the lack of parochial resources by replying that there was a quartet choir for Sunday High Mass but that for weekday services a few voiceless members of the congregation would sing the hymns. However, one of the Fathers, modestly rating himself as a "silver medal" member of Sir Edmund Hurley's choir at the Paulist Church in New York, volunteered to sing. "To sing" was the infinitive he used. When I pulled out the old tracker stops on a huge back-gallery collection of organ pipes, he ventured forth with a baritone that I tried to imagine as a silver medal ex-soprano in the familiar "Jesu Dulcis Memoria" of the Christian Brother's book. The good priest had many virtues, but breath control was not in the diadem of these. No sense of phrasing, no precise measuring of the accepted intervals between the notes of the scale. He must have lost the silver medal during the years since he had won it, for his performance was extraordinary in the fullest sense of this plenipotentiary adjective. The old tracker organ coughed. The singing Father wheezed. A coupler on the organ keyboard snapped. The left or right arytenoid cartilege of the good Father wriggled. Musically, the performance was a threnody of melodic plaints.

And that service was my debut in Chicago!

Old St. Mary's was at one time the Cathedral of the Archdiocese of Chicago. The Chicago fire of 1871 destroyed the structure which had been the Cathedral farther north on Wabash Avenue. After the fire, the Bishop purchased the Eldridge Court Church from the Congregationalists, who were moving south, and tried to convert it into a building suitable for Catholic services. For many years the partly-converted Congregational Church at Wabash Avenue and Eldridge Court served as the Cathedral. Later, the Bishop built the present Cathedral Church of the Holy Name on the near-north side of the city. Then the Eldridge Court edifice became the parochial church of the parish of Old St. Mary's, and was successful served by diocesan clergy until November, 1903, when Archbishop Quigley placed the Paulist Fathers in charge in the hope that a vigorous, distinctively American religious community would be able to serve the transient population of the district with special understanding. Also, Archbishop Quigley, realizing the devotion of the Paulists to the purpose of making the Catholic Church better understood, or less misunderstood, among non-Catholics, expected the new Old St. Mary's to offer special religious attractions to the Chicago citizenry.

Father Peter J. O'Callaghan, a Bostonian and Harvard graduate, had engineered my assignment to Old St. Mary's. It was quite irregular among the Paulists to place a student in charge of a parochial activity, but the situation seemed to be an emergency one and traditions were waived.

After my debut service, I went into the hall attached to the Church to interview applications for the new choir. It was a wretched place—floor boards warped, a single feeble gaslight scowling in a far corner, an old square piano with half of the keys denuded of their ivory mantles, and probably not tuned since the Columbian Exposition of 1893.

Two small boys composed the total of candidates. I am giving their names, because they were the first members of an organization which was to become *celèbre*, a chorus that was to assemble a great number of friends, a smaller number of unfavoring critics, a unit which was to prove to be the laboratory for retruing old principles and precepts of choral virtuosity. One boy had the surname Gasparri. He did not remain long in the unit. The other lad, John Keeley, who was a faithful member for many years and is now a distinguished judge of the Probate Court, was a postcradle infant of about six. Young Gasparri was about eight years of age.

What a start for the soprano chorus! Two members aged eight and six!

I retired from the interview feeling that if the Holy Ghost did not indicate the way, there would be no choir of boys and men at Eldridge Court.

But, of course, I knew that the Holy Ghost would indicate the way. In my boyhood at Boston, a saintly Carmelite nun, Mother Angela, had inculcated in me a sense of confident dependence on the Spirit of God. And so I went to bed on that first night in Chicago convinced that natural resources, personal talent or personal determination would not be adequate to the situation but that the Holy Ghost would "arrange."

From all appearances, the proposed Paulist Choir of Chicago looked like a Utopian dream. The Ground Bass refused to come to the surface on that first night. The odor from the southwest discouraged it. The noise of the Wabash Avenue cable cars loudly and jerkily denied it audibility. If it hadn't been for the splendid service rendered me by Mother Angela, I am sure that I would have applied for a cancellation of my commission. It would have been easy to convince the New York Superior that there was no chance for building a choral unit of boys and men at Old St. Mary's.

But the next morning (the wind blowing *toward* the stockyards), the Holy Ghost took over through Father Hopper. "Go to the De La Salle Institute on Wabash Avenue and Thirty-fifth Street. Speak to the Brother in charge. Tell him your needs and ask his permission to address the small boys."

The Brother Director received me most cordially. I addressed a group of soprano-age boys and recruited approximately twenty promising candidates. These boys, although it was summertime and they were entitled to their holidays, began the series of intensive rehearsals which, it was hoped, would have the new organization ready for an early autumn appearance. The De La Salle boys interested friends in various parts of the city, and presently we had enough sopranos to give promise of some success to the venture.

The Christian Brothers were thus indirectly, almost directly, responsible for the actual organization of the Paulist Choristers, and it is a pleasant obligation here to acknowledge this fact.

Father Hopper had the weather-beaten old piano freshened up but could not improve the choir hall. One dim gaslight continued to accentuate the gloom, and the bumpy floor boards offered hazards to the urchins when they gamboled about before and after rehearsals.

As at the Mission Church, the deadline was too close. A few weeks to remake shouting boys into dulcet agencies of music! Of course, I knew much more about the practical phases of the art of converting shouters into singers than when I began at Boston; but I was hard pressed, nevertheless, to achieve the elimination of the rough chest-tone quality, to replace it with a light, volatile but living timbre, to teach the notes of Masses, motets and hymns, and to give shape to the shapeless men's chorus that we had assembled.

There was nothing to attract good talent to the young Paulist choir. A few men accepted the invitation to join, but they were few indeed, and many of them gifted with only meager vocal resources.

Boys mornings and afternoons, men in the evenings! During the interim hours I would write the music, make copies from a three-dollar hectograph which Father Hopper proudly produced, and try to interest professional sources from which I vainly hoped to secure more and better tenors and basses.

We had begun in early June. Suddenly, in mid-August, the new choir took the definite form of a singing unit. Knowing no more about the alto line than I had known at Boston, the alto chorus was a makeshift assortment of treble voices, but the fortunate acquisition of Thomas Mc-Granahan, to whom I have already referred as being one of the two real alto boys I have encountered over the years, gave real distinction to this difficult voice part. We practiced the Responses in harmony, two Gregorian harmonized Masses (quasi-Gregorian, written by Henri Dumont), some simple motets, and processional and recessional hymns.

Father O'Callaghan, who had become the Rector, arranged to have cheap softwood pews placed in the chancel on the Gospel side. An outstanding problem was the organ. The mammoth edifice of metal and wooden pipes stood in the far-off gallery. After much calculating and some begging, we arranged to purchase a Vocalion reed organ which was placed in a good position among the pews of the chancel. The Vocalion was, as I remember it, quite superior to the average reed organ. The standard reed organ in those days played by suction through the reeds, the Vocalion by blasting or forcing the air through them. A small tube stood atop each reed and the vibrating tone of the reed was thus amplified and rounded out as it emerged through the tube. I have never quite understood why the manufacture of this unique and most satisfactory type of reed organ was discontinued.

All during those days of the summer of 1904, I was subconsciously aware of the destiny of the forming unit, but consciously I was alert only to the drab needs of each moment. Father O'Callaghan persuaded the Sisters of the Good Shepherd to make cassocks and surplices for the choir members. Toward the end of September, we were bold enough to announce the date of our initial appearance.

Remembering the Abington episode, I counseled caution about the publicity. But news had spread throughout the city that Old St. Mary's was to be the scene of a novel choral feature, and all the seats in the Church had been reserved well in advance. My memory of the sound effects of the choir in rehearsal is that the sopranos had an ethereal, lovely tone quality, although how this was acquired in so short a time I am not prepared to explain. The McGranahan alto line was like the golden light of the setting sun shining through the varicolored panes of a stained-glass window. It was an out-of-this-world loveliness. The tenors were inadequate, but the basses, Mr. Edwin Foley, a former Paulist student being the principal, were passably good.

Whenever the four harmonized parts were in close relationship, that is, when the parts were not separated by wide intervals, the ensemble blend was satisfying. It surpassed my achievement at the Mission Church. But when the parts were widely separated, as they so often are in the simplest numbers, the blend and beauty leaped across the Illinois Central Railroad tracks to disappear in Lake Michigan or elsewhere. Each part sounded as a rebellious member of a disunited family, unwilling to make any allowances or concessions.

The boys looked well on the fitting day, the cassocks and surplices being neatly cut; but the men looked like something the Columbian Exposition officials had forgotten to have removed from the Midway Plaisance in 1893. Several strange ensembles had "showed" on the Midway, but a fair-minded judge would have given my men first prize. The cassock tops permitted all styles of linen and cotton collars to show: pointed Piccadilly stand-ups, straight stand-ups, full roll-over plys, neckties, cravats, ascots. Men with beards, full, fan tails, Van Dykes, goatees; walrus, curled-up and languid mustaches. Men with shaven faces, peaches and cream! Some quite unadorned.

We had a photograph taken of the members who were to participate in the opening ceremony. A few gentlemen of more hirsute than vocal distinction had been permitted to resign on fitting day! The picture was taken in the backyard of the Rectory and includes the then young Fathers Gillis, Welsh and Mallon who had been appointed to the parochial staff.

The opening ceremony of the new choir's service to the Paulist Fathers was on a Sunday evening in late September or early October. It was an elaborate affair. First, the former mixed quartet (augmented) sang its swan song in the gallery. I played the huge, sullen organ. I remember that the augmented group of ladies and gentlemen sang the "Magnificat" which I had written for Trinity College in the preceding spring. Miss Lucy O'Neill was the soloist. She was a member of the Irish Choral Society and contributed much to establish a friendly relationship between the two potentially rival organizations. The ladies and gentlemen sang superbly that evening. It was as though they were sculpturing a fitting tomb for the quartets and mixed choruses which had rendered splendid artistic service, even though it was operatic, for several decades in downtown Chicago.

The diapasons of the organ angrily declared their disapproval of the change in the musical set-up of the Church. High string stops and flutes waved out-of-tune farewell to the two angels who at that time ornamented the sanctuary wall. The oboe and cornopean said good-bye to the high-backed Protestant pews which, without the customary middle aisle of Catholic churches, had been left when the church was altered for Catholic services. The ensemble of the organ and chignon choir announced that since Lake Michigan was being pushed farther out from the local Illinois Central Railroad tracks, they too would recede in favor of small boys and cassocked gentlemen. Chicago was changing, musically as well as topographically.

Then came a sermon by the Rector, Father Peter J. O'Callaghan. It was addressed chiefly to the new choristers who were sitting in civilian attire in the front pews. He told them of their obligations and privileges, stressing the fact that in the early Church only Levites, ecclesiastics with at least Minor Orders, were permitted to participate in the sacred functions of the Sanctuary. Upon the conclusion of the sermon, each member of the new choir approached the Altar where Fathers O'Callaghan and Hopper respectively gave him a cassock and a surplice.

With the newly blessed cassocks and surplices the choristers retired to a vesting room downstairs, and presently the new choir made solemn entry from the sacristy singing a processional hymn.* Self-conscious, nervous, concentrating on the right words and notes. Somehow they all arrived at the pews in the chancel. Confusion reigned for a few moments while the men, self-conscious because of their wives and friends in the congregation, genuflected awkwardly, went into the places reserved for soprano boys, and, backing out, hunted for their proper seats. I was working away at the Vocalion, pumping it as full of wind as rapidly moving feet could accomplish. I had a violinist nearby, Mr. Louis Brosseau, now of the Board of Trade, whose function was to play the soprano melody in a high octave, lest the small lads, being frightened at the first experience of such pageantry, fail to hold their melodic line.

The Benediction service followed, and, with the Recessional over, the initial appearance of the Paulist Choristers was a *fait accompli.*

* The Paulist Church in New York was one of the only Catholic churches in America up to that date in which processional hymns in the vernacular were sung while the choristers marched from sacristy to chancel. The *Introit* (verse of Scripture sung at the beginning of High Mass) was in the early Church chanted in procession. The Greek rites, both Uniate and Orthodox, still preserve this effective ritualistic feature. The Episcopalians in North America introduced the processional hymn to moderns, but their mother church, the Church of England, never adopted the feature in the English cathedrals.

A processional hymn, well sung, modulated carefully and presented usually as a prayer, is so effective a contribution to a solemn liturgical service that it is difficult to understand why it is not generally used. The recessional hymn, when sung as a great outpouring of praise and thanksgiving, makes a noble close for a solemn service. I have always tried to establish the difference between the Processional and the Recessional.

Chapter X   *Some Notes are Clear,*
Others Murky

THE first service of the new choir captured attention. But the interest of the congregation had not been centered upon the musical parts of the service. It was the picturesqueness and the unusualness of the ceremony that caught the fancy. The acid test was to be the High Mass on the following Sunday. Although nothing was particularly amiss on that important occasion, the consensus of opinion was that the boys would not prove acceptable substitutes for the women and that the style of music offered was drab and tended to depress the worshippers. In fact, rumors soon became current that leading members of the congregation were considering giving up their pews. There was not sufficient dramatic urge to engage the emotions. The little soprano boys were cute looking, but as agencies of music they were negligible. Etc., etc.

That was the start in Chicago. That was the beginning of the Paulist Choristers. The Ground Bass was arraigned for trial on Wabash Avenue with inadequate counsel for its defense and little sympathy for its vindication.

Presently it was necessary for me to return to Washington to continue clerical studies, and a layman was selected to function as choirmaster during my absence. Although a good general musician, he was unfamiliar with the special needs of a boys' choir, and the choir made little progress. Upon my return the following June, I found the boys in poor vocal condition, the technique of the unit ragged, and the congregation violently and volubly opposed to the continuation of the counterfeit chorus. We had built the framework of a promising choir the preceding year, but now the uprights and cross pieces did not fit together. There was no blend in any of the rilievos. Tenors and basses had been promoting a vocal feud that put to shame the mildness of the Sicilian vendettas. Charivari! Din!

During that summer I accomplished whatever repair work was possible, endeavoring to refit the pieces so that they would hang together during the following winter when again I would be in Washington, this time for the final term before ordination to the holy priesthood. I remember having concentrated on the Responses, inculcating an aesthetico-religious concept of these among the boys and men. On the first Sunday of my reappearance, I softened the general dynamic (quantitative) level of the singing, and members of the congregation told me afterwards that their first impression was that the choir had at last lost all confidence and was about to "throw in the towel." The grouchy old pipe organ still stood in the west-end gallery, many expecting it soon to resume its grumblings when the chignon outfit would have returned. The members of the congregation who thus reported their first impressions conceded that, as the service proceeded, the softer intonations of boys and men began to interest them, and that, for the first time since the preceding autumn, the potential effectiveness of a boys' and men's choir was intimated.

Ever since that time, my principal prescription for quickly remedying the ineffectiveness of choirs and orchestras has been *to reduce the quantity of tone in all the parts and especially in the treble.* There is a gremlin haunting the louder panels of musical expression, and once he's given a chance to function, the lovelier aspects of music swoon away in supine fright. Noise and music are natural foes. No peace can ever be effected between these, for their component elements are at eternal variance. For several years I had used pianissimo in the early stages of training, but it was in that summer of 1905 that I learned the real worth of applying this to an entire chorus that needed to be reprepared for immediate performances. And so, years later at Hollywood Bowl, a chorus transformed itself under the soothing influence of soft singing in a few weeks. At Boston, a few seasons ago, a chorus of one thousand ladies and gentlemen readied itself to make real music at Symphony Hall in a short time, by the same method. From one end of the country to the other, I have been guest conductor of every type of choral organization, and I have found that invariably the directing of rehearsals in the softer dynamic panels and the moderating of fortes in performance invited a spiritual effect to come through the ensembles which had not been even hinted at before. I could give innumerable instances. Later in these pages, in chronological order, I shall mention some of these.

It is relevant here to summon the memory of one such experience. This was at Chicago in 1936. Thirty-one years after the summer of 1905! I was conducting at the mammoth annual musical festival of the *Chicago Tribune* at Soldiers' Field. Chorus: one thousand; orchestra: the Chicago Symphony augmented to one hundred and thirty players! Two rehearsals. One indoors. The chorus shouting with the bombast of a stadium full of football rah-rah-ers. The orchestra pulling heavily on the high bows, and brass blowing as angry sirens announcing a Caribbean tornado! There was to be an audience of about a hundred thousand. I had not conducted in Chicago for some seasons. I was brought on from New York by the *Tribune* because of my long association with national and international enterprises in the choral field. The public was told to expect something extraordinary.

At the outset of the combined indoors rehearsal of the huge chorus and the oversize orchestra, I sensed that if I didn't pull a rabbit out of my conjurer's bag I'd have only bedlam, farrago and mess. I pulled the rabbit out immediately by the ears and stood the magic burrowing hare on its hind legs on the podium. The rabbit was, of course, a stage whisper to both chorus and orchestra that I was definitely an erratic conductor and that if any participant produced more than a piano sound, and the trebles of choir and orchestra more than a pianissimo, I would go "off my rocker," and a total eclipse of moon and stars would ensue at Soldiers' Field. The orchestra seemed to be understandingly amused, but the chorus evidently judged the tumble from the rocker to have taken place already. But, in awe and expectant curiosity, all observed my instructions, and at the performance a recreated tonal blend was projected through the great spaces of the Soldiers' Field.

This reflection about the efficacy of guest conductors employing the lighter quantitative levels with choruses and orchestras grew out of my tale about the condition of the young Paulist choir in the summer of 1905.

Then, I struggled with an unsatisfactory and bulgy chorus for several weeks, handed it over to a new incumbent, the first having resigned just in time to avoid a coronary thrombosis threatened by his dealing with the husky sons of the prairies. Then I hied back to Washington to absorb more erudition, to be startled upon arrival by the announcement that I was to train and conduct a choir at St. Paul's Church, Washington, during the ensuing high season. I had had no vacation, and the schedule of the final year at the seminary was to be exacting—an extra course at the Mission House to learn the technique of preaching Catholic and non-Catholic missions, and the superadded burden of giving three rehearsals each week to the small boys across the city, two rehearsals to the seminarians who were to provide the tenor and bass vocal lines, and Solemn Mass and Vespers each Sunday.

That was a program to get a chap "ready to be busy" the rest of his life! I'm grateful now for having been pushed into the situation because, although the days were most trying and my nerves were entertaining me with jerky spasms, I became inured to hard things. That season was a kind of final novitiate for the onerous duties of the years to come. But as the months went along and I became interested in Father Elliott's course at the Mission House, I was visited with a major temptation, and I must confess, that as far as my own will was involved, I yielded to the temptation. The temptation was to chuck music altogether and apply to the Superior to be assigned to the group of Missionary Fathers. I applied in due time, and the old gentleman, with that polished skill characteristic of so many ecclesiastical superiors, calmed me by saying that "all will be arranged satisfactorily in June." How often since have I heard the same resonant hocus-pocus. How meaningless its ring—like the sound of timpani out of key! "All will be arranged satisfactorily in June" is a code announcement to the crowd to sell you short. Most of the time in my life, either June refused to bob up or the adverb "satisfactorily" suffered a change of definition before it got hold of the verb!

But I didn't know what the old gentleman really had in mind. Closing my ears to the Ground Bass theme, I nevertheless took meticulously scrupulous care of the external details of the job at St. Paul's Church, waiting with cold patience for June to come. The calendar June came along after an eternity of months, but the old gentleman's June never showed up.

During that season in Washington, my technical facility in dealing with choirs necessarily improved. Each Sunday we sang before an international congregation. Officials of the government and diplomats from many countries came regularly with their highly cultured wives and families to the solemn services. The burden on the seminarians was heavy. To prepare and render two long service programs each week, the normal ease of Sunday being forfeited as well, was an onus of three dimensions. Gradually the seminarians began to blame me for the situation. Having tried to make clear the fact that I had had nothing to do with the arrangements, but that the financial compensation for our services was of considerable help to the Paulist community, I was still conscious off playing an unpopular role.

The requirements at St. Paul's Church included uninterrupted additions to the repertoire. This need provided excellent opportunity for composition. It became my habit after a while to compose the offertory motet for each following Sunday after breakfast on Thursday or Friday. Since the boys were all tyros, it was not feasible to program a motet for sopranos, altos, tenors and basses except for certain great Feast Days, and so I developed, by necessity, a certain measure of semiskill in writing for tenors and basses. Composition for two tenor lines, a baritone line and a deep bass line is much more difficult (if one adverts to the sound effects when the written notes are actually sung) than composition for the S.A.T.B. chorus. One is apt to assign notes to the lower voices which will be too murky for satisfactory harmonic effect. Writing for sopranos and altos alone offers a similar problem, although the difficulty of relating contraltos to sopranos, for the ear, is less than that of placing the baritones in fortunate position with the second tenors.

At St. Paul's, that winter I was put on the spot by some dilletanti who, with a smattering knowledge of Gregorian chant, had a disposition to be critical. One of these was a prominent banker of the city who regularly brought guests. Every so often he would invite a retired German organist who had definite ideas about the organ accompaniments to Gregorian chant. My first experience with the Gregorian chant had been with Frenchmen in the preparatory seminary. The French predilection for harmonizing the chant included the use of accidentals, i.e., sharps and flats which did not properly belong to the Gregorian scales. The French were devoted to what is known technically as the *tierce de Picardie,* which for the layman may be described simply as turning a minor into a major mode. At St. Paul's I had been very French until the banker complained that his German friend was much disturbed by the use of the Picardy sugar. So, to keep everybody happy, I arranged with the usher to be informed if the German had arrived. If he were in the congregation, I supplied strict modal accompaniments, not an accidental from *Introitus* to *Communio.* When he was absent, we had a wonderful time with the accidentals. Picardy was transferred to Washington. The strict, ultraconservative life of the Gregorian modes was relaxed, and the white and black keys of the organ flirted together quite outrageously. My conscience was not a bit bothered, spiritually or musically, because Gregorian chant was a complete art form before harmony began to be codified. Who had the right to dictate rules for harmonizing the chant, since chant was essentially an unharmonized style of song? In later years, however, I worked out a plan of harmonization which would be consistent with the spirit of each Gregorian mode, establishing the chordal structure according to the relationships of the important notes in each scale.

On one occasion, the adult singers nearly collapsed during the processional hymn. A tall, callow layman had joined the group. His voice had never changed, and I assigned him to the alto chorus. He was an odd looking fellow—like the first assistant of an old-time undertaker. Cadaverous enough himself to be chummy with corpses. It was the last Sunday of the ecclesiastical year, and we were singing a menacing hymn entitled "Go and Dig My Grave Today." A deaf woman was in the front pew near the door through which the procession wound its way. She was adjusting her acousticon while the sopranos were passing. As soon as she had it working, she directed it to the processional platform, and looking up beheld the Singing Cadaver, the acousticon amplifying his obituary tone quality, the text, at the moment, threatening her with a speedy six feet of earth. The combination was disastrous. The lady with the acousticon reacted as the average person of Irish ancestry reacts to the impression that a ghost is soaking through the wall. Down she went in the space between pew and kneeling bench, the acousticon and Prayer Book abandoned in the aisle. I had been playing the reed organ near the altar rail but was startled into inactivity. Tenors and basses proximate to the pew of the Swooned Lady ceased their vocal contributions to the dirge, but the sopranos and altos, including the Apparition from the Sarcophagus of Hymnody, continued their ejaculation of words and notes. The majority of the tenors and basses, after the first shock of observing the episode, resumed their threnodic harmonies, while the ushers and myself escorted the lady, the acousticon and the Prayer Book to the adjacent sacristy. Therefore, the Processional was concluded unaccompanied, and my first experience with an a cappella Processional was accomplished.

In later years I elaborated a fulsome plan of presenting processional and recessional hymns in a great variety of accompanied stanzas—a cappella stanzas with a semichorus remaining in the choir stalls, a cappella stanzas with the larger choir marching along the outer platform, etc. But the first a capella Processional was forced upon me under extraordinary circumstances.

Every once in a while during my final days at New York, when the choir would sing an a capella stanza of a particularly discouraging hymn, my ghost alto of Washington would seem to hop onto the organ console, leer at me, showing teeth yellowed in the tomb, and dash out into the nave of the church to frighten another deaf or timid female into prostration. The occasion at Washington was the first and last appearance of the Sallow Adult with the Alto Voice. Also it was the last time for the performance under my direction of that ghastly collection of rhymed meters assembled under the gruesome caption, "Go and Dig My Grave Today." I think that I must have learned a lot, unwittingly of course, about using strange voices, strange-looking anthropoids and strange texts on that memorable occasion; for, although later on in my career I did program some queer stuff, allowing chaps who were not related to Adonis to appear in my organization, and once in a while putting forth an odd text, I never made the mistake of reassembling such an array of cemetery oddments as on that Sunday forty long years agone. The sallow, callow Voice of Dracula became a mute member of the congregation,

but the tenors and basses, when spying him from the processional platform, would occasionally get B naturals and B flats confused.

During that last winter season in Washington I was doing my best
while winding up my musical adventures and looking forward to the
clever old Superior's June. We produced some signally effective choral
results. Although I was still a seminarian (a deacon at last with my own
suit and inconspicuous hat!) and the rule of the House of Studies did
not permit seminarians to waste time socially, I was perforce obliged
once in a while to ask permission from the stern Superior of the seminary
to visit a diplomat or government official with the delightfully naive old
Pastor of St. Paul's, Monsignor Mackin, who had been my father's
classmate and friend at college.

Once I was under the necessity of playing a house organ off Dupont
Circle for a dizzy assemblage of men and women, some of them obviously touched with a tint of masculine preciousness or feminine viril-
ity, and a few right out of Oppenheim's imagination. Some well-rouged,
tight-skirted, and seductive, silly sirens who seemed to be on hand
everywhere to wrest secrets from darling old generals and admirals who
were treating Washington to a fabulous riot of walrus mustaches, creaking knee joints and bulging bemedaled chests. Social corollaries to the
Spanish American war! One of these sirens—an old-timer, masquerading
as youngish, but really an ancient thrown into youthfulness by a beau-
tician, modiste, milliner and society editor—crept out of a dark corner
where the champagne had worked on a general, or maybe only a colonel,
before she could get her artificial charms to work on him, and accosted
me with a gamut of grimaces which were in the fortissimo panel. She
said something like this: "Oh! How beautifully you play the organ. You
have hypnotized me! Ah! Me! It is so complete! I mean *incomplete!*"
The sounds of the organ had probably only irritated her while she was
trying to beat the effervescence of the champagne to whatever the general or colonel called his mind. "Why do you wear that funny collar?
You are so young! You will come to my mansion in New Hampshire
Avenue tomorrow at tea time and I shall tell you how, in Europe, you
can win the Prix de Rome, study with the great masters and become a
first conductor in the Opera. I have villas at St. Cloud and Nice where
the great artists of the world—even the English!—come on Sundays at
twilight. You visit me *demain.*"

Although there was no fraternity of Harvard enthusiasts to vociferate,
I felt much as I had felt at Cambridge on the evening when I prompted
the pretty recitalist in her forgotten sequence of the Brahms song. Only
this time, there was the Oppenheim subtlety in the atmosphere. Indica-

tions that the admonitions of Sunday-school teachers were based on history! Mascaraed eyelashes. Brows curtaining diplomatic memories. I hustled for Monsignor Mackin. The tone quality of a Riviera siren had elements beyond the acoustical. These were obviously beyond the ken of an ecclesiastical youth. About as much as a small ice cube would discourage a sizzling sauté, the Roman collar influenced the spy from Monte Carlo. The Monsignor was muttering Prix de Rome, St. Cloud, Nice, Opéra Comique, etc. "Indeed, young man, come back to the rectory. I'm glad that the most notorious vampire in Washington accosted you. Good experience. But forget it, and see that you play the Psalms well tonight."

I had experience with labor trouble during my five decades in the musical arena. Just before my ordination, at the final service under my direction at St. Paul's, Washington, the tenor chorus of the seminarians' choir went on a strike. A sit-down strike. The leading tenor persuaded his associates on that important choral line that we could not give an artistic rendition of the principal number programmed. I was powerless against the influence of the labor leader.

Another strike was fomented and called in Chicago early in the autumn of 1906 by the Rector himself. I did not know of this aspect of the strike at that time. You remember that the old Superior in New York had told me that "all will be well in June." Well, June had come around, I had been ordained and I was stationed in Chicago. Upon arrival I had told Father O'Callaghan that I was not to have charge of the music. He was amused. I was sent down to Jerseyville, Illinois, to help Father Gillis on a mission. Upon my return, the Rector told me that the choir refused to sing the High Mass unless I would conduct it. He entreated me to go into the choir hall, rehearse the Choristers and preside at "just this one service." Being an easy-going chap, unsuspecting and all that sort of thing, I complied, and the "just this one service" extended itself to the long series of rehearsals and services of a thirty-six years' stretch. Boy sopranos for the major part of a lifetime. Small, undisciplined, noisy urchins to be put in order, curried with vocalization combs, and cajoled into such condition as to fit them for instrumentalities of the great art of the Muses! Toward the end of my years with boy sopranos, the sight of a youngster of choir-boy age was enough to unleash wild thoughts in my mind. Boy-choir training—murder by slow poison! The constant need of replacing boys whose voices necessarily change is one of the grievous burdens of the master of a liturgical choir. A fine choir in June. A poorer than mediocre outfit in the following September. Brilliant solo boys at Christmas, garglers at Easter. Splendid repertoire last month, nothing this month.

Once I lost a contract, which was about to be signed with a talking-machine company, because the leading soprano boys suddenly and without warning went sour vocally. The managers of the talking-machine company, listening to determine the selections to be recorded, decided not to sign the contract, and my vision of amassing capital for the upkeep of a choir school faded—as so many other mirages of financial security faded.

Another strike occurred in New York. The prefect of the sopranos was an exacting and querulous somebody. One afternoon, at the broadcast of the Catholic Hour, he and the boys had a more than ordinarily spectacular row, and the boys, without advising me, decided to absent themselves from the Lenten evening service at St. Paul's church where Monsignor Fulton Sheen was conducting a course before a large congregation. Many days were required for untangling the skein.

Chapter XI *Or Did Parnassus Move to Chicago?*

YES! Since my duties in the great metropolis of the plains kept me tethered to the shores of Lake Michigan, I arranged with Pegasus and a team of winged horses to transport Parnassus to Illinois. If the mount of the Muses had insisted on remaining in Thessaly, it would have been necessary for me to abandon my efforts to scale the peak. And so Apollo agreed to permit the transfer of the site. But the climbing proved to be just as difficult. The fissures between aspirations and achievements were just as gaping. And the winds that blew across Lake Michigan very often diverted the melodic triolets from the choir hall with the force of Hellenic mountain gales.

As soon as I set foot in the choir hall to call off the alleged strike of the autumn of 1906, I began to rehear the Ground Bass. It reclaimed my attention so forcibly that I was puzzled to understand my state of mind during the preceding year. Why had I shut off its communications? Did I not know it would be impossible for me to evade the pursuing of that mighty theme? Wraiths of the Roxbury Crusaders, the Pious Choir of Bostonian Dowagers, the Preparatory Seminary Plain Chant Choir, the men's choir at the Major Seminary, the Mission Church series of satires, the eye-rolling songsters of Trinity College, and the first group of the Paulist Choristers sneered at me for having applied to the Superior for relief from musical duties.

When I resumed these lyrical obligations, I found that the practice of the art of music was to be balanced by a full schedule of parochial activities. Sick calls at night in emergency hospitals versus Gregorian chant in the afternoons! The development of volatile soprano tone quality apposed and opposed to attendance on attempted bichloride of mercury suicides. The choir hall and an adjacent morgue. Confessions and counterpoint. Malaria, Mozart and murders! What a potpourri of contrasted elements! Boys coming from the cradle to be trained as singers, and old men dying in flophouses on State Street. Conferences with rich people about the possibility of sweeping up two-dollar bills for a fund to put the choir on a good financial basis, and overheard symposiums between "Hinky Dink," "Bath House" John and "First Search" McNally, in the nearby undertaking establishment of McNally's about the vote to be turned in by the first ward in an oncoming municipal election! A thick ragout, indeed!

I learned early that two-dollar bills were beginning to be scarce, and soon would disappear from circulation altogether. (This prediction was confirmed when I moved to New York.) The reigning Catholic aristocracy of the Midwest as well as the East wrapped up its donations to the choir in tiny rolls of dimes or nickels. The idea of supporting a Catholic cultural project evidently amused the gentry which, subscribing to the tenets of the Catholic Creed, thought it quite absurd to subscribe to the Finn-ish Hexachords of Guido of Arezzo. Of course, old Guido, as propounded and exemplified by Protestant or non-sectarian musical groups, elicited interest and two-dollar bills aplenty. Rome was still good for theology, but the non-Catholic touch was needed for present-day music!

The outlook for the growth of a superlative Catholic choir of boys and men was dim, leaden, turbid. It failed to become clearer with the years. But we struggled along. Our place on Wabash Avenue interested many classes of people. Police and politicians. Even piteous prostitutes would slither into back pews for *Benediction,* hoping against hope that some miracle would happen to snatch them from their unhappy estate. There was a camaraderie which was bound to broaden the vision of a narrow-minded little Bostonian accustomed to the holier-than-thou poses of New England. I became a better musician because of my duty days at Old St. Mary's. A spiritual something popped out of the notes of an "Ave Maria" which probably would have remained hidden if, just before the service or rehearsal, I had not been engaged in persuading some poor creature that "all was not lost, but that God would make things right." The experience of dealing directly with people's spiritual needs and difficulties, although I was clumsy at the start, made me more sensitive to the spiritual values of music. And so the Ground Bass was encouraged to resound more clearly.

The autumn of 1906 was a thoroughly bad time for the Paulist Choristers. They composed neither a good nor a bad choir. The tepidity of their choral offerings was menacing. I was frightened by the lassitude of the Choristers and the ennui of the congregation. If I were to fail to animate the choir, it would soon succumb to the stagnant finality of inertia. But what to do? In the summer of 1905, as I have already recorded, the framework of the original choir was all that remained. In

1906, all the uprights and crossbeams which any builder would require
for even a framework to remain standing had been burned by accident
or arson. I sat before a heap of ashes. It was not even easy to identify
the kind of wood which had been the basis for the ashes. Boys and men
sounded almost alike. Perhaps, if the men had not been adorned with
mustaches and girt with the corpulent evidence of adulthood, I might
have signaled sixty-year-olders to take the entrance leads of postcradle
sopranos.

The problem of obtaining enough boys for the soprano choir was
serious. The group of boys who had come from the De La Salle Academy
in the summer of 1904 was thinning out and the choir had insufficient
glamor at the time to attract new talent. In spite of industrious rehearsing we were making no real progress. At Christmastide we gave a
program of Christmas carols. This must have been poor, indeed, for I
remember clutching for encouragement at a comment of a young lady
(Miss Daisy Eager, who was nicknamed in reprisal "Miss Violet Anxious"), the irony of which escaped me for several days. After the carol
service, she came to the sacristy and rolled out this oily appreciation of
our efforts: "How ambitious and delightfully daring you are! Think of
attempting a number from Handel's *Messiah* with this choir!" Upon
my modest reply that we had not attempted an excerpt from the celebrated oratorio, she exclaimed: "But that last number, Father; wasn't it
'All We Like Sheep Have Gone Astray?'"

On a dreary morning during the ensuing week, the shriveling satire
of Mlle. Anxious was translated into direct ridicule by an unsympathetic
member of the household. At breakfast! Breakfast is not the easiest
meal. Not the best time to refer to some carol services. Not the pro-
pitious moment for an antagonistic chap to tell you how raucously Mlle.
Anxious had laughed in recounting to him her remarks in the sacristy.
The unsympathetic breakfaster even affected to imitate the fervid made-
moiselle's gestures as she pictured my manner and reaction while being
taken in. I am quite sure that the undiplomatic as well as unsympathetic
reporter-of-unpleasant-things-in-the-morning amplified the Anxious person's irony, for he held forth at length about the sopranos, dear little
lambs, wandering away from their ewe-mamas of the alto chorus, who
themselves had deserted the course tentatively followed by the bleating
rams in the tenor and bass sections. He concluded by intimating that the
performance would have made a passable Irish lamb stew if after the
slaughter a pungent condiment had been added.

But the satire and its reduction to plain language failed to disturb
me seriously. We had given a poor show. Well! forget it and do better
next time! I had trained myself not to take anything unpleasant over-

seriously in the early morning. Give the old mocha and java a chance to tune up the resistance of the system, etc. Somewhere along the line, I had picked up a good philosophy about such things : if you must construe a situation to be unpleasant, don't do anything about it until the evening. Correspondingly, never make a favorable decision about important matters in the evening. The morning frequently finds one glum and depressed; the evening too often brings elation and undiscerning enthusiasms. How often does the blunder of a bright evening dream come paradoxically out in dark cloudiness the following morning, and how frequently noontime reverses the bad decisions of sunrise time!

So I did not strut out of the breakfast room in a huff or decide to disband the choir. But I did begin to study some of the attitudes of the clergy toward enterprises which were not directly connected with the catechism. These were sometimes amusing, sometimes enlightening, sometimes discouraging. But, by and large, the Roman collar is a symbol of natural virtues, optimism and co-operation as well as of the supernatural excellences, even if practitioners of the Fine Arts are sometimes regarded as kindred to heretics.

I decided that two things must be done as soon as possible, if the choir was to be lifted out of its deadly mediocrity. First : a pipe organ must be built in the Sanctuary. Second : the choir needing publicity of a favorable kind in order to attract talent, a concert performance at Orchestra Hall, the Thomas (Chicago Symphony) Orchestra accompanying, must be arranged.

The Rector was eagerly willing to co-operate in the matter of the pipe organ. But we had very little money, our financial estate not having improved much since 1904. Finally the household staff agreed that we could find four thousand dollars for the new organ. The old scowling grumbler was taken down from the west-end gallery and sold for a few hundred dollars. Hillgreen and Lane, one of the smaller pipe organ companies, undertook to provide as much organ as four thousand dollars could erect. Both members of the firm were most co-operative, and in a short time a notably good organ stood behind the High Altar which the Rector had had moved forward in the Sanctuary. Real choir stalls replaced the chancel pews. The organ was an electro-pneumatic action type which was on the eve of being abandoned by builders in favor of straight electric action. Many of the registers of pipes were excellent and it was easy to simulate orchestral effects.

One day, the senior member of one of the greatest and most expensive firms of organ builders in North America (*not* my friend Ernest Skinner of Mission Church and later New York days!) approached me after High Mass. Not knowing which company had built our modest instrument, he waxed enthusiastic about my flute, cello and harp combinations! He said that the orchestral effect was extraordinarily convincing. What company had built the organ? Peering at the name plate on the console, he blushed, coughed and stuttered his way to the nearest exit. He seemed to be chagrined at his own sincerity. The honest praise for the instrument of a little-known company which had slipped out of the mouth of the artist tended to choke off the commercial breath of the businessman!

It's always a startling experience to catch oneself accidentally commending a humble rival, especially if one is known to look habitually with disdain upon obscure competitors. With great glee, I relayed the melodramatic compliment to Messrs. Hillgreen and Lane who had more satisfaction from the chagrin of the Prominent Builder, neatly caught in his own phrases, than from the actual commendation of their product.

As soon as the pipe organ was installed, the music at Old St. Mary's began to sound better. But the choir had not really improved, and so I proceeded to execute my plan for a concert appearance at Orchestra Hall. At that time, in Chicago, the memory of William L. Tomlins' quality work with the Apollo Club was fresh and vibrant and his successor, Harrison Wild, of Grace Episcopal Church just below Old St. Mary's on Wabash Avenue, was accomplishing fine results with both the Apollo and the Mendelssohn (men's chorus) Clubs.

I was quite conscious of the two great risks I was accepting: the financing of the enterprise, and the presentation of a program with sufficient hints of artistry to escape a barrage of acrid verbiage from the Fountain Pens of the daily newspapers.

The Rector gave reluctant consent to the rental of Orchestra Hall and the contracting for a representative section of the Thomas Orchestra. I never understood just why the Rector gave the permission, weighted with pessimistic misgivings as it obviously was. For the entire household at Wabash Avenue and Eldridge Court, many adult members of the choir, and that sometimes difficult-to-deal-with sector of the congregation which occupies the middle-aisle pews in churches of all denominations, expressed themselves as certain that I was steering my unsteady craft toward a major catastrophe. But I had set the helm and off we went on the hazardous course. Try to avoid both Scylla and Charybdis!

It was necessary first to select a composition for the performance. The then fresh and popular cantata, "The Seven Last Words of Christ" by Theodore Dubois, promised to be effective. There were melody, variety and color in the score. What was probably most important was that I *knew* both the choral and orchestral scores. I wasn't going to take any chances with an unfamiliar score of permitting woodwinds, brasses, or even strings to surprise and embarrass me on the podium with unexpected entrances.

And so I ran up a bill at Lyon and Healy's for a hundred and more copies of the Dubois work. That bill with the rental and contract price for the orchestra plagued me every waking hour of the weeks preceding the concert. G clefs, F clefs, C clefs and dollar signs got into the luncheon soup every day. Fish and ice cream began to have identical flavors. My digestive apparatus would do a somersault whenever the dinner bell sounded. It was torture even to observe the other gentlemen absorbing calories. At night in my tiny monastic cubicle, I would become suddenly wide awake, jump from a fitful slumber, seize the orchestral score, study the French horn parts, throw the score down and pick up the records of the ticket sale!

I was doing some barefoot hiking on a rough part of the Parnassus trail! The Ground Bass was exacting a heavy toll.

At least a dozen batons were broken into small splinters at rehearsals. Everybody in the house seemed suddenly afraid of me. I lost weight but was bloated with vinegar. My former smile (so bewitching!) had given place to a scowl that would do for the best "heavy" in the theatre.

It was necessary to augment the boys' chorus, and Miss Theresa Armitage selected a number of lads (several of whom were to become leading solo boys later) at Normal Practice School in the Normal Park district. She helped in the rehearsing of this section. More tenors and basses were also required, but the President of the Jesuit College of St. Ignatius came through with the major part of the College Glee Club. Michael Ahern, later defending attorney for Al Capone was one of the basses. There were not enough cassocks for the augmented chorus, and I was stymied for a while until the kind Rector, Father Byrnes, of the popular Vincentian Church on the north side, supplied the garments.

And so we went on the stage of Orchestra Hall for our formal concert debut with borrowed boys, borrowed men and borrowed raiment. All the singers had learned the notes of the cantata, but I was fearful of the bass chorus which might or might not enter at the right spots. At the rehearsal with the orchestra some of the players were amused. Perhaps (probably) at me! A second violinist asked me at the end of the rehearsal, "Why do you *shade* so much? It's louder and softer all the time. It sounds so extremely funny!" I felt, of course, like stunning the chap with a heavier-than-air baton and dropping the carcass of a second violinist into Lake Michigan, but desisted from such violent purpose, by the grace of God (Jesuit or Dominican School), and actually moderated my excessive degrees of dynamic shading.

The leading solo boy, James Kearn, now a prominent pastor at Cedar

Rapids, Iowa, was a source of anxiety. God had given this boy an exceptionally beautiful voice and an equally exceptional disposition. He learned the opening aria. A fortnight before the performance, he underwent a nose or throat operation, the surgeon indicating that the prospects of his participating in the concert were not bright. I hurried to prepare the junior solo boy, William Doody, who won laurels later, for the aria.

On the great night, we assembled in the dressing room, donned the cassocks and surplices (I wore a Paulist habit, but after a few seasons adopted the simpler attire of a single-breasted Prince Albert coat) and nervously ascended to the stage. A vast audience was there to greet us. Clergy and laity. Educators. Dilettanti! As I walked to the conductor's podium, I realized that financially we were safe, for only a minimum of "paper" (free tickets) had been distributed.

I went into the concert as water dashes over waterfalls.

How ferociously I brandished my arms! I was Leopold, Frank and Walter Damrosch compressed into one tremendous, irresistibly vital and thoroughly absurd conductor. My bows to the audience were stiff concessions to a public that should know it inhabited a lower stratum. I very nearly got "my thumb in the soup" that night. One episode of that terrific concert reminded me to watch the thumb. After a few preliminary numbers which were needed to round out the program to full concert time, we began the cantata.

With a postadolescent assurance, than which there is no greater temerity, I directed the introduction. The orchestra followed my conducting with great gallantry! Tympani rolled a crescendo and diminuendo. After a majestic gesture of the baton toward the first oboist, he played the plaintive melody which would bring in the solo boy. Having cued the French oboe player with as much pretended authority as any of Messager's or Carré's conductors in Paris have, I relaxed, dramatically leaning against the iron protecting rail of the conductor's platform, subconsciously determined to prove to three thousand persons how perfectly at ease I was; how natural and everyday-ish it was for me to be directing a great symphonic and choral ensemble. The "thumb" was getting dangerously near the shore line of the soup plate when young Kearn followed the oboe into his aria.

The charming Father Kearn's recollection and my own of what transpired differ, but since I am penning personal reminiscences, I shall naturally report my version of the episode.

Young Kearn made a beautiful start: "All ye that pass by the way, attend and see if ever sorrow was like unto My sorrow." In G minor. An undulant, fluty-oboe soprano vocal quality over a quiet string accompaniment. As young Kearn approached the end of the first movement,

I heard strange sounds. Was a saxophone suddenly interjected into the symphonic entourage? Did a couac (split reed) throw odd elements into the clarinet section? Did a French Horn player with puckered lips from too much playing run at random from high to low rilievos and vice versa?

What was taking place at Orchestra Hall with the nonchalant, young conductor relaxing in pseudo ease?

Simply—Young Kearn's throat refused to obey the reflex fulfillment of commands issued by the singer's brain to the arytenoid cartileges of the vocal cords. His voice was changing! Before three thousand people! At our formal concert debut! And with two-thirds of the aria still to be caroled!

Like a hart startled by a hunter, I sprang away from the iron rail, peered at the score, perceived that I had an orchestral interlude, sent young Kearn back to the chorus bank, called the junior Doody out and, putting him in on the right beat with only a fraction of a second to spare, brought the first orchestrally accompanied aria in the rich history of the Paulist Choristers to a finish.

Two boys, successively, for one aria!

The audience, puzzled at first and scrutinizing the printed program for enlightenment, finally realized that some historic emergency had arisen but that the extraordinary, transcending and therefore amazing resourcefulness of the young ex-Bostonian conductor had reduced the emergency to an inconsequential little *quelquechose* which it was so easy for him to handle! (Tureens of soup and ten thumbs!)

The program thereafter proceeded with amazing smoothness, and there were some really "high moments." The basses forgot to enter at wrong places, and chorus and orchestra blended effectively. The audience was thoroughly surprised. The best that the most optimistic friends had hoped for the venture was that we would not go to pieces convincingly. The professional Fountain Pens had been ready to write innocuous little news notices about a hymn-tune choir having attempted a cantata with orchestral accompaniment and escaping without fatal injury.

But the Fountain Pens scribbled merrily and at length. Surprise was expressed that such a program had been planned and performed by a Catholic organization. The critics indicated that they had been unaware of any serious interest in culture among American Catholics. Europe which was dominantly Catholic had been, of course, the nursery of the Fine Arts, but in America, the Protestants and Jews were the only legatees of the Muses!

And so we were surprisingly welcomed into the fraternity of American cultural units!

The reaction of this favorable reception of our bold undertaking on the choir itself was immediate and stirring. Boys and men strutted about as heroes. The soprano boys, who had regularly sneaked down to Grace Church on Sunday nights to fight the Episcopalian choir boys, went openly down on the following Sunday night, and according to an Irish cable-car operator who had stopped his car so that he and his passengers could observe the proceedings, it was a battle worthy of the Irish. Fierce, racial-religious, merciless, to a definite finish! According to the gleeful report of the thoroughly one-sided Irishman, Episcopalian Eton collars were torn to shreds and threads and strewn across cable-car tracks. When he gripped the cable after what was a swift resumé of the Thirty Years' War, the operator was sure that lengths of torn Protestant silk stockings of Fauntleroy choristers were wrapped around the cable, having been pushed down by the impact of battle through the midtrack slot.

The report of the operator would have made good copy for the Dublin or Cork newspapers, and many Hibernians in south-side Chicago rejoiced with exceeding great joy. But the London, Belfast and Boston (U.S.A.) papers would have carried a different story, which would have neared the truth more approximately, for at the next rehearsal many of the sturdy Paulist soprano boys gave indisputable evidence that the Episcopalian lads had functioned "true to British standards," putting up a first-class show for Old Henry the Eighth and Bishop Cranmer! Black eyes, swollen noses and lips, and purple arabesques on both cheeks attested that while the Paulist second generation representatives of Roscommon, Kerry and Waterford were dashing in, the warriors whose grandsires came from Kent, Surrey and Devonshire had met them with answers that would have made good Queen Bess smile her approval and Lord Essex cheer the antipapal boys.

I called upon Mr. Harrison Wild, organist and master of choristers at Grace Church to express regret for my boys' share in the melee. Mr. Wild dismissed the matter graciously with the unexpected comment that the fight was a good thing for both choirs and the cause of boy choirs in Chicago in general, for it proved that choir boys are not necessarily mollycoddles.

The principal purpose of the concert was achieved, the favorable publicity bringing many boys and men to the choir. Never again was there a dearth of talented vocalists in the Chicago choir.

The office of Tenebrae during Holy Week, soon after the concert, was a taxing experience. Having been reduced to the inadequate personnel of the anteconcert choir, we were hard pressed to sustain the newly won reputation. The new talent would be ineffective for at least a few weeks. It was much simpler for the Paulist Choristers, fortified with reinforcements acceptably to give what the public judged to be a difficult oratorio than to render the Psalms and Responsories of the Church's most dramatic ritual. The singing of the liturgical ceremonials is rarely accomplished convincingly or even smoothly by choirs composed of laymen. Proper chanting of the Divine Office must savor of monasticism. Only monks and levites, long accustomed to enunciating the often awkward phrases of Latin sentences in free rhythm, can carry the Tenebrae service through its long course without giving frequent evidences of amateurishness. Only choirs trained to convey the mystical elements of such profound outpourings as the *Miserere,* the *Benedictus,* the *Lamentations,* etc., are qualified to make the musical contributions to such a potentially moving Office as Tenebrae. Our first attempt at the Office was, I regret to record, more a failure than the Orchestra Hall concert was a success. It was almost impossible to hold both sides of the choir, widely separated, neatly together. While basses would be struggling with the subject of a sentence, the soprano boys, having probably omitted or elided several intervening syllables, would be finishing with the predicate. An intended disembodied effect in the *Miserere* would find the altos and tenors at variance as to the temporal values of notes or the pace at which to sing them. Even in later years, when my choristers had become expert in most styles of music and experienced in negotiating the outstanding difficulties of involved Offices, the burden of Tenebrae was more onerous than any other responsibility of the choir. I should find Bach's *St. Matthew's Passion* less of an ordeal than the three nights of the Tenebrae Office.

Besides the ease of intonation which the chanting of Offices requires, a choir must develop dependable skill in a cappella singing, for the Tenebrae is chanted without accompaniment. At the time of our first venture, we were not a good a cappella chorus. It is seldom that one hears an excellent a cappella organization. Many groups lay claim to great facility in unaccompanied singing. But many individuals and groups lay claim, without warrant, to many things. In the field of a cappella singing, the need is not only facility in keeping going without accompaniment; control of blend, intensity and color, and sureness in communicating the moods of compositions are required. A cappella singing is attempted by too many conductors nowadays. There is little stamina to much of it. Bald, feeble, flagging. Modern ears are accustomed to the rich colors of symphonic instrumentation. Therefore, a cappella choruses which fail to reveal the wealth of colors which may be found on the average choral palette cannot long hold the attentive interest of listeners. An a cappella conductor must be a master of the vocal-color scheme, of blending tints and shades, and of applying appropriate hues to indicate changing moods. The quantitative independence of the several choral lines gives opportunity for great variation in the intensities of concerted singing. But the average a cappella conductor seems to be satisfied if the singers negotiate the right notes successfully. To sing without accompaniment is presumed to be a notable feat. As a matter of fact, even a chorus of very young children can be trained easily to sing without help from piano, organ or any other instrument.

When I first directed unaccompanied singing, I was thoroughly delighted with myself for no adequate reason. Soon I learned that much research into the views and practices of the Renaissance masters of the polyphonic school would have to be made if I was to parallel the effectiveness of an unaccompanied group with the effectiveness attained while the multicolored instrumentation of an orchestra was adding luster to vocal sounds. Palestrina and his associates in the a cappella school of the sixteenth century wrote for male choirs which had cultivated greater variety of tone colors than the modern choirs of boys and men. The "Tu Es Petrus" of the great master, no matter how accurately, idiomatically and actively rendered, fails to appeal to modern audiences, when sung without due consideration of the color effects which Palestrina obviously invoked. He had both men and boys in his soprano choir. When his men's soprano section traversed the path of his boys' section, the altogether different hue of the former put the melodic line not only in apposition to, but in gentle contrast with, the timbre of the latter. In the average boys' chorus, divided to assume both of the soprano lines, there is no contrast of treble qualities. The first soprano line may drop below the second, but the now high second line sounds exactly as the first sounded, and the impression given is that one group keeps singing all the high line notes. For the same reason choirs of boy sopranos and groups of female sopranos who have not developed various tone colors fail to bring out the true content of two-soprano part madrigals.

Yes! a cappella conducting is a science and art in itself. The director least qualified to conduct an unaccompanied composition is he who feels that his chief task is to encourage the singers to continue to the finish without the help of piano, organ or orchestra. I was a passable conductor of accompanied music years before I began to feel at home in the other field.

After the temporary setback of the poor Tenebrae services, the choir proceeded happily and uneventfully to the conclusion of the most important, because the most daring, season in the annals of the Paulist Choristers. Later years furnished more spectacular events, but the season 1906–1907 gave us our real place in the musical arena of North America.

I added little to my information (so I feel now) about the art of training and conducting choirs during the following season, for it was not until June, 1908, that I had opportunity of examining the English academic principles as exemplified in the procedure in British choir halls.

The soprano boys and I had slipped into the sort of association which is most wholesome in boy choirs. In England, I was to discover, the masters have little to do with the boys except in the song school (which is the term for rehearsal hall in the choir schools), where the strictest of disciplinary codes is maintained. Once I was passing a recreation spot at Westminster in company with Sir Richard Terry, the choirmaster. His choristers were playing cricket. I stopped for a moment, thinking to compliment the boys on their fine reading at first sight of a difficult composition a few hours earlier. Terry wheeled around, waving his walking stick at me. "None of that here, old thing. We don't make free with choir boys. That may be your trick in the States, but you never work out great choirs in any case. I never notice the boys socially."

Of course I told Terry that I considered that attitude just a "sloppy dish of weak tea." As silly as wearing a top hat with a tweed jacket-suit on a rainy Monday morning. I said something caustic about how well some British choirmasters would look among other waxen figures at Madame Tussaud's in Baker Street. Maybe the distinguished polyphonist never forgave my impolite American candor. It would be pleasant to know that he did, but if he didn't, perhaps we can make it right while playing harps together in the consonances of eternal harmony. I think that we American musicians habitually annoy our British colleagues. We Americans were and are, from their point of view, estranged and rebellious colonials. Colonials! Not the highest recommendation to a Londoner!

The American attitude of a choirmaster to his choristers is generally one likely to win respect, regard, loyalty and spontaneous co-operation. If the English boys had much enthusiasm for their choral work, it was well suppressed. Perhaps on the banks of the Thames and other English streams there is more emphasis placed on regulations, work, traditions and discipline than the American boy can appreciate.

One day in the late spring of 1907, I was knocking out flies to soprano outfielders at Jackson Park. Suddenly I collapsed. An old internal trouble had long been preparing for a dramatic climax. The celebrated Dr. John B. "Button" Murphy ordered me to a hospital for immediate operation. Some of the choir boys told me after my unexpected recovery that there had been some speculation as to who the pallbearers would be, whether I would be buried in Boston or Chicago and sundry other cheerful things.

But I eluded the serving of a subpoena by immortality to join the music makers of the past.

During my convalescence, my day nurse, a lovely lady who, tiring of wasting her afternoons at teas and auction bridge, had trained as a nurse in order to fit herself for useful service to the community, put me through an undergraduate and postgraduate course in the art of dealing with people.

As the fumes of the ether became less active, some hours after the celebrated surgeon had finished his cutting, I found myself weeping copiously on the fair damsel's shoulder, while she was running fingers through the untidy haystack which I wore as hair in those distant days. "Take it easy, now. Don't be disturbed because I'm not a male nurse. I'll take good care of you."

And excellent care she did take of me, not only as a nurse but as a psychological and spiritual tutor. She told me, on the day of my departure from the hospital, that a friend of hers had had the misfortune of presenting a difficulty to me on one of my parochial duty days at Old St. Mary's. The lovely blond disciple of Florence Nightingale insisted that I was sufficiently recovered to learn that I had bungled the case, displaying stiff incompetence. I had been harsh. I had made no effort to understand the real nature of the case, giving evidence of being anxious to dispose of it quickly according to some formula I had read in a text book. The young Nightingale sang with a timbre more acute than the point of her hypodermic needle, "You are a blunderer. Why don't you qualify yourself properly to deal with human beings? I attended your concert at Orchestra Hall. Perhaps you know a little about music, but if the Fathers are going to keep you on parochial duty, for Heaven's sake read and *memorize* this book." The book was *Love, The Greatest Thing In The World,* by Henry Drummond.

When I cocked an eye to catch any relevance of the word "love" to the preceding part of her tirade, her ornithological tone quality rose to a fortissimo in altissimo. "Don't you realize that "love" is the strongest word in our language after "God?" It signifies benevolence first and many cognate ideas afterwards. You need to understand what benevolence really means."

I read the book several times within a few months, and every once in a while I reread it nowadays. Therefore, I acknowledge to my waxenhaired monitor-nurse a great indebtedness. The book and her kindly scolding gave me a new sense of direction. Even in matters musical. You see, the aesthetic and the spiritual are closely allied, and if the cold academic application of puritanical precepts be ineffective in the latter, so too is it impotent in music. Just correct notes and rhythms? Futility!

While I was in the hospital, a frail little nun, in charge of the wing to which I had been assigned, began to take an interest in the young ecclesiastical patient. This little Sister of Mercy, Sister Vivian, was not long for this vale of tears. She was tuned to the right pitch spiritually. A sort of Chicago "Little Flower." She had come frequently to Old St. Mary's and seemed to sense that I was striving to make the music at Solemn Mass more than a program of compositions rendered with good taste and technique.

One day before the angels came to escort the little Sister to Heaven, she told me not to permit any influence to divert me from the purpose to which I was committed. "Occasionally," she said, "I think that you lose sight of what should be uppermost in your mind. Once in a while you turn the loud organ on during the *Kyrie* and *Agnus Dei.* Never spoil a prayer with theatrical effects." I have carried this admonition deep in my soul over the years. It is easy for a musician to become an exhibitionist. It is difficult to avoid becoming one, if one hearkens often to the comments of the public. The dear, thrill-seeking public applauds melodrama, and if a church musician can run his sopranos up to a nice high C with a histrionic crescendo and a fortissimo *fermata,* he is likely to be popular. But Sister Vivian has been wagging a finger up there where the real relations of the Fine Arts to Eternal Truth and Beauty are clearly understood, and I am quite sure that never since her death have I allowed my choristers to roar a *Kyrie,* or to beseech God in any other prayerful text with the pyrotechnics of vaudeville vocalization.

This volume is an account of my musical experiences and impressions, and therefore I have confined myself, for the most part, to the recounting of these. But an episode occurred during those early days in Chicago which involved me as an alleged preacher. So many of my choristers, sitting in the choir stalls, and so many acquaintances in the pews, were obliged to endure my strange imitations of oratory, that this short but humiliating interpolation will serve as late atonement for my assaults on their patience.

I had been a priest about six months. The Rector rapped on the door of my little room about five minutes before the evening service of a First Friday was due to begin. "Hurry to the chapel," he commanded. "You must substitute for the priest assigned to this service. Say the Rosary, give a sermon and Benediction of the Blessed Sacrament." "But, Father, I'm not prepared to preach." "Nonsense. Hurry along. God will take care of you."

Reluctantly I donned surplice and preacher's stole. During the "Ave's" of the Rosary I tried to capture an idea which might serve as the basis for a short sermon. No idea came. If God were going to take care of me,

He was postponing indications of His solicitude. At the conclusion of the Rosary, I turned to the congregation and a torrent of words gushed forth. The choppy current came not from Heaven but directly from Noah Webster's dictionary. Nouns and verbs eddied around with adjectives and adverbs making swirling but meaningless sentences. I became rapt, listening to the lexicon pouring out its contents through my larynx. The fact that I was conveying nothing to the congregation failed to impress me. Parabolic gestures to the right and hyperbolic thrusts to the left. The bathos of rhetoric. The misfeasance of the quack orator!

An old missionary priest, having listened in the sacristy to the uncontrolled outburst, mumbled in a stage whisper as I was laying aside the vestments, "Without any doubt the worst I ever heard."

A little old lady, the parish character, awaited me in the rectory. She favored Father O'Regan, another young priest, and myself because she had heard that we were kind to the State Street hobos. She said something like this: "Father, that was a grand sermon you gave this evening. I was lifted up beyond the clouds. Even Mrs. McGillicudy, who seldom notices me, was so moved that she smiled at me. And Honoria O'Shaughnessy, whose uncle died last week, was so touched that she was like to sob her heart out. But, Father, I was glad that you made it all clair at the end, for it was damned iloquent in the middle."

God had taken care of me, indeed, but not in the manner which I expected. He had provided an opportunity for me to learn a lesson. I was long in deriving the full fruits of the lesson which was, of course, never to inflict mere words on any audience and particularly to beware of such inane practice before a congregation that had assembled to be refreshed spiritually. Gradually I was able to perceive that embroideries frequently spoil the substantial content of an address, and that, by the same token, the embellishments worked into a musical composition, if not treated with great delicacy, obscure the melodic values of a motet or symphony.

At the start of the season 1907–1908, the morale of the Choristers was much better than in preceding seasons. The "mad undertaking" of the Orchestra Hall concert caused enthusiasm to reign in place of apathy. We started off in September with the clear and encouraging, if not altogether justifiable, conviction among the boys and men (and what was more important, among the boys' parents and the wives or sweethearts of the men) that we were an important asset to the cultural life of Chicago.*

---

* Just a few seasons ago, when I was struggling to make adequate preparation for my share in the musical programs of the New York World's Fair, I called on Mr. Henry Voegli, manager of the Chicago Symphony Orchestra and Orchestra Hall for suggestions. During the long interview which he very graciously endured, he made a remark—a digression of course, which could be interpreted as confirming

Candidly, I did not think then nor do I think now that the Orchestra Hall concert had contributed anything of great value to the musical life of Chicago, but I rejoiced in the psychological effect it produced among boys and men of musical talent throughout the metropolitan district. We could now move along speedily and confidently.

During the autumn, the music at High Mass improved steadily, the new voices and consequent better balance of parts making possible the nuances upon which the vitality of music depends. We rehearsed often and long. The congregation increased and the Paulist Chorister Society of Chicago was acclaimed even by the household at the rectory. This designation of the choir as a concert unit was changed to the Paulist Choristers of Chicago in 1909, for a New York critic had upbraided us for using nouns as adjectives. The reviewer of our debut concert in New York at Carnegie Hall must have been influenced by some slight animadversion towards our Chicago organization, for in his own beloved New York, two outstanding musical organizations wore as many noun-adjectives in their headbands as we did—the New York Symphony Orchestra, and the New York Oratorio Society. The critic, although discriminating against us, was right; the nouns made the name awkward, and so, being openminded, we made the correction.

We organized a board of directors in the autumn of 1907. It was never clear, however, just what the preogatives and obligations of the board were. No matter what the decisions of the board were, all matters of importance were necessarily referred to ecclesiastical superiors. The first formal act of the board was to support me in the proposal of a second concert in Orchestra Hall. We chose Alfred Gaul's *Holy City* as the work to be performed. We were able to do much more with this composition than we had attempted with the Dubois work, although our technique did not warrant our attempting the elaborate double chorus of the second part. Arthur Dunham, celebrated concert organist who with the Thomas orchestra, furnished the accompaniments, and sneered when I announced at rehearsal that we would omit the double chorus. "But that is the only

---

the feeling that we had "arrived" with the first concert: "You don't need any suggestions from me. Use the bold imagination which changed a puny little church choir into a unit quickly to become an international force." Theodore Thomas was dead, William Tomlins inactive, Clarence Dickinson was confining himself to the quiet activity by which he and his gifted wife prepared for their truly great work in New York. Harrison Wild was tiring. And so Mr. Voegli exclaimed at the conclusion of the digression: "You and the Paulish Choristers came along suddenly and unexpectedly, and Mr. Wessels, my partner, and I agreed that a new musical instrument was born and that it would infuse spirit and *élan* into the music of Chicago and probably the country at large."

good number in the cantata !" Upon my explaining that we were not ready to perform it, he rebutted that we should have chucked the whole work, substituting something which we had the facility to sing in its entirety. Perhaps he was right. When one is without much experience, it is difficult to decide wisely in such matters. At the time, I felt it necessary to produce a popular opus, even if certain movements were omitted. And I have never agreed with Mr. Dunham that the double chorus is the best feature of the work.

The second concert with the orchestra seemed doomed to failure soon after contracts had been assumed and rehearsals begun, for the financial panic of 1907 broke. Script was being used instead of government and bank currency. Advance orders for tickets were, of course, few. The priests at the rectory were concerned, one of the Fathers promoting anxiety about the musical condition of the organization as well. This apprehensive gentleman listened to some of the rehearsals. He became alarmed. He tried to infect me with his fears. But he had been listening as a sly watcher peers over the shoulder of a painter while the crude outlines of a picture are being limned. Timid persons who have influence with superiors should be debarred from early rehearsals, for they interpret the many corrections made at initial practice periods as indications that the final product will be necessarily unsatisfactory. We did have trouble with some movements of the cantata, notably with the tricky fugue, "Thine Is The Kingdom." It was our first encounter with a fugue. At no time in the career of a choral unit may an encounter with a fugue be reasonably regarded lightly. The majority of choruses, it is fair to charge, never masters the technique of fugal singing, because the conductors do not trouble to solve the interpretative problems involved in this technique. An inexperienced group is uneasy and often frightened in the whirling eddy of independent entrances and phrases. Our boys and men required several weeks of rehearsing before they acquired sufficient confidence to guarantee the proper contributions of each vocal line. But we finally gained the confidence and could run through the choral "chase" without stumbling.

In the lovely three-part movement for sopranos and altos," It Shall Come To Pass At Eventide," I could not achieve a convincing blend, but this was due to my personal ignorance of the proper way of training and balancing the alto lines. I was urged to abandon the project. The financial depression worried the Fathers, and the apprehensions of the Father who had peered over my shoulder at early rehearsals, served to increase the nervousness of the household. But we did not quit.

Quitting is usually a poor solution of difficult situations. Often it is easier to quit than to continue. That's the reason why so many talented and educated people wallow in the slough of mediocrity. Even when the fighting is hard and the chances are clearly against you, you must fight on! If you have, in an unenlightened moment, signed to sample Joe Louis' rights, at least go into the ring. If you are put to sleep in the first round, at least you will have been game. Probably you'll come to in a hospital, but there'll be flowers from Joe to give solace. As I look back over the years, I am surprised to note the number of times I climbed into the ring to receive overwhelming haymakers. Even with a sore chin, it is better to be still working in the gymnasium than to have died of the torpor of flutter and funk!

And so we went ahead. The fugue smoothed itself out, an aromatic essence sprayed itself over the three-part number and, a few days before the performance, the box office reported that, money being easier, the ticket sale was progressing well. The performance added to the prestige of the young chorus. Critics were friendly, but thoroughly professional. It was a step forward to have interested the critics to view us without the colored glasses of charity which they had kindly worn on the occasion of our first concert.

Unquestionably, it is a misfortune for young conductors to be petted and flattered by the Fountain Pens. Honeyed phrases tend to make one satisfied with one's efforts. If real progress is to be made, the aspiring young maestro needs to be told the truth as experienced reviewers see it about his public performances. Having elected to perform for a cross section of the public, the conductor presents himself for scrutiny to the critics upon whom, at least until a recent date, the public has depended for information about the quality of his performance. I have known a few conductors about whom the critics, for one reason or another, have never written their real opinions. These musicians have made lamentably little progress from one year to another.

The Chicago critics were consistently fair and encouraging to us, at the same time candidly pointing out our faults and inadequacies. I learned soon that adverse criticism of choral or orchestral concerts is really directed against the man on the podium. The chorus or orchestra is seldom to blame for poor performances. The responsibility is the conductor's. Occasionally, it is true, an organization will fail to co-operate with its director, paying little attention to instructions at rehearsals and signals at performances, but generally, the quality of the work in public reflects the kind and degree of musicianship expounded and inculcated at the practice periods.

Once in a while a critic would fail to sense what we were trying to achieve. Some reviewers, perhaps unacquainted with the philosophy of the Ground Bass and unaware of the points of differentiation between a chorus employing boy sopranos and other types of choruses, would scribble silly sentences. My sopranos were boys, and one can achieve only certain types of dramatic expression with boys. It is unreasonable, then, for critics to complain if boys have not reached the great emotional climaxes possible only to robust female sopranos. But it is even more unreasonable for the conductor of a boys and men to attempt to perform music which relies upon such climaxes for effectiveness. Boys are incomparably effective in nondramatic styles, in impersonal music, in the ethereal and disembodied species of composition, but in works such as the Verdi Requiem, *The Damnation of Faust,* the Ninth Symphony Ode, etc., the lads are so tamely white as to disallow proper expression necessarily.

At about this time, an impression was circulated that I was employing an unnatural tone quality on the soprano line, and that my boys, as a result, would show the results of vocal injury when their voices would have changed. It required time and patience to correct this impression. Although I had not yet been to England, where I found myself constrained to solve the problem of the English boy-soprano hoot, I knew that, in the main, our soprano tone quality was acoustically correct. By this I mean that the intonations of the boys were in accord with the basic laws of the physics of sound. To elucidate: various instrumentalities of sound, of similar structure, even if the material used be different, produce similar tonal effects. If the instrumentalities are identical in length, bore and other essential characteristics, the tonal effects must be at least physically identical. Thus it is of no consequence if a flute be made of wood or metal. It speaks as a flute if it be constructed according to the specifications required for a flute-tone.

Therefore, if the vocal tubes of a boy, a girl and a light lyric female be approximately alike, it follows that these three must sing with an approximately alike tone quality. If the throats are anatomically the same, the tone quality must be physically the same. (The boy will always tend to intimate the superphysical in the implications of his tone quality more clearly than his sister, because he is farther from the glandular and emotional estate of a man than she is from that of a woman.) Musicians are mistaken, accordingly, if they think the soprano voices of boys, girls and young female lyrics are different species of treble instruments.

The quality usually associated with the untrained voice of a boy is the *unnatural* one, his natural utterances having been inhibited by misuse or abuse. Shouting, singing loudly in the middle register and reaching up for high notes with the weight of the lower notes provoke irritation in the larynx. The shape of the vocal cords is frequently changed and the tissues to which the cords are attached enlarged. A chronic constriction in the muscles and cartileges which control vocalism is established and the boy is physically unable to sing with a natural tone.

Even my friend, Willem Mengelberg, the celebrated orchestral conductor of Amsterdam, was deceived about this point. During the several seasons in which he conducted the New York Philharmonic and Symphony Orchestra, it was my pleasant privilege to associate the Choristers with his productions. Once, while he was listening to the soprano boys tuning up, he asked me to "abandon that falsetto tone." He admitted, afterwards, that he had become accustomed to the lusty singing of the boys in Holland, which he thought to be natural singing. By the time of my co-operation with Mr. Mengelberg, I was thoroughly aware that the boys in Holland, Germany and in all the Continental countries sang with a raucous Roxbury Crusaders' timbre. Mr. Mengelberg, being necessarily openminded since he was a great conductor, listened to and approved my exposition of the subject of boys' singing.

For a few seasons, however, it is certain that the charge of employing unnatural tone quality dissuaded some parents from entering their boys in the choir.

Nothing of great significance happened during the months after the performance of Gaul's "Holy City," but I began to realize that only in a choir school where boys lived in community, receiving their general education as well as musical instruction, could a superlative choir of boy sopranos be maintained. And I felt an increasing urge to establish such a school. All the great choirs of England have been trained in such schools, and there are several choir schools under Episcopalian auspices in the United States. To my knowledge, however, there is not a single institute of the kind conducted by Catholics in the Western Hemisphere. I undertook to maintain one in New York City. I shall tell later of the five years of acute anxiety I spent in trying to finance the undertaking.

Several of our solo boys were engaged that season to go to Washington, D.C., to participate in a boys' choir concert. While there we sang our first concert for a President of the United States. Not in the East Room of the White House where our later programs were given, but in the Cabinet Room, with the Cabinet in session, Mr. Theodore Roosevelt asking us to "soften the hard hearts of the members," smilingly indicating Mr. William Taft in particular.

An interesting episode occurred on that occasion. "Teddy" asked if we could sing his favorite song, "Drink to me only with thine eyes." Of course we could and did, but before beginning the number I told the senior solo boy, William Doody, a fine artist, to sing the second verse as a solo over the pianissimo accompaniment of the other voices. He flatly refused, saying, "I can't sing such sentimental words alone; it's bad enough to sing them with the rest." Quickly I tried to persuade him of the privilege of soloing before a President, but he was adamant and an enterprising well-voiced youngster named Ralph Summers took his place.

In such a song boy sopranos can underline the melody with a tranquil beauty of intonation, but the text is so far beyond their emotional perception as to be altogether meaningless. No preadolescent boy can sing "Or leave a kiss with the cup" and mean it. It's extraordinary, however, how rapidly his eager perception of that sort of thing develops when his voice begins to change, the bridge of his nose widens and his mother hands him his first safety razor.

Apropos of mothers and razors, I am reminded here of my first experiences with the removal of hirsute fluff from the cheeks. I had for some time been admiring a youth whose heavy beard showed dark and rugged even after he had shaved. There seemed to be an intriguing value in a malar shadow. An extra touch of masculinity. A sort of proof of maturity. And so I would peer in the mirror frequently to discover the first signs of tendrils on my face. The filaments were long in coming, but one day I discovered a sufficient amount of gossamer on my upper lip to send me enthusiastically to the bathroom where with a discarded razor of the Doctor's, I went through the ceremonial rite of lathering and plying the razor (I can't remember now whether I had the edge or the blunt back of the razor against the skin).

During the ritualistic proceedings, my mother appeared at the door. "Give me that thing. It's absurd for you to think that you need to shave." Six months later, she handed me the razor. "Put some soap on your face and remove those cobwebs."

The season of 1907–08 went merrily along, and having refurbished the Dubois oratorio we went into Orchestra Hall again in the spring.

Chapter XII   *Listening to the Ground Bass through the Geological Strata of England and the Continent*

THE Superior-General of the Paulist Fathers (he who had assured me once that all would be right in June) visited Chicago in the Spring of 1908 and suggested that I close the season early and hie to Europe. He was an internationally acclaimed astronomer. Being a scientist, he understood well that if I were to accomplish results of scientific-artistic value it was necessary for me to study. To make research where the history of music had written itself. Father Searle was a scholar, and scholars know that guessing about principles and precepts is a fruitless, inane and unworthy procedure, unless one is content to be a charlatan or trifler.

Going to Europe in those days was a great adventure. Perhaps like a rocket trip to a distant planet nowadays! Exciting, but also a bit frightening. London, Paris, Rome, Berlin, Madrid! What romance! Those words were not the names of mere places. To an American they were the metrical feet of a great poem. Two trochees, a spondee, two iambi! The rhythmical movement of a subtle aura!

But steamships could sink. Fogs and collisions head on occurred in the mid-Atlantic nine days out of sight of land. Forty years ago, such thoughts were disturbing. Now an ocean voyage is like a trip on the ferry to Staten Island. My Celtic subconsciousness played tag with me for the month before embarkation. I was always "it" in the game. Wondrous music floating through the vaulted arches of medieval Cathedrals. Then the spectre of an iceberg leering a few yards from the bow of the ship. The tombs of great composers and a watery grave off the Grand Banks!

The treasurer arranged for a letter of credit. Later I found that the bank in London upon which this financial document entitled me to draw was so far from my living quarters that frequently it cost me several shillings to get a pound. I was booked on the slow, old but comfortable *Arabic* of the White Star Line.

News of my going had spread through Chicago. The choirboys would gaze at me with an unfamiliar kind and degree of awe. "The Boss is going to Europe—a great man. He'll show those foreigners a thing or two." My choristers could not be persuaded that I was making the trip to learn. I knew it all already. Had known it all since I fell out of the cradle. Within a few days after Chicago had been apprised of my forthcoming voyage, I was conscious of many unusual attentions. On Michigan Avenue, during an afternoon stroll, I felt as unattended vice-royalty must feel when accosted by generally aloof dowagers and unapproachable rich bachelors. My social position rose to great heights in the metropolis, and I was invited to put my knees under the mahogany in several homes of the elite.

The social value of doing the unusual, of wrapping oneself round with so mysterious a veil as a trip to Europe, the placing of oneself under the protection of His Majesty, Rex et Imperator, was unmistakable. The hitherto unsuspected charm of a chap's manner was forthwith acclaimed, his irresistible sense of humor applauded, and the brilliancy of his dinner-table repartee reported through the grapevine of the great brownstone (or Indiana limestone!) houses. I buzzed around like a bee that finally had lit on the right flower. A delegation, a cross section of the Chicago public, accompanied me to the station to board the Wolverine which was to carry me on the first leg of the expedition.

Aboard the *Arabic* there was a large number of Episcopalian clergymen en route to the Lambeth Conference of the Church of England. I shared a cabin with an Irish-American Catholic priest of violently anti-English sympathies. He told me that I looked more like "one of those Protestant parsons" than a Catholic priest, and he made clear that the less he saw of me the better. Well! the coldness of his manner throughout the voyage was not icy enough to freeze my warm enthusiasms, so I didn't mind his pudgy animadversions at all.

After dinner the first night out from New York, I met a delightful Episcopalian clergyman and his equally delightful wife. They were young, cultured, witty, dead-in-earnest. Almost immediately they began to twit me about "papal infallibility" and to call me "Rome." This sobriquet amused the Lambeth voyagers, for within a day or two the whole fraternity and sorority (bless the latter's giggling friendliness!) greeted me with it, although I reminded them occasionally that they were advertising the papal see every time they shouted the name of the Eternal City. Mr. and Mrs. Young Episcopalian Parson and myself did the decks together the first evening. Next afternoon I awoke from a siesta in a deck chair, conscious of someone sitting on the extension. It was the fair Mrs. Parson. "Hello, Rome! Percy is always seasick. He's turned in for the voyage. Told me he took a fancy to you. Sorry about the Roman rubbish of celibacy. All the rest of the clerical collars (except the celluloid that shares your cabin) have their turtledoves along. Here's a sample of my cooing: *Coo—oo—oo!"*

Many times "Rome" and Mrs. "Canterbury York" did the decks together, sometimes arguing fiercely about the validity of Anglican Orders, sometimes exchanging impressions about sundry things. There were two Episcopalian bishops aboard and these, together with some ministers standing with them, would frown in grimacing pantomimes of disapproval whenever the Madame Parson and I would approach. The Irish-American priest perhaps concluded that I had sold out to the Church of England or its American affiliate, the Protestant Episcopal Church, leaving orthodoxy and the New Jersey coastline in the wake of the ship. At least, that was the suspicion of the seasick vicar's mate, for she reported that the celluloid often glared at her!

The denouement of this pleasant interlude on the billowy Atlantic was a facetious invitation by one of the bishops to chuck the Roman Church, to join up with them, to undertake a pastorate in his diocese and to marry either of his two pious daughters. Of course I thanked the heretical prelate for his invitation, promising to take the matter up with the Pope when I should arrive in Rome. During our many conversations, the Lady Curate, unsound in theology, showed herself solid in her views about the place of music in worship. She abhorred the type of boys' choirs prevailing in Episcopal churches. She deemed the hollowness of the average allegedly trained boy-soprano voice the least tolerable medium of expression in any of the Fine Arts. She plagued me day after day, deriding the aesthetic values which I kept insisting are possible of development in a boys' and men's choir. "Good-bye, Rome," she said at the pier in Liverpool. "Fix up your theology, and above all, get out of the business of training choirboys. See you in Heaven if you get away from the Pope."

Many years later, in a small town, after a matinee concert, an usher handed me a note. It was from a "nice little old lady," according to the usher. Written in pencil on the flyleaf of a program, it conveyed this idea: "You've done it, 'Rome.' Do you remember the Protestant turtledove of the *Arabic?* Her heretical doctrines about religion and music? I'm still an Episcopalian, but you have converted me to boys' singing. The little imps, they sing like angels."

Finally I was in England. But off to a bad start, for an old boy on the ship, having spotted me as a first-timer to England had given insistent and explicit instruction about tipping. How was I to know that behind the white beard of a seemingly kindly Santa Claus was a miser's avaricious mouth or that the twinkling of blue eyes was really the mirrored flashing of a Midas' soul? He had discoursed of the disrupting habit of Americans of overtipping. "When your luggage is cleared at the customs," he directed, "a porter will bring it to your railway carriage. Give him a sixpence only." I handed the porter a sixpence in the presence of a distinguished family of Washingtonians whom I had met aboard ship. The porter looked at the luggage stowed on the racks. He looked at me. At the sixpence. At the father, mother and daughter from our National Capital. "Blimey, if you sky-pilots can ride first class and carry real leather luggage, why in 'ell do you insult a poor man with a sixpenny bit?" In blushing confusion, which amused the Washingtonians, I stammered a hypocritical explanation: "I'm not well acquainted with the English money." But I supplemented the explanation with a half crown which brought the total gratuity to three shillings.

At Rugby I had become so thoroughly anglicized that I bought tea and biscuits for the party.

Arriving in London we all put up at the Grosvenor near Victoria Station. This hotel was to be my headquarters on my many trips to England. Before I settled down to the purposes which had brought me abroad, I fussed around a bit to become acclimated to London. This was easy because Boston was a miniature version of the English cosmopolis.

Having received the priestly faculties of the Archdiocese of Westminster, I was naturally bound by all the regulations for the local clergy. These included a prohibition to attend the theater. But when the diocesan ordinance was enacted the music halls were not included, for at that time symphony concerts were performed in them. My Washington friends, being apprised of the prohibition, insisted on my being their guest at a music hall. How the music halls had changed! No symphony! Just bawdy cacophony! Decked out in long coat, Inverness cape and top hat I arrived at the Tivoli in the Strand. My friends were already seated when I appeared. I noticed a smirk on the face of the box-office teller as he handed me my ticket. The ushers giggled as I walked down the aisle—oh, so far down the aisle—to the very first row. The entire audience was apparently startled at my entrance. A cleric at a burlesque show! Even the chap on stage who was delivering some foul stuff with cockney accent seemed bowled back on his heels.

I sat down next to the mother, a highly refined, mid-Victorian lady of great dignity. She was blushing in dread confusion. She whispered to me that we had better wait until the lights were dimmed on the house before daring to face the audience on the way out. All I have heard about the New York, Chicago and San Francisco burlesque shows would indicate that they were pure Sunday-school entertainments compared to what was offered at the Tivoli. It was against ecclesiastical law to attend a performance of a Shakespearean play or to listen to the opera at Covent Garden, but the music halls were O.K. Strange! Holy Mother Church moves slowly. Perhaps someday the English Hierarchy will learn that symphonies are no longer performed at the music halls. All in good time! Probably Father Smith in Bruce Marshall's *The World, the Flesh and Father Smith* would at this spot make a pithy point. Something like the reflection that the stupid bawdiness of the halls was probably not so lethal to spiritual sensitiveness as the subtle hypocrisies and materialistic points of view acted out on the legitimate stage in the Haymarket or Shaftsbury Avenue. At any rate we walked shamefacedly out of the Tivoli and apologized mutually for several days for having been at the show.

Quickly I went to work. Every morning, High Mass at Westminster Cathedral where Dr. Terry conducted a Gregorian proper and a sixteenth-century polyphonic ordinary of the Mass. Then I would dash back to the Grosvenor and write my impressions in a notebook. (Later a Redemptorist Father in Boston advised me to destroy the notebook, not because of the entries about English choirs, but because of the candid explosions about some Italian choirs, including the Cappella Julia of St. Peter's, Rome.)

At my first hearing of Dr. Terry's choir, I was stirred beyond the strength of vocabulary to express. Probably on account of the amazing technique of boys and men. Page after page of intricate polyphony they sang. I didn't realize at the time that they weren't making real music, for I was startled by their easy accuracy. I was remembering my many hours in the rehearsal room trying to "tamp in" even easy passages of simple pieces.

After that High Mass, I went to dine in St. John's Wood Road with Blanche Marchesi (the Baroness Caccamisi, daughter of the celebrated Mathilde Marchesi and mother-in-law of the equally celebrated Maria Jeritza), who was entertaining Liza Lehmann and several distinguished continental musicians, including Rubyo, the famous cellist. They were intrigued with my American effervescence and thoroughly amused by my reaction to the Westminster Choir. "But they can't sing," said the Baroness. "Technique, yes, but of what value is technique if they don't make music? That choir and practically all the Cathedral choirs of the United Kingdom can't sing descending semitones on pitch."

I was taken back a bit, of course, because the Baroness and her guests were all musicians of high achievement, and I was unprepared for so

severe a criticism. She proposed that we all motor down to the Cathedral
for Vespers so that she could point out to me the fact that she had been
stressing. Down we went, and her criticism proved to be correct. The
singers glided through the difficult falsobordone psalms with extraordinary ease, but the tone was hollow, a sort of sepulchral moaning, and
every downward semitone was three quarters of a tone! How luncheon
in St. John's Wood Road had sharpened my hearing!

I went often thereafter to the Baroness' home to listen to the lessons
she gave to many brilliant pupils.

She and Liza Lehmann were altogether opposed to the boy-soprano
tone quality of England. "It's unnatrual, unmusical and thoroughly distressing," they insisted. And so I began to look for more than technique.
I soon found that, with the exception of the Brompton Oratory and a
few other choruses, the English choirs were not approved by my Ground
Bass.

At Westminster Cathedral everything sounded the same. The choir
could have kept singing the same service list day after day without anyone save a specialist making note of it. *Kyries, Glorias, Credos,* motets,
all were projected through the vast Cathedral with the same monotonous
ghost tones. The only cheerful moment at the services was the Vesper
response to the *Deus in adjutorium meum intende* when the sopranos
would leap to a high rilievo over a solid homophonic harmony.

In the afternoons after the "Magnificat" at the Cathedral, I would
hop a bus and reach Westminster Abbey in time for the Anthem. The
general effect of the singing was better there, mainly on account of
Dr. Bridge's organ accompaniments which were on the string side, giving some point to the hollow hooting of the fluty boys. And after the
service at the Abbey, every day down to St. Paul's Cathedral at Ludgate
circle, where the Evensong Service began an hour later than at the Abbey. The great dome of the Cathedral took much of the hoot out of the
voices, but the sonorous organ (I forget whether Dr. Martin or Dr. Mc-
Pherson was playing at that time) almost completely obscured the voices.
I used to wonder why so many rehearsal hours were wasted when noisy
diapasons and strident chorus reeds would concur to cancel the choral
intonations. Once in a while an a cappella motet would punctuate the
service list, and the effect, colored by the acoustics of the building, was
beautiful indeed.

Father Russell, Rector of Westminster Cathedral Choir School, and
Father Hall, his assistant, were cordially kind, inviting me often to
luncheon in the refectory where both masters and boys ate.

Dr. Terry was pleasant, too, but somewhat condescending. He seemed
to be amused at first by the thought that an American could have any

valid criticism of the English choral system. Once when we lunched together, he was unmistakably cavalier. He had proposed to me that I send over a group of American musicians every summer to take lessons from him in Renaissance polyphony.

When I asked him what he would teach them, his British blood pressure, probably increased several points, for he demanded; "What do you mean, sir?"

"I mean this, Doctor. You have never answered any practical question of mine as to the proper mode of translating the notes so ingeniously written by Palestrina and his contemporaries into agreeable sounds. Furthermore, I don't think that you know the answers. You are an expert theorist, but your Palestrina in performance is hodgepodge and hash. This is no criticism of your musicianship. You are a great authority on polyphonic manuscripts and you have rendered a splendid service by restoring polyphony to daily use at the Cathedral. But the secret of interpreting the style seems to have been lost. I would rather hear your choir sing Mozart's than Byrd's 'Ave Verum.' The former makes some sense; the latter, none."

Naturally a Britisher wouldn't take kindly to such American frankness. But he was fair and a few days later admitted that he couldn't teach what he didn't know, adding that there wasn't a master in England, including the celebrated musicologist, W. S. Rockstro, Esq., who knew the trick of making polyphony sound right.

After a month at the Grosvenor I moved out to Willesden Green, North West, to be the guest of Father Herbert Vaughan, nephew of the great Cardinal Vaughan. I preached often at his church to the tittering amusement of the congregation who found great glee in my accent and the straight nonundulating intonation of Americans.

Father Vaughan bought a pipe organ which had been in the great house of one of the nobility and asked me to play the dedicatory service. There was an American organist, Ernest Winchester, a friend of mine, in London at the time. We decided to divide the program. While we were out of London, visiting the Cathedral towns, Father Vaughan began a publicity campaign of resonant dimensions. Winchester and I were leading organists of the U.S.A! No Englishman was in our class! Window cards, advertisements in the London dailies and throw-away dodgers proclaimed that at last England was to hear a pipe organ played by masters. I think the word geniuses crept into a few announcements! Winchester and I were aghast.

I telephoned upon arrival from the provinces on the day of the concert. Father Vaughan said that the organ installers were still putting the thing together. We needed to look the organ over and practice our numbers. "Perhaps at four o'clock you may practice." At four the workmen were still doing essential things, such as connecting trackers and mechanical controls. The bellows were giving trouble. These didn't seem willing to retain enough wind to keep the pipes sounding. Some hungry rodents in His Lordship's mansion had found calories and vitamins in the leather.

At six, the tubercular bellows seemed to be breathing a bit, but with noticeable rales. No thought of tuning His Lordship's calliope had entered the minds of the fatigued installers. At eight, the wind chest had sprung a sizable leak. The workmen were in a huddle inside the organ with candles, wondering how to caulk the old slide chest. But they didn't have oakum or melted pitch about, and they probably stuffed rags into the hole hoping to keep them fairly well in position by adhesive tape. At twenty after eight, the congregation already arriving, the harried workmen emerged. "That's the best we can do. The old box didn't look so bad in Hants, but it got a bad shake-up in the goods' train." I tried a few notes. Out of tune. Diapasons at concert pitch and out of tune with themselves. Flutes and strings at standard pitch, also waging a private vendetta. Pedals booming on one note, receding into silence on the next.

In the congregation were many notables of the profession who had made the long journey from the West End and even from Dulwich and Sydenham to take in the great performance.

Father Vaughan was all for going through with what was sure to be a travesty. But he was a Vaughan. That meant something in England. I argued with the indomitable gentleman in vain. And so, against my judgment and with great reluctance, I slid onto the organ bench and made the Sign of the Cross on the yellow keys. Having made note of the stops which were most violently at variance in the matter of pitch, I attacked the instrument trying to negotiate a number by the great English organist, John Baptist Calkins, which I had naïvely thought would be an American compliment to the English musical fraternity. The adhesive tape and the rags in the wind chest stood it for about sixty-four bars, and then with a final shudder which accompanied a death rattle of terrifying choking, the organ "sang its last and sang no more." I don't know where they scrapped it—perhaps near the sarcophagus of His Lordship in Hants!

Father Vaughan persuaded my mate in misery to try a Guilmant sonata on a wheezy little reed organ near the main door. It was something like trying to do the Beethoven Ninth on a harmonica. He chucked it after a few melancholy and feeble strains had begged for mercy. Then Father Vaughan suggested that I rise in the pulpit and give a discourse about the Catholic Church's contribution to the art of music. I was totally unprepared and after having been crowded into a cassock much too small, I rose and did the worst job of my before and after career. And that, in the language of "Red Mike" Hylan, mayor of New York, to the Queen of the Belgians, is "saying a mouthful." It was like talking incoherently about the "loveliness of love" or conjugating Latin irregular verbs backwards. After what seemed to be a series of eons, during which I had crossed the Styx with Charon, been sent back again, and recrossed with the obituary oarsman several times, Father Vaughan signaled me to descend from the rostrum. I haven't the slightest idea of how he caught my eye. I was rapt in a cloud of platitudes. I played *Benediction* on the reed organ while a few tired voices in the congregation gargled the texts.

The notables filed out, passing the reed organ and fixing their monocles for a better look at the miserable charlatan who had lured them from Mayfair, Dulwich and Sydenham. They probably hurried back to their whiskies and sodas while Winchester and I sipped "limonade gazeuse" at the Vaughan rectory.

What a night! Maybe the infamy of the brightly advertised organ recital has dissuaded the Vandyked monocles from reading my treatises about choral conducting. They would be justified in expecting a jack-in-the-box to leap out and cry: "April fool, even if it's August." I have been many times to England since but at a glimpse of a bus marked Willesden Green, I hie back to the horrible experience of 1908. Willesden Green and "keep your thumb out of my soup" have been twin war cries against the devils of vain glory.

During that first summer, I attended probably one hundred and fifty services at which choirs of boys and men assisted, and many rehearsals as well.

With open mind and an avid eagerness to learn, I was soon convinced that the English boy-soprano tone was wrong. I still believe, however, that the preliminary steps of the English training are sound, acoustically and physiologically, but these are merely corrective processes and cannot contribute to the development of the positive qualities of tonal excellence. The flute-tone vowel sound *oo* has been employed too much. The hoot results from continued "who-ing."

Listening to Dr. Bridges at Westminster Abbey compensating for the lack of color in his treble line by supplying a string accompaniment with the organ, I became convinced that the vowel sound *ee*, the nearest vocal imitation of a violin or viola tone, should be used with the *oo*, especially after the abuses of boys' singing have been corrected, and that *ah*, the reed vowel sound, should eventually be introduced.* This is what I was sorry that Mr. Samuel Brenton Whitney of Boston had not discovered.†

Upon my return to Chicago I introduced the *ee* sound immediately, and in a short time the quality of the soprano chorus improved immeasurably. The vibrating string effect pointed up the too hollow fluty *oo* and a lovely, alive, spiritual essence became characteristic of the Chicago boys' tone.

It was this quality that surprised Europeans when we journeyed across the Atlantic in 1912, bringing invitations to tour the English cathedral towns to illustrate its effect and the technique for producing it.

Just as one of the most ingratiating effects in orchestration is the combination of flute and violin on the treble line, so this mixture of timbres illuminates a lyric soprano's quality with a distinctive and luminous color which in certain types of music is the art's most ingratiating agency.

During that summer I learned much, too, from Mr. James Bates, of the London College of Choristers. A large number of London boys, training for several Anglican churches unable to afford choir schools, attended his classes. His solo boys were in great demand throughout England to sing the leading soprano parts in oratorios and cantatas.

Mr. Bates graciously allowed me to attend his noonday classes. He achieved a much more convincing tone than most of his colleagues in the cathedrals. He didn't employ the *ee* sound directly, using the hum on *n* which produces a color cognate to the *ee*. Furthermore, it was his custom to direct the boys early in the rehearsal in a song which would excite a simple emotion. I think that "Poor Tom Bowling" was his most frequent choice. The sympathy aroused for "Poor Tom" (I don't remember the nature of Tom's misfortunes) would communicate itself to their tone quality and the hootiness would be thus further reduced.

During my tour of the cathedral towns, I found the same standards prevailing as in London. Durham, Lincoln, Peterboro, Ely, Canterbury and York, were all about the same, but at York, under the guidance of Tertius Noble, later of St. Thomas' Church, Fifth Avenue, New York City, there was more color and warmth. Dr. Noble had an extraordinary thirty-two foot reed register on his pedals. Perhaps the overtones of this stop would climb up into the soprano rilievo and challenge the hoot. I didn't hear the Temple Church Choir on that first trip but later I found it to be a splendid unit, although the characteristic tonal defects in the

---

* Cf. "The Positive Development" in Finn, *The Art of the Choral Conductor* (Boston: Birchard, 1939), pp. 57 ff.

† Cf. p. 12 of this book.

soprano and alto lines were quite evident. The most effective choirs were the small units at King's College Chapel, Cambridge (I didn't listen to Varley Robert's group at Magdalen, Oxford), Brompton Oratory and St. Patrick's, Dublin.

I went to the Continent for a few weeks. The choirs in Paris were raucous and distressing. At the Madeleine, Notre Dame, St. Roch, St. Genevieve, and even at St. Sulpice, where the acclaimed Phillippe Bellenot had been choirmaster with Charles Marie Widor playing the massive organ, the singing left much to be desired.

I used to wonder, in Notre Dame Cathedral, why the lovely tints of the rose window didn't suggest more aesthetic tone colors to the musicians. In 1912, I was to have the privilege of feeling the inspiration which seeped through those glass panels, when playing the organ for the Paulist Choristers on Pentecost Sunday.

There wasn't sufficient time to visit Germany, the Low Countries or Spain on that trip, so I went off to Italy, expecting great things at Rome and Venice. Pope Pius X, author of the encyclical on church music, had been Archbishop at Venice and, if my memory is correct, Monsignore Don Perosi was his choirmaster.

Both Rome and Venice were disappointments. I wrote my impressions in detail, but, as I recounted earlier in these pages, I was advised by a Boston Redemptorist Father to destroy them.

I remember my first visit to St. Peter's. Arriving at the portico, I could hear lovely sounds coming from a distant spot in that vast edifice. If I had remained at the portico, I probably would not have been disillusioned, but I walked slowly toward the portable organ gallery in a transept, the sounds losing a quantum of loveliness at every nearing step. When I was as close to the singers as one would be in an ordinary parochial church if halfway down the aisle from the choir loft, I was conscious of the ugliest boy-soprano tones I had heard since I had left my Roxbury Crusaders. Crepitation! Salvos! Volleys! And the most piercing *contraltino* tonal spearheads in the alto line, while the tenors and basses could reasonably have challenged the brass section of the La Scala Orchestra in impacts and volume! How quickly I hustled out into the open, where under the serenity of the Italian sky one could feel relief, as one felt relief when Doctor Finn would put drops of hot laudanum in one's ears when suffering with earache! I tried a few other basilicas. The same tonal set-up, only some times, more so!

For my last fling at Roman ecclesiastical music (I think I had been pouting and sulking in chagrin and disappointment for days), I attended a much publicised Solemn Mass. Here, with permission from the publisher, I quote a paragraph from my *Child Voice Training in Ten Letters* * written principally for the Sisters in parochial schools and academies:

> A Bishop was to pontificate. A popular composer of church music had written a new Mass and this was to be performed by a chorus of some hundreds of voices recruited from many choirs. The great church was crowded. The singers stretched all along the triforium ambulatories on both sides of the church and filled up a large west-end gallery. The conductor leaned over the railing of the gallery and conducted the huge ensemble with a baton as long as a blackboard pointer. The *Kyrie* must have stirred up the muddiest waters of the Tiber, and the *Gloria* may have loosened some of the great stone blocks of the Castel Sant' Angelo. The boom was startling. Din, clangor, bombination! Blasts, pealings, swellings! A terrific barrage of sharps and flats, strident organ pipes and stentorian lungs. Oh! there was much reverberation along the watery road to Rome. Then came the first Versicle, *Pax Vobis*. Just at this moment a lay brother was escorting a priest to a side altar. When the lay brother reached the middle of the platform outside the altar rail, he inquiringly looked up to the conductor and singers. But they weren't having any of it. For them the next interesting moment would be the *Credo*. Then the lay brother looked at the Bishop, shrugged his old shoulders, placed his hand as a megaphone to his mouth, and shouted out with a "solitary shriek, a bubbling cry" *Et Cum Spiritu Tuo*. The poor lay brother felt that some cognizance should be taken of the Bishop's intonation. The episode made a lasting impression on me, and for many years I have stressed the importance of the liturgical Responses.

I made a beeline for Venice after the strange demonstrations in the Eternal City.

This visit to Venice was to be a pilgrimage. The memories of the City of the Canals were sacrosanct to me—Willaert, the Gabrielis and Antonio Lotti creeping out of their crypts whenever I thought of gondolas, gondoliers or San Marco's.

Mr. Hession, my first organ teacher at Boston, and his bride were on the train and we arrived at Venice together. I had long planned to make my visit to San Marco's a sort of private communion with my Ground Bass. And so I told the Hession honeymooners that I would be equivalently in "retreat" on the morrow, which was Sunday. Having registered at one of the large hotels on the Grand Canal, and having been cruelly set upon by mosquitoes which, it was alleged, came over from Lido for a bite of American beef, I tried to compose myself for the long-anticipated great experience of the morrow.

* (Chicago: H. T. Fitz-Simons Company, Inc., 1944) p. 43.

I reviewed in my mind the ancient musical glories of the great basilica. Then I sought sleep under what the Venetians naïvely termed mosquito nettings. If the long proboscies of these dread gnats had harassed me earlier by their sampling of the American meat market, their deadly, needle-like tines, having easily broken down the resistance of the so-called nettings, presently had a feast on ribs, arms, legs, and all the rest of the edible ensemble.

At three A.M. I was as hysterical as any calm Bostonian under the most aggravating circumstances could be, and lunging through the nettings, I looked in vain for a skin lotion. Finally I applied a generous dose of lather from ill-smelling soap. Having dressed and sent a tornado of cigarette smoke after the Lido long tongue-sucking species, I sat in a springless, humpy chair until about six o'clock which was the earliest hour at which a visiting priest would be allowed to say Mass.

Vividly spotted with mosquito bites, I startled the ancient sacristan of the basilica. He looked as though he suspected me of being a fugitive from Molokai who had eluded the vigilance of health officers in the Pacific, Atlantic and Mediterranean. A half dozen lire, however, relieved his anxiety, and I was immediately accorded the courtesies usually reserved for a bishop.

Extraordinary what a half-dozen coins can do!

After Mass, I repaired to the hotel, sought the manager and received from him a medicament which eased the bites somewhat but created a pungent odor. Then I made a desperate effort of the will and imagination to concentrate upon the memories of Gabreili et al.

Presently I set out for the Solemn Mass. En route, I met a pious lady from Chicago, who, observing the sorry state of my face and catching a fume or two of the antidote, gave me a small phial of a scented essence which, she said, would speedily remove the poison and embarrassment of the ill-smelling lotion. It was kind of her to baste the raw sirloin steak! I had been almost ready to hide in a ravioli mess, go over to the Lido and give the gnats a formal Sunday dinner.

Finally, I found myself in a good position in the basilica to listen to the famous choir. The Chicago lady's phial had lessened the itching and I was fairly normal for a while when the Mass began.

Ghosts of Willaert, the Gabrieli's and Antonio Lotti! Are you vampires that hide in your sepulchres at dawn? Have you never been about in the daytime since your decease to influence the services at San Marco's? You were recorded by historians as having been good men as well as artists. Why did you let a young American build up fancies about the legendary beauty of the music at San Marco's? Your spirits are alive somewhere in the eternal zone. Why don't you waft down once in a while and drive out of your famous basilica the ugly goblins that make unmusical noises there? If there is aught to this thing called telepathy, why not broadcast a sense of spiritual music to those in charge of your justly famed Cathedral? Messer Adriano, Giovanni and Andreas Gabrieli, Zarlino, Cyprian de Rore and Antonio Lotti, why have you forsaken your holy spot on the Canal? Even the doves, fattening in the Square, must have heard the story of your great music from their ornithological sires. Has the other-worldly aestheticism been poured into the by-way watercourses?

If it were feasible in accordance with the laws of Holy Mother Church, to expire then and there, be properly embalmed, and shipped back to America to be buried, I think that I should have gladly bade the world farewell. But, with the exception of the virus which the adhesive snouts of Lido had injected into my carcass and disposition, I couldn't develop anything that would interest an undertaker. A doctor, all bound round his girth with lengths of macaroni, assured me that within a fortnight the gnat virus would have disappeared altogether. And so, in spite of the terrible cheat at Venice, I would have to keep on living, or be buried without ceremonies in an un-Christian cemetery.

I toted my mosquito-scarred face to Milan, where I was much impressed by the Ambrosian Rite, exemplified at the Cathedral. The singing was better than at Rome or Venice, but very bad! Occasionally the acoustics, being ashamed of the violences intoned, would take over and put a musical sheen on a very unmusical surface.

The ceremonies seemed more convincing than the Roman Rite which is followed generally throughout the Western world. Perhaps that impression was due to the novelty of the experience.

The music, although far below the standards prevailing in England and America, was, as I have already stated, less offensive than the music I had heard in other parts of Italy and even in Paris. It was difficult then and it is difficult now to explain the low estate of church music in the country of Palestrina and the land of *bel canto*.

I left Milan for London quite refreshed.

On arrival at Father Vaughan's Rectory at Willesden Green in London, having wired en route of my arrival time, I was treated to a practical joke, presumably of a British type, for I had never heard of a similar prank executed by serious persons in America. As I alighted from the cab, I noticed a strip of carpet extending from the door to the curb. It was red. The handyman of the rectory hurried to the cab driver, not indeed to pay the tariff, but to take my pieces of luggage. Having stacked them on the sidewalk, while I was paying off the cabbie, he waved to the front windows, whereupon Father Vaughan, his assistant priests, and an awe-struck housekeeper approached to greet me at the gate, the priests with feigned respect. Said the holy villain Vaughan, "My Lord, welcome back to Willesden Green."—A bishop in the United Kingdom is thus addressed—"It is a pity, I say, that none of us here could go to your consecration in Rome! But, verily, your Lordship, we shall make it up to you here! Sarah, the good housekeeper, was overjoyed when we told her of the Holy Father's decision to make a bishop of you. She has placed the coat of arms of my late uncle, the Cardinal, in your room, being unable, of course, to get a copy of your Lordship's."

I was about to expostulate when the holy villain gave me a thoroughly British poke in the ribs. He knelt down as though to kiss the newly made bishop's ring. "My Lord, how humble you are! No ring, no pectoral cross, not even the purple stock!"

But Sarah knelt down, nevertheless, kissed the finger from which the episcopal ring was missing, burst into tears of rejoicing and fled into the house and kitchen to be sure that the roast beef and Yorkshire pudding would be just right for His Lordship's dinner.

Then I turned on Vaughan. "By the beards of all your English Kings, why did you do this thing to Sarah? I don't mind being made an ass of once in a while even if only to furnish the material for a joke. But this is as funny as the first movement of Chopin's Funeral March."

"Come, come, Finn. Haven't you Americans any sense of humor? Besides, you're Irish. You should be bowled over by the joke, what? How dour a fellow you are really! Tomorrow, I'll tell her after you've gone, what?"

"But I'm not leaving tomorrow. I'm stopping for a fortnight, until the end of the London Eucharistic Congress. You urged me to stop here and it's too late to reserve a room in a good hotel."

Then he explained. First about the so-called joke. It seems that Sarah had been impressed with the imperturbability of Mr. Winchester and Father Finn on the occasion of the humiliating organ recital. She kept talking incessantly about the restrained American gentlemen who had said no harsh word after the dreadful fiasco, and so the priests told her that the Pope would undoubtedly perceive my great quality, consecrate me a bishop, and make Mr. Winchester a Knight of St. Gregory. She was all agog during the days preceding my return.

How Vaughan straightened out the situation, I don't know, for I did depart next day on the noon train for Sheffield (Yorkshire).

But I dined once as a bishop!!

With tongues in their cheeks, the priests "lordshipped" in filibuster fashion. I narrowly escaped choking a few times on Sarah's roast beef, until finally I decided to play it out as an amateur Booth or Mansfield, and while Sarah flitted in and out of the dining room, I flayed the English clergy for an indolent lot, saying that if I didn't hear news of more zealous activity especially in suburbs such as Willesden Green, I would make a personal report, as a bishop, to His Holiness. Vaughan and the other men, some of them well in the upper-bracket years, did the choking then. Sarah would listen and look at these poor threatened ecclesiastics, puzzled that my charming disposition at the time of the fiasco could have undergone so speedy and complete a change. She looked at me imploringly, conveying the thought that really the poor men were doing the best they could to bring religion into the hard hearts of suburban Londoners. I knew it wouldn't be fair to keep at it.

And so I brought cheer to Sarah and lessened the embarrassment of Vaughan and the others by saying: "Well, Sarah, I was trying to see if these gentlemen could take a joke. There's been a lot of joking here this evening. We'll tally the score upstairs."

She beamed and Vaughan said: "No need to tally. We're outbatted."

That was rather a long yarn, but since the occasion marked my nearest though pseudo approach to ecclesiastical distinction, my American and Irish sense of humor insisted on reeling it off.

After dinner, Father Vaughan told me that he had arranged for me to give a non-Catholic mission (a series of spiritual exercises and lectures for non-Catholics) at St. Marie's large Gothic church in Norfolk Street, Sheffield, of which Dean Oswald Dolan was pastor.

Having finished this unexpected undertaking, I hurried back to London and Willesden Green for the Eucharistic Congress. My room was occupied by the Reverend X of the Paulist Fathers. And so I was obliged to seek accommodations in the Grosvenor, the hostelry nearest to the Cathedral. The best the management provided for me was a long bathroom with a cot running parallel to the wood and tin tub.

I had registered for the Congress as the representative of the Paulist Fathers before going to Sheffield and I was intent on hearing the great musical programs announced for each day. Imagine my dismay, therefore, when X, claiming his right of seniority, deprived me of my ticket of entry to the Sanctuary! I told Dr. Terry about this disappointment at luncheon on the opening day of the Congress, and he very gallantly made out a card, stating that I was an honorary chorister of the Cathedral. He advised slyly that I was *not* to sing.

Just before the opening service it was announced that representatives of prelates or superiors would have to try for seats in the nave, with the many thousands of the laity who for hours had filled the Square in front of the great Cathedral. Poor X! I don't know whether he wedged his way through the throng, but I, a non-singing, honorary member of the choir, entered through the choir school, donned cassock and surplice, was furnished with a complete set of the music to be sung and found myself in the choir loft behind the High Altar in excellent position to see and hear everything.

Tonally, I had come to expect only artificial utterances from the treble and alto choristers, but I had continued to be as much amazed by the technical sureness and facility of the whole choir as I had been on the occasion of my first hearing it.

At luncheon I asked Dr. Terry what his opening program would be. With the ostensible nonchalance of the true Britisher, shrugging shoulders as many a knight had shrugged shoulders before dashing into the fray, he said: "Oh! a bit of this and that. I'll see the librarian midafternoon. Breitkopf and Haertel promised to have copies of Max Filke's 'Ecce Sacerdos' ready by seven. My word, I hope the ink will be dry, for otherwise some of the smaller notes will be smudged, what? You know we are singing this at sight and smudgy notes raise the devil with the older men whose eyes are going off."

No rehearsal for the opening number which was to welcome back to England a Papal Legate! Straight from Rome to London, none had come as a Legate of the Holy Father since Henry the Eighth decided to have specially sympathetic satellites write up his book of theology. And Terry was going to conduct the official greetings' text without rehearsal! I think that I must have suffered much that afternoon, visualizing Terry before choristers such as we had in the States, who would need a month of Sundays' rehearsing to get two-thirds of the notes right. Immediately after luncheon I went to the hostelry aiming at a siesta, but the Reverend X was stretched out on my cot. My room at night in Willesden, my cot at the Grosvenor in the afternoon! I never knew how he had ascertained my booking, nor how, having ascertained it, he secured the key to the room for we were as much alike as Macedon and Monmouth.

The Eucharistic Congress of London, September, 1908, was probably one of the greatest religious pageants ever conducted outside of the Eternal City. The Papal Legate, many cardinals including America's venerated Cardinal Gibbons, a phalanx of archbishops and bishops, mitred abbots, superiors general, prothonotaries apostolic, and simple priests. The excitement among Catholics and non-Catholics alike in London was extreme. It was alleged that King Edward VII hustled off to the Doncaster races to be away from embarrassing and importunate invitations from the premier Earl of the Kingdom, the Catholic Duke of Norfolk, and the Marquis of Bute. The ceremonies for the many services including the Greek (Uniate) Rite had been prepared with meticulous care.

Accompanied by His Eminence Cardinal Bourne, the great assembly of prelates marched down the long middle aisle of the Cathedral to welcome the Papal Legate at the portico.

The choir filed into its place through a side door, Dr. Terry standing at the threshold admonishing us as we passed to look sharp on the bottom of page so-and-so to be on the alert for a change of rhythm, tempo and a tricky figure there. We watched in silence while the cardinals' procession found its way to the portico.

As soon as the Legate arrived, the portico doors swung open and a signal was waved to Dr. Terry who had been sitting, altogether at ease, observing the proceedings. He leapt to the podium, the organist struck a chord to establish pitch and the Westminster Choir went into the Filke "Ecce Sacerdos" *at sight* and unaccompanied as though they had sung it a hundred times. Not only the right notes, but nuances of tempo and dynamics as well. Terry himself was obliged to watch the vocal score. Not a miss nor a faltering throughout!

I had learned earlier in the summer that professional examiners went regularly to the choir schools to test the proficiency of the choristers in sight reading. Terry's outfit was top-drawer, a gold medal studded with diamonds and the bluest of blue ribbons reposing quietly there!

Presently the choir did the "Salve Regina" of Waddington (classed as flamboyant by the purists in ecclesiastical music). The voice of Bill Gee, the great Australian baritone of the choir, sent the solo part of "Eia Mater" down the sound channels of the great Byzantine Cathedral with an overwhelming effect. I brought the "Salve" back to the States and during the intervening years have given a minimum of a thousand performances of it, having orchestrated it for practically every combination of instruments.

The programs of the succeeding days were all most revealing. On the French day, French polyphony with the homophonic "Ave Verum" of Gounod, sung with what I long termed the "Westminster accent," which was in effect only the avoiding of stress on the unaccented syllables. On the German-Austrian day, German polyphony, maybe Aichinger or Eccard, with the "Ave Verum" of the Austrian Mozart. On the Dutch day, Josquin des Pres, Dufay, etc., and on the English day, Byrd and Tallis. On the day of the celebration of the Greek Rite, the choristers (I was excluded) dressed in tunics sang the Greek Liturgy, with the trebles often an open fifth and octave above the men, as though they were the regular choir of a Grecian Cathedral. All schools of music were exemplified, Dr. Terry achieving equal technical success with each style, though not an interpretative success in the polyphonic pieces which never seemed to be right at Westminster or elsewhere.

Toward the end of the Congress, Dr. Terry notified me that he was to be attacked by an unfriendly musician at a meeting of the high ranking prelates. He asked me to appear and give him a leg-up. Having arranged with the proper party, Father Makepeace Smith, S.J., I appeared on the stage at Caxton Hall, Westminster, and after listening to a green-eyed denunciation of Terry, I went forward, bowing to the presiding prelate, Cardinal Logue of Armagh, Ireland, and, having stumbled through the salutation so unnatural for an American, "My Lords, Spiritual and Temporal," I put Terry in a balloon and sent him sky high. I was quite candid, my youth being unintimidated by the crimson and purple robes, and my wrath at the unfairness of the denunciator having been inflamed "exceeding great." I could hear the old Cardinal tapping with a foot nervously on the floor. Perhaps he feared a free for all in the silly cause of music. At any rate he glared at me later in the hotel when I presented a group of Americans. Nor had he forgotten the incident two years later when I made an address, His Eminence presiding, at the Eucharistic Congress of Montreal.

My reaction to the music of the London Congress was twofold. I determined to improve the sight-reading ability of my own choristers, and to include all the types of music of which the acoustics of Old St. Mary's, Chicago, would approve. Palestrina and other medieval and Renaissance composers were excluded, because, as I hoodwinked myself then, of the flat ceiling and out-of-proportion breadth of the Church, but actually because of my lack of knowledge about rendering the beautifully composed figures into beautiful sounds. What could I hope to achieve if Dr. Terry, great archeologist and polyphonic theorist, couldn't translate the notes into music agreeable to modern ears?

At Dublin, the following Sunday, I was a guest of the Jury's at the Jury Hotel near College Green. As I was entering the rather intimate breakfast room, I spied the Irish-American priest who had been my cabin mate on the ship. He seemed more than ordinarily disgruntled at the sight of me (and that, my dear readers, is making meager use of vocabulary). In the presence of about twenty breakfasters, he shouted across the room: "Say, Finn, aren't you of Irish ancestry? You practically betrayed Ireland in that fiery speech defending the Englishman Terry. If you are going to have breakfast now, I'll leave."

My rejoinder, startled as I was, was equivalently: "Don't disturb yourself, Reverend Father, I'll tote my Irish-American-English bones over to the Shelburne. Take an extra cup of coffee, and you'll come out all right." I never saw his Reverence again, but in later dark moments, I probably suspected that he blocked my progress on the way up Mount Parnassus.

On the westbound trip, sailing on the Cunard Ivernia out of Liverpool for Boston, I ran into a social situation quite typical of the Hub of the Universe. In those days, passengers were seated in the dining saloon at long tables. On the *Ivernia*, the tables were so close together that a person rising from one table would be likely to collide with another rising simultaneously from the table behind.

During the voyage on one occasion, I rose to leave rather early. An unmistakable Bostonian lady of middle age plus rose behind me. We met head on. Snatching at her lorngette, she surveyed me as a haughty baroness has probably often surveyed a peasant. The collision was pure accident, she contributing as much to the episode as I, but remembering some of the footnotes of the gallant Chesterfield, I accepted full responsibility and with quite a good-sized bump on my forehead, rolled out sentence after sentence of apologetic clichés, to which she replied with Bostonian frigidity, "I find you very clumsy and annoying."

As the ship nosed into the dock in Boston Harbor, I was standing by the starboard rail near the Bostonian Baroness. I observed my brother on the pier conversing with an elderly gentleman who began to wave to my Disapproving Lorgnette. Then my brother waved at me. Presently both on the pier waved to both at the railing indicating that they thought the Baroness and myself to be friends.

When we cleared through the customs, I found myself with my brother in a small circle of Her Ladyship's friends. Eagerly the elderly gentleman exclaimed: "How charming for you and my sister to have crossed together. We have planned a special dinner for you two lads tomorrow at our house in Beacon Street. It will be especially delightful since you and my sister are such good friends. Jim and I have become very close, and to think that Anne and you should have become acquainted aboard ship!"

The lorgnette came up for hasty scrutiny. Fixing me with a hypnotic eye, she conveyed a command to leave unmentioned the unfortunate episode in the dining saloon and the subsequent cold relationship aboard the good ship *Ivernia*. When we arrived for dinner on the morrow, she took me aside and said in a low voice. "Too bad we hadn't been introduced formally. We could have chatted and walked the decks together. What a beastly narrow space between those tables!" Evidently the Baroness was afraid of her elder brother, who, in spite of being the Prince of Back Bay bachelors, was a real fellow, doing much good throughout the city.

When I arrived in New York, the Superior-General of the Paulist Fathers greeted me with great enthusiasm. Holding a letter in his hand, the stationery bearing the crest of the Duke of Norfolk, he asked, "How did you and X work it?"

I asked, "Work what?"

"The dinner invitation to Norfolk house, of course," he replied.

Suddenly and quickly enough to avert difficulties for the great Father X, the scene of our walk to Norfolk House during the late English dinner hour recreated itself. Having dined in a homely little restaurant in Victoria Street, the Reverend X suggested a postprandial stroll. The stroll extended itself straight to Norfolk House, the undisclosed but intended destination of his Reverence. It was known that His Grace of Norfolk was entertaining Lords Spiritual and Temporal at an elaborate dinner. Cardinal Gibbons was among the guests. A liveried footman opened to us. X said, "Present my card to His Eminence Cardinal Gibbons of Baltimore, U.S.A." The perfect-English-servant-in-livery quickly refused, stating that it was against the etiquette of Norfolk House, and for that matter, of all the houses of the nobility, to disturb a guest at dinner. "Let me have a half-crown," whispered X to me. I gave him the coin which he relayed to the avaricious perfect-servant-in-livery. The p.s.i.l. took coin and card and began a timid, slow ascent to the floor of the *salle á manger.*

Meanwhile, X darted into a nearby writing room, helped himself to crested stationery and envelopes, darted out and grabbing my arm made for the front door and the street. We went down the street afoot but in high gear, old X feeding the motor with an amazing amount of petrol. Why a bobby didn't stop us for inquiry, I don't know. Perhaps X looked as if he were on his belated way to comfort the dying. He admitted that the sole purpose of the stroll was to secure the stationery.

"But what about Cardinal Gibbons. Won't he be affronted?"

"Not at all. He'll never know about it because the footman would not have the courage to send in the card. He pocketed the half crown and forgot about the incident."

The letter which Father Searle held in hand was in this vein:

Dear Father Searle:

Father Finn and I have done well by the community at the Eucharistic Congress. We publicized the name Paulist where it had never been heard. We have just left Norfolk House, where the Duke gave one of the most extraordinary banquets of a century. We were very fortunate to be there. . . . Etc. etc.

Not a falsification in the whole letter!

Having perused the letter on the crested stationery, I merely shrugged

my shoulders, intimating that it was a trivial experience for fellows like
X and me to dine with dukes, even princes and, not beyond a calm possibility, at Buckingham Palace itself. My shrug was a masterpiece of
disingenuousness. But what could a valorous son of New England do?
Let the other fellow down, merely because he owed me a dress-suitcase
full of shillings? Or because he had taken my room at Willesden Green,
and my near-the-bathtub cot at the Grosvenor?

Chapter XIII *Great New York is Amused at Lowly Chicago*

BACK in the Choir Hall at Chicago, I industriously experimented with some of the good points of choral technique which I had observed in Europe. I was to be disappointed, however, during that season and for many ensuing seasons in the matter of sight reading. There simply wasn't enough time to devote oneself vigorously to the subject. But the Chicago Choristers were making good progress to a high ideal of chorophonic expression.

During the fall (or, having been in England, should I write *autumn*?) of 1908, Dr. Vogt's great Mendelssohn Choir of Toronto, a large group of women and men, visited Chicago, surprising the critics and concert-goers with their lovely tone quality, blend, technical virtuosity and interpretative finesse. Their crescendo through the first part of the eight-voice "Crucifixus" of Antonio Lotti was an overwhelming achievement. I remember Glenn Dillard Gunn's review of the concert in the Inter-Ocean. He was so moved by this crescendo, as well as by other features of the concert, that his usually facile pen seemed to find difficulty in writing down words which, if the richest, could only inadequately express his feelings.

Having attended all the concerts of the Toronto choir's series, I determined to take my choristers on a spring tour of the Eastern cities— to whip the outfit into its maximum of enthusiastic effort; to gain desirable publicity for a Catholic organization trying to reclaim its own Catholic music before the blasé audiences of the Atlantic seaboard; and to observe the reactions of the professional critics of New York. With this elaborate plan in mind, I booked a trial road concert at Milwaukee. In fact, we had two concerts there, matinee and evening. I was keen to make observations of the musical and deportmental attitudes of boys and men before undertaking a two-thousand-mile jaunt.

Musically, the Choristers did well at Milwaukee, but their conduct was most unsatisfactory. We played the Pabst Theatre with Milwaukee's best orchestra. Between afternoon and evening performances, some

small soprano boys stuffed paper into the bells of the brass instrument
and put cayenne or something equally tormenting on the mouthpieces of
the reeds. Usually, the orchestral players tune up before each concert,
but their instruments were on stage where they had left them after the
matinee, with the curtain up, so the players marched on immediately
ahead of the choir, and presently the opening number began. Players of
clarinets, oboes, flutes, bassoons, each blew one hysterical note, examined
their mouthpieces and laid down their instruments. Sheets of Milwaukee
daily papers rolled out of trumpets, French horns, trombones and tuba.
The tympani sounded as though the tympanist were essaying a long roll
on a stretched Indian blanket.

I stepped off the podium, signaled the players to move back and ordered the curtain down. It was a bad spot for all concerned and especially for the conductor. After much fussing and fuming, cleansing of
mouthpieces and rummaging for more wads of paper, up went the curtain and the concert proceeded artistically without further misadventure.
Of course, not a mother's darling in the outfit knew anything about the
prank which might seriously have affected the future of the Choristers,
through the professional grapevine.

In the hotel the boys raised every kind of troublesome mischief which
could be devised by preadolescent imaginations. Shouting up and down
the elevator shafts, chasing one another in pyjamas through corridors
and up and down stairways. Pillow fights. Throwing things over tran-
soms. I was on duty with a large hairbrush, but every sturdy whack I
applied to a youngster's stern seemed to pep him for further and more
outrageous activities.

Some of the adult singers were no better than the boys. A holiday
spirit seemed to have caught the choir in its grip. At one time during the
night, I went to a room where several tenors and basses were making
"close harmony," to find them giving rhythmical movement to their
chordings by pelting a young man with a very high voice with wet
towels, pillows, Gideon bibles. The unfortunate alto singer had been tied
to a high bedpost with strips torn from hotel sheets.

Altogether the Milwaukee experiment proved that, if we were to
undertake lengthy tours, the chorus should be organized on a strict
disciplinary basis. The first step in this direction was to secure the services of a prefect-escort who would be responsible for the boys. We were
fortunate in securing the services of Miss Josephine Quinn, admirably
suited by nature and experience to take over the duties. The boys were
wholesomely in awe of her from the start, for she told them at once that
she knew of the Milwaukee exhibition, and that there would be no
repetition of it. Having outlined to the boys the plan by which she ex-

pected to maintain reasonable order, she required each boy to sign a promise to respect and obey all regulations which might be announced. And the too-lively men agreed that the lack of restraint displayed at Milwaukee would not be permitted again to cause embarrassment.

And so we booked the New York trip. Easter holidays, 1909. Detroit, Niagara Falls in Ontario, Buffalo, New York, Baltimore, Washington. We tried for Philadelphia, but the Archbishop preferred to postpone our appearance there until a later tour. In New York, a publisher offered a guarantee for the first American performance of an oratorio by Father Hartmann whose compositions had been highly praised by European critics.

The New York Central Railroad sent us out on a special train. From the moment we had booked the tour, it was incumbent on someone to study the fine points of railroading in the passenger department in order to lessen traveling expenses by careful routing and to be sure of connections at junction points. The only someone available was myself. And so, a quasi musician became a quasi railroad man. It was inevitable, however, that I should eventually become a fairly well-informed tourist agent. The small boys enjoyed trying to catch me in a mistake about trains, their numbers, routes and equipment. Frequently, when a long Pullman train would roar past us in the opposite direction, a lad would ask for the number of the train.

Having observed the equipment myself, it was easy to reply. "Rock Island number three, out of Chicago for Los Angeles. Left Kansas City two hours ago." Or "Number fifteen, Boston and Albany (New York Central Lines), out of Boston for Chicago. Due tomorrow 12:55 P.M."

For this first trip which was to start the Choristers off on their long choral Odyssey, I dealt with the Michigan Central division of the New York Central, the Baltimore and Ohio and the Pullman Company. A few days before leaving Chicago, the representatives of the three companies came together to ask me if I would pay the switching charges for the chartered Pullman cars at New York. The switching movement involved a network of transfers from one road to another at so much per car per switch. The cost of the movement from the Grand Central Station in New York to the Central Railroad of New Jersey's station in Jersey City for a good-size train was considerable. When I reminded them that the New York Central had a short time before acquired ownership of the West Shore Railroad and that our train could therefore be routed on the West Shore tracks from Albany to the ferry at Weehawken, New Jersey, directly opposite Forty-second Street, and that only one switch charge would be involved, they agreed to follow the suggestion and accepted the charges themselves.

At the following Christmastide, I received a facetious invitation, signed by the three gentlemen, to become a director of each of the three companies. Music and transportation! Three beats to a measure, three cents a mile! No dallying adagios, no slow trains! Legato singing and smooth roadbeds for sleeping! Bach scores and railroad timetables!

The concert at Detroit was satisfactory, and we moved out at midnight for Niagara Falls, Ontario, where after Mass and breakfast we were to sing a concert for the Ladies of Loretto and guests in their academy which stands sentinel over the Horseshoe Falls. After breakfast, the boys went for a stroll in the nearby Victoria Park. There had been a great ice jam in the river for weeks, but on the eve of our arrival a thaw set in, causing the poles carrying the high voltage cables of the Ontario Power Company to list and the cables to sag. Two boys, having left their topcoats near the entrance of the Park, spied a short cut through some hedges and ran along this trail to get their coats. Rounding a curve between the hedges, a solo boy who was scheduled for the chief solos at Buffalo that evening fell across a sagging cable, was instantly electrocuted and his body hurtled into the ravine far below. The other lad touched the same cable but only after the electric charge had blown out.

We had a dead boy in our midst. The shock was too great to describe even after so many years. I deputed one or two of the most cool and reliable men to attend the inquest, notify the boy's family in my name, and make the necessary arrangements for sending the poor child's remains to Chicago. Within half an hour after the catastrophe, we were on the stage opening the promised concert with "Rejoice, O Daughter of Zion" by Humphrey Stewart.

What a text to deliver at such a moment! I don't remember how we pulled through the program, but immediately after the concert, I asked the Michigan Central representative to send our train over to Buffalo. Boys and men were ordered not to leave the train until a committee of men and I returned after a conference in a nearby hotel. The Reverend Father Oliver Welsh, who was making the tour with us, patrolled the station platform as a modern M.P. or S.P., allowing no one to leave the train. At the conference in the hotel, apprehension was expressed that parents would telegraph to send their sons home immediately. This would have been the finish of the Paulist Choristers, for much money was involved.

And so in spite of the heavy cloud that was tending to smother us, we decided to order all telegrams delivered to the secretary who would not distribute or read any of them until our train was well out of Buffalo for New York. In retrospect, this seems to have been disingenuous, but the accident was as an act of God. No carelessness on our part contributed to it. It seemed wise to try to fulfill the obligations to which we had committed ourselves. When the secretary finally brought the many telegrams received, we were all astonished by the unanimous approval by parents of our continuing the trip. The family of the dead boy, Joseph Cronin, was most understanding and sympathetic. Their attitude was so considerate that the memory of their telegram and subsequent conversations has ever since been a reminder of the great heights of spiritual charity which sincere people can reach.

However, we went into New York with a heavy burden on our minds and hearts.

The rehearsal with the orchestra was unsatisfactory. The soprano boys were detained at luncheon, and the first part of the Hartmann opus was rehearsed without them. A capital disadvantage. One of the great New York orchestras was playing with us. When I stepped upon the podium at rehearsal, the players looked me over with disapproving eyes. What could a young—a very young—ecclesiastic know about conducting a symphony orchestra? I should be holding book and candle instead of a baton! But I did know the difference between a bassoon and a bass fiddle, and I knew every note of the orchestral score and the relationships of the many orchestral timbres to the vocal colors.

Before beginning, the concertmaster approached the podium, and twirling the sharp end of a waxed mustache, hurled this sarcastic comment at me so loudly that all players could hear, "We are accustomed to a good down stroke for the first beat of each measure." I replied that they would get plenty of good down strokes, and incidentally they would do well to watch the upbeats, for these were more important, indicating the absence of accent. The first violins gave me a hard time. I asked them to play more lightly than the dynamic marks suggested because I was interested in underlining the inner parts. And so they proceeded to play more loudly.

At one spot, agitated by the first trumpeter, the whole orchestra became rebellious. It was a difficult movement that we were working over. The score called for *alla breve,* i.e., two beats of half notes instead of four of quarter notes to a bar. The trumpeter jumped up, crying, "This cannot be played or sung *alla breve."* Whereupon I made one of the great tactical blunders of my career. The soprano boys had arrived, and I put the chorus through the number, unaccompanied, in the *alla breve* time. Then I went to the organ and played the number *alla breve,* marking with special clarity the trumpet part. This proof of the easy feasibility of producing the movement *alla breve* put the orchestra in a most unamiable mood. It was stupid of me to have employed such tactics.

A priest-conductor, forsooth! And a youngster! And a choir from the frontier town of Chicago. Trying to show a great New York orchestra how to play!

After rehearsal, fearing the worst for the evening performance, my brother and a few adults of the choir placed piano and pianissimo signs in the orchestral parts wherever they had submerged the vocal tone quality by deliberately overplaying. This was another mistake! How much one, if he is openminded, can learn from mistakes! I learned plenty at our New York debut.

In the dressing room, before the performance, I gave a quiet pep talk to the Choristers, begging them to snap out of the depression caused by Joe Cronin's death, and the jitters brought on by the unfriendly attitude of the orchestra. Many of the singers might have thought the job of conducting the orchestra too much for me, if they hadn't sung several times with the Chicago Symphony Orchestra under my baton.

I have already recounted the silly condemnation by a New York critic of our alleged rendition of the "Alla Trinita Beata," for which we had been obliged to substitute a number in English by Humphrey Stewart. When we arrived at the oratorio, things began to happen quickly. The string section sounded as though several players had not tuned to the oboe's A. Pianissimo passages were mezzo forte plus; no attention was given to retards and every accelerando was held back by enough players to cause dreadful grinding of the tempo gears. The gears didn't mesh readily once throughout the performance. Most of the time I was forced to turn directly towards the violin section and conduct to this alone, trusting that the Holy Spirit would keep the singers and the rest of the orchestra in time.

I was having one of my worst experiences on the trail up Mount Parnassus. Occasionally, I expected a landslide to finish the undertaking and myself for ever. Large stones seemed to be rolling down from the top. Cries of demons were substituted for the tones of Euterpe and Apollo. But I kept at it! No New York orchestral hecklers were going to down me! I was of Irish ancestry and I had an impelling Ground Bass urging me on! "Come on, you double-crossing first fiddlers. Don't you realize that you're leading with your rights? Ah! there's a good wallop the bass chorus put on your chins. And here's where the soprano chorus with a dead-sure lead backed you to the ropes, and the sympathetic tympanist beat out the right time to shame you!"

There was one splendid opportunity towards the end for the orchestra to deliver a K.O. punch. The first French horn player, stiffening his lip for a mighty attack, played a wrong note. This note was important, for, following an unaccompanied passage by tenors and basses, the French horn was assigned a note which would change the key. The sopranos and altos would sing unaccompanied in the new key and presently the full orchestra would enter. Do you see the set-up?

With the French horn establishing the wrong pitch and the boys accepting it, the orchestra and chorus would presently strive to reach the climax of the oratorio in two different keys.

But the Irish-Bostonian wasn't having any of it. I signaled the boys not to enter, and beckoning my sturdy senior soprano chorister, a redhead, Frank Hartigan, who would have enjoyed trying to push the French horn down the player's thorax, to come to the podium. I hummed the right note to him. He checked by humming it back to me and went to the various tiers in the chorus bank giving the right note to the boys. *Voila!* When the orchestra entered for the climax, with furious bowing and excessive blowing, we were all in the same key, and the K.O. had failed to connect.

Leaving the podium, I was a bedraggled somebody. Physically spent, jittery nerves, frustration of artistic purpose. And on the morrow the fraternity of Fountain Pen splashed us with leaking nibs. We were the world's worst! But the orchestra, being a New York outfit, escaped censure, receiving some condolences from the most vitriolic Pens.

Off we went to Baltimore. I dismissed from my mind the hostility of the New York professionals. Tomorrow is always another day. And Baltimore, gentle, refined Baltimore, made the morrow a happy day. As I alighted from the train, a husky baritone voice behind me offered to carry my bag. Turning, I beheld young Jimmie Griffin, know as "Huncie." Two nights before, at Buffalo, he was obliged to take several encores in a soprano stunt above the high C over the chorus. His voice had changed in thirty-six hours. This phenomenon gave me my start in the study of the changing voice, leading ultimately to a technique for training changing voices to sing on the alto line.

Cardinal Gibbons attended the Baltimore concert which was given over a market in an ugly-looking hall. His Eminence requested us to sing "Lead, Kindly Light" as he did on other occasions. Curiously, this hymn was forbidden to be sung in the New York archdiocese. A Baltimore orchestra accompanied the Choristers sympathetically and the concert was the best up to date in the history of our organization. The Fountain Pens wrote enthusiastically about the spiritual tone quality and flexibility of the Choristers. No New York philippics in the *Baltimore Sun!*

Then we moved over to Washington with the Baltimore orchestra. Before going on stage at the New National Theatre, a small solo boy, Ralph Sommers, accosted me, with the manner of a prima donna, insisting that I tell the first oboe player about a mistake which he had made in a passage at Baltimore, and that such blundering, especially close to a vocal entrance was disconcerting. I relayed the admonition to the oboist who explained that his reeds hadn't been working well at that spot, adding: "A clever youngster. A real musician. He surprised the whole orchestra as well as the audience with his tone quality and authoritative assurance."

But it was not all milk and honey at Washington, for Mr. Winchester, my companion in the fiasco at Willesden Green, and Mr. Wells, my collaborator in the series of articles for the *Ecclesiastical Review* damned the performance with faint praise. The Choristers and orchestra had given a superb performance, but we sang on a flat stage, and the open flies and wings prevented the full resonance of the units from reaching the audience.

I have always tried to avoid engagements in standard theaters for that reason. A chorus needs a bank of tiers, a good back drop and a high ceiling, and must be placed as near the audience as possible. A poorly sung concert at Symphony Hall, Boston, is better for the listeners than a fine performance in any standard old-fashioned theater.

We had tried for a White House representation, but to no avail.

Back we went to Chicago, the Baltimore and Ohio making its record trip up to that date, beating its running time of President Taft's special train by almost a half hour.

The home-coming was sad. There was no merrymaking en route, no enthusiastic welcome at the Chicago depot. Joe Cronin was dead. We had suffered a tragedy on our first great expedition. Would we succumb to the blow? Were we finished as a potential national unit? Would parents allow the boys to travel to distant places again?

Dismissing such depressing speculation, I hurried to the Cronin home, where father and mother, brothers and sisters, and many relatives received me with embarrassing kindness, expressing deep sympathy for *me,* whereas I had gone out to them to try to stammer out my condolences in *their* bereavement. We sang a memorial Mass for Joseph, his choir stall filled with white flowers. I think that the family requested the Mass to be celebrated in white vestments, for Joseph was a pious boy, and had received Holy Communion at the convent a short time before the fatal accident. The season closed shortly afterwards.

Chapter XIV *A Few Arpeggios Pizzicato*

THE following season found the Choristers making steady progress to the heights of choral virtuosity. Our soprano tone quality was of the loveliest texture and infiltrated the whole unit with its spiritual overtones. Shortly after Christmas, J. Lewis Browne, then director of music at Wanamaker's, Philadelphia, and later director of music in the public schools of Chicago, announced a choral contest for the following April in Philadelphia. He invited us. It was to be a notable affair. Choirs from many places would participate. The judges would be the outstanding musicians of America: John Philip Sousa, Arthur Foote and George Chadwick of Boston, and Horatio Parker, Dean of Music at Yale University.

We accepted the invitation immediately upon ascertaining that the parents had not been unduly frightened by the tragedy at Niagara Falls. We were assigned to the top class of choirs of boys and men. How eagerly we went into the rehearsals of the appointed compositions! With what care we worked out the "Westminster accent!" How fluently we merged the two concurrent rhythms of Elgar's "Angelus!"

To finance the tour, we booked Detroit again, the Victor Phonograph Company at Camden, New Jersey, near Philadelphia for experimenting, and Rochester, New York. Also we were given a guarantee by the Wanamaker Company for an evening concert in the Egyptian Hall of that large department store.

Nothing went amiss on the tour. We had an easy first prize in the contest, and the Egyptian Hall concert impressed the audience composed mainly of professional musicians. Our "Westminster accent," as well as the smoothness of the mixed rhythm in the Elgar piece, caught the fancy of the professionals.

The experiment at the Camden studio of the Victor Phonograph Company was disappointing, however, the recording needle declining to accept the true quality of our soprano section. Even now the soprano line is the most difficult to record and broadcast evenly because of the rapid vibrations required to establish the treble rilievo. Enunciation is practically impossible above F on the fifth line, and the acuteness of the

135

timbre is unpleasantly piercing, unless the quantity is so reduced as to throw this voice line out of balance with the other parts.

On the way home we gave a concert under the personal auspices of Bishop Hickey at Rochester before a large audience. The only manifestation of prima donna jealousy which I ever observed among the Choristers was made at Rochester. The senior solo boy, Harold Dee, was programmed for his best aria: "Connais tu le pays" from *Mignon* by Thomas. A temperamental lad was jealous of Dee. He wanted to sing a solo before the great audience. Raising a row backstage during the intermission, he disconcerted young Dee almost to the point of his declining to sing. It was necessary to use strong-arm tactics with the agitator and persuasive resources with the solo boy. The aria came off well, but the agitator in the recessional hymn on the following Sunday let me know his reactions by pulling the entire soprano chorus out of the established tempo, bringing a beautifully sung service to a disastrous anticlimax.

Harold Dee helped to increase the confusion in the minds of the public about Father Francis Finn, S.J. and myself. Father Francis, a generation ahead of me, had become celebrated as the author of books for boys. Excellent books. I had read them all. Along comes Father Finn of the Paulist Choristers, a specialist in training boys. Along comes a widely publicized solo boy, Harold Dee. The title of one of Father Francis Finn's best stories was *Harry Dee*. Therefore, concluded the public, the conductor of the Choristers must have written the books! Father Francis sent me two excellent choristers from Cincinnati to the Choir School in New York.

The last occasion on which I saw Father Francis was in 1920 at Long Beach, California. I was playing the *Credo* at Father James Reardon's church, when Father Francis approached the organ bench, whispering: "I can't wait to visit with you. I'm off this minute. I want to tell you that I'm sick and tired of answering letters about training soprano boys."

Placing my foot on a wrong but resonant note on the pedal board, I managed to fling back: "I'm sick and tired of telling people that I don't know when you're going to publish sequels to *Tom Playfair, Percy Wynne, Harry Dee*, and *Claude Lightfoot*." A few times young Dee gave private recitals. His name on a window card over mine—"Harold Dee accompanied by Father Finn"—probably cheated many a youth who came to see the hero of the book and have a look at the author as well.

The Philadelphia tour and the first prize in our section solidified the Choristers' organization. We were an established national choral unit as well as a church choir.

In those days we followed the silly plan of wearing cassocks and surplices for the first part of a program which was devoted to sacred music, and college gowns with mortarboards, from which dangled golden pom pon tassels, for the second part. Some rigorists deemed it irreverent to sing any secular music in ecclesiastical attire. Even poor "Old Black Joe" had to be intoned under the golden tassels. And the "Mocking Bird" couldn't appropriately chirp its lament over "Sally" with a surplice in sight.

Years later I observed a French choir in two-fold costume. First, smocks with great red crosses in front, while they discoursed of spiritual things. Then doublets and high boots with bits of colored ribbon flowing from shoulders for the graceful little impersonal folk songs of Normandy and Brittany. What an absurd idea! To think that an organization must spend much money for the two uniforms, lest the holy garb be profaned by lovely little ditties about this world! It is like refusing to put flowers on the altar. The pretty flowers are thoroughly of this world. The Sacred Mysteries of religion celebrated at the altar are of the eternal world of the spirit!

After a year or two we outgrew our puritanism and chucked the gowns and mortarboards. Many a time since, we skipped "down St. Peter's road," held converse with "Danny Boy" and looked over Masefield's "Cargoes" on the "dirty British Coaster with the salt-caked smokestack," with the dignity of the ecclesiastical garb not affronted in the least. How silly one can be! How stupid to think that eternal values are menaced by the acknowledgement of charming and refreshing natural values! One of the inestimable worths of Christianity has been to bring the supernatural and the natural into closer alliance.

On a long trip several years later, working for French charities during World War I, we had a double wardrobe, but we never changed during a performance. We sang all concerts in the uniform of the French *poilu,* all church services in cassocks and surplices. On one occasion, however, a genial monsignor, who was presenting us in church, insisted upon the French uniforms. His church was built in unusual form. No ecclesiastical pattern had been followed. Except for the Altar and the statuary, one could fancy himself in a large theater. And so perhaps the poilu's attire was consistent with the surroundings.

The following season, 1910–1911, opened with great promise. Musically the Choristers were making lengthy strides. Beautiful tone quality on all the voice lines. I had solved the enigma of producing a definite tone quality for the alto line. The technique involved would save the treble clef quality (or at least an analogous quality) while the boy's voice was changing into the man's voice. I shall not annoy you by discussing this technique here. I have already published it in my *Art of* *the Choral Conductor.** Tenors and altos began to furnish a smooth axis around which solid basses and ethereal sopranos were spinning beautiful webs of harmony.

Considering a tour for the spring, we decided on Boston as the high spot. The critics there ranked with the reviewers of London. Philip Hale, Louis Elson, H. T. Parker. The latter, on account of the initials of his name and his uncompromising critiques of flaws and inadequacies in a performance, was known to the profession as "Hell To Pay." The audience, long used to the best in American performances, would know what we were striving to exemplify. We were specializing in Russian unaccompanied music (I was still afraid of Palestrina!): Rachmaninov, Gretchaninov, Kastalsky, Ippolitov-Ivanov, Könneman, Arensky, Archangelsky. The management of Symphony Hall, Boston, offered us a substantial guarantee for matinee and evening concerts. We accepted. St. Louis was booked along with Cleveland, Erie, Springfield, Massachusetts and Rochester, New York.

En route to Cleveland from St. Louis we had a near disaster outside of Indianapolis. A steel girder on a flat car had been wrenched so much out of position as to lie at right angles to the length of the freight train extending beyond to reach our tracks. As our train and the freight train passed, the girder ripped open the side of the boys' sleepers, directly under the lower berths. A few inches higher and a large number of boys would have been killed. The delay caused by sending into Indianapolis for other Pullmans made us half an hour late for the Cleveland matinee and correspondingly late for the evening concert at Erie, Pennsylvania.

After the concert at the latter city, several of us received another shock. A group of soprano boys elected to approach our railroad siding via a steep hill. There was a sharp curve just west of the hill. As the boys neared the eastbound track, the Twentieth Century rounded the curve and bore down upon them with tremendous speed. We screamed at the boys to move back. One lad flung himself out of the way a scant three feet from the cowcatcher of the monster locomotive.

Two near accidents in one day! Boston ecclesiastically (there had been confusion about the Archbishop's consent to our appearance), and Boston critically on my mind! This business of persevering on the ascent to the Home of the Muses was becoming a nerve-racking adventure! In the morning at Worcester, Massachusetts, we received the Boston papers. The critics had sunk sharp talons into Melba or Sembrich for her recital of the preceding evening. They didn't leave much epidermis or true skin

* (Boston: Birchard, 1939) pp. 136–144.

on her back. We were all glum. Narrow escapes the day before, and the Boston critics finding fault with a supreme artist! It was fortunate that I knew the Symphony Hall organ (it was the twin of the Mission Church organ) for with multiple anxieties harassing, I would have had a bad time trying to balance the registration on an unfamiliar instrument.

Two sold-out houses! Choristers in the pink of vocal condition. Determination and concentration prevailing. The acoustics of that extraordinarily sensitive hall abetting our efforts. The inspiriting response of Boston's cultured audiences to our well-diversified effects. All these brought elation and *élan* to the Choristers. Critics came backstage and expressed enthusiasm for the "new choral technique." Of course I hurried to remind them that it was only a renascence of the abandoned technique of earlier eras.

And the reviews the next morning and evening! Superlatives! Roget's *Thesaurus* emptied of congratulatory adjectives!

At Springfield, Massachusetts, the following day, something happened which the boys had on me for a long time. They had often boasted with the loyalty of boys, that as a conductor "I could knock 'em dead." The day was as hot as any day at the Panama Canal. In a stuffy theater we appeared for the matinee. After the spacious and resonant Symphony Hall, the theater on Court Square seemed like a tiny salon. Low ceiling. Stage without chorus banks. Piano in the pit. At that time the splendid auditorium for concerts with its well specified pipe organ had not been built. The curtain was down. The Choristers filed into their places. The curtain rose. I crossed the stage to the podium from the *wrong* side. I had developed a custom of entering from the right looking towards the audience whenever there was a choice of entrances. The habit had by that time taken on the annoying quality of a superstition. As I walked on the wrong boards to my platform, I felt that something harrowing was in the making. I stood upon the podium and bowed to acknowledge the polite but faint applause of the audience. Synchronously with my bow, a woman in an aisle seat close to the stage, rose and, screaming, fell to the floor. Ushers carried her backstage. A few minutes after the concert began, I saw an undertaker's long basket carried through the stage entrance and presently brought out, probably to a waiting hearse. With no irreverence to the lady who had met sudden death, the boys and some of the men insisted that no one with a weak heart, sitting near the stage, could withstand the shock of beholding their conductor approach the podium. Such experience would be too awe-inspiring! The magnetism that issued from his personality was too great for a coronary thrombosis to bear!

Finishing off the tour with a dismally small audience at Rochester, we arrived home having been thoroughly frightened by the two near railroad accidents.

I sailed for England on what was perhaps the last trip of the *Adriatic* as flagship of the White Star Line. Friends from Milwaukee had asked me to change an earlier booking to the *Adriatic*. Mother and three daughters, one of these rebuking me at all times for my "affected manners." I guess my manner and manners were always a bit stiff, but they were natural to me. The very dignified mother had neglected to inform me that they were going to make the rounds of Europe with a large group of females under a female cicerone. I was the only male, and a parson at that! Two of the daughters ran down the gangplank to warn me of the female-tour set-up, suggesting that I turn in my ticket and take another ship. But I wished to hear as much as possible of the music composed for the coronation of King George V, and the *Adriatic* was the last ship scheduled to arrive in time for the ceremonies. The music was made to order, and therefore lacking inspiration. But the bands of the pageant procession, with visiting monarchs, emperors, queens and empresses were impressive. I dissociated myself from the bevy of females at London.

Later that summer I played an organ recital at the College Church of Lucerne, Switzerland. I had gone down to Brünnen near the William Tell district for a few days' retreat before the concert. In conformity with the custom prevailing among the clergy in Switzerland at that time, I wore layman's clothing, except when it was required to don full dress, as at the later or second dinner hour in the major hotels.

Arriving at Brünnen with collar and tie, and ascertaining that one was not obliged to dress for dinner, I tipped the maître d'hotel, asking for a table for one in a quiet corner. The table was promised. Upon entering the dining room the first evening, the maître whispered that I must sit through my first dinner with three ladies who had requested my being placed at their table. Much demurring in the middle of the dining room would have attracted attention and been ungracious as well. And so I sat at their table. A quiet little mother. American. Two cold-looking academic (though I dare say charming) daughters. It was Friday night. The ladies declined the meat courses. Naturally I declined them, too. They volunteered no remarks in my direction save an occasional "Please pass the olives" or "That vinegar caster is handy to your reach." I made speed to be finished and rose to leave ahead of the trinity of females. As I bowed to them and excused myself, the little mother said: "You didn't eat any meat. You are too thin. A few days at Brünnen will sharpen your appetite."

Having expressed formal thanks for her gracious solicitude, with a pull at my cravat, I turned to leave when Daughter No. I or No. II sang out cheerily: "How are all the boys, Father Finn? We met you back stage at St. Louis in the spring! How about a stroll through the gardens?"

"Give me a chance to change to a Roman collar, and I'll be with you."

When I went back to Lucerne to prepare for the organ recital, I resumed the lay attire, dining ahead of the formal dinner-sitting. My single table was in a remote corner of a spacious dining hall. At luncheon for several days at the adjoining table was an American family of unmistakable distinction. Father, mother and two very beautiful daughters! One of the very beautiful daughters sat directly opposite me. She had nothing to look at save the wall and/or myself. Whenever our eyes met accidentally, she flushed with the lovely hue of an American Beauty rose. Of course she thought me to be a layman. I dined early to avoid dressing. They dined late. Evidently the very beautiful daughters were having a slow time of it, no dashing cavaliers being about to escort them here and there. On the day, the evening of which was to find me at the console of the large organ (played regularly by the Breitenbachs, father and son) the very beautiful daughters raised their voices at luncheon before Mama and Papa arrived. "How stupid and apathetic some men are. Here we need another man to go up the Rigi with us this afternoon and we can't find one."

Not being altogether dense, I caught the general tenor of the louder-than-usual conversation. Presently I left and passed the American Beauty Blusher on my way to the lift. First a wistful, then a contemptuous look. I returned a sad but sweet smile and went my way. The organ recital delayed me beyond the early informal dinner, and so I dressed in long single-breasted coat, a high waistcoat and Roman collar. Mama and Papa and the very beautiful daughters were already seated when I entered. The look of amazement, humiliation and chagrin on the faces of the very beautiful daughters is still a vivid picture in my memory.

The American Beauty Blusher went into the deepest red. Having toyed with the hors d'oeuvres, she dropped her fork, and chokingly excusing herself to the mama, papa and sister, dashed out of the dining hall. Presently papa introduced himself. He was one of the most prominent Catholics in America. I made a hurried explanation about the vogue for lay clothes among the Swiss priests, and he promised with a chuckle to straighten the situation out with the American Beauty.

At Munich, some weeks later, I was booking to Paris at the American Express office. Leaving the office I was obliged to walk through a narrow and circuitous passage. Whereupon the American Beauty and myself collided with considerable impact. At first she was quite bewildered. Then we both laughed loud and merrily, until the ticket seller looked reprovingly across his counter. Lay clothes, very beautiful daughters, an organ recital, and eventually dressing up as a junior prelate! It was all so naïve, and the memory of the episode still carries the attar of American Beauty roses. It would be fun to encounter the ladies again! Nice little old ladies now. White hair and wrinkles!

At Prague that summer I played the famous organ at the monastery of the Premonstratensian Fathers, who wear white cassocks tailored in the fashion of the Popes' cassocks. At Munich, Mme. Ernestine Schumann-Heink gave me her box for the Mozart-Wagner Festival. This was nice and balanced a disturbing experience which fell to my lot at a church in that city.

I had asked the hotel manager the location of the nearest church. He pointed across the Platz. Next morning at about seven-thirty, I went over to the church. The doors were wide open. No service was in progress. A monsignor was flitting in and out of the Sanctuary. I walked confidently forward, addressed him in my best Latin, not being intelligible in German, and presented my "celebret" (a document from the Archbishop of Chicago, granting permission to celebrate Holy Mass outside the Archdiocese). The monsignor conned the celebret quickly, asked me for my papers from the Prinz-Regenten's office, and ascertaining that I had none, took me forcibly by the arm through the sacristy to an open door. Ejecting me summarily, he said: "You are very stupid. This is the Prinz-Regenten's Chapel." And so I was obliged to seek a church where permission from royalty was not required to celebrate Holy Mass.

At the end of the summer, I was in London awaiting my sailing date for the States. One morning I read an item in the press announcing an international competition in choral music to be held in Paris the following spring. The first competition of its kind in the history of music. Counting my shillings and pence, I found that I had just enough to make a hurried trip back to Paris to try to locate the management of the competition, to sign up for it in several different classes, and to travel to Liverpool for my Cunarder, the fast, tiny and tossing *Campania*.

Chapter XV *The Ground Bass Zigzags*
Through Icebergs

I HAD made up my mind quickly to bring the Paulist Choristers across the ocean. A bold decision. As I was told many times during the ensuing months, a rash decision. How to finance such an undertaking? How to manage a large group of boys and men on foreign soil? What chance did our young organization have against Europe's best choral groups? At a Board of Directors meeting in November, my European plan was voted down. I undertook to canvass the directorate, eventually prevailing upon a sufficient number to reverse their decision, which they did with reluctance.

Announcement was made early of the exciting plan. Tentative permission for the extensive tour was granted by the Superior-General. And so we went to work to earn the necessary money. We sang innumerable concerts with a semichorus throughout Illinois, Indiana, Michigan and Iowa. Several citizens made donations. A raffle was organized. Finally we had enough money. Engagements in Europe with financial returns could not be counted as assets, because the uncertainty of our monetary status had not permitted the making of contracts or the specifying of particular dates sufficiently in advance. I had reserved space on several ships. We had the money in time to take up the option on the last ship scheduled to arrive in time for the international competition, the *Empress of Ireland*, out of Quebec for Liverpool.

Confusion, tears and a touch of hysteria attended our departure from Chicago. The *Titanic* had sunk after collision with an iceberg about a fortnight previously. Parents were anxious, for we were to take the northern lane across the Atlantic probably through the same ice floes that had caused the sinking of the *Titanic*.

Confusion developed in the concourse of the railroad station whither a large number of people had repaired to bid farewell to the boys and men. Hundreds were milling around. It seemed for a while as if we would not be able to sort out the crowd and send the Choristers through the gate in time for the train. Finally I stood on a ledge and, after a few futile attempts, put over an announcement. We permitted the boys' parents to ride with us to the last suburban stop.

I had been in the lower city from bank-opening time until train time completing financial arrangements, and was obliged to telephone one of the priests at Old St. Mary's to pack my clothes and to bring the luggage to me at the station.

A fine old gentleman, Reuben Clinton Kelley, Secretary of the Pullman Company, an enthusiastic devotee of the choir, was at the station expressing regret that he "couldn't come along this time." Just as the train began to move, he hurried to the platform, shouting: "I can't stand it. I'll meet you in Montreal in time to catch your boat-train to Quebec." And so the "Baron," as Mr. Kelley was known to the choristers, met us and accompanied us on the great adventure.

We were scheduled for a concert at Montreal in St. Patrick's Church the evening of the day following our departure from Chicago. At a small village in Ontario, the locomotive developed serious trouble. We were placed on a siding while efforts were made to correct the difficulty. It was evident that we couldn't arrive in Montreal for the concert at the appointed time. Having consulted my checkbook, I proposed to the conductor that he telegraph for another locomotive, and if necessary I would assume the cost. No other locomotive powerful enough to pull the heavy train at such speed as to reach Montreal in time was available. And so, having wired about our plight to Father Gerald McShane, the Pastor of St. Patrick's, we nervously awaited developments. Eventually we arrived at Montreal. Father McShane had wired us to be vested on arrival. All sorts of vehicles were waiting. Huge old-fashioned limousines, little model T models, coupés, touring cars, and some horse-drawn vehicles. The large audience had been apprised of the mishap and remained for the much belated program. The start of the European tour was therefore somewhat inauspicious. But the concert was good, and the patience and hospitality of the Montrealers reassuring and refreshing.

The skipper of the ship told me at the gangplank that he was not sure of bringing the *Empress* into Liverpool on schedule. One of the twin propellers was disabled. The heavy ship would have to cross the Atlantic with only one propeller against winds and seas. And besides, there were the icebergs which cautioned moderate, and at times even sluggish, pace.

This information was a damper on the enthusiasm which usually attends the departure of a great liner. We had been notified in Chicago by the United States Ambassador to the Court of St. James that His Majesty, King George V, had appointed a "command" concert at Buckingham Palace on the day of our announced arrival. It would be disappointing to us, probably not to His Majesty, if we did not arrive on time. Presently anxiety on that score was dispelled by a radiogram from the American Ambassador, canceling the command appearance at Buckingham Palace. The King of Denmark had died and all the courts of Europe would be in mourning for thirty days.

I had made a bargain with the chaperon-prefect before I could induce her to assume the responsibility for the boys on such an expedition. She was fearful lest some tragedy might occur. Boys, retiring upon her signal at ten at night, but rising by prearranged plan among themselves at about one-thirty in the night-morning, when all monitors and adults would be asleep, proceeding to unprotected parts of decks, and being washed overboard by mountainous waves! She agreed to come only after I pledged my word to co-operate in any disciplinary measures she would suggest. A necessary decision. Unpleasant, however. Involving procedures not quite snug with my disposition.

After dinner, the first night out, four small boys came to my cabin. A note from the chaperon demanded that the four lads be given a thorough spanking. There was nothing to do but to administer the spanking. But I worked out a physically merciful technique. Psychologically, there wasn't quite so much mercy in it. I produced a large hairbrush, showed it to the lads and instructed them to prepare their youthful sterns for a memorable encounter with the polished back of the brush. Two at a time. The first pair entered the cabin, the other waiting outside. I instructed the pair to lie face downwards on the bunk. They were trembling as with the ague. Finally, having delayed almost to the point of cruelty, I said to one of the pair, "Are you ready?"

A feeble "yes" was audible.

Thereupon I walloped the other fellow! Both bodies rose several inches from the bunk. Only one was hit—not too hard—but with adequate resonance. The struck and unstruck let forth synchronous cries of terror and anguish. The pair awaiting their turn in the companionway were ashen pale when I invited them for their taste of the brush. The same technique. Spank two boys on one stern. Tough for the fellow chosen to receive the hardwood brush-back on his epidermis. But psychologically just as punitive for the other lad who vicariously felt the impact. Of course I never explained to the chaperon my disingenuous technique. Nor to the boys. Probably both thought that they had been walloped, though one was conscious of the experience longer than his mate. No boys were washed overboard. No dangerous breaches of discipline came to my attention!

I ascertained that boys were sent up for spanking for any failure to observe the chaperon's regulations, even the slightest. A coat left on a chair instead of being hung in the closet was good for a rear-end blister or two. Sixty seconds late for a meal meant sixty seconds of torture. To the spanking was often added solitary confinement in his cabin for a "repeater." The rigid discipline of the chaperon soon established at least overt obedience.

Passing through the ice floe, we counted thirty bergs, some large, some small. One towered on the horizon as Notre Dame Cathedral towers over the Ile de France. The master of the ship brought us to Liverpool nearly on schedule. Since we had not booked any professional engagements in England and the command concert was not to take place, we had nothing important to do in London. A few English choirmasters, including Dr. Terry, gathered in the lounge of our hotel to listen to the soprano chorus. The conviction prevailing quite generally among English choirmasters about boys and soprano tone quality was, in effect, that only English youngsters could make the right treble sounds. They seemed to be bewildered by the elasticity, compass and dynamic flexibility of the American boys. There was much polishing and refitting of monocles. The masters attested their surprise, not in words but with blushes of confusion. A long crescendo on a high C from pianissimo to forte plus, followed by a similar dynamic progression on the C below the treble staff (where the English boys are especially ineffective) seemed to nettle some of the maestros who left abruptly, having forgotten some of Lord Chesterfield's recommendations.

That night we had a long crossing from New Haven to Dieppe. No cabins. Bunks along the length of the ship. A rough sea. Seasickness. Little sleep. Solemn Mass in the morning at Notre Dame Cathedral in Paris. A bad proximate preparation for one of the most widely publicized ventures of any choral unit in the history of music! A special train from Dieppe to Paris which was delayed a few times to allow regular trains to pass! What a night and early morning!

It was Pentecost Sunday. I prayed to the Holy Ghost. Perhaps the Spirit of God answered, for the Ground Bass came through with insistence and persistence. Paris was in gala attire. Flags flying. Multitudes of people in the thoroughfares. The Cardinal Archbishop was to pontificate. Many thousands arrived early at the Cathedral to hear the American choir. Probably some came to scoff. How bold of an American unit to dare to sing in the greatest cathedral of La Belle France! How inexplicable on the part of their Cardinal Archbishop to permit such an invasion! What would the great stone walls, arches and triforia cry out if they could cry out. What words of reproach would come from under the cardinals' red hats hanging high above the Sanctuary if the cardinals were not mute in the mortuary crypt! Oh! yes, some came to scoff. I know not if we influenced them to remain to pray, but I do know that many remained.

The special train had been very late. I suggested to the chaperon that she bring the Choristers immediately to their hotel, where we had wired for a light breakfast to be in readiness. After the quick breakfast, the Choristers were to vest in cassocks and surplices and go directly to the sacristy of the Cathedral in taxicabs. I said Holy Mass at the Cathedral and was awaiting the arrival of the choir when a verger called my attention to a procession of surpliced boys and men crossing the Place de Notre Dame with American flags flying in front and in the rear. Taxis in sufficient number to accommodate the large group were not available, and following the suggestion of the hotel manager, the chaperon brought them vested to the Cathedral via the *métropolitain,* the subway of Paris.

The great Cathedral was crowded. It seemed that every available inch of space was occupied. In the triforium ambulatories, the number of people assembled would have constituted a congregation, a large congregation, in any sizable city church. Musicians were there. From the Conservatoire. From the opera. Enrico Caruso, the celebrated tenor, was in a row of seats close to the chancel. From the Comique. From the Chanteurs de St. Gervaise. Vocal teachers. Composers. Organists. Patrons of all the arts, and a cross section of the diverse components of the population of Paris.

I remember making the Sign of the Cross over the organ keyboard as I seated myself on the bench. The start of the Procession was a memorable moment. In conformity with a regulation of the Archdiocese of Paris for the Paschal season, we were required to sing the "Regina Coeli" in procession around the vast edifice. The chancel organist warned me of what he called the impossibility of keeping in time with the Choristers when they would be at distant spots. He suggested an unaccompanied setting. But I had had much experience in synchronizing organ and choristers by beating the time with resonant pedal notes; by carrying important melodic lines on sturdy low-sounding pipes, pointed up for definition and elasticity by the contribution of violinlike stops; by allowing for the hiatus between the speaking of the pipes and the hearing of these by the choristers by anticipating the notes. The procession came off well. When I heard the chorus singing from the far-off tribune, I was amazed at the floating, volatile and otherworldly effect.

Presently, in the chancel, we began the Solemn Mass. The organist, a most gracious gentleman, asked if I were familiar with the complete nomenclature used on the stop knobs of French organs. I was not familiar with this nomenclature, for except in France, and perhaps in Spain and

Portugal, the names of the stop registers were German or Italian, with only a few names in French. The organist volunteered to help me with the registration. He sat beside me at the console. Misadventure Number One was chargeable to that arrangement.

The gentleman beside me reached over to turn a page shortly after the beginning of the *Kyrie*. He lost balance. His left elbow struck the low notes on the top manual, proceeded to the middle-register notes on the second manual (this was the great manual from which the loudest stops are controlled on a three-manual instrument) and finished on the high-, piccolo, clarionlike piercing timbres of the lowest or choir manual. What this accidental sliding through practically the major part of the compass of a pipe organ and its many tone qualities did to the melodies and harmonies of the choir cannot readily be imagined. One would have to hear the cacophonous medley to appreciate its violent challenge to the intonations of the Choristers. I recovered from the shock, quickly realizing the stupidity of concentrating on the misfortune of an accident the nature of which was probably discernible to a considerable portion of the congregation.

The boys and men had been seasick on the Channel. I was obliged to use all the devices at my disposal for keeping them true to pitch for accurate attacks and for the application of the nuances of interpretation. I had just warned the soprano chorus of the need to sing *above* the notes, by playing a measure or two of their voice part on a high flute, when misadventure Number Two presented itself. I should write *himself,* for a venerable priest, evidently in his dotage, appeared across the chancel in the doorway to the sacristy. I couldn't spare time to look him over, but some of the Choristers reported him later as being of vacuous eye, in sort of a trance. I remember his shuffling across the chancel, past the Cardinal's throne, to the side of the organ case at my right. In a moment he had drawn out from a compartment in the organ case, a huge old-fashioned bass fiddle with only three strings (modern string-basses have four strings). These strings were thick. They could make a notable racket if vigorously plucked pizzicato or played forte with the bow. Spending only a few seconds to tune the enormous menace, he began to play the bass part of the *Kyrie* which we were singing—before many thousands of people and standing almost in the middle of the chancel. It was reported to me later that the Cardinal was manifestly ill at ease. A deacon of honor descended from the throne and with the assistance of a couple of acolytes and the verger escorted the poor old priest to the sacristy along with his big bass fiddle.

Two such mishaps in quick succession. Under such circumstances! All the Choristers, however, remained undaunted, intent upon fulfilling their responsibilities. Nothing unfortunate happened during the rest of the Solemn Mass. That is, nothing novel in my experience. But a near mishap threatened to take shape when the baritone soloist began to flatten and I was obliged to transpose. The key into which I was forced to modulate was the six-flat key. Many black notes in the final chorus, especially on the pedal keyboard. I had never played the finale in that key. What to do? I took a chance that all would get my signal to await another signal before beginning the finale. All understood. I modulated back to the easier key and we finished without a catastrophe.

As the Choristers became accustomed to the surroundings, their control of tone quality, rubato and dynamic changes increased. When the *Benedictus* after the Consecration floated pianissimo to piano to pianissimo with undulating grace through the Cathedral, I knew that my Ground Bass theme was explaining itself to the thousands in the congregation, including a goodly number of the scoffers. One could tell from the stillness in the nave, the only audible sounds being the disembodied intonations of the choristers.

Since the turn of the century, when the Concordat between the Quai d'Orsay and the Vatican had been broken, the wearing of surplices in the streets of France was in transgression of an explicit law. Cassocks, yes; for the French clergy had worn their soutanes in the streets in accord with a centuries-old tradition. The soutane was the ordinary garment of clerics. But the government proscribed surplices except at religious rites in churches.

I had forgotten about this interdict.

The organization made such a striking impression on observers that I was urged, after the Solemn Mass, by an American resident of Paris, Countess Spotswood Mackin, to have the Choristers fully vested whenever they appeared in public as a formal unit. I acquiesced. I was inviting difficulty. Difficulty accepted the invitation.

On the day following our concert, we sang before President Fallières and his cabinet in the Jardin des Tuilleries. As on Sunday, the Choristers arrived fully vested with American flags flying. When the program in the Jardin was finished, the Chief of Police hurried over to me and snarled a command to me to take the Choristers out of the Jardin immediately, vociferating with Demosthenean eloquence that we were transgressing a law of "la République." I began to realize the unwitting folly which I had permitted. We were about to depart when I noticed the large number of competing choruses and bands taking positions for what promised to be a parade. The chief barked another order to leave. Nodding my obedience, I swung the choristers into the first position of the marchers and led the parade through the Jardin, in step with an inspiring band behind us, to the right in the Place de Concorde, and again to the right down the Rue de Rivoli. The parade, I learned later, was to go as far as the Bastille.

Americans were leaning from the balconies of the popular hotels, the Crillon, the St. James and Albany, the Continental, the Meurice, etc. Much cheering and waving of American flags. The band behind us, catching the spirit and borrowing *élan* from our countrymen did a French version of "Dixie." But when we arrived at the Place Jean d'Arc, I decided to take the Choristers out of the parade. Taxis to the Hotel. Presently came a telephone call to notify me that I would be visited by a police inspector. When he arrived, he had in hand a copy of one of the French daily papers. An editorial urged my arrest and imprisonment for bold defiance of the antisurplice law. I pleaded forgetfulness and was reminded by the polite officer of the incompetence of the plea. My Celtic imagination became active. A French dungeon! Darkness and dankness! Rodents! Tepid water and moldy crackers! All alone save for the pacing guard! I began to regret that I had not allowed the whole organization to remain in the parade until it reached the Bastille where we could all have been locked up together behind and under the historic battlements.

And what of the morrow? The competition at two o'clock in the Theatre du Châtelet! How long would I be in durance? Should we cancel engagements in Rome? Send the boys and men home via Havre or Cherbourg?

It was a tight spot. One of the tightest. The polite police officer suggested that a member of the Chamber of Deputies might come to my rescue. Lucien Milevoye responded. After much telephoning, conferring and gesticulating, he finally convinced the Sûreté that the stupidity of the young American should be overlooked, and that for diplomacy's sake, it would be unwise to build up the unintended transgression into a criminal offence.

What a relief to feel the French shackles drop off, even if the fetters fell only from my imagination! What surcease of terror to bring the chimeras out of the dungeon into the fresh air of freedom! I was hardly in top condition to conduct at the competition the next day. But the combination of Ireland and New England brought strong fibers to the fore and when I began to conduct, the pictures of French police officers, of prison pits, and the guillotine surrendered to the aesthetico-spiritual concepts which I was determined to create or re-create.

We were allowed to sing only in the Division d'Honneur, although I had registered for other classes. Many notable organizations were in our division. We were permitted to appear last among the contestants. I went early to the Theatre du Châtelet where Sarah Bernhardt had achieved her greatest successes, in order to observe the work of other conductors and to note the acoustical singularities, if any, of the Theatre. The choirs, to which I listened, were placed too far upstage, much of their quality being obscured and resonance decreased by the flies and wings and ceilingless setting. Each conductor stood on a podium almost atop the footlights. Our turn having come, I instructed the Master of Ceremonies to arrange the Choristers in a compact bloc as far downstage as possible. Then I went out into the theater itself, chose a place on the ramp between the orchestra stalls and from this excellent position, a point of vantage for judging acoustical as well as artistic effects, I led the Choristers through the program. The arrangement of the Choristers and my superior spot for conducting concurred to set forth the best resources of the choir.

At the conclusion of the first number, "Ave Maris Stella" by Grieg (a fairly simple number on paper, but dotted with many vocal and interpretative hazards), the perfunctory applause which had greeted the efforts of other choruses was significantly lacking. A few seconds (these seemed as minutes) of solemn soundlessness. Then an outburst of acclamation. The Ground Bass had resounded throughout the Theatre, the spirituality of the boy-sopranos' voices and the euphony of their volatile timbres over the undervoices found awed response in the subconsciousness of the listeners. As one of the judges, Mr. W. G. McNaught, musicologist and critic, I think, of the *London Times* described his reaction: "The singing didn't come from any particular place; not from the stage or the floor or the ceiling. The sounds seemed just to happen; the group on the stage gave the impression of listening rather than of singing."

Our group was awarded First Prize in the Division d'Honneur and on the morrow we were feted in the Hôtel de Ville where Sèvres vases were presented as the trophy. I was awarded the *Palmes Academiques.* Mr. McNaught suggested that upon the completion of our engagements in Italy we make a tour through the Cathedral towns of England to demonstrate our approach to the choral art. But I was keen to return the darlings to their mamas and papas in far-distant Chicago. Delaying in England, giving one-night stand performances, had not lure enough to offset the manifold anxieties which necessarily beset the managing director of a group of boys and men in a foreign land.

After the program at the Theatre du Châtelet, the choir was entertained *and* entertained at the salon of Miss Sarah Lawler, with a glamorous Countess pouring tea. The personnel of the organization, at least the adolescent and adult sections, were more interested in "sight-seeing" the Countess than in any of the historical places upon which tourists usually gaze in awe. The Choristers had ears that could prehear beautiful sounds and throats that could produce them. They also had eyes. Even a specially small tot of about ten kept his eyes on the Countess. Putting his dark curly head on his arms, these being on the tea table, and looking like a Botticelli cherub, he stared at the lovely lady. For once in his life, he was not interested in refreshments. Sweetmeats failed to attract his attention and when we were asked to sing he was loath to leave the tea table and the Countess. But he sang to her!

Several professional critics and the composer, Isadore de Lara, whose opera *Nail* was being performed in Paris at the time, were there. Having heard us in the great auditorium of the Châtelet, they were interested in our technique for adjusting balance, blend and dynamics to the relatively small space of the salon. There was no opportunity to explain this in detail to the inquirers, but I indicated the basis of the technique. Proper tonal balance in a chorus depends ultimately upon control of quantity. I have a series of signals which indicate the degree of quantity desired. The singers are trained to accommodate their dynamics to these signals. In a small room, I naturally call for a softer prevailing level, making crescendos and diminuendos very conservatively.

I might have added, if there had been time, that the pitch of unaccompanied numbers would probably be raised to advantage under a low ceiling, and a brighter than usual tempo followed. What had interested the congregation at Notre Dame Cathedral and the audience in the Châtelet was the aura which seemed to emanate from the melodies, harmonies and timbres in progress—that transcendental, psychic something which attracts and holds the intuitive awareness of people.

Our organization had unmistakable flaws in its structure at that time. While the tenors and sopranos were excellent, the bass chorus was not a well-blended unit. Naturally, on such a long tour we were obliged to include in the personnel some men whose chief recommendation was their availability. The alto chorus was less effective than in later years when the technique for training countertenors had been applied to all singing on the important alto line. By sundry means of balancing and fusing, we were able to distract listeners from particular inadequacies and to convey an over-all impression of aesthetical worth.

Throughout the many years of my professional activity with choruses, I have been seeking in vain for satisfactory answers to these questions: *Why don't choirmasters make real music with their choirs? Why are they satisfied with unmusical tone qualities? Why complacent with mere structural correctness, the right notes, clean-cut attacks and releases and outbursts of volume?*

Choral music nowadays masquerades as a pauper among musical agencies. I write "masquerades" because chorophony has in reality a wealth of resources. Altogether unnecessarily it abases itself in rags. Its fine raiment hangs in closets which are not locked. Only shut. Modern choirmasters have not been interested in examining the fabrics so skillfully tailored by the greatest musicians of past generations. In the treasury of chorophony lie forgotten the golden traditions of music's richest era.

The Ground Bass is not the theme over which current choral singing is developed. Nor are there many widely publicized symphony performances influenced by the theme.

The melos of concerted music fails to reveal itself. Timbres are misused. The natural qualities of voices and instruments are extended beyond their structural capacities to the point where musical communication ceases. And the monotony of unrhythmical procedure from start to finish! The ceding by middle-part voices and instruments to the high trebles and sonorous basses of the prerogatives which belong to the inner parts and upon which the mystic appeal of true music depends! The wide interstices between the choral and orchestral lines! The mad pressure put on fortes! The unregulated or mechanical application of nuances of tempo and volume which is substituted for the patternless spontaneous variations urged by the nature of the score or the circumstances of the performance!

The inadequacies and positive blunders in the direction of choral singing today challenge the musicianship of conductors for explanation. Perhaps the less spiritual aims of the modern world? Perhaps the content of people generally with the lick-and-a-promise way of doing things? Perhaps the drifting away from secure moorings of all the art forms? Who knows?

I am sufficiently an optimist to believe that this transitional period which has not favored the best purposes of the arts will soon have elapsed. The Ground Bass theme is academically correct. It remains for the professional practitioners of chorophony and symphony to expound the theme. Now! *Otherwise the theme may be lost!*

There were many excellences in the work of the competing choirs. In the Division d'Honneur, however, there was an excess of weightiness, a plodding, earnest pursuit of surface items. In other classes, facility in sight reading, technical virtuosity, and at-homeness in difficult pieces were notable. But there wasn't much *music!*

After Paris, off to Italy.

Guardian angels probably came down to steady the adult section on the last night in Paris. That gay Capital of Hedonism beckoned tenors and basses to a merry evening. I was worried about the early start for Turin on the morrow. My announcement at dinner about the train time

(7 A.M.) and the need of retiring early (not in the morning, but that night!) was received with respectful coolness. The chaperon and some of the senior adults spoke individually to the men, pointing out that if they missed the train, they would be stranded in Paris.

Boys and men were aboard the train next morning in good time. Several waggish lads, young and old, talked *at* me during the journey, making satirical allusions crescendo to the delightful time they had had in Paris. These gentle satires had no sting, for the men were happy to have won the prize and thoroughly content with the opportunities provided for relaxation.

In Paris, many of the boys were talking among themselves at the Hôtel de Ville before the awarding of the prize when, unperceived, I slipped into the room. One lad was querulously demanding of the others: "How long do you suppose the Boss will keep us here? Why can't he represent the choir himself and let us out?" This question, amusing in itself considering the place and circumstances of our assembling, revealed an aspect of boy psychology to which I had not adverted. Do your job well. Have it over with. Eliminate all fuss and formalism afterwards. Chuck the public congratulations. Forget the whole thing. Enjoy the recess until the bell rings for the next job. Through the ensuing years, I was to learn that ceremonious rites, such as public welcomes by mayors, the presenting of the keys to cities, parades such as those in San Francisco from the ferry to the City Hall and through the downtown district of New Orleans, irked the boys more than any other particulars on the list of agenda. I believe that a normal boy endures a public reprimand with less embarrassment than extended and extravagant compliments. It was almost a surprise, at Rome, after the concert for Pope Pius X, not to discover signs of eagerness among the boys to be done with it.

The attitude of boys to ceremonious felicitations does not mean that a "regular" boy objects to having good work acknowledged. In fact, his sense of fair play demands this. He expects rebuke for faults, accepting it as just. But he needs a simple acknowledgement of efforts diligently made. And so, over the years, I developed the habit of disclosing my satisfaction at a particularly well-delivered number by blowing a little whiff over the tip of the baton. Many choirmasters err in this matter, failing to express appreciation while often violently decrying, protesting and inveighing.

Once in a while I have been a visitor at rehearsals, at which no word or sign of commendation was offered by the choirmaster. I dare say that sometimes I have personally presided over rehearsals in truculent mood. But this is a grave mistake. If such manner of conducting practice periods be chronic, the choirmaster cannot evoke from his singers the qualities of music that are its greatest charm.

At Rome, the Choristers had a heavy schedule. Our first appearance was at the church of San Silvestro in Capite, the only church administered in Rome at that time for an English-speaking congregation. We sang the Solemn Mass. After a processional hymn down the center aisle, the Choristers mounted a narrow stairway to one of the most cramped choir lofts in which I have been called upon to conduct. As most of the Italian church organs of that time, the instrument at San Silvestro's was old-fashioned, inadequate and puzzling. The close confinement in that loft brought on so severe a headache that I begged to be excused from a formal dinner at the North American College. The Choristers were to sing at the College in the afternoon. I decided on aspirin and a siesta. The room clerk promised to rouse me in time for the concert. When the bell rang, I arose with alacrity and dressed as I was accustomed to dress for concert appearances in America—long single-breasted coat and high waistcoat. I forgot that I was in Rome where the clergy wore cassocks and feriolas in public. As I arrived at the College, the Choristers were filing into the Sanctuary, where, standing on the altar steps, they would sing to the audience seated in the nave of the chapel. Cardinals were present in crimson robes; archbishops, bishops and monsignori in purple; priests and seminarians in black cassocks. I was the one individual in the assembly who was not dressed in the traditional ecclesiastical attire. And it was in a chapel! In Rome! Before high-ranking prelates! I was conscious of my transgression of the strict Roman custom only when I faced the hierarchical congregation.

Was I heading for trouble in Rome for not wearing the ecclesiastical dress? I had had trouble in Paris for permitting the Choristers to appear in vestments. A "yes" mistake in France! A "no" blunder in Italy? A funny world! Well, I'd wait and see. Meantime, skip it and make the cardinals concentrate on music rather than on vesture. Chorales and not cassocks. Perhaps if I could persuade the Ground Bass to assert itself with convincing clarity, my civilian longcoat would lengthen to the measurements of a soutane! I was far from being at ease. At least during the rests I was aware that I had stumbled against an obstacle on the uptrail to Parnassus. And just at the time when the going should have been easiest.

Fortunately, I escaped any serious consequences to my unwitting disregard of the Roman traditions. Perhaps my friend, Bishop Kennedy, the Rector of the North American College, relayed my explanation to the cardinalate and the episcopate. Save for a delightfully satirical note from Bishop Kennedy in which I was admonished not to appear in Rome again without ecclesiastical attire, I heard nothing about the matter. But at the papal concert, I observed some sly glances of disapproval from some of the ecclesiastical musicians present. Although properly garbed on that important occasion, I may have impressed the aforesaid ecclesiastical maestros as at least a subconscious iconoclast, willing if not eager to overthrow standards of ecclesiastical propriety and the Italian criteria of musical worth as well.

A concert at La Salla Pia with an orchestra including many players of the Augustheo Orchestra, before a cross section of Rome's ecclesiastical, professional and concert-going groups, revealed the organization in control of its best resources. Monsignor Rella, assistant of Monsignor Perosi of the Sistine Choir, brought the boys of that famous choir to the concert. He told me afterwards that he had offered a lira to any Sistine chorister who could catch one of my boys inattentive to me on the stand. I asked him what his temerity had cost him. He replied that he had not opened his purse. Well! his boys hadn't seen what I saw. I don't remember ever to have conducted a performance during which it was not necessary to signal to both boys and men for better attention.

The concert before Pope Pius X in the Throne Room of the Vatican was, of course, the greatest experience of that tour, and in fact, of all the tours of the Paulist Choristers. We were nervous. Nervous with awe. The thought of appearing before the Vicar of Christ, within the hallowed precincts of the Vatican was not indeed intimidating. For in the sense of exciting real fear, the saintly Pope was a gentle, kindly soul. But the signal honor of being permitted to sing before the successor of St. Peter affected the whole organization differently than any other episode in the record of the choir. Even to see the Pope is a great event in the life of a Catholic and of the majority of non-Catholics.

The Pope is not only the head of the Church, the Bishop of Rome. He is a symbol of all things that are Catholic. Doctrines, moral principles, practices and the essence of Christianity. The Christian history of nineteen hundred years seems to be retold in the person of each successive Supreme Pontiff. And so the small boys as well as the adults were in sober mood on the eve of the concert. A solemn silence prevailed in the dining room. There was little scampering about the hotel. Boys and men retired early. Many went to Holy Mass and received Holy Communion the next morning. It was almost with too grave mien that the Choristers went from their hotel near the Quirinal, across the Tiber, and having passed the historic Castel Sant' Angelo arrived at the portico of the Vatican. Papal guards, resplendent in colorful uniforms, and monsignori of the Vatican household, welcomed us and escorted us to the Throne Room.

The Vatican houses the Sistine Chapel where the most celebrated singing body in the history of music still assists at all ceremonies in which the Pope participates. The Sistine Choir!—with its unbroken continuity from the fourth century, in spite of the transfer of the Papal See to Avignon, 1305–1376. The choir in which singers were clerics, priests, bishops; in which, from the fifteenth century, most of the singers were composers, the leading composers of their eras. The choir from whose personnel instructors were sent to distant lands to inculcate the musical principles and practices expounded and followed at Rome by the masters under the custodianship of the Church. The choir whose archives preserve the records of great men: Angelo, Abbot of Santa Maria de Rivaldis; Elziario Genet; Boccapadule; Dufay; Palestrina; Vittoria!

Yes, the Paulist Choristers of Chicago with a scant and inconsequential record of eight years had arrived at the historic fort of the Choral Art! Young Americans were to dare to sing among the ghosts of the greatest choristers of Italy, the Netherlands and Spain! Little wonder that we were agitated. Were our consciences plaguing us for the effrontery of raising puny voices under the direction of a young Nordic conductor in the surroundings of the renowned Cappelani Cantori of the Golden Age of choral music? Did the trepidation with which our reluctant feet mounted the grand stairway stem to a sudden realization of presumption, impertinence and calamitous imprudence? There were a few moments when at least the seniors of the group, including myself, wished ardently that we were anywhere else in the world. On a desert island. In a jungle pursued by beasts of prey. Snowbound by enormous avalanches in an isolated Alaskan ravine. Anywhere except at the threshold of the Throne Room!

One who has not had the experience cannot comprehend the quality of the nervousness that had overtaken us. Not that we were fearful of stumbling through the pieces, of singing wrong notes or offpitch. Not that there was doubt about exemplifying our normal standards. But that we were hoist by our own petard. By our own contrivance we had pushed open the door of the Throne Room of the Pope! Would it soon shut on our departing figures with such a slam as to noise our humiliation to the world?

But there was no retreating. No turning about and fleeing swiftly down the Grand Stairway. The Swiss Guards and the Chamberlains of the papal household flanked and followed us with impelling "forward march" courtesy. At length we crawled, a thoroughly bewildered outfit, into the allotted places in the Throne Room. Presently His Holiness arrived. With a casual glance but more than a casual smile in our direction, He mounted the Throne and an attendant signaled me to begin the program. The charm of the Pope's smile had dispelled our morbid nervousness. With the sounding of the first chord, it seemed natural to be there. If the ghosts of Palestrina, Anerio and Baini had soaked through the walls, they had brought nothing of the eerie with them. They must have been smiling along with His Holiness. Probably Palestrina was amused at the youthful American conductor! A friendly monsignor had warned me to omit examples of Italian polyphony from the program lest, transgressing the prevailing Italian conventions of interpretation, we invite ridicule. Although I had been convinced for some years that the modern Italian approach to polyphonic interpretation was not the authentic Italian approach of the Renaissance, I had nothing better to offer and so I had had no intention of trifling with the great Italian heritage of polyphony. The warning of the monsignor was well meant but needless.

I began to conduct programs of polyphonic music a few seasons later, but not until 1925 or 1926 did I finally come upon a plan of interpretation that has seemed since to be in accord with the probable scheme of the polyphonic period.

The Pope was pleased. The tone quality of the sopranos particularly arrested his attention. Some American priests in the audience heard His Holiness making comments to those near Him. It was reported that He asked a well-known Italian musician to explain why a comparatively new organization from America which was presumed to lag far behind Europe in appreciation of aesthetics could produce tonal effects with boys that even the Sistine Choir did not produce.

The rumor of this alleged question of His Holiness spread quickly through the choral fraternities of several countries, and soon I was boycotted by many conductors. Earmarked as an innovator. A disturbing Somebody. "He tried to show the Sistine Choir how to sing!" "He hoodwinked the Pope, by tricks and sham effects, into believing that the Sistine should copy his boys' timbres!" "His hat is too small for him." Etc. etc. The et ceteras grew into a long series of satires and sarcasms which took years to spend itself. I was often called "Doctor" and not infrequently "Monsignor." Once, a year or two after the European tour, the newspapers of a certain city played up an absurd item to the effect that Rome had cabled me to take over the Sistine Choir in place of Monsignor Perosi. The publication of these trumped-up tidings caused me much embarrassment. I received telegrams, some of congratulation, others warning me to decline the honor and a few bristling with sardonic spines.

I knew, of course, that I should have to pay, in personal uneasiness, for the publicity which would accrue from the European venture and especially for the papal endorsement. But I was too young to realize how great the cost or the number of years before the debt would be amortized. One must always pay, in advance or afterwards, for any undertaking which receives favorable publicity. Particularly if the undertaking involves some developments unpleasant for one's colleagues.

After the program in the Throne Room was finished, we were momentarily disturbed by what seemed to be the abrupt departure of His Holiness. Descending from the throne, he went quickly through the doorway. Presently he returned with the official photographer of the Vatican. Pope Pius X had spied the photographer and, instead of summoning him by messenger, went personally to fetch him. This act of simplicity was most impressive.

But the Pope may have been a little confused that morning. I trust that we had not caused the confusion. He seemed to forget that His infallibility was confined to matters of Faith and Morals. Authoritatively, He gave precise directions to the photographer, indicating the spot upon which to set the camera's tripod. The photographer volubly objected. He gesticulated with characteristic Italian vehemence. He told the Pope that the tripod should be placed elsewhere. His Holiness leant deaf ears to the expostulations. "Place it here, as I told you." That was a fiat.

Then began a series of pantomimes between His Holiness and the cameraman. Up and down went shades. A difference of opinion about the proper lighting for the photograph waxed divertingly. After several up and down trips of the shades, the papal plan prevailed. His Holiness directed the Choristers to group themselves in a certain formation which provoked a hopeless shrug of the photographer's shoulders. And the picture was taken. With the light coming from the wrong quarter. With the camera in the wrong place. With the Choristers so placed as to exclude many from the camera's field of view. It was a most gracious thought, the Pope's idea of having an official photograph of the Choristers with Himself. But the picture would have been a success if the photographer had been allowed to take it according to the canons of his craft. I spent much money in various places and with many photographers in an effort to have the Vatican plate improved. In vain.

Before His Holiness finally left the Throne Room, He gave His Apostolic Benediction to each of the Choristers. There was a non-Catholic lad among the sopranos. When the Pope neared him, I mentioned that the youngster was a Protestant, whereupon His Holiness chucked the lad under the chin, and placed both hands on the lad's head. He also focused a most benign smile upon me!

We descended the great stairway in a mood different from the disposition of mind in which we had made the ascent. All was well! The great undertaking had come off without mishap. The Choristers, especially the boy sopranos, had approved themselves to the aesthetical discernment of the Pope! It is true that there were some dour glances hurled at us by a few musicians (harmlessly—for the moment, however).

We proceeded to the Consistorial Hall where we had agreed to sing a program for the Secretary of State, Cardinal Merry del Val. He had invited guests from the royal family and many of the Italian nobility. His Eminence was pleased. After having sung in a sprightly manner, the success of our appearance before the Pope adding *élan* to the intonations, the Cardinal drew me aside, thanked me, and opened a copy of *Le Monde Illustré,* a weekly magazine that had extensive circulation on the Continent. He pointed to a picture of the Choristers flanked by American flags, taken in the Jardin de Tuilleries on the occasion of our appearance (in the forbidden vestments) before President Fallières and his Cabinet. His Eminence remarked that this feat (wearing the surplices in public) was the first stroke for ecclesiastical diplomacy since the breaking of the Concordat with the Vatican by the French Government. His Eminence asked me why I had decided upon the plan and if I had not been apprehensive of difficulty with French authorities. He laughed loudly and merrily when I recounted the story. But, with somber expression, his black eyes flashing, he warned that I should have to expect much unfriendly critique and hostile manifestations from many quarters as a result of the European trip as a whole.

I remember his having asked me if I thought I could wiggle my way through the narrow lanes and obstructions which would presently make tranquil progress impossible. Not knowing at the time just how narrow the lanes could be, and never having encountered such obstacles as were to come, I suppose that I assured His Eminence that I'd wiggle through somehow. Well! I did wiggle through. But that's about all. A few abrasions decided to leave perpetual mementos. The trip to Parnassus is quite an adventure!

We set out for Naples and home after the Cardinal's concert. The ship was flea-ridden and the captain unfriendly. He had assigned a private deck to the boys where they could frolic and caper without annoying other passengers. On the second day out, however, the chaperon took issue with him during his inspection of the ship. I overheard some of her remarks.

With the volubility and directness acquired by years of schoolteaching, she complained to Herr Kapitan (the ship was a German liner) of the inadequate service given by stewards in the boys' cabins. She enumerated several items of neglect. "You saw yourself, at the inspection yesterday that these berths were not properly made up? Why have you done nothing about this? If matters don't improve I shall report you to the New York office."

Although we were on the Mediterranean, the heart and soul of the Teutonic skipper froze with resentment. Maybe he translated into some acerb bit of Goethe the "scornful eye of derision" with which he silently answered her, tramping off with heavy tread. He amended the shortcomings of the service, but deprived the boys of their private deck space. The ship tossed and rolled on the long crossing. Many were seasick.

During the voyage "Baron" Kelley and I had poked some fun at the strict chaperon and her associate, the wardrobe mistress, for these excellent ladies enjoyed "moonlight on the inland sea" with some of the senior tenors and basses. When the boys had been tucked away for the night, the "Baron" and myself would hear echoes of spontaneous harmony coming from the boatdeck. Lilting ballads with well-sugared texts. Eros seemed to be conducting the performances. Although I am sure that the ladies enjoyed being bantered, they decided to pay us off in full. They invited us to a dinner in a private dining room on the eve of disembarking. We were counseled not to partake of food at the regular dinner hour. The special menu later was to be extraordinary. And that's what it was, exactly. For the "Baron" and I, primed for a hearty late dinner by an hour's promenading in the wind and famished at ten o'clock when summoned to the orgy by a steward, sat down (without the ladies) to a platter of oversize sour pickles. Nothing else save a note from the chaperon: "Our wit is as keen as yours." Kelley gulped and dashing for the smoking-room bar, said: "Yes, but much tarter!"

At quarantine in New York harbor, an announcement from the bridge informed us that on account of a cholera suspect in the steerage, all passengers would be detained for at least twenty-four hours. The Choristers were scheduled to give a concert that evening at the Church of St. Paul the Apostle in New York City. The Superior, having been apprised of the situation, secured special permission from the Mayor for a speedy clearance. New York City's little welcome steamer, with a senior doctor of the Health Department aboard, came alongside and soon, after a special examination, our party was declared free of infection and assembled for disembarking. Herr Kapitan was taken back a bit by this evidence of the Choristers' status in the mind of New York's officialdom. Hurriedly the Nordic seaman became friendly, gushing, shaking the limp hands of the Choristers with vigor to impress the city officials with his friendly regard for our organization. As the little steamer was casting off, Herr Kapitan leaned over the rail from the quarter deck, waving farewell. Boys and men, with unrehearsed but synchronous movement, acknowledged his farewell gesture with the traditional "nose" gesture of derision. Should I blush to confess that I did not rebuke them for the preciously vulgar performance?

Gaily decked buses brought the organization from the Hoboken pier to the Fifty-ninth Street church. By concert time, the great edifice was full to capacity. The local Paulist Choir divided the program with us. Both units, drawing upon their full resources, exemplified their characteristic approaches to the choral art. The New York critics, who had belittled us on the occasion of our debut in Gotham three years previously, did a back somersault admiring, complimenting, congratulating. It was enlightening and amusing to observe the influence of European approval on the Fountain Pens. Of course, three years of intensive rehearsing and scores of public performances had refined the singing of the Choristers, but the differentiating features of our concerted work were well indicated on the earlier occasion. The tonal qualities which add spiritual sheen to acoustical timbres; the blend and balance which leave no gaps between voice parts; the fluency and spontaneity of nuances of expression—these traits marked the singing of our unit in 1909 as well as in 1912 and through the ensuing decades. At any rate, New York had finally forgiven us for being a Chicago organization.

Before leaving for Chicago, we experimented with gramophone recording. But the experiment was as unsuccessful as our earlier essay with the Victor Company at Camden, N.J. The spiritual tone quality of the soprano chorus eluded the needle of the phonograph. We were too happy, however, in the realization of a safe return to this country to be depressed by the failure to make satisfactory records, and we boarded the train for Niagara Falls and home in pleasant mood.

A rumor had been current in New York that Chicago was to give us a formal welcome. This was to include a parade in vestments down Michigan Boulevard and across the Loop to the City Hall. I tried to circumvent the plan. It seemed silly. Ballyhoo. Legitimate publicity for a good cause is reasonable, but parading through metropolitan streets to evoke from the general public cheers for something in which the general public was not interested seemed to lack dignity. I craftily arranged with our railroad representative to have our wardrobe trunks sent on ahead with instructions to place them in a remote storeroom where they would be claimed in due time, but to hide them from the ecclesiastic responsible for the parade! This overzealous ecclesiastic was traveling with us, and he doublecrossed me. Sensing that I might do exactly what I did, he wired the stationmaster in Chicago to have a locksmith open the trunks and to have the vestments laid out according to sizes, awaiting our arrival.

Special police lieutenants of the Chicago Police Force, Fourth Degree Knights of Columbus, "Hinky Dink," "Bath House" John and other potentates of modern Midwestern Rome were on hand to greet us and to see that plans were carried out precisely. Two of the young Fathers from Old Saint Mary's, masters of the jocular, possessed themselves of the victoria in which I was supposed to be conveyed to the City Hall. These droll padres, attired in long coats and wearing top hats, bowed to the people on the sidewalks all the way. I was obliged to walk. This episode occurred thirty-four years ago, but whenever the memory of it is stirred I feel as ridiculous and conspicuously idiotic as I did during the parade through the thoroughfares. Every once in a while I felt called upon to doff my hat to spectators.

It would not be unreasonable to conclude that professional claques had been engaged to cry out bravos at important intersections. There was an inexplicable hullabaloo. I sensed that I was giving a superlative performance as a strutting peacock. During the last few minutes of the parade I looked to neither right nor left. Upon arriving at the City Hall, the Choristers were seated in the chairs of the aldermen and I was placed in the regular position of the Mayor. His Honor made a speech. District leaders from the First Ward and other Democratic areas scattered roses of rhetoric through the Council Chamber. Chicago was mindful of its debt to the Paulist Choristers! The cultural purposes and attainments of the great American inland metropolis had been certified by the Choristers! Father Finn, still a very young man, had reassembled and modernized the choral ideals of past centuries! That sort of oratory. After an unsparing coating with compliments, we were permitted to disperse and find our ways homeward.

The European tour was finished. What was actually accomplished by the undertaking, I don't know. Perhaps little. Probably a reawakening of interest in choral music among a few conductors here and there. Certainly nothing of permanent significance.

Both Bishop Kennedy and Cardinal Merry del Val asked me if I had requested the Pope to suggest to the Hierarchy of American bishops that they establish our unit as a National Choral Institute in which Catholic organists and choirmasters might learn the principles of choral technique and become facile in interpreting Gregorian chant, polyphony and modern liturgical music. I was obliged to reply that I had asked the Pope for nothing. Both prelates had been surprised at my reply. It seemed almost incredible that I could have planned and carried into effect such a venturesome undertaking as a trans-Atlantic journey with many small boys without a tangible compensation in view.

"You mean," asked Bishop Kennedy, "that you get nothing from this widely publicized expedition save the publicity itself, the elation of winning the prize in Paris, and the honor of singing before His Holiness? Why didn't you ask the Pope for something? He was disposed to grant you any reasonable request."

I remember replying that the Pope had conferred a degree upon me.

"What can you do with that?" asked the Bishop.

Chapter XVI   *My Work Was Not*
"*All Play*"

OFTEN, in after years, I wondered if I had not wasted the energy spent in accomplishing the European tour. Was Bishop Kennedy right? Had I lost a golden opportunity for establishing my work on a substantial basis? Had I managed the enterprise without long range vision? Did I allow myself to become so immersed in the eddy of petty details as to be insensible of the lasting advantages which might accrue?

When I was floundering in a chaos of financial worries from 1918 to 1923 in New York, I would often reproach myself for having missed what should have been the main objective of the European trip. It was small consolation to tell myself that I was not and never could be an opportunist. When heavy clouds banked on the horizon and the Choir School which I had conducted for five years in New York was on the eve of its closing, it was not refreshing to think back to the day in the Vatican when I probably could have secured from His Holiness an authorization for a national foundation. How simple would have been the financing of a great institute commissioned by the Holy Father! How inevitable its development into a great centrifugal force of spiritual and aesthetic culture! If only I had looked beyond the momentary features of the trip. If only I had concentrated on enlisting the services of specialists who would have taken care of the details which absorbed my attention on the tour! Petty cash. Enough for daily needs in the monies of different countries. Assigning berths in sleeping cars and cabins on liners. Settling disputes about seniority and turns in claiming the better rooms in hotels. Checking the health of all and examining menus so that boys and men would have a balanced diet. And withal, keeping the unit musically fit, playing the organ, conducting. Nevertheless, allowing the potentially valuable and enduring effects of the tour to escape attention!

My first experience with the psychological phenomenon of frustration came when I began to suspect that the Choir School was a failure because I had failed to gather the fruits of the European tour, rich fruits ready for garnering and so near to one's hand!

From the beginning of the 1912–1913 season the Choristers were much in demand for concerts in the Middle West. But there was considerable sniping to dodge. A sort of guerrilla warfare was in progress. From behind choral hedges, Gregorian staves and contrapuntal figures became shots that were aimed to belittle, to weaken and perhaps to force us into inactivity. But the shots were only pellets which often stung but could inflict no serious injury. Our programs were picked to pieces in Letters to the Editor columns. As program-maker, organist, conductor, I was an egregious mountebank, an itinerant quack dispensing worthless nostrums. I was written up and down as America's leading antagonist to the Pope's plan for reintroducing Gregorian chant at Solemn Liturgical Offices. I was caricatured as a devotee of the insipid in choral expression. But we kept going. Naturally we became wary. Sometimes not sufficiently wary. A communication, for instance, to one of our best newspapers, trounced me energetically, over head and ears, for conducting Eric De-Larmarter's song about the devil. The Chicago composer had written an ingenious musical setting of Robert Burns' satirical skit, "The De'ils Awa' with the Excise Man." How undignified for a Catholic organization, under the baton of a priest to sing such an unseemly song! Instead of confining itself to the great spiritual library of the Church's motets, this notorious (rather than celebrated) chorus sought applause from an unbecoming text and a jingling tune! If I had been adequately on the alert probably I would have eliminated the harmless little ditty from the program, for I knew that in that particular city, shotguns were kept loaded with little wads of disparagement against our coming.

All this, of course, reminded a chap to "keep his thumb out of the soup." And it was a good prophylactic to the organization, preventing infection by the bacilli of self-complacency. The Choristers had a long route to follow before attaining genuine virtuosity. Personally, I knew that there were steep trails ahead on the ascent to Parnassus. As a matter of fact, our experiences up to date, had begun to convince the thinking members of the organization that we had just made a good start. Nothing more.

But we were hounded and haunted by publicity. The appearance of a semichoir in a little hamlet would bring comments in metropolitan newspapers. If the best foot were not always kept forward, we not only heard about it, we read about it. When I preached, comparison was made between my efforts in the pulpit and on the podium. "What the Preacher is Like" was the heading of a column in a Chicago newspaper. One day in Lent 1914, the columnist looked in at Old St. Mary's during the noon hour. I was playing the organ at the Benediction service and a quartet of men was singing. In the evening, the same columnist, noticing a crowd of people entering the church, decided to look in again, intrigued by the fact that there two large congregations had assembled on the same week-day. It had fallen to my lot to give the evening sermons during Lent on the same recurring weekdays. The columnist was interested in my ap-pearance in two roles on the same day, and wrote a lengthy article in the morrow's paper.

That article was a real blow. The writer was complimentary. Too bad! Beginning with that article a situation gradually took shape which some months later eased me out of Chicago for almost a year. But more of this anon.

My recollection of our choral activities for some seasons after the European invasion is that they followed a pattern, a pattern designed to assure steady progress toward the control of the best elements of chorophony. We gave many concerts in Chicago under the direction of America's unique impressario, F. Wight Neumann. Mr. Neumann regu-larly brought to Chicago the world's leading singers and instrumentalists, as well as the Metropolitan Opera Company of New York, and many Symphony Orchestras. A concert under his management, unless it were a debut recital, was certain to bring out a representative audience.

The first concert in Chicago after the European tour was sold out days in advance. On the eve of the concert, we were notified that Cardinal Farley, Archbishop of New York, en route to San Francisco, wished to attend the concert. Mr. Neumann was embarrassed. Not a box available. Nor a stall for that matter. He summoned me to his home where after much telephoning we finally persuaded a box holder to relinquish the box in favor of His Eminence. Mr. Neumann made an appropriate pun for the occasion, calling the concert his "red-letter concert," for he had the Cardinal's box draped in cardinal crimson and a deep red carpet laid across the sidewalk from the foyer to the curb. Certain adjustments were hurriedly made in the program, His Eminence expressing a desire to hear some of the pieces sung at Notre Dame in Paris and before His Holiness.

That first post-European appearance in Chicago on the concert stage was the beginning of a long series throughout the Midwestern states. At Duluth a mammoth audience greeted us. On the same tour, after a journey on Lake Superior, we played Fort William, Ontario, to two of the smallest audiences in our records. But we were learning to take everything in stride, and the size of the audience rarely affected the artistic efforts of boys and men. Of course a gala occasion, a great audi-torium and a capacity audience would add *élan,* but less inspiriting cir-cumstances would not persuade to slovenly performance. Nevertheless, we did come to dread matinees.

There is something about a matinee, even in the concert halls of great cities, that depresses. Once the program is in progress, the attitude of the participants improves, but, after rising in the morning until the curtain goes up for a matinee, one feels emptied of enthusiasm. The day is "heavy" until the afternoon performance will have at least begun. Many actors have told me that the morning of a matinee performance was the time when the most pessimistic thoughts beset them; when memories of unpleasant things would come vividly to mind; when things in general took on drab hue. And on a rainy day, the prospect of a matinee could turn an ordinarily pleasant chap into a testy growler. Matinees in small, old-fashioned theaters were especially dull things to think about.

It would be easy to write reams of ironic script about afternoon performances in villages and small towns. The ladies bringing their knitting and sometimes a small child or two who would carry the soprano top notes higher to the tessitura of an infantile wail. Stuffy, ill-ventilated auditoriums. Inadequate quarters backstage. Often an upright piano in the pit. "Upright" save in its pitch. Tuned at Christmas and perhaps at Easter. Usually a flat stage. No chorus bank. The conductor's stand the size of a soapbox and crowded onto the metal blind of the footlights. A few dilettanti affecting interest in the classical items on the program, but the majority bored, waiting for the second half when the solo boys would begin to pluck high notes from the rafters and the chorus would intone in soft, sweet harmony the old familiar part songs. Yes, it would be interesting to discourse of the psychological effect of the Wednesday and Saturday matinees on a troop.

I read recently an article by Ethel Barrymore in which she referred with nostalgia to her "barnstorming" days, but I don't recall that she had much enthusiasm for the after luncheon performances. As I wrote above, the prospect of the performance was more burdensome than the performance itself. This may be a neat point for psychologists to debate, but I admit candidly that Wednesdays and Saturdays on the road were to me days to be encircled in heavy black on the calendar. It always seemed more difficult for me to guide the chorus away from pitfalls in the afternoon. I was usually convinced in advance that the Choristers would flatten at matinees, and although they rarely sang off pitch even under the most untoward circumstances, the likelihood hung over me all morning like the sword of Damocles. And a matinee in a small town, after a concert on the preceding evening in a great city and after a bumpy sleeping car ride on a spur line! Perhaps after a greasy breakfast-luncheon in a dingy restaurant. Perhaps in a theater where the management had posted signs such as: THIS STAGE DOOR HAS THREE HINGES.

USE ALL THREE. BY ORDER OF THE MAYOR. FINE $5. DO NOT SPIT ON THE
FLOOR, ON STAGE OR BACK STAGE. BY ORDER OF THE MAYOR. FINE $10.
Even the retrospect invites the doldrums.

After the Duluth and Fort William performances, we found ourselves
on the Mesabe Range in Minnesota. I shall omit the name of the particular place where we had three strange experiences, for one of these was
unpleasant, having to do with flat little insects which feel at home in
beds. The ugly creatures on this occasion forced the entire organization
to spend the night in lobby chairs.

One of the experiences was memorable in a better connotation. We
had approached the theater in a matinee mood, although it was evening.
The townsmen did not seem to be the type of citizens who would be
interested in our singing. Through the peephole in the curtain, we could
see a large audience of miners assembling. After a hurried consultation
with the librarian as to the possibility of changing the program which
was weighted with serious compositions, and ascertaining that he had
not brought along many simpler folk-song numbers, I decided to give
the program as arranged. The first two or three pieces brought no
response from the audience. "If these were too heavy for the miners," I
thought, "what of the next numbers? Palmgren's 'Finnish Lullaby' and
'Sorrow,' Könnemann's 'Neath Our Earth in Gloomy Hades' (in which
the Russian composer contemplates Hell as being populated only by
women and girls!) and the 'Singet Den Herrn' fugue of Bach?" I
couldn't spend much time in pondering. We went into the Palmgren
lullaby. Queer chordal progressions. A bit too dissonant for the average
American ear at that time. Being fearful, perhaps, that there would be a
rush for money back at the box office, I must have conducted the piece
with great care. The last chord was trying to find its attenuated pianissimo when the miners began to shout their approval, to demand an
encore and generally to give evidence of great satisfaction. Each ensuing
number of the recondite style evoked bravos. I think that we did the
Bach fugue at least three times.

In the second part of the program, I was hard pressed to sustain the
interest of the listeners, for the simple lilts and lays had little appeal to
them. I learned after the concert that the majority of the miners were
Finns and accustomed to hear the best repertories. On other occasions I
observed similar reactions in audiences the appearance of which would
not tend to convince one of its culture, but on the Range those apparently
simple people from the country of Sibelius gave me one of the major
surprises of my musical career.

The third experience was the temporary loss of two soprano boys.
The town was surrounded by open mines and the boys had been ad-

monished not to descend into them. At train time, two lads were missing. One was a solo boy nicknamed "Tom Thumb" (he was a tiny tot when he joined the organization). But, small as he was in stature, he had acquired huge dimensions as a mischief-maker. Once, during an organ interlude before the final vocal measures of an aria which he had been singing with great artistry, he learned over into the next row of choir-stalls in the chancel and planted a solid wallop in the ribs of a boy who had been plaguing him. Well! Tom Thumb and another youngster went off on their own that morning on the Mesabe Range, descended into the mine, could find no immediate way of leaving and were temporarily lost, as far as we were concerned. We left word with the local constabulary to search for the boys, and, when found, to send them along on a later train to Superior, Wisconsin, where we were booked for matinee and evening. The lost were found and they reported at the close of the matinee. The stern chaperon insisted that I tan the disobedient boys who had caused such anxiety. After I had raised a few memento blisters on one of the rear ends (Tom Thumb's) we went over to Duluth to ser-enade Maud Adams in the hotel lobby.

The famous actress was playing *Peter Pan* and as she came across the lobby she radiated that spirit of immortal youth which she interpreted so convincingly in Sir James Barrie's work. It was a delightful experi-ence to sing for the lovely lady. She most graciously acknowledged our little tribute, and the management was so pleased that he made our organization his guests for dinner. A free dinner in a first-class hostelry was a novelty, indeed! Then back to Superior, not far away, for the evening concert and for the night train to Dubuque, Iowa.

In the morning, we were delayed between country towns by a wash-out. For several hours we waited for the repairing of tracks. A few men went to the nearest town to fetch dry sandwiches and weak, lukewarm coffee. Finally, we were on our way again.

Then an aftermath of the Tom Thumb episode occurred. As we rolled along by the Mississippi, the chaperon fell asleep. A large leghorn hat reposed on the rack above her. The afternoon was warm enough to re-quire the windows to be open. Tom Thumb studied the sleeping chaperon. He studied the open windows. He studied the leghorn hat. He studied the flowing Mississippi. Probably he thought of the vigorous tanning which the chaperon had ordered. Suddenly, although many were watch-ing him, myself included, he took the leghorn hat from the rack, brought it to a window frame in which the pane was pushed all the way up, and hurled the hat with accurate aim into the muddy waters of the river.

Awaking from her nap, the chaperon discovered the loss and immediately demanded information. No one in the car knew anything about it! Had someone hidden it as a practical joke? The leghorn was even then probably being carried along by the fast current and was possibly within her field of view. She questioned each member of the unit. Evasion. No lies. Just shrugging shoulders. Tom Thumb's face was as innocent looking as that of a Boticelli cherub. Everybody was waiting to observe my reaction to the episode. When the chaperon plied me with her questions, I stood my ground with the most amiable and sympathetic hypocrisy, evading direct answers.

Our arrival was too late at Dubuque to permit her opportunity for purchasing any kind of headgear, and the large dignified lady was obliged to walk the Main Street of the Iowa city with a cute little tam-ó-shanter which she borrowed from the accompanist. Although the era was well past the Victorian, women were not yet accustomed to walk about without hats, bonnets or scarfs on their heads. Tom Thumb had avenged himself.

During that period, 1912–1914, the Choristers made their first appearance at Portland, Maine, where, under the auspices of Bishop Louis Walsh, a great audience assembled as his guests at the Civic Auditorium. The Bishop was interested in demonstrating the centuries-old Catholic approach to the liberal and fine art of music. He announced through the papers and from the Catholic pulpits of the diocese that Catholics would be welcome at the Solemn Pontifical Mass at the Cathedral, but that non-Catholics only would receive the free tickets of admission to the Auditorium.

The plan seemed feasible on paper. It did not work out smoothly, however, for the Cathedral could accommodate only a small percentage of the people who sought admission. And at the Auditorium and in the surrounding streets large crowds were milling around. Many thought that at the last minute, doors would be opened for standees. The throng of expectant listeners was so great that the Choristers found difficulty in reaching the stage door. Personally, I was delayed for a considerable length of time by the congestion. It was necessary for me to identify myself before police officers would permit me to proceed. Finally, a police captain opened a wedge through the throng and played interference while I gained the last few yards to the goal.

At only one other indoor concert (El Paso, Texas, 1918) did we experience such difficulty. Forcing our way into a concert hall where we were to entertain the very hordes that were preventing our arrival!

At the Portland concert, with the skillful assistance and accompani-

ments of one of America's best organists, Mr. William McClellan, and
favored by the fine accoustics of the Auditorium, we gave one of the
best performances of our career up to that time.

The last stop, en route homeward to Chicago, was at Grand Rapids,
Michigan. The weather had been inclement for days. Many soprano
boys developed laryngitis. At the matinee the soprano chorus began to
weaken noticeably. In the middle and lower registers I could not keep
the voice line to the pitch. An evening concert was to follow. Then a
sleeping-car jump to Chicago where on the morrow we were to sing the
Solemn Mass at Old Saint Mary's and give a gala concert in the afternoon under the management of Mr. Neumann.

Having conferred with Miss Mary Anderson, our brilliant accompanist, and a few seniors of the organization, I decided to telephone Mr.
Neumann to postpone the concert to the following Sunday. He would
have just enough time to reach the newspapers before the deadline for
the city editions.

Mr. Neumann listened. He listened with deaf ears. He ridiculed the
idea of postponing the concert. "Keep faith with your public. What does
it matter if the whole organization is disabled? Put them on the stage.
Have them sing as much or as little as they can. Good-bye."

My conferees were as much disturbed as myself, and so we put in another call to the uncompromising impresario. Evidently he had given
instructions to the long-distance operator that he would not accept another call from Grand Rapids. We were in trouble. The weather became
violently worse. Cold rain. Piercing wind. Drafts in the theater when we
went back for the evening effort. Leading boys could speak only in
whispers. The laryngitis had extended to the men's section. The lyric
tenors sounded like hoarse fog horns. As I went on stage I felt that the
icy blast must have come from Mount Parnassus! One could almost
hear the gusts screaming that they had left us undisturbed long enough;
that we had been having too easy going; that it was time to impress upon
us that no humans could scale the Mount of the Muses without interference. *Ad astra per aspera!*

I had had enough experience with storms along the trail to Parnassus
to know that if I didn't plow through that gale with all the strength
and resources at my command, I would make a spectacle of myself and
the unit then and there and on the morrow as well, inviting ridicule.
And so I changed the program, eliminating what I could of pieces that
demanded much loud singing in the middle and lower registers. I substituted high-register numbers, so that the sopranos and tenors could intone the notes with the margins of their vocal cords, almost in falsetto
fashion, avoiding use of the membranes above the true cords, as much

as possible. The tissues near the true cords were inflamed; therefore, exercise them as little as possible. Somehow, we delivered a program. The audience was at least agreeably impressed. We certainly did not receive an ovation, but to have pulled through with any degree of aesthetic acceptability was as surprising as it was gratifying.

Probably I learned much that night at Grand Rapids. First, I learned from Mr. Neumann's insistence on the Chicago concert that one should not fail to fulfill obligations because physical difficulties threatened to make fulfillment onerous and perhaps defective. Second, I became aware of several devices by which strain on the cords could be lessened. Some of these devices were related to the physiological functioning of the larynx. The high rilievos instead of the low. The responsibility for volume effects placed upon those whose voices were normal. Some devices were psychological. For instance, the playing of the treble parts of accompaniments in higher-than-written octaves to create and abet an impression of volatile lightness. The underlining of certain fundamentals in the bass vocal or piano line to suggest to the higher voices that it would be fairly easy to sing their notes which in many instances were already contained as harmonics in the notes of the basses. A smile of satisfaction from the conductor when a particularly hazardous phrase was safely if not impressively delivered. Such devices.

The Grand Rapids episode was a milestone in my journey to the Mount, and when it was over I may have shouted up to Apollo and Euterpe: "You can't keep down an Irishman with a German impresario. Next time you must try a tornado to knock me off the podium."

In Chicago the next morning, I chose a list of easy pieces for the Solemn Mass. At the tune-up backstage before the Neumann concert, the sopranos and tenors revealed almost normal throats. The laryngitis had "gone with the (Parnassus) wind." Later and often, Mr. Neumann twitted me about my long-distance call. Before guests like Fritz Kreisler, Cleofonte Campanini and Egon Pollak, he would tell of my panic at Grand Rapids. These artists and others who were regaled by my troublesome experience, although kindly and sympathetic, would banter with: "How are the little soprano boys tonight, Father? Are their delicate throats comfortable? It's a cold night. Don't you wish to telephone their mothers to put flannels soaked in camphorated oil around their cute little necks?" Once in a while I would make a fair rebuttal. With Campanini, for instance, for canceling a performance of *The Jewels of the Madonna* because of a throat ailment suffered by the prima donna Carolina White. With Egon Pollak for eliminating part of a Wagnerian score because his solo trumpeter had developed a cold sore on his lip. With Mr. Neumann for permitting a prima donna to have the vocal score of an opera trio altered so that a minor part singer would take the high notes. With Fritz Kreisler for having debated once about the advisability of playing a scheduled concerto because he was physically below par! Grand Rapids became a symbol.

The moments after the matinee there had been acutely distressing. The successful delivery of the evening program brought enlightenment. Reference to the episode was a source of much facetious and delightful repartee at Mr. Neumann's salon. This salon was probably one of the most interesting focal points of social activity in the country. No affectations. No lorgnettes. No stupid regard for alleged caste. Merit and achievement alone were recognized there. With a charming wife as hostess and a most engaging child-daughter, an atmosphere was created at Mr. Neumann's that was unique. Guests were unanimous on this point. Kreisler, the great violinist, talking sociology and politics, avoiding music as though the subject would spoil the evening with its professional implications. Mme. Carreño, the virtuoso pianist from South America, discussing the fauna and flora of Latin America. Mischa Elman, cosharer with Kreisler of world honors for violin playing, elaborating on the different psychological traits of Teutons, Slavs and Latins. And the child-daughter dropping a big mechanical bug, which she had bought in Hamburg, into my coffee to plague me as I set forth on some blustering gasconade about nothing in particular.

For several seasons the Choristers had been specializing in Russian music for concert use. There is a spiritual aura about the cherubic hymns of pre-Bolshevik Russia which the tone quality of our organization could make readily discernible. Once, after a concert at Orchestra Hall, Chicago, Mr. Charles R. Crane, later Minister to China, came back stage to express his appreciation of our interpretation of the Slavonic idiom. He had spent much time in Russia and highly valued its culture. A short time before coming to greet us at Orchestra Hall, he had imported the major part of the personnel of the Russian Cathedral choir of New York. The noted conductor, Dr. Gorokkof, and several unusual singers, including an octavist * or two, were in this group.

Mr. Crane was keen to promote interest in the Russian culture generally, and in the a cappella music particularly. He urged me to go to Russia. To the Synodalny. To study with Alexander Kastalsky, the leading authority on Russian music. I determined to follow Mr. Crane's suggestion.

Although the local Superior of the Paulist Fathers opposed my going, the Superior-General at New York granted the permission. Perhaps the

* An octavist is a basso whose intonations extend to the octave below the normal bass-line.

local Superior at Chicago felt that more singular moves on my part would increase the publicity which, as I have already reported, had been excessive since the European trip.

Passing through Chicago, many people from distant parts would stop over to hear the much-advertised choir. The telephone would ring frequently on Saturdays, visitors inquiring: "Is this Father Finn's Church?"

"No."

"Is this the headquarters of the Paulist Choristers?"

"This is the headquarters of the Paulist *Fathers.*"

"Will the Paulist Choristers sing at your church tomorrow and, if so, at what time?"

"Well—yes—at eleven in the morning and at eight in the evening."

It had really become an instance of the tail wagging the dog. There was nothing I could do about it. But while I was abroad, others thought up something to do about it.

I went to England at this time, rechecking its chief choirs and listening to operas in English under the amazing Sir Thomas Beecham, and after a fortnight there I left for the Continent. At Berlin, having secured a ticket for the weekly fast train to St. Petersburg (now Leningrad), I found myself with several days to idle away. Austria had sent its ultimatum to Serbia apropos of the assassination of the Archduke at Serajevo. I went each evening to the Unter den Linden where the common people were making antiwar demonstrations. The people knew what the Austrian note to Serbia implied.

One day I was lunching with a group of American friends at the Adlon. An attaché of the American Embassy was present. We talked of our plans. I mentioned my booking on the train for Russia and my hope to arrange transportation homeward via the Trans-Siberian Railroad to Vladivostok, and thence over the Pacific to Seattle. As we were leaving the table, the attaché said softly to me: "If you don't ask any questions, I'll tell you something important for you to know."

"No questions, of course. Fire away."

"Don't go to Russia," he advised. "Try to leave Germany as soon as possible, via Holland for America."

I thanked him and betook myself to the travel agency where I had booked for Russia. No space was available on a *wagon lit* for any place in Holland for several days. At the agency I was advised to wait, to hold my booking for St. Petersburg. The war clouds would soon pass. The whole disturbance was a tempest in a teapot, etc. And so I waited, instead of having taken a seat in a third-class railway carriage across the German frontier to Flushing, Amsterdam or Rotterdam. War was suddenly declared. A moratorium on paper money was announced by Germany. This meant that no change would be given for mark notes. I had had most of my cash transferred into German one-hundred-mark notes under advice from the railroad agent, for German money then was bringing a sizable premium in Russia. The money which I had not cashed was awaiting my call in the American Express office at Paris. I wired Paris to send me a draft for gold to Berlin. No answer. Critical relations between Paris and Berlin had developed. I cabled America to wire a gold deposit to a German bank. No answer.

Besides the paper marks, I had only a few gold pieces and some silver when war was declared. Presently the gold and silver were gone. Having been obliged to offer a hundred-mark note in a cafe (about $24) for a sixty-cent meal, and receiving no change, I realized that I was in a tight spot. I decided to use up my paper money to reach a neutral country. I notified my friends that I was departing, my first stop to be Leipzig. They (five American ladies of a distinguished family) were heading for Dresden with a vague hope of arriving in Italy somehow and boarding a ship at Genoa for the United States. I arrived late at Leipzig. At about one o'clock in the morning I was awakened by a great commotion in the Rotz Platz upon which my room at the hotel gave directly. War had been declared against France, and the Germans were doing a snake dance through the Platz, singing the patriotic songs of the fatherland with great gusto.

The ladies at Dresden went into a bit of a panic. How to reach home when so many countries were becoming involved in war? They wired me, the only male available, to hurry to Dresden and escort them to safety. It took one of my fast diminishing hundred-mark notes and thirteen hours to accomplish a trip which would normally require a couple of dollars and a couple of hours. I was greeted by the ladies (all non-Catholics but members of a coterie in New York and Chicago from which I was not ostracized) as a deliverer. Would I hie to the *bahnhof* and beg the passenger traffic manager to place us on a train for Holland?

"How about money? Has anyone any gold?"

The senior of the group immediately dispelled anxiety on that score. "I always knew," she said "that one day my money belt would justify the long years I have been wearing it on my travels." She ascended to her room to loosen the belt, and descended forthwith to hand it to me. "Take it and bring us safely home."

Many compartments in the belt. Each three and a half inches deep. Each filled with gold coins. A fortune! The moratorium did not include refusal of silver change for gold coins. And so I went to the *bahnhof* to plead the case.

A most gracious gentleman was in charge of all train service out of

Dresden. Eventually he was free to listen to me. He issued tickets for the train next evening for Flushing, where we could board a channel boat for Dover, England. I nearly bungled the matter, however, by offering the traffic manager a gold coin as a gratuity. He refused indignantly. He scowled at me, deliberated a moment as if pondering the worth of depriving me of the tickets, but finally with a disapproving grimace he dismissed me. We had the tickets and would leave on the first part of our journey to safety at six the next evening, Sunday.

One of the ladies, who was accustomed to listening to the Choristers in Chicago, asked me to escort her to the Solemn Mass at the pro-Cathedral in the hope of hearing a good German choir. Evidently she had expected to hear music of the sort she had heard on other jaunts at St. Thomas Kirche in Leipzig. The ceremony was elaborate. The Bishop blessed the Catholic uhlans who were about to leave for the invasion of Belgium. But the music was dreadful! Just sustained utterances! No hints of the German musicianship which had developed an Aichinger, an Eccard, a Bach or a Brahms!

At a critical moment in the world's history, when World War I was beginning to set the stage for the greater World War II, when the animal savagery of mankind was sticking its ugly head out beyond the veneer of civilization under which it had been lying partly concealed— at such a moment, it was curious to find oneself wondering, in the pro-Cathedral at Dresden, if the real potentialities for spiritual awakening and progress had *ever* been consistently evoked from religion, education and aesthetics. Of course, Christ did not achieve an overwhelming success with His Sermon on the Mount! Nor did the rectors of the eighty-one universities flourishing at the time of the Reformation promote the inculcation of the principles of the trivium, which included logical thinking, so widely as seriously to influence the judgment or the sensing of values among the lords and vassals of the feudal system! Nor, yet again, did the architects, sculptors, painters, poets, liturgists or musicians, with all the alleged spiritual appeal of their temples of worship, their statuary, their madonnas and angels and saints, their dactyls and trochees about eternal truths and the lovely melos of sounds thought to be tuned by the smile of God, turn the minds of men away from the contemplation of the worldly embellishments of riches and power.

Christ startled His hearers when He abrogated the philosophy of an eye for an eye. He left it to His apostles and their successors to inure men to the opposite philosophy of the Beatitudes. Over the centuries, the Church zealously tried. Over the centuries men improved a little, but not enough to avoid the world cataclysm that, from the pro-Cathedral at Dresden, one could see was to convulse the world.

In times of peace, between the wars that harassed neighbor-nations, the pursuit of knowledge and the appreciation of culture was wont to give specious promise that all was well with mankind. But something was missed somehow, somewhere. Religion, education, aesthetics, the only spiritual forces which can lift men from the slough of the carnal, the selfish, the cruel—why had these failed, in almost two thousand years of post-Christ opportunity, to make deeper impressions on Christian nations? One could answer by admitting that human nature is too heavy and inert to be leavened en masse by even spiritual forces. That would be a wrong answer.

At the moment in the Dresden pro-Cathedral, I dismissed the more comprehensive aspects of the problem and concentrated on the inadequacies of music as a leavening agent. What had we missed in setting forth the melodies and harmonies which should help to temper and tame the wildest impulses? What was it precisely about the so-called music in progress at the pro-Cathedral that made it seem a proper accompaniment to the blessing of soldiers' lances? It was rough and discordant. So too was war. There was arrogance in the voices. There would be arrogance in the uhlans as they poised their lances to kill. There was no give and take between the vocal parts. There was no reasonable interchange of policies, ambitions, assets between the belligerent countries. Yes! the music was bad. War was bad. There is a perfect equation between singing off pitch and living off pitch.

As I left the pro-Cathedral, my non-Catholic friend depressed by the threatening cacophonies dispensed in the choir loft, I consulted my Ground Bass. Can human beings be really exalted to an awareness of spiritual values by music? Perhaps its appeal is only to the superficial emotions? Is it sentimentality that is awakened rather than spirituality? Perhaps. One would have to meditate seriously on the point. If only a sentimental glow could be induced by the consonance of sounds contrived by exacting efforts and rigorous routine, why waste one's energy? Sentimentality is mawkish. A certain dosage of it acts as an emotional emetic. It tends to provoke disgust. And so on my long journey homewards, I tried to take stock of the value of the things which I had been undertaking with such lavish expenditure of physical, mental, and temperamental resources. Long before landing at Quebec, I had decided that the appraising of the worth of one's efforts was too involved an exercise, that all life was veiled in some degree of mystery, and that the only reasonable thing to do was to continue to struggle for the realization of the ideals which had stimulated for so long. Nevertheless, and in spite of this resolve, every once in a while I would find myself back in the pro-Cathedral at Dresden, especially on days when there was little to hearten me.

Perhaps the frequent trips back to that church in Saxony sharpened my scrutiny of the means which I was employing to make clear the validity of the Ground Bass. I began to examine every aspect of both the choral and the orchestral mediums of musical expression. The psychological reactions of diverse types of people to many styles of composition and methods of presentation. The relationships of fast and slow, of a slight increase or decrease of pace in certain phrases or parts of phrases. The effects on listeners of quantity of sound. Quickening without increasing volume. Retarding a tempo without diminishing the volume, and diminishing without retarding. The aural spectrum of choral and orchestral tone colors. The interdependence of one tone color upon another for balancing the vibrancy of strings, the white roundness of flutes, the twang of reeds and the expansiveness of horns, trumpets, trombones and tubas. The kinship of chorus and orchestra and the apposition of these, including organ registration, when both are employed together. I spent much time in pursuit of information about these and other points comprised in the complete art of concerted expression. Probably I harassed my choristers with an uninterrupted series of experiments, which many perhaps recognized as deliberate interpolations in the agenda at rehearsals.

My experience up to this time had been almost exclusively with boys and men. The meager information which I had acquired about female sopranos and contraltos, from my efforts with the venerable ladies of Boston shortly after I had crawled out of the nursery to that later with the orb-rolling damsels at Trinity College, was obviously inconsequential. I had not really entered the broader field of choral activity. I had merely stood on the threshold looking in. But one must have experience with all kinds of choruses if one is to understand and control the potential effects of choral singing. It would be unreasonable for one to consider himself a master of orchestral euphony, if he had studied and experimented only with a group of string players. It would be equally stupid for a bandmaster who had never dealt with the string instruments to fancy his knowledge of the reed and brass instruments to be sufficient for conducting a symphony orchestra. The boy-choir director should know by actual experience just what features differentiate a boys' from a women's soprano choir. I began to look around for opportunities to work in the broader field. A few engagements to conduct mixed choruses were offered and accepted, but there was not sufficient time before performances for me to delve deeply into the differences between soprano choirs of boys and women to make these undertakings valuable.

Finally, a major opportunity was thrust upon me. It seems not rash to suggest that in every shifting of the sands there is a providential purpose. And sometimes, in retrospect, one is tempted to view outstanding interludes in an established routine as more than inconsequential, especially if during such interludes one develops a new and more enlightened point of view. Those whose lives are guided by religious faith are wont to see the Hand of Providence in changes of a status quo when such changes have been the occasion if not the cause of progress.

Chapter XVII *I Hear the Ground Bass in a More Complete Tonal Spectrum*

WHILE I was in Europe during the summer of 1914, it was decided by the local Chicago Superior that the Paulist Choristers would profit by the direction of a new conductor. Upon my return, therefore, I sensed immediately that it was better to make no serious plans for the ensuing season. Before Christmas I bade the choir farewell. I had obtained permission from the Superior-General in New York to spend a year in Spain, a neutral country and one rich in musical literature and traditions. My luggage was sent to a ship at a New York pier, but upon my arrival in New York the Superior-General asked me to abandon the trip in view of the possibilities of the war involving many countries then neutral. And so I went to Toronto, Ontario, bringing along an invaluable henchman, Horace Anderson.

Mr. Anderson had been a member of the Paulist Choristers since 1905 and was thoroughly conversant with our ideals and choral technique. Therefore, when I took temporary charge of Lourdes parish in Toronto, I invited Mr. Anderson to coach the soprano boys there. Within a few months these boys gave local proof of the validity of our convictions about training chancel choirs. Our plan is based on a few fundamental principles and the precepts for applying these are simple.

At the request of many Catholic members of Dr. Vogt's celebrated Mendelssohn Choir, I organized a chorus of about one hundred women and men. Within a few weeks of its inception this new unit was in demand for feast-day services in churches, for concerts in and around Toronto, and for participation in the dedicatory services of new organs. Of course, the majority of the singers, being members of Dr. Vogt's choir, brought a ready-made technique to me, and the rehearsals were for me more of a recreation and an opportunity for learning facts about comprehensive choral possibilities than exacting tasks.

I began to perceive from the start that the color scheme of timbres on the soprano and alto voice lines includes many more tonal tints and shades in choirs of females than in choirs of boys and falsetto altos. I had known this to be true theoretically, but I had never had actual experience in applying the knowledge. Boys, normally, must be restricted to light flute, string and very light oboe timbres. Occasionally a boy gives evidence of richer tone colors, but it is not safe, except under the protective vocal discipline of a choir school, to cultivate the richer qualities. One of the most harassing difficulties which plague the average master of boy choristers is their habitual misuse and abuse of their voices outside the choir hall. Boys shout. They converse with one another, often at the distance of half a city block, in the fortissimo panel. They tend naturally to make such extravagant demands on the muscles, tissues and cartileges of their throats that a choirmaster's chief concern is to subdue their intonations. Therefore, the broader tonal colors are a hazard, even if they could be developed artistically. Since, however, rarely does one encounter a boy with more than the light timbres indicated in unforced vocalization, a choirmaster has only a Hobson's choice in the matter.

But with women on the soprano line, I soon noted that all of the colors of the treble sections of a symphony orchestra invite employment, except in very small units or in choirs of nuns whose chanting in their convents is restricted to almost colorless intonations, eventually effecting the equivalent loss of broader tones. In the Toronto group of about thirty sopranos and twenty-five singers on the alto line, I found it easy to display the iridescence of an orchestral rainbow. The sopranos could furnish all the six timbres of the instrumental trebles. These timbres are proper to the flute, oboe, clarinet, French horn and violin, including the trumpet in the category of dramatic sopranos.

On the alto line there is more distinctive tone color in a chorus than in an orchestra, for in the latter the alto instruments in present use are weak and lamentably inadequate. A composer for orchestra needs must build an alto line synthetically. He must borrow energy from treble and tenor instruments. In a choir of boys and men, if the alto line is to compare at all in richness with the other voice lines, the choirmaster must frequently assign second sopranos and first tenors to the voice part, embarrassed by the same necessity that requires an orchestral composer to reinforce violas and English horns with second treble instruments such as second violins, second clarinets and third French horns; and tenor instruments such as cellos, bassoons, second French horns and high trombones. The falsetto alto in a boys' and men's choir is a monochrome. It is not so feeble as pale. The viola and English horn, the proper orchestral altos, are not so pale as feeble.

But in a chorus of twenty-five bona fide female singers on the alto line

(I don't include what I have come to designate as *esses* *), one finds pigments from which to extract the most variegated timbre-hues. Over vibrating tenors and under a polychrome soprano line, it was a source of startling satisfaction to find an alto line with every tonal shade of purple, from opaque darkness to a semi transparent magenta. Contraltos with a round fullness of tone that suggests the umbra of "sable-vested Night." Contraltos, not quite so round-voiced, giving the chiaroscuro of earlier posttwilight hours. Mezzo-sopranos with the low range of contraltos, but scintillating with rays from a midafternoon sun finding their way through cirrus clouds. Other mezzo-sopranos with such brilliant overtones that the brightness of noonday is intimated. And the combination of noon, evening and midnight! What a paradox of effects! Bewildering but satisfying. Light and darkness blended, not into an inert greyness, but into a tonal chromatism full of life and substance diffusing a lovely radiance.

The correlation of this rich-hued alto line with the tenors afforded opportunity for much study and experimenting. It is a simpler task to arrange proper apposition between countertenor altos and a tenor chorus. That marked personal consciousness of aesthetical and emotional reactions which is characteristic of women, (reflecting itself in their vocalization) is not present in the intonations of male altos. The tone quality of these is pallid (except the converted altos of the English cathedral type). How much of the darker shade of the contralto should be employed when reedy tenors predominate in the tenor line? When the more blunt types of tenors compose the majority? How many mezzo-sopranos will balance a true contralto? How temper the distinctive vocal features of both contraltos and mezzo-sopranos when those of either group seem excessively active? Which type of alto-line voice is the better for specific styles of composition, contralto or mezzo?

These and many more questions pertinent to the artistic employment of a female alto-line chorus require answering. I did not know the answers when I arrived at Toronto. One could not answer from restricted experience with countertenors. It was necessary then and there to seek the answers by the trial and error method. And so, at Toronto, I was introduced to the art of choral expression in its more comprehensive inclusions. My ostracism from Chicago, therefore, and the imposed necessity of pursuing my studies in a broader field provided an advantage which otherwise I would have missed.

The Toronto unit was not conscious of my experimenting. At least I

* ES : Encumbered Sopranos who, without true alto-line quality, consider themselves to be altos just because they have long preferred to sing in the lower compass.

felt that I was disguising my attempts to ascertain the best combinations of colors to produce certain effects. The ladies and gentlemen were very gracious, but in retrospect I can see little grimaces of amusement, when, after having called for flutish sopranos and mezzo-sopranos on the alto line to italicize a phrase in rehearsal, I would change the color scheme at a performance by softening the flutes and mezzos while underlining the string sopranos and the darkest contralto tonality. Perhaps, and sometimes, indeed, probably, I would alter a color relationship because of acoustical conditions about which I had begun long since to interest myself. In some halls, in some types of composition and in some harmonic relationships, an apposition of tonal tints, which is notably effective under different circumstances, is altogether unsatisfactory. For example, on a wet night at Town Hall, New York, one might need strings and reeds to dominate the soprano line and a heavy alto shade to balance the acuteness of the trebles, while on a bright night at Symphony Hall, Boston, the string soprano timbre would be too piercing. Flutes would be indicated here, perhaps, with a brilliant mezzo-soprano on the more hidden part to give it opportunity to project itself through the arresting high part. Perhaps, however, after having called out the flutish sopranos and the mezzo alto line at rehearsal, I would decide that the combination was malapropos, and make a mental note to use another color scheme at the performance.

At any rate, the personnel of the Toronto chorus gave me splendid opportunities for testing. Some of the findings of those days have been incorporated in my final scheme of choral expression; others were abandoned in favor of conclusions accruing from the accumulated experiences of later years.

During the months spent at Toronto, I had many preaching and lecturing engagements. Preach at Lourdes on Sunday morning and Sunday evening. Lecture about music or some aspect of telepathy or spiritism, the latter subjects attracting sharp interest at the time, on Monday evening. Rehearse on Tuesday evening. Play the dedicatory recital of a new organ in or near the city, and give an address of the place and purpose of music in the Liturgy of the Church on Wednesday evening. On Thursday and Fridays, conferences with Sisters in various convents. Saturday afternoon and evening, confessions at Lourdes.

This pattern, with alterations as to days and hours, kept me busily engaged. Also, at Newman Hall, the Catholic Club of the University of Toronto, where Father Thomas F. Burke, later Superior-General of the Paulist Fathers, was Rector, I presided over the rehearsals and performances of a glee club of young women and men. In connection with my work at Newman Hall, I first faced the problem of curing sopranos of the deadly fault of singing sharp. My previous experience with out-of-tune intonation was confined to flatness. Up to that time I had not realized that vocalists could as readily be at variance with the pitch by adding vibrations to notes as by subtracting from the requisite number. I was only partially successful in remedying the defect in the glee club, but my attention had been called to the failing, and the efforts made then to correct it led to the more successful enterprise of ensuing years.

The rectory at which I lived in Toronto was near the home of the Archbishop. Frequently he would drop in to chat. We had several interesting shadow-boxing bouts about the place of the Fine Arts in religion. He was a very spiritual man. His spirituality was based on convictions. There was little of the imaginative or emotional about him. It used to amuse him to poke fun at me. In public, once, I had him at a disadvantage. Accidentally. He was presiding at the dedication of a new organ in one of Toronto's largest churches. Having played part of the program, I descended from the organ gallery and gave an address from a small lectern-pulpit which was flush with the dais on which his episcopal throne was placed. Suddenly, as I threw out a gesture full-circle in his direction, he turned towards the pulpit, and coming a bit too near the orbit of my arm, his biretta and the back of my hand met in violent collision, His Lordship's purple headpiece coming out second best in the encounter.

Shortly afterward, he assisted at a Holy Name rally at Lourdes Church. Over a thousand men were in the Church. They sang lustily together. With stentorian voices, the organ booming and the leader of the congregational singing egging them on as a cheer leader spurs the fans at a football game, the thousand hearty males shouted out sentences to God. At dinner, later, the Archbishop *thought* that he had me at a disadvantage. Before several monsignori, pastors, curates and leading Catholic laymen, he accosted me in something like this vein: "The other evening, you were so keyed up about the value of specially prepared and performed music in the services of the Church, that you reached out and knocked my biretta off. Oh! I concede that you didn't do it deliberately. But I said to myself: 'He's making an awful fuss about this matter. Fuss enough to knock a bishop's biretta onto the floor. I'm all for congregational singing. The highfalutin singing of choirs and the playing of fancy pieces on large pipe organs are only distractions to worshippers.' Now, tell me, before this assembly of intelligent and educated men if you are not forced to admit that what we heard at the Church this afternoon was not infinitely more edifying than all the pretty pieces your choir sang the other night and all the noises you got out of that expensive pipe organ?"

My reply was in effect: "Your Grace, you will be kind enough, I am sure, to debit the accident to the biretta to my natural awkwardness. I'm really a very clumsy fellow. I'll admit to have been interested in the points I was making for the cultivating of a spiritual type of music in the Church, and if the accidental toppling off of your biretta (I'm glad that the zucchetta didn't go, too) emphasized those points, I'll not lament the accident too morosely. Now as to your challenge about this afternoon's edifying service: the great climax of the congregation's participation in the service was their singing of Father Faber's 'O Paradise.' The men liked the tune. It's an excellent melody by a fine composer of hymn tunes, R. A. Turton of England. The first verse whetted their appetites, and when the second stanza started they were all for giving it everything they had. The first stanza was only a rehearsal for the second. But in the second, what volume! What relish! What dash and enthusiasm! Please note, Your Grace, that the volume, relish, dash and enthusiasm were for the melody, not the text. Did you, perchance, advert to the words of the second stanza? You asked me if I didn't think the congregational singing more edifying than the motets of a choir. Permit me to recite the second stanza of the hymn which edified you so much.

> O Paradise! O Paradise! *'Tis weary waiting here.*
> *I long to be where Jesus is,*
> To see, to feel Him near.

Now, Your Grace, in this friendly atmosphere, I dare to answer your question directly. I think that the congregational singing this afternoon was as dramatic an example of unconscious pharisaism as I have ever heard. Intent on the melody they shouted out their eagerness to be out of this vale of tears, to have done with this weary life. They were proclaiming a falsification, for there wasn't a man among them who, if he felt a cold coming on, wouldn't have stopped at the corner drugstore to purchase a remedy! The performance, Your Grace, was pretty close to material blasphemy. I don't convict the men of formal blasphemy, because they weren't paying any attention to the words. All they cared about was the tune. Does that answer Your Grace's question?"

The Archbishop, a Nova Scotian, had a dry sense of humor. Stroking his archepiscopal chin thoughtfully, he replied: "Well! you knocked my biretta off once, and now you tackle the old Archbishop himself. Gentlemen, let's say grace!"

Perhaps my reply to the Archbishop seems more of a retort than an answer. But His Grace enjoyed a bit of banter, and good-humored personalities often punctuated the repartee when he was present. And besides, his challenging question provided opportunity to emphasize some thoughts about the proper use of hymn texts. The hymns sung in the vernacular in most Catholic parishes, where the members are in majority of Irish or English ancestry, are textually inferior to the great hymns of the Roman Breviary. The popular effusions in English during the last three quarters of a century have been increasingly vapid. They ooze feeble flavors, affectation and sentimentality. Frequently the versification is unskilled. The tunes and harmonizations are often so trivial that many non-Catholic musicians express surprise that the Church, under whose sponsorship the art of music developed over the centuries, permits their use. The simple elegance of Gregorian chant hymns, the settings in harmony and counterpoint of the great Catholic masters, and the generally high ideal of musical utterance of earlier eras are, indeed, affronted by repudiation in favor of paltry, scrubby substitutes provided by untalented, untrained and therefore ineffectual adventurers.

The subject of hymnody is important. In most of the non-liturgical services of the Church, such as special devotions, novenas, etc., the hymn is an outstanding and influential feature. Weak texts, setting forth flabby points of view in out-of-step syllabification, put to bleached tunes or harmonies are not the stuff of which hymns should be made! There is a thesaurus of hymnody in the Church of which not only the people but the Church musicians seem unaware. It has been a privilege, throughout my career, to draw upon the resources of this treasury. The hymns of the Breviary and many others worthy of being incorporated there, have composed the repertoire of our processional and recessional hymns in the best English translations available. The pleasant tilt with His Grace of Toronto gave me opportunity of making a gentle but tallying thrust.

After my term of service was finished at Lourdes Church, I moved over to the Paulist Church in Toronto, where for a few months I was engaged in mixing diverse elements. I felt like a Jack-of-all-trades. Parochial duties. Preaching. Teaching at the parochial school. Playing the organ at Solemn Mass and Vespers. Training the gallery choir of women and men. Inaugurating an auxiliary choir of boys who soon began to sing Responses and other short parts of the Vesper Office.

Every second Sunday at the Solemn Mass, two altar boys with acolytes' candles (liturgical license!) met me at the foot of the choir-gallery stairway after the *Gloria,* and escorted me through the middle aisle to the pulpit. My arrival on the rostrum thus suggested to the congregation that I was to make an ex cathedra pronouncement notwithstanding the probability of my dispensing only a few platitudes. Even if one had carefully prepared an outline for the pulpit discourse, the distractions accumulated in the choir gallery would at least smudge the outline, and by the time the formal procession to the pulpit had been accomplished, the proposed continuity of the discourse would have dissolved into a congeries of irrelevancies. If the fugue at the end of the *Gloria* had required special attention, the beginning of the sermon would find my subconscious mind still occupied with the fugal subject, answer, countersubject, episodes and stretto. If the *Credo* promised to trap the singers in nets of sixteenth notes, the peroration of the discourse would foreshadow the fact to the congregation.

Although it is well to have had a varied experience, especially in one's formative years, it is disadvantageous for a specialist to be active for a lengthy period in unrelated fields of endeavor. His specialty suffers. He becomes a hack. Probably in his own field he gives a slightly better account of himself than in others, but his keenness is blunted. He is required to give thought to so many subjects that he cannot concentrate on any. His energy is diffused too widely. Even if he continues to produce satisfactory results actually, the feeling that he is trying his hand at other activities, many of which require specializing, is disturbing. He is liable to lose the sense of authority which an expert should possess if he is to achieve true success in his specialty.

I had begun to feel a hack. Although I tried to focus my interest and attention upon the musical work which was my chief responsibility, I was often too fatigued by other activities to bring enthusiasm or freshness into the choir hall. Therefore, when I was reappointed to Chicago, a new local Superior being in charge, I asked to be relieved of regular service in other departments of parochial enterprise.

Chapter XVIII *Final Experiments with a Boys' and Men's Choir in Chicago*

UPON arrival in Chicago after an absence of eleven months, I found the soprano section of the choir in poor condition. The musician who was directing the choir during my absence, although an excellent pianist and theorist, knew practically nothing about chorophony. The boys, therefore, had lost much of their tonal excellence. There were just enough boys left with the timbre which had become distinctive of the Paulist Choristers to serve as an exemplar for newcomers who had been singing raucously with an unqualified chest tone.

After several weeks of peremptory insistence on the fundamentals, the choir reassumed its former, and, I must add, unique mastery of expression, to be fair to the boys and men who worked so steadfastly to achieve that mastery. Presently the choir was giving evidence of an approach to the highest ideals of the choral art. My months at Toronto had been fruitful. I had ascended higher on the trail to Parnassus. While, of course, I did not try to borrow richness from the Toronto women's treble-staff lines, I was almost subconsciously impelled to develop in the boys the supertotality of their safe, natural vocal qualities. Without subtracting from the volatile character of their tone timbres, I was able to increase its warmth. From that time until my final relinquishing of the conductorship of the Paulist Choristers at New York in the autumn of 1940, the soprano quality of the boys was acclaimed throughout the country by critics and laity alike as an extraordinary medium of musical communication.

During the winter of 1916 the organ at Old St. Mary's was rebuilt. A skyscraper had been erected on ground adjacent to the site of the Church and the sinking of caissons to a depth of about a hundred feet to support the immense structure occasioned much damage to the organ. Pipes looked like miniature leaning towers of Pisa. Cracks appeared in the wind chest, and the console was divorced from amicable relations with the tubes, wires and other essential fittings of a pipe organ. The new Rector decided to improve the whole plan of the sanctuary. The Altar was placed against the wall. The organ pipes were installed in two sections, one on the Gospel and the other on the Epistle side. The keyboard was put below the floor of the Sanctuary near the altar rail, with a paneled wood screen to conceal the gesticulations of the organist from the congregation. From the new position of the organist, it was possible for him to see the ceremonies. For some years I had conducted the music from behind the Altar. The timing of many starts of sung numbers of the services was by conjecture. I would have to guess. Was the Deacon ready? How far along had the incensation of the Altar progressed? Was the celebrant waiting for the organ to cease sounding so that he might intone the Pater Noster? Etc., etc.

As I said, the new position of the organ console at Old St. Mary's, Chicago favored greater intimacy between the essential and the musical parts of the religious exercises. Personally, as the weeks went by, I felt my reactions to the liturgical ceremonies increasing in sensitiveness. Behind the Altar, one would miss many things which in front were inescapable. And so, in fulfilling its primary purpose to increase the solemnity of religious services, the choir grew and waxed ever stronger. The activities of the Paulist Choristers in the concert field were proposed in the beginning as a means to an end, not as an end in themselves. The end was definitely to improve the unit as a church choir by interesting talented singers to become members, and, incidentally, to emphasize on the concert stage those properties of music which, because spiritual, might influence clergy, musicians and laity the country over to improve the standards of church music in the churches.

Musicians who have not been required to preside over the musical portions of religious services from positions affording no view of the ritualistic proceedings cannot fully appreciate the disadvantages involved. When the organist beholds the progress of the incomparable drama of the Mass, he is most likely moved to at least some degree of unction. Unless he be a dullard, artistically as well as spiritually, he will probably be sensitive to the growth, through varying moods, of the liturgical phrases of the Sacrifice. His music will thus have some chance of underlining this growth. *Kyries, Glorias, Agnus Deis,* etc., are more likely to seem integral parts of the ritual, emerging necessarily as well as opportunely from rites and spoken prayers, than interpolated concert numbers. In my opinion, if a *Kyrie* fails to sing the supplication of the people for God's kindly mercy, it has no place in the agenda of worship.

Musically, the service must proceed *pari passu,* i.e., consistently, with the spirit and intention of the Liturgy at every step. A pianissimo chanting of the Creed is a wishwashy attestation of faith. A defiant howl to

God to forget our transgressions is not only an evidence of arrogance (perhaps unwitting) ; it is crude and rude disdain for the fitness of things, which is the true basis of aesthetics. How often one feels, during a religious service, that the musical offerings are altogether out of place! If only the organist would disconnect those blatant pipes! If those shouting sopranos and snarling tenors would temper their vociferation so that one might be conscious of the Divine! If only that prayer for peace in the depths of the soul had not been delivered by the choir as a "leading lady and chorus" number of a muscial comedy! If only the music of the Church would suggest religion!

From 1915 to 1918, we reached the peak of our achievement as a Chicago organization. Later, in New York, the Paulist Choristers were destined to pass far beyond the highmark of Chicago. But during the final seasons in the Windy City, the boys and men attained a blend of tone colors, an elasticity in expression and a convincing authority in execution, especially in the homophonic style of composition (the style in which one melodic line is sustained usually by one vocal part throughout, as distinguished from the contrapuntal or polyphonic style, in which each vocal part develops its own melody). Later in New York, when I felt that I had personally begun to understand the tricky business of making the more involved style *sound* right, we became specialists in the interpretation of polyphonic music.

Our concluding days at Chicago were made memorable by several interesting episodes. In addition to the sung services at Old St. Mary's where large and representative congregations assembled each Sunday, we gave many concerts under most favorable conditions. Among these were programs at the University Club of Chicago. The audience there —seven or eight hundred men, graduates of the best universities, all appreciative of cultural values of the fine arts—was good and stimulating for us.

Shortly after I became a member of this club myself, I was appointed chaplain of the Base Hospital Unit, the medical staff of which was made up of physicians and surgeons belonging to the Club. Upon inquiring as to the nature and extent of my duties as chaplain, I was informed that only in the event of some local disaster, such as the Cherry Valley tragedy of some years before, would the Base Hospital Unit be required to function. We were registered as members of the Reserve Medical Officers' Corps. What a surprise when, in April 1917, the United States becoming involved in the war, we were shifted to the Reserve Officers' Corps! This meant active duty.

Physically I was not eligible for active service because of lameness resulting from infantile paralysis. However, I was ordered into a captain's uniform and told to report for drill at Battery B. Before I could go to a tailor to be fitted for a uniform which I knew I would never wear, the War Department decided to reorganize the Hospital Unit which at that time included a large number of Germans, some of these having been naturalized only a few weeks earlier. There was a strong Teutonic flavor to the speech of many. During the months of reorganization I contributed to the war effort by bringing my choristers over the country for the relief of French war suffering, and to stir up patriotism in the more remote places.

When Bishop Mundelein, Auxiliary Bishop of Brooklyn, N.N., was appointed Archbishop of Chicago and installed in the spring of 1916, we were invited to participate in an installation event which became widely known afterwards as the Soup Banquet. Poisoned soup was served to the many hundreds of guests at a banquet given to His Grace by the Extension Society, of which Monsignor Francis Clement Kelley, now Bishop of Oklahoma City, was President. The banquet was given in the Cathedral Hall of the University Club.

Monsignor Kelley, a gifted litterateur, had written a dramatic poem for the occasion, entitled "The Death Dream of Père Marquette." I was commissioned to set the poem to music. We were to sing this offstage, while professional actors were enacting the scenes in pantomime. The rehearsal on the eve came off well enough, but on the morning of the banquet date, Monsignor Kelley telephoned early requesting my immediate presence at the Club. Ararngements required changing. About two hundred guests in addition to those already provided for must be accommodated. This involved using a smaller stage for the actors and shifting it to a different spot. Under the altered conditions, where would I place the Choristers, portable organ, etc.? How would the Choristers enter with the originally planned middle aisle occupied by tables for the extra banqueters? I did not delay to have a substantial breakfast.

We fussed around the Club through the morning including the lunch hour. Only at the start of the banquet did I realize that I had not eaten since the preceding evening. Sitting just below the speakers' table, at which the most distinguished of the guests, clerical and lay, were placed, I avidly consumed a plate of very savory soup. One must say in light of later developments that it was too savory. Too alluring. Delicious as a glass of a specially prepared Borgia wine which, according to legend, had toppled many a cardinal, doge, and mere feudal lord to his final supineness.

Not more than sixty seconds after having consumed the palatable concoction, I began to feel strange. Lightheaded! First, a bit youngish, that is to say, on the giggly side. Then, much older. Many years older. A senile veteran watching his gravediggers! Having fasted so long, the essence reinforced with arsenical poison attacked the unprotected lining of my stomach with fierce vehemence. As the soup gathered fury for another attack, I had a moment of quasi lucidity. I spoke to the gentlemen at my table, saying that I would have to excuse myself to descend to the corridor below in order to check a detail of the oncoming performance.

"Nonsense," said Mr. Neumann who had "nonsensed" me out of canceling the Chicago concert when I telephoned from Grand Rapids.

"Nonsense," chimed in Dr. John B. Murphy who had cut a physical "nonsense" out of my abdomen with a scalpel.

"Nonsense," cried several others at the table. "You're directly under the eyes of His Grace, the new archbishop. You must remain here. Your choir will not arrive for at least another hour."

Presently I could see the gravediggers again, and rising with a "Manners or no manners, gentlemen: here I go!" I sped with gathering haste to the safety of an anteroom. When I came-to, Mr. Newman, Dr. Murphy and many others were staggering into the little room. Groans. Moans. Clutchings at the abdominal regions. Ashen complexions. Faintings! Pleas for medical attention. The soup had broken down the best-mannered of the guests. Exit. Flight. The attacks would come in spasms. During one of Dr. Murphy's good periods, I helped him to return to the banquet hall where he hoped to be of assistance to other stricken banqueters. He threw off his dress coat, rolled up his shirt sleeves, and with many of his medical colleagues undertook to minister to the poisoned company. Few escaped the effects of the poison. The banquet was finished at the soup course! Rather a unique episode in the annals of "Les banquets de Gala!" A few of the guests died shortly after the banquet, their demises being charged to the soup by many. But I have always thought that they expired from natural causes.

After about half an hour, I decided to try to salvage something of the wrecked program. Monsignor Kelley had returned for a few moments, during a good spell, to the speakers' table. I followed him, suggesting that I fetch as many Choristers as possible from the lower corridor to make a least a noise in the Hall. Even a noise might help! He urged me to hurry.

As I passed a dignified old bishop, a friend of my family, the prelate stopped me saying, "Willie," (this vocative nearly induced another spasm) "isn't this a scandal?" I agreed, of course, that there was something sufficiently wrong about the situation to be so designated. The prelate in gay purple continued: "Of course, I mean that it is scandalous for grown men, leaders of the people, men of high professional repute, to make such a scene. Why don't they exercise their will power and control themselves? You see me. I'm staying right here! Willie, the will!"

Having neither time nor taste for His Lordship's thesis on the controlling power of mind over matter, I hastened to fetch the Choristers. As we were ascending the marble stairway and the senior soprano chorister, himself decked out in hierarchical magenta according to our tradition, reached the top step, His Lordship, having left his thesis on the Value of Volition at the speakers' table, was reeling without sense of direction in the outer hallway. Volition died a quick death. The arsenic had landed a solid solar plexus, and the poor old academic bishop and the magenta-gowned chorister mixed in skirmish which only the cinema might adequately portray. It wasn't a pretty scene.

When the choir was placed behind the screen and the pantomimists had taken their places on the stage, we began to sing about Père Marquette's vision of the great development of the West. I was pumping away at a little reed organ. A Club page stood near by, alternately placing over and removing a topcoat from my shoulders. Chill. Fever. Arsenic and consommé. Marquette's dream. Finn's nightmare. The Rockies advancing upon me from Colorado one moment. The next, the Pacific Ocean sending a tidal wave from Santa Barbara to engulf me! Indian tomahawks poised to kill missionaries in the desert. A feverish thirst persuading me that I was lost without a canteen on the hot sands. Actors continuing to make gestures on the stage. Choristers singing flats and sharps. Basses trying to harmonize with tenors; sopranos soaring to top notes; countertenors struggling with the dream fantasies of the modernistic chords with which I had vitiated the score! Nobody caring. Nobody listening. I could speculate on metaphysics. On psychology. On the relationship of the physical and the mental. The world was a mess. Banquets! Borgia and poisoned wine! Ptomaine from fish! Or was it soup? It was strange that the soup was so delicious—and all that sort of thing! Finally a kindly soul wrenched me away from the little reed organ and guided me homewards. And the installation banquet of His Grace of Chicago was written down as one of the major botches in the history of festivities.

It was natural to suspect that the soup had been poisoned deliberately. A yarn soon connected a certain alleged anticlerical, who had been dismissed from service in the Club's kitchen a fortnight before the banquet, with the dastardly purpose of trying to murder about eight hundred prominent men, the group including prelates of the Church, high officers of the State, and leading professional and business men. The newspapers played up the affair in headlines. My family wired me to know how I

liked being dead. A tepid reward was offered for the arrest of the suspected criminal. He was in a dozen places at the same time. Leaving a
train in Omaha, boarding one in Kansas City. Hiding behind bales on
a New York pier seeking to board an outgoing ship. Soon, however,
interest in the anticlerical waned. And Chicago added the soup banquet
to its already long list of unsolved mysteries.

The following summer saw our first experiment with a vacation plan
for the Choristers. I had decided that I wanted something better than a
camp, and from the first announcement of the plan I referred to the
proposed abode as a "villa." I had in mind a spacious, roomy mansion,
perhaps a hotel which the heirs of an estate no longer wished to operate.
No tents for us. None of the roughing it that seemed to be part and
parcel of real camp life. Private rooms for boys with baths between the
rooms. A large assembly hall for rehearsals and recreation. A light, well-
ventilated dining room. Broad verandas. A private, sandy swimming
beach. Proximity to the city. We talked it out privately and publicly for
months. We raised enough money through concerts to finance an elaborate establishment. But we were doomed to suffer acute humiliation,
for the only place within a hundred miles from Chicago that could accommodate our crowd, providing swimming and boating facilities, was
an abandoned ice house at Crystal Lake, Illinois. The ice cutters had at
one time occupied the main building which was probably originally a
large barn.

We tried diligently to improve the sleeping quarters. Berths in three
tiers along walls. Primitive sanitary arrangements. Kitchen equipment
suggestive of the caveman epoch. Windows and doors refusing to close
snugly. The *tout ensemble* of our "summer estate" ridiculed the boastful
pretensions of operating a villa for the Choristers. And yet, in spite of
the crude ugliness of the ice house, the summer spent there was probably
the happiest experience in the history of the Choristers. A camaraderie
developed. Boys took care of their own sleeping quarters. Everybody,
young and old, performed menial tasks. I drove a battered model T Ford
through the farming country gathering carrots, spuds, corn and coal. I
should have become an expert in managing staccato, for my Ford engine
vocalized only in staccato shocks of its glottis. Visitors flocked to the
place.

Each week day morning, after the chores were done, there was a
rehearsal. Thus the boys were kept fit vocally and additions were made
to the repertory. We gave concerts throughout the neighborhood. Farmers from miles around drove carriages, small Fords or Maxwells to listen
to the choir singing in bandstands in village squares. We became a

number one rural attraction. The farmers liked the high notes of the sopranos and the close harmony of tenors and basses singing familiar songs. Our programs therefore scintillated with simple melodic music.

For the following summer we made early arrangements in the same general neighborhood for an old hotel. Although living quarters and culinary facilities were better than at the ice house, neither boys nor men were so well pleased. The keynote at the crude ice house was informality.

During that second summer, I introduced Sunday evening concerts in boats on the lake. I called these concerts "Venetian Nights." Why Venetian? I don't know, because it was in Switzerland that I had become acquainted with this delightful form of musical diversion. It was necessary to work out a practical scheme for keeping the boats in correct alignment as they were rowed slowly along. It wouldn't do to get boats with sopranos mixed with crafts carying basses. The conductor's boat must be kept steadily in the same relative position to the singers. Our course would have to be governed by the direction of the wind. To sing into the wind would of course be stupid.

Crowds of people thronged the lake shore each fair Sunday night. We would start about half an hour before sundown and continue singing through the afterglow and conclude under the canopy of the night sky. The Chicago newspapers gave much publicity to these Venetian Nights and many visitors made the journey from the metropolis to be refreshed by the romance of choral music accompanied only by the gentle undulation of the lake lapping the shore. When the afterglow had finally surrendered to the night, I would conduct with an electric flashlight baton. Every once in a while the rowers of different boats would get their oars entangled, and the consonance of voices was momentarily challenged by shouts of warning or the thud of wood against wood. We had a near-capsize one night when a restless soprano boy essayed to change places with an equally restless companion.

The local Pastor, Father Joseph Lonergan, for whom we had been singing concerts throughout the county, organized a group of young ladies to "tag" the listeners on the shore. The parish was the beneficiary of the tag donations, so we were all pleased that our singing on the water was of more than artistic value.

Once near Elgin, Illinois, on an ait of the Fox River we gave a memorable concert. Memorable, because the audience was assembled on near-by roadways and on the bridges connecting the ait to the shores and because a solo boy climbed to the top branches of the tallest tree on the little isle to toss out his limpid high notes. The chorus, standing below, provided harmonic support while his phrases seemed to come out of the sky itself.

The two summers at Crystal Lake helped immeasurably to increase the family spirit among the Choristers, the added formality of the second summer promoting a feeling for domestic etiquette. An esprit de corps which proved an invaluable asset in the great undertaking of the Six Months' Tour was fostered by the community life of the boys. Naturally, little groups of boys whose temperaments blended easily were formed in our organization as in all others, but the necessary give and take of daily contact of all the boys with one another developed mutual understanding and a spirit of teamwork throughout the unit. Our rehearsals during those summer months were leisurely practice periods.

Not pressed by the need of learning new pieces for immediate performance, it was possible to perfect the minutiae as well as the broad contours of interpretation. Frequently both boys and director assumed an *ars gratia artis* attitude towards the practices. We enjoyed simplifying ostensibly intricate movements. A certain aura hovered over phrases of Mozart, César Franck, Rachmaninov. We caught something of the spirit of the music that was living under the notation. Facility in sensing the latencies grew rapidly and upon our return to the choir hall at Chicago in September, 1917, the organization was able to reread the whole repertoire with greater sensitiveness.

The intonations of the Paulist Choristers had begun to give off an afterglow. A sort of nimbus which seemed to continue after a sound had ceased. Probably five hundred and more critics in daily newspapers during the ensuing years discerned and wrote about this mystic tonal nebula. Perhaps the acoustical overtones were blended with allusions that came not from the timbres themselves but, as the attar rises from the flower as a whole, from the very concept of the choral art which telepathically had been inspiriting the singing.

The validity of the Ground Bass theme was making itself unmistakably evident. The long pilgrimage to Parnassus, while not destined to reach the peak, was fruitful, many exotic souvenirs finding their way back to our choir hall.

Professional musicians would sometimes shake skeptical heads and, wagging fingers with academic stiffness, query as to what we were trying to add to the written music. Often we welcomed organists and conductors to the rehearsals, and almost as often we heard comments such as this: "The mere technical processes which you employ cannot be responsible for the other-world effects achieved. The same processes are used elsewhere, but the same result is not produced." It was always difficult to clarify our points of view about musical expression, for these did, indeed, include more than systems of vocalization, blending and interpretation. They not only included, they were based upon and inevitably derived from, the truth of the Ground Bass. Just as all the melodic fragments, harmonic developments, contrapuntal figurations and over-all aesthetic effect of the Bach Passacaglia stem, indisputably, to the theme written on the opening page of these memoirs.

One might successfully discuss the deep truths underlying the successful practice of the other arts, because these arts speak in the open to the reasoning mind. But music whispers confidences to the soul. It addresses the emotions. It affects the intellect almost inconsequentially. Therefore, music is too complex a medium to permit of harnessing in the words of formulae.

Deep, moving musicianship cannot be attained by concentration on the externals of the art. Great composers experience moments of inspiration. Occasionally a truly great soloist comes across the horizon. John McCormack was one. He possessed a musical intuition. But inspired and intuitive artists are rare. Especially in the re-creative field. The conductor is a re-creator. Not being endowed with genius, we merely talented re-creators must try to borrow from genius some elements which will complement and supplement our mean-average gifts. This is why a musician, who would become a great conductor, must wed himself to some all-absorbing Ground Bass. As the years pass, a philosophy of music must develop. Besides the surface techniques, an appreciation of the inner potentialities of music as music must grow.

Externals frequently fail to produce convincing results. *The conductor needs to conduct from within.*

It used to irk me vexatiously to be obliged to overhear conversations in trains or restaurants between groups of singers. "I get my top B flat by feeling it start in the region of the diaphragm, etc." "Oh," another counters, "I just think of the *fausse nasale* and send the note high into the resonance chambers." "But," the rejoinder of a third, "Professor Homophonios taught me to gape a high B flat. Yawn on pitch and there it is." Once in a while, especially at breakfast in a crowded little village restaurant, I would feel impelled to exclaim! "Fiddlesticks! Why fuss about top B flats? How about your middle B flats and all the notes in your middle voices where the real music lies? Let me hear you sing right there!"

Goldsmith wrote: "Little things are great to little men." I am prone to believe, after so many years, that singers, players and conductors are wont to magnify "little things," to underline minutiae at the expense of the whole and to sacrifice substantial content to face values. I don't wish to convey the thought that a musician or any practitioner of the fine arts may neglect technical details. By no means. I mean this, simply but emphatically: unless, as a musician matures, his techniques indicate that they are only facile means of communicating impressions and moods, they are as silly as tinsel. Furthermore, when techniques are honestly used as means of communication, they tend to perfect themselves. What began, perhaps, as a formula, develops into a canon of procedure, the urgency of which is irresistible. Processes and precepts adjust themselves almost imperceptibly to expanding emotional and spiritual feelings.

A chorus and a symphony orchestra can reach out to the hearts of people with electromotive force, if the conductor and participants are moved from within. But if a performance be only an exemplification of technical excellences, its valid and valuable purpose is frustrate.

The Paulist Choristers from about 1917 to 1940 were unconsciously singing from within. At rehearsals, vocal exercises and all phases of the craft of perfecting the choral unit seemed to spring from that necessity. Certain vocalises would suggest themselves as needful at a given moment, not principally because their form would tend to correct a present fault or make more sure a superficial refinement, but principally because these vocalises seemed to guarantee a greater degree of tonal fitness to communicate an idea. Thus, if the *Recordare* from the Requiem of Mozart were in preparation, almost instinctively I would assign vocalizations which included passing discordances. For the communicability of Mozart's musical reaction to this text depends upon the degree of feeling for dissonances and their resolution into consonances developed by conductor and chorus. It is not only a matter of proper regulation of the volume of sound applied—a little louder here, a little softer there—it is more than that. In the *Recordare,* for instance, the altos must *feel* the tug of the dissonant bass note G as it enters against their F. If the altos fail to *sense* the conflict between fear and hope which Mozart is limning here, the mere addition of a crescendo on the alto F will not create the impression intended. *Intensity* must demand the *crescendo.* Intensity comes from the thought; volume is only an acoustical phenomenon.

The outstanding reason for the ineffectiveness of many choruses and orchestras is ultimately to be found in the failure to develop intensity of feeling. Often nothing but sound comes through the notes. The emotive power of the art is too profound to be revealed by the mere physical vibrations of tones. A Ground Bass must send up something substantial.

During the six months beginning January 1, 1918, the Choristers sang in public two hundred and forty-one times. Such an uninterrupted series naturally brought finesse to their control of techniques. I wrote "naturally" although I am well aware of the likelihood of extended touring, with its many consecutive performances, becoming a hazard to artistry. One success after another disposes an organization as well as individuals to take success for granted and thus to become less alert. But if the spirit of a stirring Ground Bass has become resident in the very heart of a chorus and if the conductor maintains a strict routine of corrective rehearsals, the chorus will naturally profit by a long series of performances.

Looking back over the engagements of that arduous tour, I am forced by facts to record that the Choristers maintained an extraordinarily high level of alertness, and that, even under the depressing conditions of fatiguing travel, inclement weather and food not prepared by Parisian chefs, we followed a strict routine of rehearsals. Never, even at a matinee on a rainy day in a small town did we knowingly lower our standards. Therefore, each day brought its meed of improvement.

I had developed a code of signals by which to communicate directions, clearly and simply, to the Choristers. One couldn't always conduct a number in the same fashion. Page four, at the great Exposition Auditorium in San Francisco, might need a crescendo by the second tenors. At the theater in Waco, Texas, the acoustics might require the second tenors to omit the crescendo in favor of the baritones or first altos. Thus it was necessary to "sing off the stick." Each performance provided a different set of surrounding circumstances, and one of my tasks on the podium was to signal the adjustments and readjustments indicated. And so, for the application of greater or less degrees of volume, I usually followed this easy plan:

(a) Left hand flat, moving from shoulder to shoulder = pianissimo to the entire unit; if held flat toward a particular group, this group was to sing at its softest.
(b) One finger up = piano, soft but not pianissimo.
(c) Two fingers up = mezzo forte.
(d) Three fingers up = forte.
(e) Four fingers up = fortissimo.
(f) Gradual opening of hand = crescendo.
(g) Gradual closing of hand = diminuendo.
(h) Sliding of left forefinger down the baton = more attenuated pianissimo.

For a number of years I used some amusing signals to recall certain devices of vocalism to the group. A T, formed by placing the left forefinger horizontally over the perpendicular baton, meant Tetrazzini, the name of the great coloratura who sang her high notes with her chin down. And so at the T sign, chins would be lowered to relax the throats for top notes. Another signal of this type was a capital G which I undertook to form with left forefinger and thumb. This G recalled to the Choristers the wide opening of the mouth for which Geraldine Farrar was celebrated.

Blanche Marchesi had warned me, during my first trip to England, of the tendency of voices to sing descending tones too far apart, and ascending tones too close together. With this warning in mind, I devised a signal to prevent such bad intonation. As a descending figure would approach, I frequently snapped my middle left finger against the thumb to remind the singers, especially sopranos and basses, to *think* the descending intervals close together. After some years of this constant snapping, a chronic soreness developed in my left thumb. Even today the thumb resents being bent back even slightly. To recall to the Choristers the need of thinking the ascending intervals sufficiently high above one another, I used the converse gesture, snapping the finger away from the thumb.

With this set of signals for the left hand, the right hand being free to indicate the time and tempo, I was provided with a code of directive and suggestive instructions which would immediately and clearly convey to the choir the needs and interpretative intentions of the moment. It was easy, therefore, to vary the readings of numbers in various halls. Hints from acoustics and other varying conditions could easily be accepted and followed. But is was amusing sometimes (more often distressing) to observe some other conductors using these and similar signals. Unless the techniques to which they referred had sprung from a real understanding of the score, the running up of one, two or three fingers, sliding down the baton, etc., are extravagantly vain expedients. Occasionally I have sat behind a conductor whose fingers danced a caprice from start to finish. Nor rhyme nor reason. Loud here—four fingers. Suddenly soft there—one finger, flat hand and a slide down the banister. Random gesticulation. Presently, of course, the restless fingers, ceasing to convey any serious intention to the singers or players, were altogether ignored.

All this is apropos of the futility of techniques *if there be nothing valid to express*. My long trip to Thessaly made clear with noonday lucidity the fundamental truth of all art, and especially of music, that craftsmanship, technical skill, aptitude in using the tools of expression are valuable only in the ratio of the value of the thing expressed.

Once, on the long tour about which I shall write presently, I was quite charmed by the naïveté of a little lady, the music teacher of a town where we had sung some concerts. She was the town's music teacher. She had been for long. The local Euterpe. She knew her harp strings! She had met Caruso, had visited a New York studio where an expensive sorcerer was wont to vend gold bricks to a rich clientele. She had seen Dr. Walter Damrosch conduct! And she wasn't being taken in by this Paulist Choir with its conductor who made such funny motions with his left hand! All this information had been relayed to me by the town's Cholly Knicker-bocker.

She had announced that she would sit as close to the organ console as possible during the Solemn Mass with which we would conclude our visit to the town. I spied the little mid-Victorian. Eagerly she watched my every movement. Occasionally she would jot a note on a pad. I was under a piercing and ruthless scrutiny. On my way down from the organ gallery at the end of the Solemn Mass, I passed her. She had hypnotized a group of the village grapevine tenders. I was dressed in ulster and muffler with snow glasses already in place. She or her satellites did not recognize me.

As I walked past, she was declaring: "That man is certainly overrated. There is absolutely nothing scholarly or worthwhile about his work. This minute I have come from watching him. It's only a matter of one finger, two, three or four fingers. He hasn't another trick in his whole bag."

Yes, dear little lady, that's all I can carry in a bag, but maybe I know where there's a good sized closet in which one can store things! It is important for artists to have commodious closets.

Chapter XIX   *The Ground Bass Takes a Transcontinental Tour*

O N JANUARY 1, 1918, the six months' tour of the Choristers began. The expedition was undertaken as a humanitarian and patriotic service. Dressed as French soldiers, the Choristers sang for the relief of French victims of the war. In the majority of the places visited,
the bookings were managed by local war chest boards or other patriotic
organizations. The tour involved many responsibilities and some hard-
ships were necessarily suffered. Many thousands of miles of railroading.
Blizzards, snow, rain, mud. Frequently unsatisfactory housing. All possible varieties and qualities of food. Waiting on station platforms for
early morning trains. Hurrying, after belated arrivals, through snow
drifts to little theatres. Difficulties with the transportation of wardrobe
trunks. Sickness among the boys and men. Trying to sustain a high level
of artistry when the morale of the group was low. Extracting music from
throats inflamed with laryngitis. Putting on a show when everybody
wanted to be in bed. Yes! we went up and down the gamut of pleasant
and unpleasant experiences. The scale was chromatic, indeed. Going up
in sharps—that was enlivening. Coming down in flats (sometimes double
flats demanded to be held for extra beats!)—that was disheartening.
But, all in all, the sharps and flats were disposed in such harmonious allocation that no chorister or member of the staff, to my knowledge, regretted having made the tour.

Reflecting upon the probable values of that undertaking from this distance of almost thirty years, I am convinced that it was a significant undertaking. I was still young enough then to be bold. I suppose that without plenty of daring and probably an extra dash of temerity, we who
outlined and managed the long series of concerts would have been over-
dismayed by the prospect of bringing a group of one hundred and ten
boys and men, with chaperons and schoolteachers, through the United
States and Canada on an itinerary of six months' duration. But the au-
dacity seems to have been justified. In addition to the humanitarian and
patriotic ends served, the cultural influence of the tour in so many parts

of North America catches the memory's eye. We were exercising an apostolate, an apostolate for the basic truths of a definite musical creed. For the certainties of a great art. We aimed, everywhere and in all circumstances, to interest professional and lay listeners in such aspects of our belief as convincing tone quality, blend and balance, elasticity, aesthetic and spiritual communicability. The Ground Bass over which these memoirs are being written was stressed as the principal tenet.

Rarely did the Ground Bass fail to come through. Sometimes it showed itself in startling clarity. On many occasions the singers seemed to draw upon hidden sources of tonal beauty. One could tell that melos was controlling the emotions and appreciations of the audience on those occasions.

I am going to specify here some of the occasions on which my boys and men produced extraordinary effects without conscious effort; effects which seemed to reveal themselves as lovely lights quietly make their presence known. The Choristers will be pleased to recall these especially memorable instances—at Carnegie Hall, New York, at the evening concert in February; at Massey Hall, Toronto; in the old railroad station at Richmond, Virginia, while the remains of a much-beloved Protestant Episcopalian bishop were borne from the train; at Richmond, too, in the Arena; in the great Hall at Atlanta, Georgia, where choir boys from the Protestant Episcopal Cathedral brought a wreath to the stage; at the vast new auditorium at El Paso, Texas; at the evening concert at the Civic Auditorium, San Francisco; at Balboa Park, California; in the Cathedrals of Salt Lake City and Omaha; on the Santa Fe platform at Needles, California, for the local Indians; in the concourse of the railroad station at Kansas City before boarding the train for the last ride of the trip; at the Chicago Auditorium, in front of one of the greatest audiences in our records, for the final concert of the long tour.

One number sings its beauty in the fastnesses of my memory whenever I indulge in reverie about the tour: the "Cherubic Hymn in D" by Alexandre Gretchaninov. Many times I was so rapt in the utter loveliness of the tones that were floating around that I wonder how I managed the mechanical details of conducting. Probably the most satisfying musical moments of my life up to that date were during the performance of this number at Carnegie Hall, New York. A trio of New York notables, Drs. Frank and Walter Damrosch and Dr. Walter Henry Hall, came backstage to report that they had been strangely moved. Sarah Robinson Duff, renowned teacher of opera divas, including Mary Garden, pointing to the Gretchaninov number in her program book, remarked with Arcadian simplicity; "That was the most exquisite musical experience of my life."

Kurt Schindler, of the Schola Cantorum, found the motet an "adventure in heaven."

In later years there were moments when the Choristers created an even more unmistakably mystical atmosphere, notably at the Metropolitan Opera House, New York, in 1929, when for the first recorded time the abellimenti of Allegri's *Miserere* were sung elsewhere than in the Sistine Chapel. But the Carnegie Hall performance of the "Cherubic Hymn" in 1918 found me scaling a high crag on the Mount of the Muses. Somehow, on that night, I could understand myself. Some achievement!

We left Chicago on a very stormy day. Awaiting the signal to entrain at the La Salle Street Station, boys and adults seemed to be shrouded in gloom. Often, on many later departures from that station, I have seen the picture of the group, depressed at the thought of so long a tour, walking nervously about. There was no element of romance in the prospect of going from town to town in the Middle West and in the Eastern states. The large cities were all much like Chicago, but Chicago was home. The small towns were hardly distinguishable one from another. Main Street. Churches. A couple of hotels. Restaurants. A theater or two. But always concerts. Every evening and several afternoons a week. Including the church services at which we sang, there was a total of two hundred and forty-one appearances in one hundred and eighty days. Some interest was expressed among the members about seeing the deep South and California, but many weeks would have elapsed before we reached either of these sections.

Once the train had pulled out, however, we settled into a better mood. The opening concerts, matinee and evening, at South Bend, Indiana, found both boys and men determined to give a fine account of themselves.

I took a priest-prefect along who had complete responsibility for the boys. He arranged with our schoolteachers to hold classes aboard train if we were rolling, or at some parochial school assembly hall, if we had arrived in a town by midmorning. It is interesting to note that no boys failed to pass the school board's examinations at the conclusion of the tour. Two school hours each weekday except Saturday; small classes and concentration! (The instructors had enough of a gentle and commanding air to capture the attention of the boys. Not a negligible degree of charm!)

It would be tedious to write at length about this tour. There was so much sameness to the days and nights. Once in a while we would have a gala night, as at Carnegie Hall, New York, or at Toronto where the Governor-General of Canada occupied the vice-royal box. A private concert for His Eminence, Cardinal O'Connell, at Boston, was an interesting feature of our weeks in the East. At St. Patrick's Church in Washington, officials of the government, ambassadors, consuls and high ranking officers of the armed forces assisted at Solemn Mass. I played the organ at which one of my best teachers, Armand Gumprecht, had presided years before. Ambassador Jusserand of France spoke to the Choristers, thanking them for what they were doing for his country and pleasing them by saying that their rendition of the "Marseillaise" was full of French verve, that he had not heard a more stirring performance even in France.

Generally, however, it was just town after town. Monotony. You know. That *monotonous* monotony!

Our group certainly did sing the national anthems of our allies with most telling effect. I think that we revealed every musical thread of patriotism that was woven into the "Star Spangled Banner." By retarding the tempo in some spots and accelerating it at others, we were able to convert the awkward and not overengaging melody of the anthem into a spirited tune. Throughout the tour and afterwards we had many requests for copies of our arrangement of the piece. Of course, we sang the traditional arrangement except for the banal high note tossed off by the sopranos (now officially deleted), but the variations of tempo and dynamic strengths led listeners to think that we had our own special setting.

We could do things with the Canadian anthem, too. And "Rule Britannia" was so fiery as to cause surprise that any save subjects of His Majesty could hurl such an imperative to the British sea power. Occasionally, then and in after years, some of the Irishest of the Irish-American men would refuse to sing "God Save The King." One chap used to worry me when, in the presence of British officials, he would strike a bellicose attitude on the stage, folding his arms, pressing his lips closely together, and generally calling attention with melodramatic effect to his anti-British silence. Fortunately, no complaint was made by officials, but various impresarios were wont to be anxious.

Our progress through Indiana, Ohio, Pennsylvania, New York and New England was difficult. Snow for weeks. At Buffalo, drifts were so high that boys and men were obliged not only to cancel an engagement to sing Solemn Mass at the Cathedral but to miss assisting at Low Mass in the near-by church. We said the Rosary together in a sample room. Beginning at New York, we strewed boys and men over the hospital areas. For a month or more I was disturbed by anxiety for sick members who had been left behind for medical treatment and nursing. Two boys at New York. Diphtheria. Several in Connecticut towns. Influenza. Rhode Island and Massachusetts claimed some. At Boston City Hospital we had two boys with scarlet fever. These lads did not rejoin the group until we arrived in Texas, many weeks later.

In Boston we added a registered nurse, capable and devoted to the boys, to our traveling staff. The lads nicknamed her "Aspirin Annie," because she often gave the aspirin tablets.

At Boston, after the scheduled appearances, we declared a holiday. A few days for rest and recreation. During this period the unit got its second wind. When we left the Athens of America for its humble neighboring city, Worcester, Massachusetts, everybody felt better. The great strain had been the initial weeks and especially the New York City appearances. But the amazing portraits of early American generals and statesmen which adorned the walls of the concert hall at Worcester stiffened us up again. What luxuriant side whiskers! It was hard to beat "three-to-a-bar." Those ancient laddies with the Lord Dundreary's looked like "two in a bar," and much at home!

At least I, personally, was much affected by the glaring, staring mustachioed heroes who presided over the functions at that New England city. The next day, at Holy Cross College, I squared the account with the sabre-bearing officers. Having given a lively concert for the students at that renowned college, I availed myself of an opportunity which the President of the college unguardedly offered. He said something like this : "What can I do to show my appreciation for the great treat you have given the boys?"

Without hesitation, having been a college student myself and being a priest, not easily frightened, I replied with Thespian delivery : "Give the students a whole day holiday."

The President was stuck of course, but the students had the holiday and our concert went into the records of the college as a very great success.

We went on from there to other Massachusetts towns and back to the Syracuse, Auburn and Geneva districts in New York State for the concluding days of Lent.

Emotionally, the tour began to lag. In fact, to sag. Sing, sing, sing! Rainy Eastern Mondays! Dusty Southwestern Tuesdays! Make pretty sounds every day! We had been singing a cappella or with piano accompaniment for many weeks. The music began to pale and to pall on us. There was too much sameness in it. With the acoustics of Carnegie and Symphony Hall to add color to our intonations, those major concerts were gratifying. But ordinarily, day after day, night after night, to intone without accompaniment was a bit on the savorless side. Like Irish stew every day without salt. We became fed up with a cappella singing. What a couple of fiddles could do! A battery of violas and cellos! A quartet of French horns rouging up the ashen faces of ghostly sopranos! How we would have welcomed bassoons and trombones to spatter a few daubs of color into the tenor section. And how cordially would we have greeted string basses and third trombones and tubas if they had joined us to make us oblivious of the deadly, onerous, oppressive tone quality of the bass chorus. This section of the choir was very fine actually, but the monotony of hearing it daily without the pointing up of associated colors became a mental strain.

Never before, in our record as a concert organization, had we given so many a cappella concerts. Generally, on other tours, we had had an orchestra every other day or so. But on the six months' trip no orchestra. Ever. Anywhere. It was bald, very bald, excessively bald unaccompanied chanting. Of course, the audiences couldn't be as sick of it as we were, for they listened to only one program. Perhaps the boys and men did not realize, as keenly as I did, the incompleteness of our programs. On the stand, every number, to me, began to sound the same. Fugues, canons, counterpoints, major and minor modes, high keys, low keys, fast tempos, slow tempos—all seemed alike. I would find myself checking off the numbers as they were finished. Only five more to go. Not too bad. Finally, only one more to go. What a relief!

After a while, naturally, I began to be inquisitive about this restless dissatisfaction of mine with unrelieved a cappella singing. Subconsciously, I had been an "orchestral" musician for a long time. I fancied that I could hear all the colors of a symphony orchestra whenever a simple four-part chord was sung. I had come to need violins, violas, cellos, flute and oboes to season the choral harmonies. As a teen-age organist, I knew that registration on the organ was one of the most influential agencies of music. Well, registration on the organ and orchestration are first cousins! They are definitely blood relatives. Perhaps they are closer than cousins. Yes! I believe that they are brother and sister. Which is male and which female, I won't hazard a guess. Koussevitsky would say orchestra for the male. Dupré would probably cry, *les orgues*. At any rate, the vibrancy and highly colored flashes of orchestral color are missing in a cappella singing. Perhaps this is one reason why Monteverdi went to Rome in the seventeenth century to argue with the Pope to ease up on the ecclesiastical restrictions which had retarded the more picturesque development of music.

Here is an indisputable fact: in spite of the feeble protests of faddists or anaemic amateurs who still argue for unrelieved a cappella programs, *the public gets all it can politely endure of unaccompanied singing in a few numbers.* Hundreds of concerts are the plinth upon which this conclusion stands.

After leaving Boston, I examined my reactions to the music that we were purveying to audiences. I found it to be without enough savor. Probably then I began to think, more ardently and eagerly, in orchestral terms. I know this definitely: never since that tour have I been satisfied with the tonal colorlessness which a choir of boys and men produces. Although I had known the technical phases of orchestration for many years, I had never fully realized its psychological aspects until the spring of 1918.

Organ registration had captured my fancy from the first lesson I received from Mr. Hession. It became a specialty of mine. After a few years, I could get whatever of tone colors there was to be gotten from any box of pipes. This is not boasting. It is merely the statement of one of the facts of my musical career. It would have been strange, indeed, if the thought and hours of experimenting which I devoted to the subject had not netted facility.

Except on Sundays and on a few occasions—as at Symphony Hall, Boston; the Civic Auditorium at San Francisco; Balboa Park, San Diego; the auditoriums at Portland, Maine and Oregon—we sang unaccompanied or with piano accompaniment. Throughout the tour at the Sunday services, it was enlivening to hear the tone colors of the organ complementing the vocal timbres.

As the tour proceeded, I would catch myself fancying that an orchestra was adding its tones. Perhaps I even conveyed to the Choristers some of these imagined colors. For instance, during the progress of a long tenor melodic line, it was easy to guess what the influence of cellos and clarinets would be.

My sister Agnes recently said to me: "I think that all your life you have been *groping* for something." Yes! that was it and always has been over the years. Reaching for something. For tones that were not physically there. To grope thus makes the exercise of music difficult. By the time the trip was finished, I was a confirmed choro-orchestral or orchestro-choral conductor. I began to lecture about the twinship of chorus and orchestra, prescribing study of orchestration for choirmasters and choral technique for maestros of the symphony.

Therefore, it was amusing to read in *The Musician* of August, 1944, a critique of a book of mine * remarking that "it is rather unexpected to encounter a book that is ostensibly as comprehensive as this from the hand of one who throughout his career has been associated almost exclusively with choral music."

There is a big point here. It shouldn't be unexpected to discover a cho-

* *The Conductor Raises His Baton* (New York: Harper, 1944).

ral specialist thinking in terms of orchestral music. In fact, if he fails to think in these terms and if he neglects to apprise himself of all aspects of orchestration, his management—not the kind of management that develops from the *mental* preaudition of instrumental colors which are needed to make the musical spectrum complete—of a chorus is limited. Limited to the kind of music which he can actually hear coming from singers' throats. Orchestration not only opens the ears to other sounds; it promotes a feeling that other sounds are really hovering in the neighborhood of those physically intoned.

Does this sound a bit vague? Is it confusing? Is it a reflection that you would have deleted if you had been editing these memoirs?

Perhaps it is a little confusing. Perhaps it is impossible to convey in simple words just what I mean.

You see, music is a mystical agency. It has tones, overtones and undertones. It comprises not only what can actually be heard by the ear, but harmonics that can be correlated only through the medium of highly sensitive mechanical measuring instruments. The essential quality of music is in those elements that cannot be heard by the unaided ear. How strange and paradoxical!

Ask any professor of physics. He will tell you that what makes a violin tone a violin tone is not what leaps directly to your otic nerve when the bow is drawn across the catgut, but what happens in the intangible ether, where overtones with certain mathematical frequencies, in certain set series and in certain intensities coalesce and send down to that vibrating catgut string the over-all, in-all and under-all timbre that makes it a violin sound.

Ask any acoustician or organ builder to tell you about the almost mysterious effects that overtones have upon the audible tones.

Music is made up not only of patent elements, but of latent elements as well. It is in the bringing to the surface of as many of these latent things as may be possible, that great musicianship consists. Right notes, correct time, good harmony, well-modulated vocalism, etc.—all these are necessary to a fine performance. But they are not enough. To produce a convincing performance, and I mean by convincing the kind of performance that speaks forcibly to the aesthetical sensibilities of listeners, one must rise to the stratosphere of tonalities where inexplicable things are happening; where the eerie is normal. One must descend, too, to the vaults of the undersoul where profound truths live. Truths from which the fabrics of life and art are woven.

Music is superficial in the sense that it requires a flawless surface complexion. Its surface traits and contours are what first attract the ear. *But music is superficial only in that sense.*

Here I am going to write again the Ground Bass theme, for it is timely to have another look at it: *Music* (after religion and racial prepossessions) *is the most powerful spiritual instrumentality by which human beings can be moved.* The synthesis of some things heard, and many things unheard but sensed. The combination of the obvious and the enigmatical. The scale of the natural climbing through the preternatural to the supernatural.

That is why in the failure to sense the out and beyond elements and values of music one produces only counterfeit sounds.

And that's a good reason why ever since the six months' trip I have urged choral conductors to become expert directors of orchestras. A conductor's responsibility to stimulate the listeners' most highly refined susceptibility places upon him an obligation to draw upon all the resources of music with which he can make himself familiar. If he doesn't want to be that kind of a conductor, he should retire from musical activity and devote himself to a less exacting enterprise.

On each Sunday during the long tour the choir sang Solemn Mass. For the second half of the trip we had two more priests along—Father Peter Moran of the Paulist Fathers, and Father Stephen McPadden, Pastor at Geneva, New York. The latter brought complete sets of Gothic vestments. Thus we were able to exemplify the impressive Liturgy of the Church in many places where people had never had opportunity of witnessing it. In small towns, it was a privilege to place all our forces at the service of the pastor. And so we'd take over completely. Celebrant, deacon, subdeacon, master of ceremonies, acolytes if needed, preacher, organist and choir. Protestants, as well as Catholics, would come in great numbers to the solemn services. One of the most gratifying memories of the tour is the thought that we could and did bring this spiritual experience to many in remote places.

At one town in the South, the pastor, a zealous priest and cultured gentleman, declined to consider our offer for the Solemn Mass unless we would accept a stipend. He couldn't afford a stipend. The parish was poor temporally, but certainly rich spiritually. But he insisted so resolutely that we capitulated. He said that he would give us all over the ordinary Sunday collection. He was pleased as a boy who had knocked a home run, when, after having counted the collection, he presented me with a check for thirty dollars. The entire collection had been thirty-three dollars and some cents. Imagine! The regular collection only three dollars plus! We prevailed upon him to accept our thanks—and the money back.

Some amusing incidents occurred as we wended our way across the country. At a certain Southern town, the pastor met us at the railroad station, explaining with unctuous piety that the audience would be small. He had not used the publicity material. No stories in the newspapers. Window cards, three-sheet and twenty-four sheet posters had been left in bales backstage. He was obviously a simple man. He was so *good* that I shall not try to paint him with a more picturesque adjective. He said that he didn't believe in publicity, but that he and the good Sisters of the school and hospital had prayed every morning and evening that the Lord would fill up the enormous auditorium. Of course, we sang to vast unpeopled spaces. The simple priest concluded that it had not been God's will for a large audience to gather. How pious people can so readily discover the Eternal Will of Almighty God has always mystified me. At any rate, that night we performed for the priest (the Sisters were not allowed to attend), a few altar boys and the janitor who probably did not sit through the program.

At a town in Virginia, we were booked at a large auditorium not far from an army cantonment. A group of soldiers was in the audience, having been intrigued probably by the name "choristers." Perhaps, they expected to attend a musical revue with a couple of rows of New York chorus girls adding terpsichorean *élan* to the music. How gravely disappointed they must have been to see a group of boys and men march out and settle into the serious business of interpreting classical music! Presently, they could endure the strain no longer. Precisely at the discordant climax of Archangelsky's "Meditation on the Day of Judgment," where it was my custom to indicate a *grande pausa,* one of the military lads rose and said in a loud voice: "This is a H—of a show." They clattered out and collected their money at the box office.

At New Orleans, we were met at the station by a committee who quickly placed us in open automobiles, saying that our train was very late. Actually, our train was on time. I could not understand the ado and fussbudgeting of the men in charge of what turned out to be a prearranged parade through the important streets of the city—but a parade featuring Charlie Chaplin.

I was seated in the tonneau of the car which the throngs on the sidewalks estimated to be Charlie's car. They didn't enthuse over me. I was no substitute for the popular comedian. Who could be? And especially in a Roman collar? Deadliness! Of course, nowadays it would be different. Since Spencer Tracy made the Roman collar acceptable in *Boys' Town* and Bing Crosby did even more in Leo McCarey's inimitable *Going My Way* and *The Bells of St. Mary's,* the clerical garb would not elicit the frowns and scowls and sardonic satires that I experienced on my "pinchhiting" ride for the little comic of the silent films. Chaplin and Finn got mixed up in the Delta city. And I didn't enjoy the confusion.

Old Baton Rouge, Louisiana, and then Texas. Nine stops in that state. From Beaumont to El Paso. The audiences were easy to sing to, and although the schedule was hard, we took it in the long easy stride of the traditional Texan. At Austin we had fun with the acoustics of the Capitol where we were pleased to sing a program for the Governor. We could hear chords floating about under the dome while we were singing different chords in the concourse on the street floor. But the effect was not disturbing as was the running back and forth of chords in the Coliseum at St. Louis, about which Mr. Campanini had warned me. I don't remember feeling the need of using the special devices which I was forced to employ in the Missouri city.

I have a vague recollection of sensing a sort of patronizing attitude on the part of the audiences at San Antonio. There seemed to be a little more of the thing one has to sing through at Boston and Philadelphia. Probably it was only an impression.

But sometimes impressions are true notions stimulated by facts. I remember, in this connection, an incident in the Auditorium at Chicago. The opera *Faust* was to begin. The basso Auguste Huberdeau had asked me to meet him at the theater before the performance. We descended together to the trap upon which presently he was to rise to the stage for the old-fashioned entrance of Mephistopheles. Faust was singing above. Then the chorus sang. It was about a half tone off pitch. I exclaimed to Huberdeau: "Gus, that chorus is very flat, I hope the chorus master will check them, or they'll ruin the performance."

"Nonsense" he rejoined, allowing no criticism of his beloved opera company. "It is only an impression that you have. Listen! They are truly on the pitch." I sent him up on his trap hoping that he would not follow their example and sing his lead a semitone off.

At any rate, the San Antonians and the other Texans whom we encountered were in general a kindly people, and it was a pleasure to sing for them.

All through the South and Southwest we found that audiences were interested in the best we had to offer. Of course, the "Mockingbird" lad was sure to receive an ovation, and the other solo boys came in for a good share of applause.

One of these solo boys, Billy Probst, was a stunt boy; that is, he was not entrusted with important arias or arioso pieces. Later, when we had moved to New York, he became a very brilliant aria boy. Some potential solo boys were not quite ready for public performances. Richard Finn was an attractive lad, with unusual voice, and, after some weeks of public appearances, he became a dependable member of the solo staff. Another lad, Hallet Dolan, discovered himself to me as ready for public singing at the rehearsal on Easter Day at New York. He developed with amazing rapidity into a top-grade artist. He was among the greatest solo boys in the long history of the Choristers. He had voice, intelligence and fine feeling for interpretative fitness.

But, generally, the audiences in Texas were more intent on the motets than many audiences elsewhere.

At El Paso, a throng reported at the entrance to the new auditorium which, I think, we were dedicating that evening. So many crowded into the aisles, with all available seating space occupied, that the Fire Chief came on stage and announced that if the "extras" did not leave the hall immediately, he would order the concert canceled. Some determined Texans looked and acted as if they didn't mind in the least if the performance were called off if they were to be excluded. Finally the extras were prevailed upon to go, and the program began. At Portland, Maine, some few years earlier, we had difficulty with overcrowding, but this was principally in the streets surrounding the Auditorium. The El Paso Fire Chief talked to me in such a tone of voice as to intimate that I was personally to blame for the confusion. But we had a good time, sang a fine concert and said a reluctant farewell to the Lone Star State.

Only one more town before entraining for the legendary land of palm trees and orange groves—California. The cinema industry was in its early phases, then, and so no thoughts of glamorous Hollywood competed with the simple idea of going to the loveliest part of our country. As a matter of fact, after one of the concerts at Los Angeles, an agent of a picture company approached me with a request to discuss the feasibility of our making a picture. It would have been a silent, of course, and no good purpose would be served by our boys and men going through a trumped-up scenario with me trying to ride a charging steed. It would have been only a publicity stunt, and there was more conservatism about stunts then than nowadays.

At Albuquerque, New Mexico, we nearly lost a leading tenor. In less than the few hours from breakfast to concert time, he had fallen in love with a New Mexico charmer, decided to marry her and settle down in that locale. Some of his colleagues told me of the situation, as we waited on the platform for the train. "Sighing like a furnace," the smitten young man was on the platform bidding adieu to the group. He avoided me assiduously. However, knowing that he would make a great error in judgment by acting so precipitately in so serious a matter, I told the men to lift him bodily onto the train. They complied.

Presently I sought the sobbing chap, telling him that if he felt the same way a week later, I would send him back to Albuquerque. Next evening he sheepishly approached, saying that he was very grateful for having been deterred from fulfilling his insensate plan. He was a splendid fellow who had had a touch of Southwestern romance, underlined by the flashing eyes of the señorita.

We had one other case like that. A baritone, this time, was wounded by a sharp dart from the bow of Eros, in Montana, where one would scarce reasonably expect to come upon quick-working romantic influences. He was all for remaining in Butte, but we shanghaied him to Salt Lake City. He recovered completely in that city, where, in years gone by, matrimony, much matrimony, was highly favored!

We had no real casualties at any time during the long tour, although a small boy narrowly escaped death when a speeding express rushed through a Texas town while we awaited our train. God was good to us. We had had much illness in New England and New York State, but the patients recovered, and "Aspirin Annie" kept the outfit in order with the little pellets of crystalline compound which she dispensed. It became a legend that she could remedy any disorder, save a broken bone, with the white tablets.

When we crossed the Colorado River, dividing Arizona and California, we were looking straight into the setting sun. It was a lovely eventide. The great river bringing the cold power of the north to the warm sensitiveness of the south. The end of one desert, the beginning of another. We crossed the river and were at last in California. There was something about being in that great state that is difficult to tell. Not only its high mountains and low valleys, its flowers and fruits, its mighty ocean coastline, its curiously beautiful nooks such as Carmel-by-the-Sea, gave the assurance to Easterners and Midwesterners that California had a definite personality, unique and proper to itself, but also the pictures one could see in the sky of Father Serra and his Franciscan companions making the long trek from San Diego to Sonoma, establishing the great chain of missions. The climate and history of California had, even before the days of the Hollywood exploitation, captured the fancy of people who lived in less of a fairyland. And so, when we alighted at Needles, we were under the spell of an aesthetical reverence.

Navajo Indians had been notified by the Santa Fe officials that we would sing our first California concert for them on the platform of the railroad station. My impression of this informal concert for the Indians is that both braves and squaws were puzzled if not amazed by the sudden bursting into harmony of a large group of boys and men. Probably they had not heard such sounds before. Small boys climbing the heights and basses sinking to profound depths. The very high and the very low together. The young and the old. And all the while the red of the setting sun making strange consonance with the silvery ripples of the great

Colorado River nearby. One could not be sure of the reactions of the Indians. When the trainman signaled us to reboard our sleepers, the Chief acknowledged our offering with a courteous, resonant *basso-cantante* "Ugh!"

Our first professional concert in California was in Balboa Park, San Diego. There was a mammoth audience. Humphrey Stewart played the organ with us. I had conducted his *Nativity* (first performance with orchestra) years before at Chicago with the Chicago Symphony Orchestra. He was "doing us one back." And how well he did it! I was obliged to concentrate on conducting from the angle of out-of-doors audibility. It was no easy matter, in those days, for a conductor who was not well experienced in al fresco concertizing to make a composition sound right. Various voice lines would seem to disappear suddenly. A gust of wind in the wrong direction would carry all voice lines out of hearing. Suddenly the direction of the wind would change and augment a delicate passage into an unlovely noise. Probably the serious attention which the al fresco difficulties forced me to give to the mechanics of conducting was good discipline for me, because for many weeks the choir had really been conducting itself, my contribution from the podium being a hint or two about acoustical conditions and an occasional frown or smile. When I left the stand at Balboa Park, I knew that I had had a thorough workout.

We started on the long series from Long Beach, California, to Victoria on Vancouver Island in excellent condition. We were at our best. Morale was good. Enthusiasm and interest in little things replaced the deadly apathy with which we had gone through some weeks of concerts at the beginning of the tour. But apathy had never interfered with the validity of our performances. It meant only that we found it hard going. Drab railroad rides. Drab theatres. Occasionally drab audiences. But along the Pacific Coast we walked, thought, talked and sang as though charged with electricity. Alternating current one day; direct, the next. High voltage. And the flashes were felt all along the Coast, through the San Joaquin Valley, and clear through Oregon and Washington. In fact, the electrification we took on in California lasted for the rest of the tour, making it possible for us to present our finest over-all program at the Chicago Auditorium on the last day of June.

The Sels-Floto Circus were our friendly rivals up the San Joaquin and beyond, playing the same towns on the same days as far as and including Oakland. The boys watched the circus parade a half dozen times, noting the features so keenly that they would prophecy whether or not such and such an act would give a good, mediocre or poor performance that day. The circus players whom I met daily in the railroad stations impressed me most favorably. Traveling and working with a carnival must be a tough experience and I am glad to record here that the many performers with whom I had casual conversations were refined and often genteel people. We couldn't attend their performances because our units were working at the same time, but some of their trapeze, tightrope and equestrian performers managed to come back stage for a number or two each night. The "Mockingbird" was frequently in peril of being mothered to death. "What a darling little boy!" a fair equestrienne would exclaim. Etc., etc. But though he was an exceptionally fine and reliable lad, he certainly was not a "darling." Two-fisted. Real. But the facility with which he could run up and down the ladder of roulades in the obligato over the chorus, and the simplicity of his manner, made audiences generally think him "too cute for words."

There are not many outstanding features of the Pacific Coast series to record. Some interesting incidents come to mind, but the series as a whole was just consistently satisfactory day after day. At Los Angeles, we, on tour for France, sang the Solemn Mass in the German Church at the urgent request of the German Rector. An out-of-doors concert in a clearing of a great orange grove at Monrovia was a delightful and unusual experience. At San Francisco, the Choristers paraded in uniform from the Ferry Building to the City Hall where the Mayor gave us the keys of the city. At that time, the official organist of the great instrument at the Civic Auditorium was enforcing a regulation of his own which forbade other players to perform on the organ there. So, when Mayor Rolph had presented the keys, Mrs. Cecilia Cudahy Casserly, very active in promoting cultural undertakings in San Francisco, and at that moment, ranking officer of the Red Cross, spoke up: "Your Honor, Mr. Mayor, this means that Father Finn will be permitted to play the great organ?" Mr. Mayor had given us the freedom of the city, and therefore acquiesced graciously.

Mr. Clarence Eddy, celebrated American organist, gave a luncheon for me at the Bohemian Club. Many organists and conductors attended. When I told them that I was to play the mammoth organ, they unanimously urged me not to make the attempt. "You'll find all the controls mixed up. Right side gadgets are on the left. Mr. ——— had everything changed around so that no one but himself could manage it." I thanked them for their solicitude and warning, but I knew that the combination of Mrs. Casserly's will and the old sturdy New Englandism would force me on to the bench. And of course it did. I went up some hours in advance of the performance to examine the instrument and to make a diagram of stop and controls positions which I memorized.

There was a vast audience. As great as the audience a week earlier for that peerless combination, Galli-Curci and John McCormack. The arch-bishop, governor, mayor, judiciary, presidents of colleges, a cross section of the very varied citizenry of San Francisco.

Good old Mr. Eddy was in a row near the stage. I played the opening number, a fairly simple and therefore safe piece such as the "Grand Choeur" by Theodore Dubois. It went along uneventfully. I had set as many gadgets as possible in the afternoon. No terrifying blasts unex-pectedly coming from loud trombone pipes. No sudden discontinuances of sound when I made a shift from one tone color to another. I knew that Mr. Eddy was very nervous. I think, too, that he was irritated by my boldness. But when I finished without mishap, he beamed a cordial smile upon me, and when I descended to the stage to begin to conduct, he led the great audience in another round of applause. That was a great night for us. If we had not been schooled into almost automatic control of our resources by five months of consecutive appearances, we might have failed to come through with the kind of a performance demanded by the occasion. The soprano boys mesmerized the throng, and the solo boys were as effective as the leading divas of the Metropolitan Opera would have been. It was amusing, during ensuing days, to hear com-ments about the parity of effectiveness of Galli-Curci and the little "Mockingbird."

After a heavy schedule at Sacramento where again we sang in a state Capitol, we left the land of sunshine (plus fog!) and went northwards. At Portland, Oregon, Archbishop Christie took us in hand. He gave us plenty to do. Morning concert for the Sisters. Regular matinee and evening concerts. Solemn Mass next day at the Cathedral.

Then Tacoma, Seattle, Bellingham, Victoria, Vancouver.

By that time we had become so thoroughly accustomed to producing mystical effects and to influencing all audiences in about the same man-ner and degree, that we paid little attention to comments, either from the people or from the press. We have in our files the reviews of the Fountain Pens covering the entire tour. It is interesting to note that the Pens all wrote in the same style. The professional critics in the East, Midwest, South, Southwest and the Far West made almost identical comments, choosing the same features to discuss, such as the spirituality of the over-all effect, the disembodied volatileness of the soprano tone, the unification of each voice line and the blend of all the lines with no gaps between.

I had learned long before, that, after the single voice lines have been properly developed, a system for fusing all lines must be worked out and applied with painstaking care. There are too many wide interstices between the component voice lines of most choruses. Through these interstices the mystery of concerted music slips away. Therefore, there must not be any interstices. I have not yet ceased to look for further means, beyond those already long in use in my various singing units, for improving the fusion of the parts. Sopranos borrowing from and giving to basses; altos from and to the tenors and vice versa; minor chords telling major chords to be calm; majors telling the minors to cheer up. We devised a scheme for rehearsing symphonically, to wit, with a concord of colors which would be mutually complementary and supplementary. This technique has been published.* But I am still seeking and searching. The recent announcement from the scientists of the American Bell Telephone Company, that instruments have been constructed which produce tones never heard before, indicates the wide field of research that any zealous conductor of choral or orchestral music must plow.

One of the most contributory factors to the oneness of a chorus is frequent singing in six and eight parts. In multipart compositions the voice lines are close together as a rule, and such closeness establishes a kinship between parts which is not disturbed when the harmony is open and the parts at a distance from one another, as in three and four part music. As a family close-knitted at home is never really separated even when members are at opposite ends of the world. The four-part singing of the average chorus suggests the lack of solidity which is characteristic of a family, dining together and going through all the other motions of living together, in which there are few common interests and no reciprocal enthusiasms.

Our programs for those many months included much intimate multipart singing. Gradually we were able quite unwittingly to evoke almost the same aura from a four-part as from an eight-part chord. Blend had become a personality trait of the unit. Teamwork in all its implications. No great gap between sopranos and altos, through which one might drive a model T.

Therefore, the concluding weeks of the long tour brought no surprises because of press notices or private comments. Musicians frequently asked questions about the basic system upon which we operated. But it was futile to attempt to explain in a few sentences principles and precepts which by that time we were following by second nature. Routine was observed almost without effort by boys and men. Rarely were members late for appointments. Ahead of time in theaters and at railroad stations. No serious disciplinary problems. And so we headed happily eastward for the final part of the tour. Not much more to do.

* Finn, *The Art of the Choral Conductor* (Boston: Birchard, 1939).

Spokane, Helena, Butte, Salt Lake City, Omaha, Kansas City and Chicago. The Solemn Mass at the Cathedral in Salt Lake City for Bishop Glass was a beautiful ritualistic pageant. At Kansas City, the heat was intense. We might have been back in the San Joaquin Valley of California. But the Midwestern heat seemed more oppressive. And we were perspiring with the hot eagerness to be home! The two days at Kansas City seemed a fortnight. We sang good-bye to the "road" in the concourse of the railroad station, and the mighty chords which emerged from the large chorus were as great music as any we had made in New York or San Francisco. Of course it was not good-bye to the road for many of us, because we had consummated arrangements to leave Chicago to establish headquarters in New York, and the long years of barnstorming ahead make the Kansas City "good-bye" a satire, in retrospect.

However, at the moment and for many of our singers, the farewell to daily railroad jumps, matinees and evening performances was real. There was some display of emotion even among the older men. They were glad to be through, but there was a sense of reluctance to be finished with so great an adventure. That funny psychological ragout: glad sadness or sad gladness! Many lifelong friendships developed from the association of boys with boys and men with men.

One factor which had contributed to the successful conduct of the tour was the spontaneousness with which the boys avoided the men and the men the boys. We had made no announcement about this matter, but in spite of the friendliness which all had for all, the wholesome arrangement of boys with boys and men with men just happily happened.

At a suburban station in Chicago, I was notified that the father of two boys had been dead some months. Would I please tell them the sad fact? And so the last responsibility of the six months' trip was difficult and depressing. Great crowds met our train with much cheering and general ballyhoo. The final concert took place at the Auditorium Theater on the afternoon of June 30 before a sold-out house. Members of the organization who had been unable to make the tour reinforced our ranks. Arthur Kraft, one of America's greatest lyric tenors and a most successful present-day teacher, slipped into the tenor line with the ease of the true artist. It was a gala day. The group that was to accompany me to New York was allowed a week's leave at home. Then this group would depart for a summer villa which I had engaged near Peekskill, New York, where young candidates from the Great Metropolis would join them. The New York continuation of the original Chicago organization would begin there.

Fourteen years as a Chicago organization! We did the spade work there. We planted the seeds, and during the six months' trip had the satisfaction of observing the Ground Bass prove itself.

From 1910 to 1940 the Paulist Choristers had the good fortune of the enthusiastic services of an archivist, Mr. P. M. O'Connell of Chicago. He moved to New York with the Choristers in 1918. He prepared many books of records and critiques which preserve the story of the organization. His ardent interest in the chorus was almost sufficient in itself to urge the boys and men always to maintain the highest ideals.

Here ends the first half of my musical career. I had learned much. But I had and still have much to learn. Certain progress up the slopes of Parnassus, but much sliding backwards. Persistent seeking and groping found me fairly well on the trail of the Muses.

But how far, how very far from the peak where Apollo and Euterpe tuned their lutes!

Chapter XX   *How Will You Like Man-hattan for a Home, Ground Bass?*

BOUND for New York! Drawn there by the magnetic needle of the greatest city in the world. It was one thing to invade New York for a few days, giving carefully prepared concert programs, and quite another to be heading there with the prospect of taking up permanent residence. Chicago was and is a large city. The second city of our nation. But it was and is a second city. New York is not only a first city, but *the* first city, the metropolis, the cosmopolis of the world. A first anything is necessarily different from a second. There is a gap which one cannot span psychologically.

Many have achieved success elsewhere, only to locate in New York and suffer discomfiture, disappointment and decisive defeat. Oh, yes! Big toad in fourth, third and second cities, but tadpole in Gotham! Sopranos, contraltos, tenors and basses who had warbled to the delight of villages, towns and cities, thinking themselves good enough for the Big Town, were annihilated by it. From small hall-bedrooms, hundreds have gone back home to help in papa's grocery store and to sing in the local choir. Conductors who wielded ebony batons with ivory tips in the hinterland, daring the cold, pitiless, and altogether derisive attitude of the Manhattaners who could make or break one, have hidden themselves in obscure positions, earning pittances instead of amassing fame and fortune, and in many cases have bought tickets for the lowest price transportation back to the hometown.

I was thinking about such unpleasant things as I drove from Chicago to the summer establishment where the Chicago and New York boys would meet for preliminary efforts to establish a great treble unit for the New York Choristers. I could not forget our reception by the New York critics in 1909. Arthur "Bugs" Baer, in a recent edition of the *New York Journal-American,* indicates the trend of the thoughts which beset me during that journey and the truth which all who have tried to work in the artistic crafts in New York keenly realize. Baer's wisecrack sums up the relevant facts thus: "New York is a city of subways and skyscrapers—either above everything or below it." Yes! in New York, you're high up or low down. You're great, very great, or small, very small. Of course, if you belong here, or, having come from afar, do not strut about like something important, New York lets you ride the buses and street cars on the surface, paying no attention to you. But strut or puff your chest out a bit, and New York will either toss you with cheers to the top of the Empire State Building, or drop you through the nearest air vent of the subway.

Of course there is a lot of fake about it all. But, there it is! If you're good, you must be always better. If you're mediocre, look up the timetables.

Well! we were coming into such a place. No more meeting friendly friends in the Chicago Loop who would exclaim: "Oh! how *divinely* the Choristers sang last Sunday!" Or: "What a magnificent concert you gave at Orchestra Hall last week!" Rather this in New York, if, by chance, anyone recognized you save the nearby traffic cops:" Are you living in New York now? Have you a choir? Yes? Well! one day I'll probably get around to hearing it. Toodle!"

New York, at the time of our arrival well over a quarter of a century ago, boasted of several celebrated musical organizations. The Philharmonic Society and the New York Symphony Orchestra, with the orchestral ensemble of the Metropolitan Opera House, sometimes masquerading as the Victor Herbert Orchestra. The New York Oratorio Society. The Musical Art (a cappella) Society. The Metropolitan Opera. Chamber music quartets. Several loudly acclaimed church choirs, such as the choirs of St. Bartholomew's, Grace Church, the Brick Church, St. John the Divine's, etc. The choir at St. Patrick's Cathedral was not then regarded as a musical unit of significance, although before 1904 it was well esteemed. Several conductors were firmly established as the ne plus ultra's of America: Drs. Walter and Frank Damrosch, Louis Koemmenich, Toscanini, Stransky, Miles Farrow, Arthur Hyde, Dr. George Edward Stubbs. Kurt Schindler was beginning to draw a kindly radiance from the spotlights. Henderson, Krehbiel, Gilman, Pitts-Sanborn were forecasting the triumphs or penning the obituaries of performers. Belasco, the Frohmans, Dillingham, George Cohan and the Shuberts were calling the turns in the theatrical world.

An insularism which was and is definitely Manhattanism prevailed. If one stepped on the soil of the island of the Astors and Vanderbilts from an ocean liner incoming from the Continent, one might have a fair chance of displaying his goods, but the unfortunates, speaking Midwestern English upon arrival at the sarcophagus of the Indians who had sold out the terrain of Manhattan for liquor, were well advised not to bother opening their sample-cases.

Yes, my friends, it was and still is a hazard of dimensions to set up shop in New York. A Van Dyke beard, a semi-intelligible broken English, press-agent publicity from Paris, Milan or Berlin (London did not count for much in New York, although in Anglophile Boston a recommendation of Covent Garden sounded well!) would boost a chap for a few weeks. A gangplank interview gave a newcomer at least sufficient time to hunt for that subtle force, that potent essence, that altogether indispensable patronage, which the rich or socially elect could furnish. But alighting from the Erie, the Lackawanna, the West Shore, or even the New York Central or Pennsylvania, the newcomer would sense almost immediately that marked cards would be used in the New York game, and that he did not know the markings.

That's a picture of the locale in which we were about to take up our abode. Leaving Chicago, a great city as far as population can make any city great, where human and fraternal feelings dominated lives and efforts; moving to New York, where much would depend upon artificial standards—upon money, upon the prestige of being invited to social functions on the aristocratic streets traversing Fifth Avenue, upon one's acceptability to the Dowager Queens and Top-hatted Dudes. This was a line of thought which depressed me all through the trip eastward and for many ensuing years.

Well! we had started for the First City and its ice floes! Good luck or bad luck, approving or disapproving dowagers, we were going to lay our Ground Bass as a cornerstone amid all the queer noises, physical, temperamental and psychic, of New York, the Great Enigma of the modern world!

PART TWO

Chapter XXI *The Ground Bass Goes into Fugal Development*

PERHAPS the frequent reference to the Ground Bass during the telling of the first part of this story was a bit irksome. But since that basic theme was and still is the impelling force of my musical activities, it is not unreasonable to allude to it occasionally. In this second part of the tale, the Ground Bass shows itself with increasing clearness, because, as in the Bach theme of the Passacaglia, to which I likened my motivating theme, it manifests itself in all sorts of positions and circumstances. Bach worked his theme out, for its most potent and substantial effects, in the fugue with which he concluded the opus. Do you know what a fugue is?

Many concertgoers know, as well as the average musician, that a fugue is a strict form of composition, in which one voice line announces a subject, another voice line answers this subject in a different key, a third voice line repeats the subject in the original key (sometimes delayed by an ornamental episode) at a different pitch, and the fourth voice line, higher or lower than the second voice line, answers in the second key. Then, after the four voice lines have presented the original theme, many developments, embellishments and ornate figures appear, the main subject, however, being always hinted at, and often clearly underlined. The word fugue is derived from the Latin *fuga,* which means a *"flight."* As Percy Scholes puts it, in his *Oxford Companion to Music*: "The idea seems to be that the opening of a composition of this sort gives the idea of each 'voice,' as it enters, chasing the preceding one, which flies before it." The last part of a fugue is usually a stretto, a movement in which the material is gathered into close quarters, each voice line following more closely upon the heels of the others than in the first exposition of the theme.

This definition of a fugue is not academic. But it is the kind of definition proper for these pages. This book is not a textbook. I must remind myself continually that it is a collection of reminiscences put together in

227

such fashion as to underline a basic explanation, viz., the motivation
which urged me to risk the perilous journey to the home of the Muses
and to persevere in the ascent of Mount Parnassus even when knees and
knuckles were abraded and the going was hard.

In this second part of the account of my journey, I find the Ground
Bass, or motivating theme, manifesting itself much after the fashion of
a fugue. All the essential elements have long since entered. Many epi-
sodic tassels have been appended and I can see the stretto coming around
the bend. I hope that the stretto will assemble itself effectively.

There was a lot of fun in the unfolding of the theme up to 1918.
In spite of inadequate resources, we were a rich organization. Rich in
the loyalty of the members. The boys and men were made of a special
material which God probably keeps in Heaven for special purposes.
They were determined, urbane, sensitive to aesthetics, spiritual. So,
when the boys who were to form the nucleus of the New York chorus
were told that they could have only a few days' holidays at home, there
was little demurring. They would be gone practically a whole year this
time. They would live together in a choir school. Sort of humdrum. A
new experience. Different from flitting from town to town as on the
six months' tour. But they were anxious for further adventures with
the Boss.

Before arriving at Chicago in June, I had arranged with my brother-
in-law, Ignace Panzer, to rent a summer place whither the Chicago boys
could immediately repair to meet the New York lads who with them
would make what we optimistically hoped would be the greatest choral
unit of its kind in the history of music. Mr. Panzer chose the most
suitable place he could find near New York City, in the short time at his
disposal. But it wasn't much of a place. It was too far back from the
Hudson River to make swimming arrangements easy and comfortable.
There was a vast acreage. A gas engine pump which was supposed to
furnish the water supply to the main house and cottages was usually out
of order. My principal recollection of that summer of 1918 has to do
with this pump. Of course, I was motoring into the city almost daily to
play the organ at St. Paul the Apostle's Church, giving morning and
evening rehearsals to the boys, and making trips to Peekskill to keep the
larder replenished. But the outstanding memory of that summer was the
persistent capriciousness of the pump. Perhaps that was a good thing
for me. I had just finished one of the greatest tours ever undertaken by
a choral group, and was in the initial stages of building a New York
organization into the dimensions of virtuosity. It was probably psychologically advantageous to be obliged to concentrate on hydraulics and
gas engine pumps, being forced off an engrossing aesthetic front a good

part of the time for a few weeks. "Pressure and valves, 'Willie'; not timbres."

We arrived at the Oscawanna, New York, summer place early in July. Soprano boys from St. Paul's Church in New York came out to be examined as to their adaptability to our purposes. The boys' and men's choir at St. Paul's had enjoyed a splendid reputation as a Gregorian chant choir for many decades. Under the direction of Father Alfred Young, C.S.P., and Sir Edmund Hurley, the choir had become favorably known to the hierarchy of the country and was commended by all liturgists who attended the services in large numbers. This choir sang the Gregorian chant in the now abrogated style, using the Montreal edition. Long and short notes were sung almost in the fashion of modern music, whereas, according to the findings of the monks of Solesmes, all notes of whatever shape should be sung with practically equal temporal value. The Paulist Gregorian Choir sang much of the chant in harmonized version, too.

The boys and men had developed a commendable facility in singing Sir Edmund Hurley's ingenious arrangements. And Sir Edmund supplied organ accompaniments that were amazing. Sir Edmund was an extraordinarily fine musician. What is known among the directors of boy choirs as the "unqualified chest tone" was the prevailing timbre of the boys. Soprano boys who could put extra resonance into low notes addressed their arytenoid cartileges to the alto parts. As a student, going through New York, I used to be much impressed with the general effect of the liturgical services at which this choir assisted. The Paulist services had long been the finest exemplification of the Liturgy to be observed in North America. But the singing as singing left something to be desired.

When the New York boys came to Oscawanna for examination, I found myself on a difficult spot. To be hypercritical about these boys' vocal condition would have savored of smugness; perhaps of arrogance. And yet to admit boys, wholesale whose vocal mechanism had been damaged by coarse intonation on the New York streets would have been to invite defeat for our New York undertaking.

It was important that, at the first feasible moment, the reconstructed New York Paulist Choristers would appear, exemplifying all the excellences of the former Chicago unit. We were brought to New York to solidify those virtues and to expand as a group could be expected to expand only in such a metropolis as the First City.

The plan of transferring the Paulist Choristers from Chicago to New York was in the making for some three years. Sir Edmund had been failing in health. In 1915, during my sojourn at Toronto, I was summoned to New York to play the Easter services in his stead.

In 1916 Mr. Charles M. Schwab invited a group of the Chicago Choristers to give a program at his Riverside Drive mansion, indicating on that occasion that it would give him satisfaction to underwrite us if we were to move our headquarters to New York. Mr. Schwab, his organist Archer Gibson and myself had a few conferences at various later dates. Patently, Mr. Schwab wished to be our patron in New York. Sir Edmund Hurley died in April, 1918, and Father John Hughes, Superior-General of the Paulist Fathers, notified me to report to New York immediately upon the conclusion of the six months' trip, to assume the direction of the New York Choristers. Father Hughes and Monsignor George Waring, Vicar-General of the then recently organized Military Ordinariate, co-operated in the matter of securing a substitute for me as Chaplain of the Chicago University Club's Base Unit Hospital. Being physically unfit for military service, I was easily removed from the active list, although to this day I have never received any official discharge papers. Perhaps I could collect back salary for all these years? Probably not! In spite of having been notified, while at Los Angeles, by the War Department to report at Fort Des Moines, Iowa, on July first, I was later instructed by a Paulist superior to disregard the notice, considering my physical lameness, and to proceed to New York.

Well! I arrived at Oscawanna with the fully developed plan of opening a choir school. The operating of such a school had been my determination for years. The records of all the superlative boys' and men's choirs in the history of music indicate a choir school to be a prime necessity. By superlative choirs, I mean the great institutes whose names have been associated with the highest ideals of music. The Sistine. St. Stephen's in Vienna. St. Paul's, London. St. Thomas Schule, Leipzig. Canterbury. Westminster. Durham. York. Ely. Etc.

The choir school was the great historical background for the developopment of choral virtuosity.

Considering its importance in the history of concerted song, and the place it had in my plans for the Paulist Choristers, I think it opportune to set down here a few facts concerning this unique type of school. Tradition has it that Pope St. Sylvester in the early fourth century established a school of this sort, and that in the sixth century Pope Pelagius II co-operated with the Benedictine Fathers in the maintenance of a choir school near the Lateran Basilica. In the same epoch, similar institutes were founded at Reichenau, St. Gaul and Metz. The establishment of these *scholae cantorum* extended soon to England. In England, the choir school received its most comprehensive development. The school at Windsor (St. George's Chapel) was opened by royal mandate.

St. Paul's Choir School in London has probably served as the outstanding model for modern schools.

The advantages accruing to a choir from a well managed choir school are manifold. First there is the good discipline of the choristers. Not only correct conduct, but correct thinking about conduct. Then comes the *esprit de corps* which is more readily fostered in such a school than where the boys are merely assembled on certain days for rehearsing. Add to these the further advantages of a private education in the humanities, the prevailing atmosphere of quiet which discourages vocal abuses, the daily opportunity of vocalizing, the learning of the theory of music and the mastering of a great repertory of compositions. In a choir school the urbaneness of the art as a whole is appreciated. Sensitiveness to the latencies of music is indisputably an invaluable asset in choristers, and the growth of this in a school where boys live together, almost as monks, is assured as an inevitable by-product of the other features.

No great choir of boys and men has endured long without the background of a specially directed boarding school, with the possible exception of Brompton Oratory, where a day school was maintained. Perhaps, too, the Temple Choir of London is an exception. I am not clear about its history. Since the Reformation, the Church of England has operated the choir schools founded by Catholic bishops or monks. With Catholic foundation money! The only outstanding Catholic choir school today, within the limits of my knowledge, is at Westminster Cathedral, London. Goudimel, Palestrina, Giovanni Annimuccia, Ingegneri, Kuhnau, Bach and the other master singers and composers of the polyphonic and Handelian era were each at one time or another entrusted with the care, keep and supervision of the education of soprano boys.

In my first days in England I came quickly to the conclusion that if a truly great choir employing boy sopranos was to be reared and maintained with any degree of permanence, a choir school would have to be established necessarily. And to emphasize this I put it in Latin: *Ex necessitate rei*. So, when I left Chicago for New York, I had clearly in mind the founding of such an establishment. Of course, the European and English schools were all endowed. I had no endowment. I had nothing but the orally expressed interest of Mr. Schwab (he kept his pen in his pocket), the reputation of the Choristers, and the possible co-operation of wealthy Catholics in Gotham on which to rely. It turned out that these resources were too thin a substitute for an actual endowment.

But I'm getting ahead of my story. The fact is that we arrived at the summer villa at Oscawanna, did the necessary things preliminary to reorganizing and in late August moved into New York City, having rented from the Guggenheims the charming little Gothic house on the corner of Seventy-second Street and Riverside Drive. Number Three Riverside Drive!

We were all quite set up about the undertaking. We were one block south of Mr. Schwab's house. Some people said that I had selected that spot with the deliberate purpose of being so close to the tycoon that he would be ever conscious of the boys' nearness. But the fact is that Number Three was the only suitable place available, near enough to the Paulist Church to simplify the matter of transportation.

Sight-seeing bus drivers would call out to the passengers as they passed, "Number 3—the Home of the famous Paulist Choristers." The boys loved to hear that. So did I!

We moved into the quaint Gothic house before it was possible to furnish it adequately. Presently, however, we had a full complement of simple furniture. Our refectory was arranged in unusual fashion. Long tables had been constructed which ran along the walls on three sides of the room. The boys sat at tables on the sides nearest the walls. This made quite an unusual but serviceable arrangement, for the waiters (the boys themselves in turn) could readily serve the viands from the outer sides of the tables without reaching over the heads or shoulders of seated boys. No one had his back to anyone. We all were in full view of one another. I had seen this arrangement at a luncheon program which we sang for Mrs. James T. Harahan of Chicago some years before. At that luncheon, the hostess moved her chair from one spot to another in the unoccupied zone, and was able to see and converse freely with all her guests.

We started off well. The servants were admirable. Good food and well prepared. We had a little private chapel and a splendid rehearsal room. Regarding the latter, however, I remember the strange phenomenon of the inability of the boys to sing E natural on the fourth space true to pitch. Probably an acoustical idiosyncrasy of the room accounted for this, because in the churches and halls in which we sang we had no difficulty with the note.

We had arrived in New York with a reputation for high choral achievement. The public would expect us to sustain that reputation. It would surprise the public and do us harm to appear in church services and at other public functions without our reputed excellences unmistakably discernible. Of course, we had the soprano tone quality of the large number of boys who had come from Chicago. The New York boys would gradually cultivate the same timbres and general tonal facility. Also, our alto line was well taken care of, for several countertenors from the Chicago unit soon reported at Number Three. But we were faced with the immediate need of organizing a tenor and bass section which would speedily fit into the tonal picture of the boys and countertenors. This constituted a real difficulty.

Many of the young tenors and basses of New York were in the armed forces. Older and experienced men had already been signed up by New York churches. I had only a limited number of applicants whose vocal and technical equipment were in any degree promising. Eventually I assembled a motley chorus of adult singers. Many of these gentlemen have since passed into the other world, so it is not ungentle to them, on my part, to aver that some of the sounds to which they gave utterance could only with excessive latitude be classified according to categories of musical intonation. Mournful, threnodic wailing on the tenor line; hollow, sepulchral droning on the bass line. Altogether, a choral caricature. But what to do? One had to have tenors and basses and so I took on these strange sound-blowers with the feeble hope that I might recreate their vocalization. As far as the adult section was concerned, we started off badly. At Solemn Mass at the Paulist Church, I would shiver and shake with apprehension whenever an important phrase that depended upon the tenors and basses for effective presentation would appear.

The funny old two-manual pipe organ in the Church was called upon to qualify these peculiar tone qualities of the men's section in every piece undertaken. After a while, however, Mr. John Finnegan, tenor of St. Patrick's Cathedral, a fine lyric artist and a zealous worker, joined us for evening services and concerts. Then the Armistice came. From that time, the men's chorus began to improve and before the end of the season we had an admirable assortment of voices. The first few months were almost terrifying, however, considering the high esteem in which the Chicago unit had come to be held, and the nature and number of engagements which we were obliged to accept.

Monsignor Michael Lavelle, Rector of the Cathedral, from the start directed to us all seekers for Catholic participation in musical programs. The first of the highly publicized programs in which we took part at his request was at Old Madison Square Garden. It was the last financial rally of the war by combined religious agencies. Catholics, Protestants and Jews all collaborated in a mammoth drive for funds.

I was notified of our assignment to represent the Catholics in the musical program at the last moment, so to speak. All the good places had been assigned to other choruses. The nook reserved for the Catholic chorus was under a balcony. It would have been disastrous to sing there. I went to the Garden, told the Irish caretaker that the Protestant choirs had the best places, and that it would be shameful to let the Catholic choir appear at so great a disadvantage.

"Leave it to me, your Reverence. The old judges' box which is used only at the horseshows will not be occupied. I'll clean it up and see that your boys are escorted to it. It's the best place in the whole Garden."

And such it was. A chorus of a thousand voices sang several numbers from a spot on the main floor. The effect was thuddy, weighty, unmusical. We had only a small unit relatively, but perched high in the judges' box, and with the special effects which I had learned to evoke in mammoth auditoriums, it was easy to "take the house" from the other participants.

The influenza epidemic of the fall of 1918 struck at us full force. My sister Catharine, who had been very popular with the soprano boys, died in the early days of the epidemic. So many funerals were scheduled for St. Paul's Church that the Fathers were obliged to cancel High Masses. The soprano boys fell victim to the dread disease, and we spent many anxious days and nights worrying about them. The doctors in attendance agreed unanimously that the chest development and pulmonary strength which had come from our breathing exercises, and the general manner of breathing while singing, contributed much to the resistance of the boys. Our star solo boy, Hallet Dolan, was the most serious case. All the boys recovered, but the passing of my sister cast a gloom over the household.

Mr. Schwab had been appointed chief of the Emergency Fleet Corporation, and I decided to postpone the discussion of our affairs with him until the war would be finished. Meantime, I had the task of financing the undertaking. A certain income was accruing from the sale of our Columbia Gramophone records which the company had advertised extensively on "twenty-four sheets," in connection with our World War I concerts across the country. Soon, however, this company went out of business to be reorganized later. Our income ceased. And so we were obliged to go hither and yon on any kind of a musical engagement that would net us money. Almost every Sunday evening, having sung the Solemn Mass and afternoon Vespers at the Paulist Church, we would go over to Brooklyn for a sacred concert in a church or school auditorium. I think that the co-operation of the Brooklyn clergy kept us going under that first year.

Every once in a while, we would go out for a few days on the road. Scranton, Pennsylvania, New Years' Eve—one of the worst concerts I ever conducted! Tenors and basses at their most dreadful low. Rain. Poor acoustics. An inconsequential program of Christmas carols. Rarely over the years had we given such an inferior performance. The circumstances seemed truculently stacked against us. But we forgot it soon.

There was a series of concerts to be prepared and given with the

Russian Symphony Orchestra. Modest Altschuler, the conductor of the orchestra, was a fine musican and an excellent conductor, but, without adequate financial resources, he could not keep the personnel intact. At rehearsals we would have certain string and woodwind players, for instance, but at the performance an unrehearsed group of substitutes would take their places. A concert at the Lexington Avenue Opera House with the Russian Orchestra taxed whatever of talent and ingeniousness I possessed. A very pale affair! Another, at the Brooklyn Armory, with Marcia Van Dresser, and a large number of players who had not rehearsed our material, was equally anaemic, while a few appearances at the New York Hippodrome brought us as close to disaster as we could risk coming. At the Hippodrome, Hallet Dolan, saved the situation. Although singing some of his arias to the uncertain accompaniment of the scrub orchestra, his voice and consummate artistry raised the concert as a whole to a fairly high level.

About this time, a fine deep basso, James Byrne, later Borough President of Brooklyn, joined the ranks. Friends of his, good and experienced singers came with him, notably, Nicholas Sebastian Murphy, who developed a great loyalty to our unit. Joseph Scanlan, Fred Rover and other Brooklynites swelled the ranks of our men's section. Until the close of that season, however, we did not travel much from New York. There was one short tour of a week that brought us to Toronto and Ottawa. When we arrived in Toronto, we were singing as well as the former Chicago unit. Our programs were more catholic, however, for we had added a repertoire of sixteenth-century compositions.

I think that I have already stated that I had determined to try my hand at Palestrina and the other polyphonic composers. The acoustics of the Paulist Church in New York would help to bring the voice parts into alignment, in spite of my ignorance of the idiomatic manner of presenting the polyphonic style. In large buildings, the New York group had soon developed facility in making the polyphonic style fairly agreeable. Our polyphony at that time was probably as good as that in Westminster Cathedral, but, as I intimated in the first part of these memoirs, Sir Richard Terry at Westminster, as well as the other polyphonic conductors of England and the Continent, had failed to discover the sixteenth-century secret of making the style as attractive to the ears as the compositions on paper were to the eyes.

At Toronto, although the chorus had gone beyond the sort of achievement which was characteristic of the Chicago chorus, we experienced a depressing setback. During the six months' trip the Choristers, numbering twice as many as constituted the New York group, wore French uniforms. We had had a backdrop of white silk with the flags of all the allies arranged in an effective arc. The Governor-General had been in the vice-royal box. Massey Hall had been in festive attire. Eclat and *élan* were in the atmosphere. But this time, the singers were attired in cassocks and surplices. There was no backdrop of brilliant flags. There was no Governor-General. It was a straightforward, ordinary choral concert without any extraneous features to bolster the program. We were greeted upon our entrance from backstage with polite but unenthusiastic applause. Those of us who had made the six months' tour knew that something was wrong from the start. Later I analyzed this, finding that the audience was disappointed in our general appearance. We looked like a "requiem choir" about to chant some lugubrious phrases in the minor mode. And we were numerically half the size of the choir of the preceding year!

Sensing the surprise and quasi chagrin of the audience, I threw myself energetically into the task of trying to produce the finest choral music of my career. It wouldn't do to offer a passably well-performed program. We faced the necessity of doing a superlative job. And I think that's what we did. But Toronto didn't think so. During the intermission, friends and acquaintances came to my dressing room, looking rather sheepish and speaking in subdued tones. One had the impression that they came to offer condolences. "Cheer up, old fellow. Time will heal all." That sort of thing. When I went back to the stage for the second part of the program, it was hard to escape the conviction that obsequies were actually in progress, and that the late lamented was the Paulist Choir.

I tried to inject all the merriment and brilliance I could invoke into the secular numbers. Solo boys, at their best vocally, seemed rather to be intoning elegies at a bier. There was the quiet of bereavement throughout the great auditorium. And all because we *looked* different. Looking different, we must be different. Therefore our singing was different.

A friendly critic of the Toronto press came to my room at the end, and, waiting for all others to leave, put it to me directly: "What's the matter, Father? Has something happened to your outfit?"

My answer was just as direct: "We've improved musically; look at the program. We wouldn't have risked that a year ago. And our sopranos are more fully developed, without having lost the distinctive lightness of their tone quality. But we have a smaller number of singers—fifty-five against the one hundred and ten of 1918. But quantitatively this chorus reaches the same level of dynamic strength as the larger one, which I always strove to keep below its full potentialities. We dress differently, and we are a smaller unit. That's all."

The critic was convinced and gave a splendid review on the morrow.

This experience focused my attention upon the matter of numbers and appearance. I was to learn from similar experiences that the North American public was and still is impressed by great size.

The first question musicians or laymen ask me about my choir is: "How many voices?" A large number impresses. A relatively small number smacks of inferiority.

On that short jaunt to Canada, we gave a concert at Rochester, New York. Contrary to my usual custom of declining social invitations on the road, I accepted a dinner invitation from the priest who was presenting the concert for a parochial benefit. The large coliseumlike building was sold out. We were to have a gala audience. At dinner the conversation covered a wide field of topics. The subject of music and choirs was omitted. The guests probably sensed that I didn't enjoy talking shop, answering questions about training boys and reminiscing about our years before the public. But the pastor was alarmed. He expected me to talk about nothing else save the problems connected with boy-choir conducting and the evening concert.

After dinner, he called me aside, nervously querying as to whether I expected to give a first-class performance. I assured him that such was my intention and expectation. "But," said he, "you're much too calm. Do you realize that the best citizens of Rochester will be in the audience? I should think you would be very nervous." I pointed out to the agitated gentleman that I was so accustomed to conducting before large and distinguished audiences that it was second nature to walk out to the podium and, altogether free of apprehensions, evoke from the Choristers their best resources of throats, minds and hearts. This good priest, however, kept bobbing into my dressing room every few minutes before the opening number, trying to urge me to surpass anything that we had ever before achieved. "The Governor has just arrived." "The Mayor's party is in the foyer." "The Bishop and Vicar-General have taken their places in a box." "Are you sure that the boys are in good voice?" Etc, etc.

A few more moments of that sort of thing would probably have made me so nervous that the performance would have been affected disadvantageously, but when we went on stage and got off to a good start, the tremulous pastor became quite tranquil, leading the audience in a prolonged round of applause.

There was only one other occasion in my many years of concertizing upon which an effort to make me nervous was unwittingly made. At Rochester, the pastor was merely overanxious, and interpreted my easy manner at dinner to indicate indifference. But on the other occasion, early in our Chicago days, a layman whose naturally dictatorial manner was fired by many highballs, entered the dressing room at Orchestra Hall and begged me not to let the boys sing off pitch or the tenors and basses to make wrong entrances. He was too well known to make forcible ejection charitable tactics. And so he sank into a chair, keeping up a melancholy chant, the leit motif being that it would be a horrible experience for him to hear us do a bad job; and that furthermore he ardently hoped that in conducting the orchestra I wouldn't get the fiddles and flutes mixed up or the bassoons and kettle drums. From time to time during the concert, I caught a glimpse of him in a centre box, sometimes alcoholically asleep, sometimes wringing his hands, imploring me to be careful.

During our first few years in New York, the Ground Bass, the theme of the fugue, was still on the bottom voice line, so to speak. I mean that I was working out again the familiar problems of training new boys and new men into such a singing unit as would make choral music convincing and aesthetically moving. I had been through all the experiences involved a few times before. But now I had the extra worry of financing and managing the Choir School. Lack of space made it impossible to conduct the school classes in our house at Number Three, so the boys attended the excellent school of the Christian Brothers not far away.

A few concerts at Mr. Schwab's residence were interesting, especially those for the Bethlehem Steel Company dinner and a great function given for the Emergency Fleet Corporation. Several appearances for the Pennsylvania Society at the old Waldorf were also notable events. We sang there for the General Pershing, Marshal Foch, Cardinal Mercier and other receptions. Also a program at the home of John D. Rockefeller, Jr., in the interest of a postwar charity was memorable. And the singing of a "Te Deum" on the steps of the great library building at Fifth Avenue and Forty-second Street for the homecoming of New York's own Sixty-ninth Regiment, of which Father Francis Duffy was Chaplain, was a gardenia for each one of us.

The first season in the great Eastern metropolis passed quickly. The boys seemed happy and the experiment with the Choir School gave promise of real success. But Mr. Schwab decided that he could not go along with us financially to the extent of subsidizing the undertaking. This decision was a severe blow to me, for the financing and development of the undertaking necessarily became a personal responsibility. I had only my wits, and these didn't make a large parcel, upon which to fall back. But we had started, and I was resolved to carry on until it would become sadly clear that the venture was not feasible.

At the end of the season, I booked a three-weeks' trip through the Hocking Valley to Cleveland, and Detroit. At Detroit the Chicago boys went west for the summer holidays.

Upon my return to New York, I began to look about for a more spacious home for the Choristers. Finally I discovered Libby Castle, on the north end of Manhattan Island, perched high on Fort Washington Avenue between Broadway and Riverside Drive, not far from Dyckman Street. The castle had been built many years before by Boss Tweed of Tammany Hall fame. It was a replica of some old German castle on the Rhine. Minarets, towers and a most forbidding aspect generally. Frequently upon entering the medieval-looking mass of stones, I would find myself almost expecting halberdiers to rally around; to have the bridge thrown across an imaginary moat; to have guards salute and a valet remove my armor. My little coupé would seem to be rather a fiery steed which a groom would lead off to the stables.

The place was, indeed, a veritable tower of illusions. It was probably the most romantic pile of stones in the Western Hemisphere. Overlooking the Palisades, with the majestic Hudson River flowing by to the sea, remote from other buildings save a convent, E.K.G. Billings' abandoned racehorse stables, and the celebrated Barnard's Cloisters, we seemed to be living in an era long since past. As boys marched into the dining-room, it was easy to fancy them to be Hapsburg children on a visit, or Hohenzollerns, Guelphs or Ghibellines.

When the venerable Mrs. Charles R. Crane, wife of the Minister to China, or Mrs. John Mackay, widow of the Mackay who made the great silver "strike" in Nevada, would visit the castle, it was difficult not to see in these ladies archduchesses or marchesas, and when the young ladies from the Brownson School came to a dance, they flitted in and out of the pre-Raphaelite apartments as ladies-in-waiting to queens or attendants to princesses. And when the librarian would enter the rehearsal room, carrying copies of a motet of Mozart, the great composer himself could have been calling, with his manuscripts, upon Haydn at the castle of the Prince of Esterhazy. Palestrina often seemed to be sitting at his desk in the Villa d'Este, and John Sebastian Bach often set tempos for us from his clavichord in the music room of Prince Leopold of Anhalt-Gothen.

Yes, that castle belonged to a long-ago epoch. As soon as one would leave the highway and arrive at the porte-cochère, it was easy to go back over the centuries. No wonder the boys developed a choral technique that was characteristic of other generations. No wonder there was a mysticism in their intonations. In New York and in the twentieth century actually, but by the suggestion of their surroundings, mystically in the cinquecento period. Perhaps the old masters liked to hear their music being rehearsed in such an atmosphere. Perhaps by a sort of mental telepathy from the other world, they could convey to us, living in that feudal building, a clearer concept of their compositions. At any rate, outside the castle we were moderns, and inside a very fair representation of medievalists. Probably the boys themselves were not so conscious of this as the adults, particularly myself.

During the summer, while the boys were on holiday, it was my wont to place the castle at the disposal of the Holy Cross Sisters who taught in the parochial school of the Paulist Fathers. But there were two Sisters who were afraid to sleep in the great building. Ghosts! Wraiths from the Thirty Years' war soaking through the walls! Creaking boards and the sighing of weird winds through the casements in the upper towers were too much for these two Sisters to endure. The Superioress gave them permission to return each evening to the convent on Sixty-first Street, hot and noisy though it was sure to be.

Shortly after we moved into the castle, an episode occurred which is funny enough to recount. The Superior-General had given us a larger-than-life-size picture of Mary Magdalen. We were coerced for strategy's sake to hang the vivid picture. The artist had given to Mary an extraordinarily lush head of hair. Much too much hair for a human being. Much too golden-red. He had also presented her with a pair of eyes that looked like miniature moons, and a red slash of a mouth that could have gobbled up quickly all the Don Juans of her period. She was pictured at the foot of the Cross. Tears as large as old-fashioned cobble stones were dropping from the moon-orbs. Altogether a most remarkable picture. An extraordinary achievement, even if one did have to seek another word to replace "art" in describing it! This horrific thing had been hanging by a cord which was worn thin; at least it could not carry the weight of Mary's hair without protesting occasionally. A few times at Number Three the picture had dropped to the floor. One afternoon at the castle, I was chatting with my sister Mary when a great crash resounded through the building. A small boy dashed into the room, looking wildly excited, crying out: "Miss Finn, a terrible thing has happened. Mary Magdalen has fallen again!" And in a school for males!

During our four years at the Castle, we maintained a full staff of teachers in both grade and high school departments. Father Owen Mc-Grath, of the Paulist Fathers, having finished service as a chaplain in World War I, was appointed headmaster of the academic department. I added the extra job of prefect of discipline. This latter office did not involve much unpleasant responsibility, for the Paulist Choristers in the Choir School were a well-behaved group, holding high ideals of personal conduct, and appreciating the rather easy code of regulations. In fact, thinking over this point, I am impelled to state that, from every point of view, the boys and youths were a most exemplary lot.

Of course, once in a while, a lad would kick over a bit, but on such occasions Father McGrath would pounce upon him. And the Father was a real pouncer. His pet torture for a chap caught in some even trifling transgression was to campus the unfortunate for a week. This meant that the lad was deprived of such permissions as going to the cinema and leaving the premises for an afternoon stroll or a visit to the city on holidays. The Father was so strict that a misplaced towel or a minute's tardiness in reporting for classes, meals, etc., would stir his wrath. Sometimes I found difficulty in taming the reverend prefect. Father McGrath was a master of Latin and Greek. He was a contemporary of mine at the Boston Latin School. An athlete, having been quarterback on the Dartmouth eleven, he developed great interest among the boys in outdoor sports. We had a fairly fast baseball team which played high school teams in many cities while we were on the road. He permitted a school store to be operated by the boys. Smoking was allowed to the seniors, and every once in a while a small soprano boy would be caught with a cigarette. When I saw a youngster with his tribute to Lady Nicotine in evidence, I forgot about it. Nor did the other boys play stool pigeon. But if Father Mac saw him, the kid was due for campusing and a few wallops from the hair brush.

With Father McGrath on the faculty were Father George Callahan, an excellent teacher and an accomplished pianist, Mr. Albert Callahan, his brother, professor of mathematics, and Mr. William Tierney of Philadelphia. The Misses Marguerite and Anna Cowhey completed the teaching staff. I mention the ladies last, to give them honor, as an archbishop is honored by the last place in a ceremonial procession. These two sisters accomplished signally successful results. Miss Marguerite was in charge of the grade school division. Under the tutelage of this staff, the boys made speedy progress in the academic branches. We were incorporated as a school under the Board of Regents in New York State, and, if my memory is right, no boy failed to pass the Regents' examinations. The chief assistant in the musical department was Anne Wolcott Williams, a pianist and general musician of brilliant achievements.

Once the routine of the Choir School was established at the Castle, it seemed as if the institute was as well organized as any of the great English choir schools. Except that the latter had endowments, and we had no money. We had plenty of hope, but the New York banks wouldn't let us draw checks against that! And the plumbing at the Castle was so bad, rust choking the mains, and the water pressure frequently so low, that only a gifted satirist could properly describe the inconveniences, anxiety and general confusion often endured. But, considering the facts that Palestrina, Bach and Orlando Gibbons were obliged to put up with primitive sanitation, etc., and that in the Castle, as already noted, we sensed, after a theosophistic fashion, the presence of these great musicians, we were not justified in complaining too loudly. It wouldn't have done much good, anyway.

Running a choir school is an expensive undertaking. The boys pay their board and tuition with their voices. But these, as *hope,* couldn't be deposited in the bank. I was harassed at all times by the specter of bills. Night after night I would prowl around my room, which looked out over the New Jersey Palisades, nervously, and some times almost hysterically, trying to figure out ways and means of improving the financial condition. I tried about every thing I could devise or others suggest. My imagination pictured the Hudson River feudal barons who some generations before had sailed up and down the river with their rich cargoes. Didn't Phillipse's ship strand somewhere near the shore just below us with a hold full of Spanish gold? Maybe the boys could dive in and locate the sunken craft?

The legend of the buried Indian relics a short distance to the north was intriguing, too. Some of the relics would bring fabulous prices from antiquarians. But we didn't dive for the Phillipse gold or dig for the Indian tomahawks and pottery. We took into the school some non-singing paying pupils. But the only way of meeting our needs, even partially, was to tour. And so, one week in every month, we were on the road. It was worse than the six months' trip, because we were returning often to the same places. As a troop of jaded Thespians is wont to return to places where they are sure of an audience, and to which the railroad fare is not prohibitive.

Beginning with the autumn of 1919, we were free to leave New York immediately after Solemn Mass on Sundays, for the Vesper service had been eliminated from the service program at Fifty-ninth Street. The people were losing interest in the Liturgy. The Psalms irked them. And the congregations were so small that the local Rector decided to give up the long chanting service. Thus, we were free to fill Sunday evening engagements as far away as Boston, Washington or Albany. Sunday evening was probably the best time for a sacred concert, or any kind of an artistic recital.

John McCormack and the Paulist Choristers seemed at that time to be appearing in Boston more often than other attractions.

A plan of tours was gradually worked out. New England gave a vague promise of being our El Dorado. The entire troup knew the sequence of stations between Boston and New York by heart. A few lads claimed that they could tell by the curves just where our train was at a given moment. We could have done an excellent map of New England for Rand, McNally. Too bad we didn't think of that!

With good luck in the smaller towns on the Boston mileage, we could net two thousand dollars a week. Boston gave the guarantee. We played "on spec" (speculation) in the smaller places. The guarantee payed the railroad, hotel and payroll expenses. The tenors and basses were necessarily all professional singers. The few volunteer adults in our organization were not free to travel, making their livings at occupations in New York.

While we lived at Number Three, Victor Herbert, who used to drop in to the Vespers at Fifty-ninth Street, would talk to the boys on Riverside Drive. He tried to catch them napping when he would ask them to identify a certain Gregorian mode which he hummed. He was popular with the boys. Strange, but he never entered Number Three to chat with me! Perhaps he had heard that it was the orchestra temporarily carrying his name that had almost ruined us in New York in 1909!

Although the Washington mileage was about the same as the Boston, we rarely netted as much money from tours in that direction as from the trips to New England. Once in a while we would take a longer jaunt. Chicago twice. Louisville twice. Indianapolis. Pittsburgh. Cleveland. The concerts were uniformly good. But they were so much alike that few interesting memories stand out.

We were constantly running into John McCormack. On many occasions we either preceded him or followed him in a town. His manager, Dennis McSweeney, was a patron of ours, but John avoided us. I never knew just why. Perhaps the rivalry of two attractions that appealed to the same type of audience is the explanation. At any rate, he declined to sing with the Philharmonic and Radio City Orchestras under my baton. I always liked the man, personally, and found it a privilege to write an appreciation of his art in the *Catholic World* of November, 1945, shortly after his demise.

In June, 1920, we started off on a postseason coast-to-coast tour. The boys were instructed to copy the route as posted on the bulletin board and mail it or bring it to their homes. Young Adolph LeMoult, an excellent lad and one of New York's leading florists now, seemed to be slow in copying the route. I asked him: "Doctor, haven't you got the itinerary ready yet?" "Oh, yes, Father," he replied, "all except my under-wear."

Sleeping cars for seventy nights! Knights of Columbus or Y.M.C.A. provided bathing facilities. We were given the keys of the city at St. Catherine, Ontario, and feted overabundantly by the Knights at Winnipeg and Vancouver. Our long trip across Canada showed the Canadians to be keenly interested in the classical forms of music and especially in the unaccompanied motets of the Palestrinesque style. Before going into Canada for a three weeks' tour, we stopped at Duluth, where the lynching of three Negroes had so disturbed the populace that the attendance at our concerts was poor, and the local impresario was unable to pay the guarantee. This was a blow, for we not only lost the profit that would have accrued from the engagement, but we went into the red because the trip to Duluth was not on our main-line ticket. And so we were working for the railroad!

In spite of the interest displayed by the Canadians in our programs, that second transcontinental trip was the most tedious and unsatisfactory experience of my musical life, before and after. I practically lost my sense of humor in the Canadian Rockies. I am not sure that I ever found it again. I guess that I began to pull grimaces on that trip. I have not laughed much since. What used to be a smile is now, and has been for a long time, a wry puckering of the lips.

Temperamentally, I was never one to laugh easily and certainly not boisterously. And that California-Canada tour, plus the whole episode of the Choir School, left me "besieged with sable-coloured melancholy." I don't mean of course, that I went around scowling and forlorn, or that I pouted or moped. But the cheer had thinned out. I couldn't find much to be merry about. Most of the boys and men felt the same way during the tour, and we were glad to wind up the venture at Kansas City, where we sang in an open building adjoining a carousel and not far from a bandstand where Sousa's marches and Straus' waltzes offered a strange background for Palestrina and Bach.

We remained at the Castle for three more seasons. But, after the lugubrious tour to the coast, I knew that the show would be over presently.

We continued to make great progress as a singing unit, however, and gave several concerts with the Philharmonic Orchestra and Barrere's Little Symphony. We were often at Carnegie Hall, the Metropolitan Opera House and the Brooklyn Academy of Music. Richmond, Virginia, was good to us on several occasions, as was Washington, D.C. At the

White House, we sang in the East Room for Presidents Wilson and Harding.

Once at Washington, my aunt, Sister Paulina of the Visitation Convent in Georgetown, invited us to sing at the Academy. It was her Golden Jubilee year, and I was happy to arrange the concert. Besides the nuns, the young ladies of the Academy were present. At the conclusion of the concert, Sister Paulina, a tiny parcel of consecrated humanity, pattered up to the stage, and, placing her arm around my neck, said: "First I want to thank my darling little nephew Willie. And then I must thank the boys, the men and the *tenors*." The effect of this statement on the boys was overwhelming. They had been waiting for such a plum for years. The girls in the audience had a grand time. The tittering was fast and furious and ominous. I am sure that the boys called me "Willie" after that, and I know from the admission of some of the girls later on (mothers and young grandmothers now) that I have been known as "darling little Willie" from one end of the country to the other. The Georgetown Visitation Convent was and probably still is among the best and most popular educational institutes for young ladies in the United States.

A slip of a girl, somewhere in the far west, San Francisco, or Los Angeles, asked me *sotto voce* not long ago: "How's darling little Willie?" I used to become irate when the sobriquet was used, but nowadays I can endure it. God knows I was never a "darling little Willie." Willie— what a dreadful name to wish on a helpless babe! He has to carry it all the way through! Sometimes it makes him wonder if God hadn't intended him to be a her. Perhaps dear auntie's salutation threw my voice up a few notes. It has never seemed baritonish since that dreadful afternoon in Georgetown. Well! dear auntie's little Willie went down a year or two later and celebrated her funeral Mass. But she owes me something, and I trust that she'll persuade a nice angel to come down and visit me to tell something about the techniques of the heavenly choir.

"Darling little Willie." What a pet name! Maybe I'll use it as a *pen* name! A column in a newspaper ought to go well over such a nom de plume. What "D. L. Willie" thinks about music in New York. Or about the roaring of tenors and basses at the Metropolitan. Or about expensive, loud-singing, unmusical musical societies' so-called concerts. Or about screaming, fat sopranos, warbling off pitch at Town Hall recitals. Or what Willie predicts as the net result of this modernistic stuff they are calling by the misnomer "music." Yes, a column might kick up a sort of Winchell fuss with so cute a byline!

The concerts at the White House always elicited much enthusiasm from both boys and men. We gave three altogether besides a reception from President Hoover who permitted his picture to be taken with us.

After our concert for President Harding, he told me a story which ran like this. While he was editing and publishing a newspaper in Marion, Ohio, he was frequently invited to give public addresses. The best choir in the district, which often shared the program with him, was the Catholic choir of men and women of St. Mary's Church. After Pope Pius X issued his *Motu Proprio* about church music, which requested that the clergy use boy sopranos instead of women, President Harding noticed the change in the personnel of the choir. He spoke to the priest-prefect of the choir saying: "I notice, Father, that you have abandoned women in the choir."

"Not one," answered the priest!

Usually the professional concerts in Washington and some other cities where the stage was not provided with chorus tiers, were not signally successful. Singing on a flat stage, especially when there is no ceiling in the set, always puts a chorus at a disadvantage. It is difficult to balance the tenors and basses with the sopranos and altos who generally sit in front. Also a high percentage of resonance goes off into the flies and wings. And the conductor, in order to place the singers as far forward as possible, must conduct right atop the footlights. Usually this arrangement makes it impossible for him to see the first line of choristers and vice versa.

All during those trying years, I was making progress in the more subtle phases of musicianship. I have rarely let a day go by without a period devoted to study and research in the latencies of the art. Orchestration! Registration on the organ! How clearly my thinking about choral musicianship included these! I worked daily on orchestral manuscrips, arranging many compositions for various combinations of players. On many occasions we used these at Carnegie Hall and elsewhere.

I was talking recently to Dr. Walter Damrosch, the grand old gentleman of the conductor's podium. He remembered engaging us for a concert with the New York Symphony. I had made all the orchestrations except one. This had been done by the composer, a warm friend of Dr. Damrosch's and dean of music in a great university. At the rehearsal with the orchestra, the good Doctor asked me who had made the orchestrations. I told him that I was the guilty party. He said, "A youngster like you? You have placed the instruments in ingenious positions. But one orchestration is very bad, and I don't want you to use it. Give it to me, and I'll fix it up." I handed him the one which he had indicated, being amused to observe his surprise and chagrin on discovering it to be the work of the great dean. When I told him of this episode recently, he laughed with a rich heartiness, saying something like this : "Well! you certainly caught me that time."

I developed a great interest in the viola and cello. These instruments in the string choir of an orchestra have the same place in the ensemble as the altos and tenors in a chorus. I discovered that by giving prominence to these rich instrumental and choral colors, one would achieve an over-all effect quite impossible of attainment if the treble instruments were given too acute prominence, or the string basses and low trombones and tuba allowed to assert their parts boldly.

I never knew an outstanding violist personally, but Robert Ambrosius, of the Chicago Symphony Orchestra, and John Mundy, of London and New York, cellists, were good friends of mine. On some tours, I included a cellist, Paul Schoessling of the Chicago Symphony, and a great friend of Victor Herbert, who was a cellist as well as a composer.

One of the first things I observe about a conductor is his treatment of the viola, cello, second clarinet, English horn and tenor bassoon sections. Next in importance, for my aesthetic taste, are the second violins and the second and third French horns. The rich tonal effects which these instruments produce in the alto-tenor compass seem to carry the principal impressiveness of music generally. The top instruments, as the first violin, the flute, oboe, first clarinet and often the first French horn, contribute so many more vibrations per second on account of their higher pitches, that the treble line easily becomes too piquant, distracting listeners from the subtle beauty of the middle parts. I have always been conservative with trumpets and tenor trombones.

Because of this preference for the lower strings, I became known to the personnel managers of orchestras as a "viola faddist." Often I have been twitted about this in various parts of the country. And in conducting both choruses and orchestras, I have developed a concentration on the middle parts. Frequently, I admit, I conduct to these and let the upper and lower parts go their own way, if they are not making too much of a racket, and are keeping in proper perspective.

This middle-voice tendency of mine has amused many, especially considering the reputation of the Paulist Choristers and other groups of mine for soprano tone quality. And my trademark or symbol (it's on the covers of all my books, and compositions) has brought many questions. Here is the symbol: FF of course means fortissimo.

It also stands for *Father Finn*. And the F clef is, of course, the bass clef. How explain a symbol that seems to contradict my principal notions? Well! it's a paradox! My firmest conviction about training a chorus is that it must be vocalized pianissimo (PP) in the preliminary stages of training, and that always the rehearsing should be done on the softer side of the dynamic scale. "Father Finn" has come to mean pianissimo to many musicians across the country, but I make it signify fortissimo (FF). A paradox is a good means of underlining a thought or precept.

And the bass clef? Our records show that for many years I was fanatically concerned with working out a volatile, disembodied, aesthetico-spiritual soprano tone quality not only with boys' voices but with the voices of female lyric sopranos as well. It was our soprano chorus that interested America and Europe. Hundreds of critics have written about it. Why then not use the treble staff, the locale of the sopranos, in my symbol? If I had chosen a symbol a quarter of a century ago, I daresay that the G clef would have been used. But my symbol is of relatively recent origin. I had come to know that the soprano part is the canopy over the other parts, save in strictly homophonic music (where the soprano part carries a tune all the way, and is supported by the harmony of the other voices).

I had been engaged in conducting much contrapuntal music (one part being often as important as another) and had become acutely aware of the distortion effected in this style of music, if the top parts in either chorus or orchestra were allowed to dominate. Furthermore, I had begun to appreciate keenly the acoustical fact that the lower notes shoot off their own high notes (*harmonics*) and that the treble notes were often just reinforced overtones of the low sounds. And so I adjusted the soprano tone quality accordingly. I watched over this quality with great zeal. I came to sense in advance a possible departure from the right quantity and timbre, and a technique for preventing or correcting an inferior tone became second nature. But, you see, I had been meditating on all phases of tone quality since I had first heard the choir at the Boston Cathedral. And the experience of hearing the wrong timbres in England and on the Continent, as well as in America, had sharpened my appraisal of quality. Quality, especially soprano quality, such quality as would float over the altos, tenors and basses with a mystic intimation, became an obsession with me. For years I sacrificed other needs to the supreme need, for me, of refining the treble intonations.

Critics didn't approve of our diction (this word is used now instead of enunciation) for a long time. My search for quality was responsible for the lack of clarity in pronouncing vowels and articulating consonants. But I didn't care. Finally, and that's a long time ago now, I realized that I could go no further with tone quality. I had experimented with every scheme for controlling the potential beauties of soprano quality. Then, I turned my attention to diction, and to many other phases of the choral art.

But quality must always be first in music. Texts must be projected clearly, especially in the liturgical prayers and hymns of the Church, but if the quality is poor or even below its possible effectiveness, I think it better to have the liturgical texts read rather than sung. It has been difficult to persuade musicians that the first need in music is aesthetic quality. The average choral conductor is a rank infidel in this matter. Musicians of good technical achievements frequently are observed conducting choruses that make the most ugly noises. And they seem to be unaware of this. A chorus, and particularly a soprano chorus, curtailed of its fair proportions, is not a medium of musical communication. It is only a miscellany of disheveled voices emitting twangs and sonorousness that have no kinship with art. And the orchestras, too, have been going sour on this point for a long time. When occasionally, it has been my good fortune to conduct an orchestra in which several of the first desk players seemed to be intent upon producing real quality, and therefore keen to accept from the conductor hints as to the dynamic ratios, it has been as if I had gone off on an angel's back to the eternal home of St. Cecilia, Palestrina, Vittoria, Pergolesi and the many other spiritual musicians, to listen for a while to those celestial harmonies that we expect to hear in Heaven. Of course, dear St. Cecilia is ranked among musicians (what a funny anachronism, St. Cecilia pictured playing a modern pipe organ!) only for the sake of poetic legend, but maybe she sings soprano as guest artist occasionally with the seraphs!

Well! I was growing in the direction indicated in the last few paragraphs. Perhaps beyond my natural talent, for I always was conscious of very limited gifts in music or in any other line. But constant thought, serious and uninterrupted application, and dogged purpose frequently lift a man higher than his natural stature.

It was delightful as well as instructive to slip into the last row at Carnegie Hall when an orchestral rehearsal was in progress. How quickly the difference in conductors would show itself! Damrosch, Stransky, Gabrilowitch, Monteux, Stokowski, Harty, Toscanini, Walter, Mengelberg! How easy to classify them properly, even if not according to the categories in which ballyhoo or prejudice had placed them. One man intent only upon incisive entrances. Another concerned chiefly with altering the players' traditional understanding of tempos. Another interested only in verve or the succulent passages of a cloying adagio. And with due respect to all the men mentioned and many others, I must say that Willem Mengelberg seemed to me to be more interested in refining quality than the others. Gabrilowitch was a close second. I don't imply that the others were not attentive to quality altogether. But many focussed their first and chief attention on the mechanical features of concerted playing.

And I often strolled into rehearsals of choral societies, and into the practice rooms of greatly acclaimed choirs of boys and men, frequently to emerge puzzled as to why the maestros were giving so little thought to the very essence of music.

Standing before an orchestra, for me a first violin and a flute would equal one boy soprano. Viola, English horn and top bassoon would look like a good countertenor alto. Cellos took on the form of string-tenors, second French horns of reedy tenors, and second clarinets of the dry-throat tenor who usually sings on the second tenor line. And standing before a chorus, or seated, playing the organ for it, I was in imagination before an orchestra, voices and instruments being in the same apposition. And I found myself playing the organ, each season more orchestrally. Even with the wonderfully orchestral instrument, with mechanical aids to registration, which Mr. Ernest Skinner built for me at Fifty-ninth Street, New York, it was quite a fatiguing task to change the stops as frequently as orchestral scores required. Playing and accompanying at the same time. Trying to conjecture the liturgical procedure from behind the Altar. Transposing from one key to another to assure true-to-pitch intonation on wet days or when the choir was "off feed." Although I had ceased to smile much after the California-Canada trip, my interest was as intense in the promotion of choral ideals as ever. Even the burden of finance didn't blunt my sensitiveness to musical loveliness.

We sang oratorios once a week for years in Lent. It was a joy to study the orchestration of these and to duplicate it in the organ registration. Even the harp effects were available, more clearly than in an orchestra, where the other instruments frequently submerge the light tones of the harp. On the organ, the registration can be adjusted to permit the harp to come through effectively. And the Deagan chimes! How the people loved the chimes! If I failed to use them for a week or two, complaints would come in to the Rector, and I would be requested to let the bells ring out. After a while, I worked out a duet form in which chimes would ring a third or a sixth above or below stops of various timbres on another manual.

Organists would come from distant places. Many asked me why I used the violin, viola, cello family of stops when accompanying the sopranos while these were singing without the other voices. My reply was that in addition to the fact that the most frequent form of orchestral accompaniment employs the strings more regularly than the woodwinds or brass, the flutish character of a trained boy soprano is so likely to assert itself, that I found the pointing-up effect of the string choirs most helpful in neutralizing the baneful timbre of the "fluty" boy.

Also I would frequently play the melodic line of the sopranos on a full stop, but an octave lower than written. This gave a satisfying impression that the boys were only singing the octave harmonics of the low organ stop. There were other devices on our organ which enhanced the vocal effects in progress, notably the Unison Cancels. By canceling the regular pitch of a stop, throwing it up an octave and down an octave, one gets an extraordinarily beautiful combination of high and low, with the boy sopranos singing in between the top and bottom octaves. Miles Farrow, my friend at St. John the Divine's, was so opposed to this scheme, however, that he had the cancels removed from his console. Well! every man to his own choice! I was so engrossed in tone quality that perhaps I found in strange combinations, that did not approve themselves to others, aids to the ethereal loveliness of timbre, for which I had been so long groping, and which by the goodness of the Lord I finally found. I have written out and published the main points of the technique which I eventually employed to produce our distinctive tone quality, but techniques are of little value unless employed in connection with a *clear end in view*. No choral conductor, by the mere use of systems or vocalizations, can evoke a bewitching quality from his singers. He must have thought about it, for a long time. He himself must have seen with his ears, the sort of sounds he plans to educe from his singers. He must have lived with tone qualities in the otic chamber of his imagination. Otherwise he can produce only mechanical phonation. He needs a Ground Bass to convince him of the raison d'etre of music. The exercise of the art, when it's not poised firmly upon a Ground Bass, is analogous to a system of philosophy which is not based upon logic, and not dissimilar to a so-called religious cult that omits belief in God as its starting point.

Music is the strangest of the arts. It has many secrets. It keeps its secrets well hidden below the surface. You can't use a mechanical drill to get below this surface, like drilling into the ground for oil. You need a mental probe, a psychological auger, an aesthetic perforator to break into the surface-texture of the arts, and for music, and its psychic elements, you need also a divining rod. There's no use boring until you have thought so much about the procedure that instinctively you know where to break in.

This is an age of steel and concrete. It seems to me that the loveliness and persuasiveness of music is encrusted by a solid cover of reinforced concrete. Of course, occasionally, something wonderful and glorious pops up through a break, but most of the time, it's just noise repercussing against the concrete cover. Do you think me pessimistic or unduly critical? Perhaps some of my sentences justify that impression. But I'm not really a pessimist or a hypercritical censor of the musical situation of this era. I simply fail to observe the influence of the Ground Bass that has stirred me on the average solo or concerted performance. Perhaps the art is being overcommercialized. Or perhaps, it's sour grapes with me, for not having become better friends with its commercial aspects. Perhaps, if I had, I would not have been obliged to close the Choir School, or to have struggled through later years with inadequate funds.

The Choir School was given up finally in 1923, at the close of the season. Just before the finish, the Board of Regents gave each of the fourth year high school students a diploma of graduation. I went to Europe and upon my return I was stationed at the uptown church of the Paulist Fathers, where I reorganized the Choristers. All boys from distant parts, except two, Thomas Moran "Peggy O'Neill" of Trenton, New Jersey, and Brendan O'Callahan of Rochester, New York, returned to their homes. The two boys who remained were the plinth upon which we reared the reorganized group. A great solo boy, Jack Huber, went back to California. Thomas Coates to Chicago and Edward Guilfoyle to Cincinnati. Father Francis Finn, S.J., of the boys' books fame, had sent me young Guilfoyle and another nice lad whose name I have forgotten. The strength of the choir, while we were at the Choir School, was in the group of boys from distant cities. During the five years' conduct of the school, we gave scholarships to boys with exceptional voices in various parts of the country and Canada. We announced tests for interested applicants in practically all the large cities which we visited on tour. The personnel of the Choir School, thus, included boys from many parts of North America. Successful applicants were not always material for brilliant solo work, but they were the real choir-boy type. And so, on the closing of the school, I had a tough problem to replace them.

Efforts were made by friends, such as Mrs. John McElroy of Providence, Rhode Island, Mrs. Charles Mitchell, wife of the president of the National City Bank, New York, and Mrs. John Mackay and her son, Clarence, of the Postal Telegraph Company, to finance the school. But Catholic New York was in need of so many eleemosynary institutions that we could not get official approbation for an extensive campaign for money. I was conscious from the start of the choir school of much unsympathetic criticism for undertaking what seemed, to those who knew nothing of the history of music to be a fantastic project. An effort of the Superior-General, Very Rev. Thomas F. Burke, C.S.P., to rally a group of wealthy Catholics to the support of the foundation was soft pedalled effectively by some who later on expected me to work miracles with a scrub personnel. But that's all right! They did not know, and therefore could not understand.

Mrs. Mitchell, Justice Morgan O'Brien and Clarence Mackay addressed His Eminence, Cardinal Hayes, with a proposal to make our Choir School an Archdiocesan establishment, which could quickly be developed into a national institute. By this plan, the choir boys of the Cathedral and several other large metropolitan churches were to be trained in the institute, the organists of the participating churches to be on the musical faculty. Musicians from other dioceses were to be invited to study the art of choral technique, organ playing, Gregorian chant, polyphony and all the subjects of which a first-class church musician should be master. These would return to their dioceses prepared with a practical scheme to raise the standard of Catholic music from its very lowly estate. But for a variety of reasons the Mitchell-O'Brien-Mackay plan fell through a vent into the subway.

Another proposal went awry, also. Monsignor Lavelle, who had a keen sense of what we were attempting to accomplish, suggested that I combine the Cathedral and the Paulist choirs into one great unit, one half singing at the Cathedral and the other at the Paulist Church. This would entail the necessity of my appearing personally about half the time at the Cathedral; and so I lost that chance, too.

I guess that I was becoming accustomed to losing games to superiors. I had begun to lose seriously in 1913, when the Archbishop of St. Louis wanted me for his proposed choir school but was afraid to place a Religious-Order priest in charge, because of the uncertainty as to whether the Order would allow him to remain long enough to build the institute into a solid establishment. And I lost with Archbishop Mundelein of Chicago, because the Superior in New York told him that I was to be transferred to New York. All the games were scored at forty-love. I was on the "love" end. The "loveliness of love"! It would have been wonderful to have had a forty once! Well! that's all finished and a good many other things, too! A man must never weep with tears that fall from the eyes. But even a thoroughly masculine specimen can't prevent the lachrymal glands of his subconsciousness from exuding doleful drops.

During those years at the School, the Choristers developed an amazing facility in all styles of music. We sang often with orchestras in difficult programs. I remember especially a Symphony of Mahler which we did with Mengelberg four times. I had not yet found the key to the proper interpretation of Palestrina and the other great composers of his time. But we were making the polyphony sound fairly well in the great Paulist Church.

Some years later, when I finally discovered the secret of conducting medieval and Renaissance polyphony, we brought the great congregations back over the centuries to listen to that extraordinary music with the ears of medievalists. Our church might have been the Basilica of St. John Lateran, in Rome in 1500 A.D. Or the Chiesa Nuova of St. Philip Neri where Annimuccia and Palestrina frequently conducted the afternoon *Laudes Spirituales,* the forerunner of the oratorio. But, while, we were not bona fide polyphonists at the time of the closing of the choir school, we had achieved such choral facility that we could take on a difficult assignment with an orchestra with only a few days' notice. The boys loved to sing the difficult scores. Carols and lilting lays usually bored them, and they sang them with less finesse than the most difficult counterpoints of Bach. Once through was par for learning the notes and rhythms in the Choir School. I was amazed myself at the speed with which they put together the double chorus "Sanctus, Hosanna in Excelsis" of the Bach B Minor Mass.

We used the *moveable do* system for reading music, and except in very modernistic music, this system is simple and certain. Some of the professional men used to marvel at the facility with which the youngsters would master an intricate score. The sopranos and countertenors were much "faster studies" than the tenors and basses. If a soprano boy made a blunder in public, or even a notable one at rehearsal, his colleagues would harry him for days. And if I put my foot down on a wrong pedal note on the organ, or pulled a raucous stop by mistake, the whole soprano chorus would stare unforgivingly at me as though I were a hopeless amateur. And sometimes a solo boy would ask me for a different combination of stops, if he had been dissatisfied with my registration on a previous occasion. Oh! yes, those choir-school boys knew the choral business from A to Izzard. Gradually during those years we became a regular feature of Catholic charity affairs, of civic functions, and of most of the patriotic programs which were designed on a large scale. Of course, we never received any money for these things. In fact they were liabilities, for we were obliged to pay the adult singers. Later on, after radio developed, we had a much worse time of it, but I'll postpone telling about this.

When we were on tour, as I have already indicated, our baseball team played the high school teams of various cities in the spring and early autumn. Father McGrath gave us a bad moment at Indianapolis. Our regular catcher was indisposed and Father Mac, a semipro catcher in earlier days, went behind the plate for us. He looked like a fat boy in his baseball togs. We were a run behind, and when an Indianapolis lad was coming in from third base to home, Father Mac deliberately stepped onto the base line, and obstructed the runner, knocking him down. Father Mac wasn't going to let an Indianapolis school beat the Paulist choir school. The whole Indianapolis team rushed up to the plate. A giant of a youth called Father Mac a bad name. Father Mac began to stab at him with his gloved fist, waiting for an opening to land a haymaker. While they were mixing it, I jumped over the stand and shouted to him: "Finnegan,"—he was in the batting order under that alias— "you're benched. Out of the game." He looked up surprised, and his distraction gave me an opportunity to pull off his opponent to whom I apologized for the whole team. The lad was a decent chap, and said Okay. Then I asked the umpire to declare the game forfeited to Indianapolis.

We had plenty of publicity in the sports columns before and after. And the choir was calm enough to sing a May Festival program with the Russian Symphony orchestra, Henry Hadley, coconductor!

Chapter XXII *The Ground Bass Serves Reluctantly as a Theme For a* Marche Funebre

A FEW months before it was evident, with the finality of absolute certainty, that the Choir School would be closed, Otto Kahn, the head of the great banking firm of Kuhn and Loeb, sent for me. He was the chairman of the board of trustees of the Metropolitan Opera Company, and well informed about the major musical undertakings of the whole country. He told me that at a meeting of the board the Paulist Choristers were mentioned favorably, that the several gentlemen found in our organization indications that the choral art could be restored to a high plane and to the place of dignity which it had long since forfeited to the Opera and Symphony.

He said further that the board expressed interest in our financial condition. Was the Catholic hierarchy or some unrevealed angel taking care of us?

I made haste to assure him that no one was taking care of us; that I was as a medieval alchemist, trying to turn copper into gold, for we needed to make every penny look like a twenty-dollar gold piece. He remarked that the old alchemists were not egregiously successful. I told him that I had not exceeded their achievements, although I had made a few coppers look like nickels. He replied that the Catholic Church, a very rich organization, should finance the Choristers. I disabused him of that unwarranted notion, pointing out that practically all Catholic institutes were sorely handicapped by lack of money, that frequently the parochial schools were a severe strain on the parochial exchequer. That the hierarchy was zealously trying to establish and maintain the essential foundations, such as hospitals, houses of refuge, orphan asylums, etc., and that until the day would have dawned when all such needs had been supplied, it was unreasonable to expect that money would be diverted to a musical enterprise.

Being a practical man, as well as an aesthete, he grasped the situation.

Of course, I immediately put it to Mr. Kahn that the leaders of cultural activities in New York might be induced, by such men as composed the board of the Metropolitan, to raise an endowment fund for us, especially considering the well known fact that our activities were not only *C*atholic but *c*atholic as well, that Jewish and Protestant units were studying our methods, and that all choirmasters of whatsoever denomination were welcome at our rehearsals and at the classes in choral technique which I had begun to conduct in New York and in other cities in the country. But Mr. Kahn said no. The Opera and the Symphony used up all the ducats that rich New Yorkers were willing to devote to music. I must look within my own church for support. He inquired as to net earnings from concerts. I told him. Also I told him that I couldn't continue the strenuous and nerve-racking job of arranging and conducting concerts all over the land. That the one-night-stand idea had become most objectionable. That neither the boys nor myself could endure further the continual hopping about, and serving of ragouts of motets and madrigals to the dilettanti of distant small towns. That railroading had become a menace to the health and nervous composure of all concerned. The interview ended on that note. It was good to have elicited interest from Mr. Kahn and the board, but it wasn't good enough to keep ham and eggs on the choir school table or to pay the professors.

Before I went to Europe and the choir school was formally closed, we did a three weeks' tour through the Maritime Provinces. What a tour! It seemed like an ironic wind-up of our great plans. I thought, years before, that we had taken about everything that touring could produce. But I was mistaken. The railroad schedules were frightful. Before-dawn-starts in rickety daycoaches. And a boat trip in an oversize canoe from Prince Edward Island to Pictou, Nova Scotia. And the theatres along the Restigouche Valley! And the tiny inns. And the salmon diet. Plus the greasiest potatoes ever set before an Irish group! And on the hottest day, three concerts, because the Mother Superioress wouldn't allow her community to attend the afternoon concert. We were like the teams that used to play the New York subway circuits. Only we didn't have the subway. We bounced violently over rough roadbeds, delayed at stations, bolted food at railroad restaurants and generally had a "wonderful time." A good trip in a good ship, however, from Yarmouth, Nova Scotia, to Boston Massachusetts, where an Irish customs' officer, noticing the wording on a window card which a boy had lifted in a Canadian town, called out to his colleagues: "Pass the whole crowd through. They're the Paulist Choir from New York!" And addressing the boys, asked: "Where is the kid who sang the 'Little Red Lark' last winter at Symphony Hall?" Jack Huber of California was indicated, and the customs' officer shook his hand: "I feel as good as I did when I shook the hand of the great John McCormack a few seasons back!"

Five hours on the familiar route between Boston and New York brought us back to the Castle, our last return to the great medieval looking Towers. The lares and penates had flown. The place looked as though it would house only ghosts henceforth. And such were its tenants, until it was rased a few years later to make room for the landscaping which is now the beautiful Fort Tryon park with the new Barnard Cloisters suggesting "old ideas" on the top of the hill.

The original Barnard Cloisters were a few hundred yards to the south of the Castle. Mr. Barnard, the celebrated sculptor, had had an old abandoned monastery in the south of France rased and shipped to New York, where he had it refabricated in its original form. Only one New York brick was needed to complete the reconstruction. We had the pleasure of providing the music for an old French masque in the Cloisters, and Mr. Barnard, living close by, would frequently drop in at the Castle to listen to rehearsals and to chat. An extraordinary man, Mr. Barnard.

"How did you develop that tone quality?" he once asked. When I explained to him that I meditated upon all phases of aesthetico-spiritual tone quality, and had finally been able to differentiate between mere acoustical timbres and vital, intrinsic quality, he told me of his scheme for working out the strange sculptural effects which he achieved in the famous statue of the conflict between good and evil which stands, I think, in Central Park, New York. He said that he meditated so constantly on what he was trying to bring out of a mass of stone, that he finally arranged to shut out all distractions. Whenever he was out of the studio (from which he had excluded all light), he would be blindfolded. This, because he wished to behold physically and mentally only the astral bodies of the two men who posed for the statue. If he had seen anything else during the long period needed for the completion of the work, he said, the concept which for many years he had been building up about the composition would have been destroyed. Blindfolded he was led to and from his bedroom, where he sat in darkness in the evenings for many weeks. He ate alone. He lived with the etheric vitality of his ideas. And so he was delighted to learn that our tone quality, which, he claimed, reached down into the fastnesses of his soul, was not the result of mere mechanical technique. Perhaps he never fully escaped from the control of the seeing in the darkness idea, for we often noticed him strolling slowly along the familiar paths on our hilltop with his eyes closed, feeling his way with a walking stick. Once in a while, in the spring or autumn, he would stand outside the rehearsal room, through which, the windows being wide open, would float the strains of a beautiful motet, and he'd cry out "Capital! Please have the boys sing it again." I was much impressed with validity of Mr. Barnard's plan for intimating the mystical, and I probably devoted myself with increased zeal to the pursuit of my own ends.

Well! we left the hill. The boys from distant places went home. I went to Europe, and the choir school succumbed to the pressure of poverty. Mr. Barnard died. Those in charge of the plans for the new park took down the French bricks. What stands now a little farther north, as the Cloisters, does not look familiar to me. Something is missing. There are no latencies, for me. There is none of the Barnard "seeing in the darkness." There are no disembodied, volatile, hypnotic intonations of small boys up on the hill. Things were finished up there, and I never drive over the familiar route in these long-after years without wondering why we had not been able to carry on. Of course the city authorities would have evicted us to fulfill their plans for the park. But perhaps, if we had been financed, an adequate spot could have been found for us up there. Water under the bridge!

When I returned from Europe, (I made some reference to this a few pages back) I reorganized the Choristers with local boys, moving to the uptown church of the Paulist Fathers, where the process of rebuilding could be, and was, accomplished without the trying critiques which would have harassed us in the great basilicalike church at Fifty-ninth Street.

The reorganized chorus sang its first service at midnight Mass on Christmas, 1923, and continued singing the Solemn Masses and Vespers until January, 1925, when we moved back to Fifty-ninth Street. From the uptown locale, we went to Boston and to a few other places for concerts. That was too bold a thing for me to have planned, considering the previous virtuosity of the Choristers. One Boston critic chided me for my rashness. But perhaps it helped to hurry the rebuilding.

We were chosen to provide the music at the home-coming reception to Cardinal Hayes, after his reception of the Red Hat. This rather surprised New York. Some musicians, and a fair scattering of the clergy had predicted that "Finn will never build up another unit like the celebrated one. He's finished." Well! We were far from being finished. There were years of comprehensive undertakings ahead. The radio! The cinema! The great services at the Paulist downtown church. Programs with great orchestras. The Silver Jubilee Concert at the Metropolitan Opera House. The Diamond Jubilee programs of the Paulist Fathers. The world-wide broadcasting from Radio City for the opening of the Holy Year for Pope Pius

XI. The New York World's Fair. Countless charitable, municipal and
governmental appearances. Demonstrations in illustrating methods to
large classes of professional conductors and organists. Bach, Brahms and
other great masters to be interpreted on the radio for special commemo-
rations! Oh! yes, we were far from being finished, but the "sweetness and
light" had gone wherever bubbles go when they burst.

There were two funerals on the Castle grounds. One was solemnly
pointless. It was the interment of a dog. But there were mourners and
pallbearers in the cortege. Although one satirist placed a sprig of dog-
wood on the grave, and another, condoling with the owner of the deceased canine, remarked that its passing was a "dog-gone shame," the
poor dog was interred with ceremony. Whether there was pathos or
bathos emphasized is of no importance.

The other funeral was without rite. With no mourners but myself.
Without pallbearers. The satirists were not present in body, but one could
feel their psychic presence. It was my last night at the Castle. No moon.
No stars. The empyrean was not blue; it was black. Nor was it as a
"sphere of fire." It was as a cascade of ashes. For I was burying my hopes
for the choir school. Apollo and Euterpe threw soprano and tenor parts
over the tired old Ground Bass, and the trio did a heavy dirge on the top
of Washington Heights. The Muses went off, as rich relatives depart, assuring me that there would always be room for me on Mount Olympus.
Of course, I knew that I would draw an uncomfortable cot if I accepted
the invitation, probably not in the palace, but in the forgery of Vulcan!
I can still hear the clods of earth fall upon the casket of my planning!
Perhaps the planning and the hoping had not lived altogether in vain!

But "thick-ey'd musing and curs'd melancholy" would only make the
days more gloomy and the nights ruthlessly longer. So with Masefield's
"Trust still to Life, the day is not yet old" for a prod, I started anew.

Chapter XXIII *The Ground Bass and the Movement Back to Gregorian Chant*

I HAVE been urged by many to tell of my observations of the movement to restore Gregorian chant to its old place of dignity officially initiated by Pope Pius X, in his encyclical letter about church music. In the earlier pages of this volume, I referred to the unworthy state of church music prevailing in repertoire when His Holiness issued that *Moto Proprio*. But unbecoming and unsuitable as the types of Masses, concerted pieces and solos undoubtedly were, in practically every country there was often a high degree of general musicianship exemplified. There were hundreds of virtuoso choirs singing in the west-end galleries. Right here in our own country, the musical offerings at some of the prominent Catholic churches were comparable to the very best performances of opera and oratorio choruses. At old St. Matthew's in Washington; at St. Patrick's in the same city; at St. Patrick's Cathedral, New York, in the days of Archbishop Corrigan; at the Church of the Immaculate Conception and the Mission Church in Boston; at St. James' in Chicago, as well as in some other less widely known churches, the singing and organ playing were of a high order of excellence. Women, well-trained women, singing on the soprano and alto lines. The best tenors and basses available on the lower lines. Organists who were accomplished executants, graduates of European conservatories, skilled in the best traditions of organ playing, and masters of theory, counterpoint and orchestration, presided at the keyboards. Men who were in the class of César Franck, Guilmant and Widor who gave such repute to the ornate church music of Paris. Yes! though the repertoire was wrong, the performances, in a popular if not liturgical sense, were right. They were so attractive musically that they distracted the attention of listeners from the Altar. That is why the Pope wrote his condemnation.

When the wrong repertoire went out, the wrong kind of performance came in. Gone with Haydn, Handel, Hummel, Rossini and Gounod, were all the excellences which are needed to make any style of music acceptable to people of aesthetic appreciations. When the women left the choirs

(I am referring particularly in these observations to the conditions which began to prevail in the United States and Canada, though there was little difference in other countries with the exception of England), boys assumed the soprano parts. And who knew anything about training boys here, except Episcopalians? Many of the best Catholic musicians assumed positions in Protestant churches. Hordes of untrained performers took their places. So-called organists, who would play an occasional B flat on the pedal board when there was a fifth Sunday in the month. Piano players who knew nothing of organ technique or registration. Choirmasters popped up from remote hiding places to train the boys and men. Choirmasters who were altogether without knowledge of the choral art. Men and women unqualified by every canon of true musicianship for the Herculean task of making the reforms seem reasonable to the people were put in charge of choirs by the clergy, who were trying their best to conform to the papal decree. Alleged boy sopranos choking on easy soprano notes, making deafening fanfares of ear-rending sounds. Volunteer tenors and basses putting old Stentor to shame, smashing into Gregorian chants like express trains into locals. And almost overnight, the Protestant, as well as the Catholic public knew that the music in the Catholic churches had deteriorated to an unbelievably low level. The liturgical movement and Gregorian chant were blamed for the deterioration. Unfairly, certainly! But the inferior singing and playing were associated in the minds of the laity with the reforms instituted by the Pope. Small boys were dressed in cassocks and surplices and, seated often in the Sanctuary, they would howl out the Gregorian melodies which they had learned by rote. But they were *not* singing Gregorian chant! A very poor counterfeit, indeed! And with wretched vocalism!

Several schools were opened where the chant was taught. Many choir directors, including large numbers of the Sisters, attended the courses. Some of these schools were staffed with first-class teachers. Others were unfortunate in having faculties not adequate to the undertaking of imparting practical information. Among the first-class schools, one thinks immediately of the Pius X School of Liturgical Music, under the direction of the dynamic and well-informed Mother Stevens, a Madame of the Sacred Heart Order, and also some institutes conducted by the Benedictine Fathers. Generally, however, diplomas from the schools did not mean that the graduates were masters or mistresses of Gregorian chant. Such masters, as graduates of the Counterpoint Department in the New England Conservatory of Music, would be in the field of imitation, canon and fugue. Or graduates in piano playing of the Curtis Institute, the Peabody Institute or the Juillard, would be in that of Chopin, Bach Beethoven and Liszt.

The pedagogy in Gregorian institutes was frequently too pedantic. Doctrinarians discoursed in archaic terminology of points which needed simplification. The nomenclature of the chant built itself up into a menacing vocabulary. Fundamental points about rhythm often were presented so abstrusely that students emerged from the courses in a state of distressing confusion. Various schools of thought about the interpretation of the Gregorian notation abounded.

Although the *Liber Usualis,* edited by the Benedictine Monks of Solesmes, was made the official version of the ancient chants, all other versions being abrogated and universal use of the same melodies thus assured, there were countless different points of view as to accentuation, crescendos and dimuendos, tempos, and dynamic variations in general. One Doctor of Gregorian Chant would try to promote one concept, and another would underline the opposite. Various systems of organ accompaniment for the chant were sponsored, and many books with accompaniments were published. One by ABC followed an accentual harmony, supplying chords on important notes, and using frail inversions of fundamental chords with passing notes to keep the thing going, so to speak, while another by XYZ employed all kinds of descants (the association of other melodies with the chant in progress) which distorted the chant almost beyond recognition. Only in comparatively recent years have real masters of the art of supplying a background of chords to the monodic chant appeared on the scene, such as Dr. Bragers of the Pius X School in New York, and the celebrated organist of Montreal, Dr. Lapierre. A Sulpician priest from the seminary in Montreal, Father Thibault, is now presenting all the basic and idiomatic aspects of Gregorian so clearly that, at this writing, it is reasonable to hope that genuine progress will soon be made in the matter of restoring authentic understanding of the chant. Recently, I observed Father Thibault and Dr. Lapierre at work before classes in a Vermont summer school for Sisters, where I had the privilege of being associated with them on the teaching staff. These gentlemen are practical. For many years the teachers were mainly theoretical.

And so, during the decades which have elapsed since the issuing of the encyclical letter by Pope Pius X, in November, 1903, the efforts to develop a distinctively effective type of church music met with little success. Congregations expressed dislike for the raucous singing, the two-finger organ playing, *and* the Gregorian chant. The movement did not have a fair chance. And furthermore, ultra-rigorists, archaists, leaders more Catholic than the Church, retarded progress by condemning modern music in toto. Some were so fanatical as to cry down from the housetops all who were so irregular as to program anything written after the early era of polyphony. Some were even distressed by the tortuous counterpoints of the great Palestrina. A choirmaster who would use the *"Ave Verum"* of Gounod was anathema. And yet this number is just as spiritual in effect as the sixth mode *"Ave Verum"* in the *Liber Usualis!*

I was among those most vehemently attacked by the severe purists. In magazine articles, newspaper items and on lecture platforms, I was dubbed the chief heretic on this side of the Atlantic. The written and spoken censures failed to disturb me. I knew what I was doing, and this was in accord with the best traditions of the Church, and as a fruit of the Ground Bass my efforts were directed intently and intensively upon the task of restoring church music to an aesthetic estate. Without aesthetic quality, music could never wield a spiritual influence over men. It matters not what the repertoire may be, exclusively Gregorian, Gregorian plus the bald medieval polyphony or the richer polyphony of the sixteenth century, or modern music, if the rendition of the repertoire lacks those qualities that make music music. Excessive devotion to archaism, for its own sake, often tends to develop smugness. There is a savor of puritanism in the promoters of the exclusively Gregorian repertoire, which is essentially non-Catholic. Pope Pius X made clear in his encyclical that modern music as well as Gregorian chant and polyphony are worthy of use at the liturgical services, if the compositions are not melodramatic, sentimental or disruptive of the liturgical texts. In the repertoire declared improper, the settings were, in the majority, histrionic, melodramatically emotive, romantic and frequently ruinous to the continuity of a Mass text, an Antiphon, and often even to a hymn. Many repetitions occurred. But even in polyphony, to which Pope Pius X accorded the second place in the gamut of suitable church music, if one were to count the number of *Kyries,* intoned by the independent polyphonic lines, the total might often exceed that of a Cherubini Mass. However, Cherubini went out for other reasons, chiefly the operatic style and the great length of choral and orchestral figures. Beethoven's Missa Solemnis and the Bach "B Minor," although punctuated by many movements as spiritually oriented as anything written by the master a cappella polyphonists, are not only too long for liturgical service, but far beyond the talent of church choirs.

The whole movement got off to a bad start. The hierarchy was interested, moderately, in instituting the reforms decreed. But it has been difficult to persuade Their Excellencies that the first step towards satisfactory church music is the training of choirmasters in the art of choral technique. Their Excellencies have been satisfied if the Sisters and the leading directors took courses in the chant. The fact that neither the Sisters nor the lay directors were generally able to evoke musical sounds from their singers did not impress the bishops. Gregorian chant! Have the boys and men sing that, and all was well! This was an error in judg-

ment. It would be as reasonable to commission alleged stained-glass artists to put the windows in a church, provided they pictured only saints or
religious scenes, with no consideration for their technique or lack of this,
as to place the music of the Church in the hands of Gregorianists who are
altogether unequipped to give instruction in the fundamentals of choral
singing.

Another tendency which has acted as a drag upon the progress of
church music has been the passion for the heavy and sad in vernacular
hymns. Minor chords dominate the staves in most of the reform hymn-
books. Even the "Mexican Glide" waltzes which filled the unexpurgated
books were preferable to the ponderous, dull and melancholy-laden airs
and harmonies which our rigorous puritanical editors and compilers have
offered. No doubt, a lilting "Mother Dear, Oh! Pray For Me" suggests
more the gay raiment of a senorita south of the Rio Grande than the white
mantle of the Blessed Virgin, but at any rate there's something sunshiny
about it. Too often the puritans let loose thunderbolts of depression.
Overcast skies blotting out hope. Minor thirds in low areas, telling how
glum and dreary everything is in the other world. No joy in religion! Is
this the primary tenet in the subconsciousness of these hymnists?

The restoration of church music to its noble place among the arts
which are presumed to serve religion can be accomplished only when the
approach to the art is influenced by the conviction that beauty, spiritual
loveliness and cloudless happiness are the foreground and background of
eternity.

This is a suitable place in these memoirs to consider the general musicianship of the Reverend Sisters, upon whom as a body has fallen the
responsibility for the musical accessory of public worship throughout the
land. For many years, I have had excellent opportunities for measuring
the dimensions of the Sisters' knowledge and skill in the exercise of the
art of music. Among the Sisters who have presided over musical activities, as specialists, I have often found a marked degree of natural ability
and superior training. Except in one important department! Of course,
there are many Sisters who, though not musical specialists, are called
upon to conduct the classes in singing in parochial schools. But the case is
same with the lay teachers in public schools. The teachers of reading, 'rit-
ing and 'rithmetic are frequently required in the grade schools, to go
through the same motions of singing teachers as the musically trained
teachers. One cannot reasonably expect satisfactory results in music from
a teacher of history, whose knowledge of music is limited to such basic
points as the sequence of notes in the *do, re, mi* scale, and the influence on
pitch of sharps and flats. There are not enough trained specialists in either
parochial or public schools to teach music in all the classes. But I am inter-

ested here in telling of the qualifications of the specialists. Among these, the musicianship is certainly on as high a level as that reached by the supervisors of music in public schools. In fact, I am convinced that there are many more brilliant performers, and theoreticians in the convents than among the supervisors.

The Sisters who give lessons on the piano are, by and large, artists themselves, trained for years by the great masters of the instrument. They play the piano themselves with the master touch and facility. Also, the teachers of the violin rank with the good teachers at conservatories. I have not encountered many brilliant organists among the Sisters, but I take genuine pleasure in calling attention to the remarkable achievements of a little Franciscan Sister, Sister M. Theophane, of Alverno Music School, Milwaukee. She can outplay most of the celebrated recital organists in Europe and America. The Alverno Music School is an extraordinarily well-staffed institute of music, graduating pupils who would not come out second best in a contest with the best from the New England Conservatory, or Juillard, Curtis or Peabody institutes.

But in the multiple phases of choral musicianship, the nuns as a rule, are as unqualified as their lay colleagues. They have not had the opportunity to learn. Personally, it was necessary for me to institute a thorough search for the information I needed. There didn't seem to be any one around who knew chorophony from its fundamentals to its broadest ramifications. The chorus and the orchestra are to the Sisters what the irregular verbs of Latin are to a first year student, who can translate about forty percent of *Viri Romae*. The lay musicians, generally, know little about chorophony or symphony. Ask an average organist to suggest a balance of flute, string, reed and horn sopranos, singing over a contralto-mezzo-soprano chorus. If he does make a suggestion, this will usually be the fruit of hopeful conjecture. Ask him to arrange quickly a four part hymn tune for strings, double-reeds, single-reeds and French Horns, and he will probably discover that he's late for an appointment. Concerted musicianship has not in recent decades stimulated the interest of the great majority of instrumental players or vocal soloists, either outside or inside the convent walls. It is time for qualified teachers of choral and orchestral technique to hang out shingles. They would probably build up quite a trade after a short time, for Sisters and lay practitioners of the art are becoming increasingly aware of their shortcomings.

In the many summer courses I have conducted, and about which I shall write later, the Sisters have been among the most alert students. I hazard a guess that the number of Sisters to whom I have lectured on the choral art would total a minimum of two thousand. It has been possible at least to open up a new vista for them. Many are now *thinking* about chorophony. About tone quality, blend and the resources of interpretation. There is less guessing. Guessing and gambling are cousins-german. Too often one guesses wrong. Too often a man puts his money on the wrong horse.

If I have assisted the sweet Ladies of God by sharing with them some of the facts which I garnered on the trip to Parnassus, it will be a source of happiness on some eternal day to learn this. It required several years to convince the Sisters and lay students, too, that my experience qualified me to deal with the problems of ordinary choirs. My choristers were ac-claimed as extraordinary, and I was presumed to be working, over the years, with exceptionally fine voices, with plenty of money to prosper my undertakings. Save in a few instances, we did not have remarkable voices. And as for money, well! you've already learned that "I had plenty of nothing" but nothing wasn't plenty for me.

In concluding this chapter, I quote from a program note in the book of words distributed at a great concert given in 1945 by the Chicago Sisters and the Chicago Symphony Orchestra:

"As the other art-forms have been gadding about, roving without sense of direction, confounded by misleading criteria, succumbing to the increasing influence of neo-paganism, so, too, the art of music has gone astray, floundering in eddies of noise, bereft of its elegances, ad-dressing itself to the devotees of hullabaloo, and generally invalidating its primary worth. Since the Sisters compose a great sector of the army of the Church Militant, it is reasonable and practicable to rely upon them for aid in guiding music back to the flower-strewn paths so long deserted."

Chapter XXIV *The Ground Bass and the Radio*

THE reorganized chorus moved back to Fifty-ninth Street in January, 1925. Broadcasting was developing at the time into a major industry. Soon we were giving programs on the principal wave lengths. The Paulist Fathers were having their own radio station built. WLWL was planned as a medium for giving instruction about the doctrines and practices of the Church.

I was placed in charge of the musical programs of the new station, but my tenure of office was short lived. Having been instructed to permit only first-class soloists or groups to broadcast, I set about fulfilling the instructions literally. This was a mistake. Except in military units, perhaps it is an error in judgment to be meticulous in carrying out instructions. It might be better, at least more politic, to try to interpret the spirit of the orders, and fret less about discharging them with precise exactitude. I don't know. It would be an interesting point to debate. But I do know that at station WLWL following the instructions exactly failed to win approbation from those in charge.

I would give auditions to singers and instrumentalists, turn my lists in with approval or disapproval of the candidates indicated, and a few evenings later be surprised to hear one of the disapproved warbling or scraping the fiddle on our wave length. Friends of friends were favored. It would be a mistake, I was told, to blackball applicants who were recommended by prominent persons. Female organists who also sang (a little) would come from Westchester County, New Jersey and Connecticut, with letters introducing them as great artists. "She has been organist and soprano soloist at St.————'s for thirty years." That sort of thing. But when she and the other kindred she's and he's let loose the Schubert, Gounod-Bach or Luzzi "Ave Maria," the full thirty years were epitomized in the intonations. And so I suggested that I should resign. This terminated the existing arrangement.

But the Choristers broadcast the Sunday evening services from the

Fifty-ninth Street Church. We gave many programs on week nights also. I think that the station continued in operation for twelve years. From September to June, I was responsible for the Sunday evenings.

In the beginning, we had some amusing and some distressing experiences. Once, the engineer dashed into the choir hall where we were practicing the next number, during a sermon, and shouted at us something like this: "How do you expect me to put you folks on the air right? You sing loud and then soft. Sometimes, the Gospel side is louder than the Epistle side. Sing everything the same."

On another occasion, during a midweek broadcast, an assistant to the engineer came down to the Sanctuary, looked around, and detached the microphone from the sopranos' side, spoiling what had been up to that moment our best broadcast.

Engineers and acousticians were just learning the basic principles involved in broadcasting. Everybody who sat in the control room at WLWL and later at the National Broadcasting Company studios experimented with us. Microphones here, not there! Next time, there, *not* here! Certain types of music could not be clearly put on the air. I'll discuss this point when I tell of our ten years on the National Broadcasting Company Catholic Hour. And in different parts of the city, and with superior or inferior receiving sets, the effects produced were startlingly at variance. Once a priest complained to me that I should not have allowed a solo boy to sing without an organ accompaniment. He had been listening in Brooklyn. Another priest, tuning in from the Bronx, upbraided me for overplaying, almost completely muffling the small boy's voice. I was usually playing too loudly or too softly at the same time!

We soon came to dislike broadcasting, realizing that our characteristic style of singing might or might not be reproduced. What sounded well in the Sanctuary or studio was often reported as inferior on the air. Our best repertoire frequently made the poorest material for the air. Involved numbers suffered from "confusion of tongues." A soprano passage when attacked by a bass phrase entering just as the listeners were becoming accustomed to the soprano timbres would fade out altogether, or become so opaque as to be only a blur.

Once the director of WLWL entered the choir hall to censure the boys and men for coughing while the broadcast was in progress. He gave quite a dimensional tirade. Working up a great choler during his speech, which had to do with self-control, he completely lost control of his voice, and, first spluttering, coughed his way out, to the delight of both adults and urchins.

For about four or five seasons, the Choristers gave many concerts for the financial benefit of the WLWL station. Most of these concerts were in nearby towns. It seemed that the majority of musical forays into New Jersey were on rainy nights. And we were often requested to sing numbers that were popular with the priests at Fifty-ninth Street and therefore broadcast on WLWL, becoming known thus to the New Jersey audiences.

One of the bête noires was "Good Night, Sweet Jesus." This particular piece, with its very saccharine melody and soft-hearted text, was hard to fit in with Palestrina, Bach and Brahms. But when Henri Marcoux, baritone, well known to the radio audiences, would address his larynx to the second-verse solo part over the glucose harmony of the other voices, audiences would be hypnotized into the most delightful reveries. Palestrina and the others could not compete. This piece evoked from a satirist much caustic criticism in the monthly calendar of the Fifty-ninth Street Church. On the day of the appearance of the lampoon, circumstances placed me on the spot, for the Rector and another priest of the local community requested it to be sung at the evening service. Relatives would be coming in from out of town, and would be disappointed if the number were omitted. We sang it, of course, but the author of the satire judged that I was thus answering his comments, and carefully avoided having breakfast near me for at least a fortnight.

A signally successful Rector, Father Henry Riley, was in charge between 1925 and 1931. He invited the then young Dr. Fulton Sheen to preach the Lenten course at our great Church. And he supported every effort of mine to maintain the choir at the highest possible level of artistry. On the Fulton Sheen Sunday evenings, the great Church would be filled to capacity long before the hour appointed for the service. Father Riley and I, after the choir had finished the preliminary part of the service, would fill up the Sanctuary and priests' choirstalls with men and women who had been standing in the aisles. Sometimes the number of these was large enough to make a good congregation in a smaller church.

One day a boy from Canada called on me, asking for an audition. He had an extraordinary voice and consummate mastery in using it. Father Riley heard him from a nearby corridor. Beckoning me to confer with him, he told me to take that boy on, no matter what it cost. The boy was Joseph Laderoute, probably the greatest soprano solo boy ever heard in North America. He is now one of the tenors at the Metropolitan Opera House, New York. With Fulton Sheen, the choir at its very best, and young Laderoute singing the great oratorio arias, Fifty-ninth Street became the chief competitor of the Metropolitan Opera's Sunday night concerts. Once Armand Crabbe, great Belgian baritone, well known to New York audiences, joined our already highly effective forces. His appearance was announced in the newspapers, and on that Sunday night, Fifty-ninth Street, Columbus Avenue and Sixtieth Street looked like Broadway on election nights.

During those years, in addition to our broadcasting from WLWL, we were engaged to sing on many commercial programs. The National Carbide Company invited us for their Bach, Brahms and Mozart nights. These were the most satisfactory broadcasts I ever conducted, for things were right. Usually, on all our extra radio appearances, there was something amiss. Most frequently the rehearsing of the orchestra was restricted to an altogether inadequate period. Hardly sufficient time to give more than a "cue" rehearsal. Certainly not enough to blend orchestra and chorus or to perfect the details of interpretation. How often we went on the air with pages of unrehearsed copy!

But with the Carbide Company, we could rehearse with the orchestra as often and as long as we found it advantageous. The *St. Matthew's Passion* program was a thoroughly artistic performance, and the Brahms and Mozart selections were almost as satisfactory. After the *St. Matthew's Passion* broadcast, I was descending in the elevator at the old National Broadcasting Company building on Fifth Avenue. I noticed one of the cellists in the elevator, and thanked him for his co-operation. He was a Jew. He patted his cello with one hand, wiping away a tear with the other, and saying something like this: "Oh! it was so beautiful tonight and at the rehearsals, too. My cello, it loved to play the music of Bach about the death of Jesus. The chorus and the orchestra were as one perfect instrument. You know, many Jews admire your Jesus. How my heart melted when we played 'Bleed and Break.' "

And there were many performances for Al Jolson and the Shell Company, for George Washington Coffee, for Palmolive Soap, and for Kate Smith and the March of Time. Sustaining programs for National Broadcasting Company gave us opportunity for historical concerts—Gregorian chant, the polyphony of the middle ages and the Renaissance, Bach, Mozart, Handel, Haydn, etc. All this, plus the preparation and singing of the service music at Fifty-ninth Street, kept us actively busy. We found that for a four-minute number of average difficulty, if the broadcast were to do the piece and our organization justice, two hours of rehearsing were required. Two hours in our own choir hall before going to the studio for another hour's balancing at the microphones. There wasn't much fun in it. Plain hard work. Nothing amusing to laugh about. Just routine.

But the great concerts at Carnegie Hall and the Metropolitan Opera House made up for the dull moments of broadcasting. Concerts with the New York Philharmonic, and Barrère's Little Symphony. Great audiences. Diverse styles of music. Programs that made the boys and even the professional men eager and sometimes worried, such as the Ascendo ad Patrem Mass of Palestrina; the *Miserere* of Allegri; the premier of a work of mine; the Mozart and the Brahms Requiems.

The Ascendo Mass was performed at our Silver Jubilee concert at the Metropolitan. I had come upon the secret of presenting polyphony. It is not within the scope of this book to expound the technique for interpreting this great style of music. Those who are interested are referred to a recent book of mine * in which all the principles and precepts involved are discussed. However, the fact that I had been unsuccessfully seeking the convincing, idiomatic manner of rendering polyphony for many years, and the circumstances under which the secret revealed itself to me will probably hold the attention of some readers, especially that of former Choristers. Overnight they must have observed that I began to emphasize aspects of the style which I had never mentioned before.

We were invited to sing an a cappella polyphonic program at Wolsey Hall, Yale University. Only music of the Middle Ages and the Renaissance was listed. I began to conduct in my usual fashion, conscious, as always before, that I was missing something essential in my interpretation. When we had been singing for about quarter of an hour, I became aware of unfamiliar, strange, but highly satisfying effects coming from the chorus banks. The Choristers, warmed up by the first two or three motets, suddenly began, on their own unsuspected initiative, to unfold the polyphony with a new technique. (I judged later that this seemingly new technique must have been the old, lost technique of the cinquecento musicians). Gentle crescendos and diminuendos recurred at similar places in the composition. Glidings into the first notes of phrases instead of addressing them with destructive impacts. I went offstage, made a few memoranda on paper, and presently co-ordinated these into what I am firmly convinced is the reconstructed technique of Palestrina and his colleagues.

At the date of our Silver Jubilee concert, the Choristers had been singing the polyphony with the new-old technique for some seasons. It was announced that we would sing in unequal temperament, viz., just intonation which, for example, makes F sharp and G flat two different notes. On the piano and organ keyboards and on all keyed wind instruments, such notes are identical. Otherwise the size of the keyboards would be too large to be manageable. It is said that small children can sing scales more perfectly in tune than their elders whose intonations have been tempered by the equal temperament of the piano. I knew that, if only a single note were struck on the piano to establish the pitch at

* Finn, *The Conductor Raises His Baton,* (New York: Harper & Bros., 1944).

the beginning of a piece, my choristers, so long accustomed to singing without accompaniment, would presently settle into the more correct intonations of unequal temperament. Physicists at nearby colleges were interested. It was reported that some of these had special tuning forks made by which to test the accuracy of our acoustical pitch. I had observed, in the Fifty-ninth Street Church, that the true acoustical pitch provided a vitality to the singing that was missing with the tempered pitch. The difference is not discernible as a notable difference to the average listener. It is too subtle. But subtlety and latency being among the determining if elusive forces of music, the conductor of an a cappella chorus must take them into account.

We prepared the Ascendo Mass with great care. There are many upward skips of an octave in this Mass, but never two wide skips in succession on any one voice line. The octave jumps were hazards. Not vocal hazards. Accentual hazards. To ascend an octave is a surreptitious invitation to accent the top note. In this Mass, such accentuation is destructive of its polyphonic character. And so we practiced with zeal. Considering the significance of the Silver Jubilee concert and the ideals which we had been essaying to promote for a quarter of a century, I took pains to see that no detail which might influence the effectiveness of the music would be left unchecked. And so, I visited Artur Bodansky, seeking suggestions as to the best stage setting. Mr. Bodansky had been senior conductor of the German operas at the Metropolitan for several years and also choral director of the Friends of Music. I had been dissatisfied with the setting provided for the Choristers on many occasions at the great opera emporium. It was hard, from the conductor's podium, to sense the effects I was trying to produce. Much of the resonance seemed to be absorbed by the scenic wings and the flyspace over the proscenium. Mr. Bodansky advised against the use of the regular chorus tiers, suggesting that we use the Toscanini false stage which that maestro had arranged in the orchestra pit. It could be elevated to a height not quite level with the stage. It was in front of the footlights. That seemed to be a reasonable arrangement, and I decided upon it. A curtain was to be dropped behind the Choristers, preventing the sounds from stealing off backstage. But alas! I failed to check one detail, viz., the kind of curtain to be dropped.

The audience that assembled for that concert was the sort of audience one dreams about in optimistic moments. A cross section of the concert-going public of the world's greatest metropolis. Standing room only and little of that. The Pope instructed the Apostolic Delegate in Washington to attend the concert. Cardinal Hayes was there. Many archbishops, bishops, monsignori. Conductors of opera, symphony and oratorio were there. Many of the several Four Hundred groups that confuse the make-up of New York society were represented in the boxes. The Diamond Horse Shoe was all aglitter. We were to sum up, after twenty-five years of concentrated effort, in a practical demonstration, what we had discovered and mastered of the medieval and Renaissance choral excellences. Interest was keen among the critics and choirmasters.

And the concert started badly! As we wound our way through the intracies of the first long section of the concert, I knew that something was amiss. On such a brilliant occasion. "O dark, dark, dark, amid the blaze of noon!" I hadn't checked the kind of drop curtain! The stage manager had provided a heavy velvet curtain, a fabric with a thick, fuzzy, plushy pile. Every thread in its nap seemed avid to swallow the liquid tones of the singers, and especially of the soprano boys. If I had not made the grievous blunder of changing the routine which I had followed for years, I would have ascertained before beginning the polyphonic pieces that only a higher than usual pitch would counteract the muffling effect of that thirsty velvet screen.

Several men and women had urged me to place a Gregorian chant at the top of the program, saying that we should pay tribute fittingly at the very beginning to the official music of the Church. It had been our routine to begin concerts with the unaccompanied "Emitte Spiritum Tuum" of Franz Schuetky, programmed as "Invocation Motet." The structure of this motet affords excellent opportunity to the conductor for judging the effects of low and high pitches, crescendos, diminuendos, accelerandos, rallentandos, prevailing faster or slower tempos, and the relationship of the various vocal lines to one another, in the hall and under the circumstances in which the ensuing program would be sung. Franz Kneisel, of the celebrated Kneisel Quartet, had interested me years before in ascertaining the acoustical state of a hall at the outset. Against my better judgment, I followed the urgent advice of the monitors and discarded the harmonized motet for the unison Gregorian chant. Only the adult voices sang this chant. It was therefore impossible to make calculations which would show the course to pursue when the soprano boys would make their important contributions. And so I indicated a key too low to defeat the eager velvet, and chose a slower tempo than I would have selected had the "Invocation Motet" been used.

It was a dreadful experience to stand in front of the great chorus and realize that its excellent vocalism was being neutralized. I was reminded of this experience recently, while reading a detective story, the main point of which was the deadening of the sound of a violin by pouring varnish through the *f* openings.

Presently I accelerated the tempo. The faster pace lent some animation to the proceedings but not enough to defeat the inimical backdrop. At the end of the first long piece, naturally, I remedied the situation, but the first twenty minutes of the Jubilee concert seemed like eons of slow-moving fragments of eternity.

A few seasons later, in the same Opera House, we sang the celebrated *Miserere* of Allegri. Perhaps no single composition for a cappella chorus was ever guarded so strictly as this setting of the Fiftieth Psalm. Written for use at Tenebrae in the Sistine Chapel, the complete composition was not heard outside that famous chapel until comparatively recent years. There are many legends about efforts of choirmasters, and even princes and kings, to secure copies of the verses known as the *abbellimenti*. Mozart and Mendelssohn are said to have copied them from memory. At any rate, these difficult and highly ornate decorative figures were not heard in America, if my knowledge is correct in the matter, until we rendered them, first at the Fifty-ninth Street Church and later at the Metropolitan and elsewhere. I was long debating the wisdom of undertaking them.

Finally I decided that a certain small group of singers could manage the strange movements. When we gave the great composition at Fifty-ninth Street, the congregation was much impressed. A professor of the Catholic University, who often said that music irked him, was in the congregation. He told me later that those mysterious tonal arabesques that traced themselves in sound behind the High Altar had moved him strangely. He was curious about the structure of the ornamentations, but upon my trying to explain this to him in nontechnical language, he said that he'd rather not try to understand, that hearing them was a spiritual adventure.

When we brought the composition to the Metropolitan Opera House, New York musicians were much more excited than Gotham's music masters usually allow themselves to become. On the evening of the performance, I was worried, because Jack Kearney, the solo soprano boy, had himself been worried for several days. He was required to touch the high C, in the dead center of the pitch; to glance at it, so to speak, with his vocal cords. It would have to be in perfect tune with the C an octave lower sung by the alto, for when the soprano would release his high note, the alto would continue to sustain the lower one at the same time, the upper pitch seeming to continue, which would be, of course, a harmonic or overtone. For the soprano boy to be in perfect concord with the alto and his harmonic required an altogether unencumbered vocalism. Free physically and mentally.

But Jack began to worry. Anxiety, especially among trained soprano boys, usually is such a strain that they can hardly escape singing such high notes sharp. At the last rehearsal, Jack would climb to C sharp, and since the undervoices were true to pitch, the discord was a painful cacophony. I didn't know what to do. Finally, I told Jack to remain off stage until time for the *Miserere,* and asked Mr. Harry Moyle, one of our basses and formerly a patter-bass with the Savoyards in London, to entertain the boy while we were singing the preliminary numbers. Mr. Moyle distracted the lad with the patter songs of *Pinafore, The Pirates, Ruddigore, Mikado,* etc., and when the boy came on stage for his ordeal, he was completely relaxed and soared to the heights with great ease and safely true to pitch. A later experience with the Allegri setting was not so successful, however, for another solo boy was so frightened that he sang high above the top note, and I was obliged to shorten the number before a large audience at a Sesquicentennial Concert in Constitution Hall, Washington.

In the spring of 1929, Pope Pius XI was reported to be preparing an *Apostolic Constitution* concerning church music. There was much speculation in the United States as to how forcibly His Holiness would insist upon the employment of boys instead of women in church choirs in compliance with the *Motu Proprio* of Pope Pius X. Some bishops here and elsewhere had expressed the opinion that there was a dearth of choirmasters qualified to train boys. The fact that these bishops were right in their conclusions had not impressed the major part of the American hierarchy. Although I had long championed the aesthetic worth, as well as the liturgical convention, of the use of boy trebles, if properly prepared, I was and am emphatically opposed to the use of boys whose only qualification for musical service is the circumstance of sex. And so, somehow (I don't remember just why) I was deputed to travel to Rome to confer with Vatican officials on the subject.

Having sailed at midnight on the ill-fated ship, *Paris,* of the French Line, we found ourselves stranded the next morning, and, I think, for the greater part of two days, on the mudflats off Brooklyn. The trip was thus lengthened, but I profited from the extension of the voyage by association with two gentlemen of different backgrounds and interests— John Erskine, then recently resigned from the Chair of English at Columbia University and beginning his tenure of office at Juilliard Musical Foundation; and Raymond Michel, a Parisian formerly on the staff of Andre Tardieu, liason officer for the French in New York during World War I. Mr. Erskine was adept in two media of communication, English and music. Monsieur Michel was well trained in the diverse psychologies of a homogeneous people—the French, and a heteregeneous people—the Americans. I learned much from these gentlemen. From

Mr. Erskine, the relationship of an adjective to a noun, and an adverb to a verb, suggesting the association of a melodic arc to a main theme. A parenthesis clarifying a sentence much after the fashion of one vocal or orchestral line explaining simply what a profuseness of notes and parts had been confusing. And from Monsieur Michel, the spontaneity, effervescence and delicacy of the French mentality contrasted with the stolidity and prosiness of a people dominantly Ango-Saxon and Teutonic. Perhaps I began to consider items of interpretation which had escaped me before. The relationships between parts of speech from the point of view of eloquence. The relationships of contrapuntal figures. The need of one point of view in reading a French or Italian score, and another in reading one from the pen of an Englishman or German.

Upon my arrival at Rome, several gentlemen from the Vatican called upon me. Signs displayed in conspicuous places in the hotel asked guests to refrain from tipping the employees. My recollection of the signs is that they were worded in beseeching phraseology. I was sure of the English, of course, and of the French, too. Of the Italian I wasn't so certain. But I was impressed by what I concluded to be a plea for strict observance. Ten per cent would be added to one's bill in lieu of the traditional gratuities. When I settled the bill for the first luncheon with the representatives from the Vatican, the waiters seemed unfriendly, and I thought to see covert glances exchanged between the monsignori. Next day, after our order had been placed for a considerable period of time without service, I sought the manager, who complained that I had failed to tip on the preceding day.

"But what of the signs?"

"Dear me, those signs don't mean a thing! Give two dollars' worth of silver and I'll send the coins out to the pantry. Then the service will be prompt."

I handed over the gratuity, and the *garçons* rallied around quickly. What a folly to have interpreted the ubiquitous signs literally! Probably it is an error in judgment to understand words in their first and explicit dictionary definitions. Maybe as with the language of diplomacy, one should "say what you don't mean forcibly but artfully." At any rate, having remedied my mistake, food came, and we continued our discussions of the day before.

It was interesting to observe the polite interest of the Italians in my point of view, which they obviously regarded as typically American, and therefore, amusing. In Rome, the notion of women singing in churches, by the necessity of centuries of tradition, would be judged a diverting whimsey. Men and boys only! Monsignore Perosi must have experienced the need of reorientation when first he waved his baton over the soprano chorus of females for the production of his oratorios. I am reminded here of my mother's distaste and perhaps chagrin when she watched me directing the Medievalists, a choir of women and men. It was fantastic for one habituated to using boys for the soprano chorus to appear suddenly on a New York podium conducting women! I think that she always had an excuse for absenting herself on the occasion of later concerts with the daughters of Eve.

Well! I unfolded my point of view, arguing that certain remote and sparsely settled places could not furnish boys for the High Mass and other church services, and that furthermore, there were as few maestros qualified to teach the boys, at least in the United States (I can't understand why I intimated that elsewhere there were many!), as there were lilies of the valley at the North Pole. We ate the tasty offerings of one of Italy's best chefs, and discussed the subject at hand with most delicious ragout of urbane Oh's and Ah's.

Cardinal Lepicier, Prefect of the Sacred Congregation of Religious, was an important member of the papal advisory staff. And so I called upon him at his humble quarters near the Basilica of St. John Lateran. Having been stationed for years in London, His Eminence spoke English with fluency and elegance. "So you are Father Finn? Can you prove your identity?"

"Here are my credentials, Your Eminence."

"Easily forged! I'll test you. If you are Father Finn, you will be able to play the organ for me." Thereupon a lay brother brought a little dress suitcase reed organ into the room. "Play something by Bach."

"Your Eminence, this organ has a scant two octaves and a half on the keyboard and of course no pedal notes." But, thinking the situation to be a cardinalatial prank, I pumped as much wind into the instrument as the tiny treadles made possible, and played the subject and answer of the Bach Little G Minor Fugue.

"Play for me the Gregorian scales, naming each as you play it." A chap on the rack in the kindly days of the Inquisition had no more thorough catechetical examination than I endured, although I soon perceived that His Eminence was deriving much amusement from the proceedings. Finally, he ordered the organ away and said equivalently: "This was absurd, but I was having a little fun and testing you psychologically at the same time. You are dogmatic in your statements about music. You give vigorously enough. I wanted to find out how much you can take. Now, what shall I tell the Pope?"

I requested him to ask the Pope to allow some latitude in the matter of using boys in the soprano choirs. He agreed to make the recommendation, saying that one could easily become so liturgically minded as to lose the sense of proportion needed for dealing with special situations and circumstances.

My recollection of the Apostolic Constitution finally issued by Pope Pius XI is that it stressed two principal points, viz., that the liturgical text must always be given the place of honor, never the music, and that the Roman pronunciation of Latin was to be adopted in all parts of the world.

During the years following the promulgation of this Constitution, choral conditions have remained about the same. Perhaps it would be inaccurate to insist that no progress has been made. But it is clear that the resources at hand in the average parish in cities and fair-sized towns are not being adequately developed. During the last decade, a larger number of Catholic musicians have shown interest in the delicacies of choral technique than in the earlier years of the reform movement, but, except in few instances, a high degree of artistry is not exemplified.

For many years I had been conducting intensive courses in all the important phases of chorophony throughout the country. At first it was depressing and astonishing to note that the registration of Catholic musicians for the courses was, on the average, fifteen per cent of the total. Once I gave a winter course which involved a weekly round trip journey of five hundred miles. There were ninety-nine non-Catholic musicians in the class and *one* Catholic.

Some of the truths of the choral art, however, are beginning to influence Catholic choirmasters in many places, for a noticeable reduction in noisy performance is evident. Even a negative virtue has value, but the positive virtues of the art are not made manifest. Certain priests in charge of music in the seminaries are becoming aware of the fundamental principles of concerted singing. And the Sisters are improving each year. Later on I propose to discuss the relationship of the Sisters to the status of music in Catholic churches and schools.

In March, 1930, the Catholic Hour was inaugurated through the co-operation of the National Council of Catholic Men and the National Broadcasting Company. The names of Archbishop Schrembs of Cleveland and Monsignor John J. Burke, C.S.P., organizer and chief secretary of the National Catholic Welfare Conference come immediately to mind in connection with this undertaking. Both of these prelates are deceased, and I esteem it a privilege to pay tribute to their initiative and boldness in embarking upon what many thought would be a disastrous enterprise. How to finance the weekly programs? How to guarantee a consistently high standard of broadcasts for fifty-two Sundays a year? Where would the proper type of speakers be found? Who would accept responsibility for the music? The National Broadcasting Company donated the use of their broadcasting facilities, otherwise the project could not have been undertaken. In the beginning, at Monsignor Burke's prompting, the National Council of Catholic Men provided enough money for good musical programs. But we were obliged to pay the tenor and bass singers stipends below the prevailing rates in the studios. For orchestra, we had a string quartet which we could not pay for rehearsals. Therefore, our broadcasts were done with only a few moments' practice for balance before the microphone.

In this connection, I recall an amusing comment by a man more given to sarcasm than to constructive criticism. After one of those broadcasts for which we did not have the money for orchestral preparation, he said to me: "Do you realize that with your orchestra you don't get anything like the effects that Toscanini gets from the Philharmonic?" We had four players, unrehearsed. The Italian maestro had about a hundred with daily rehearsal.

When the economic depression was at its worst, our budget was reduced to so low a figure that we were obliged to eliminate the four instrumentalists, and to offer a pittance to the adult singers. Under the circumstances, which naturally one could not gracefully explain on the air, it is remarkable that we were able to produce the artistic results which the large listening radio audience acclaimed. Two or three times a year, the National Broadcasting Company would donate a well-balanced orchestra with one hour's rehearsal time, and with a chorus augmented through payment by the Choristers' slender resources, we would make quite a grand splurge. But most of the time, for ten long years, the Catholic Hour was a dreary task and an undertaking full of hazards for an organization as well known as the Choristers.

Letters from all parts of the country commented on the music sung. It was difficult to please all the listeners. Some complained because we did not adhere to strictly liturgical music. Others found that we offered too much Gregorian chant and polyphony. Popular hymns, with little to recommend them either in texts or musical settings, were demanded by many. When we acceded to this demand, we were promptly rebuked by listeners interested in a better type of hymnody. All in all, we managed to please the outstanding majority of listeners, but our very efficient secretary, Miss Marion Loughlin, was busy tabulating the divers and diverse tastes of the many who sent us letters.

Soon after the instituting of the Catholic Hour, I realized that the boys and men of the Paulist Choristers would be unable to furnish the music for fifty-two Sundays a year. The soprano boys would have summer holidays, and the need of an ever-increasing repertory would demand so much rehearsing, in addition to the rehearsal time required for church services and concerts, that I decided to organize a group of ladies and gentlemen which would share the work. This unit was very satisfactory. Since it would sing so much music of the polyphonic style, it was immediately named "The Medievalists." The young ladies had no objection to being called by that name, but they were much chagrined when a facetious critic wrote a review of one of their stage concerts, dubbing them "The Mid-Victorians." Our lassies didn't mind association with the long-ago Renaissance, but they rebelled at being identified with the not-so-long-ago stiff, starchy, prim and smug affectations of Victoria's era.

It was easy to lyricize the sopranos' voices, so that they could produce a volatile tone quality comparable to that of the boys. In fact, the singing of one unit was often mistaken for the singing of the other. I remember one appearance of the Medievalists which confused many critics. We accepted an invitation to provide the music for a masque given by the Countess Scherr-Thoss in the ballroom of the Plaza Hotel. We sang offstage. The only reference to the music on the printed program was that it was under my direction. The audience assumed that the Choristers would sing. After the performance, which was beautifully given by the ladies and gentlemen, a distinguished New York lady, who had long been a patroness of the Choristers, told me, in the elevator, that she had never heard the boys in better form." But where are they? I don't see any of them about." So I pointed to some of our ladies and asked the enthusiastic patroness to meet some of the "boys."

The Medievalists took over the summer programs, and for a few years alternated with the boys during the high season. Also, the ladies and gentlemen gave a series of historical concerts on the Blue Network. The unit was fast developing into a virtuoso choral group, and would undoubtedly have become one of the notable small choirs of the epoch, if, as usual, we were not handicapped by lack of funds. The ladies and gentlemen made their livelihoods by singing, and I could not offer them stipends sufficiently large to warrant their foregoing good commercial opportunities. And so it was necessary to disband. Again it was the financial phase of the undertaking that defeated purpose.

I was becoming inured to poverty by that time, and I venture a guess that if a large endowment had suddenly been thrown in my lap, I would have become, at least gently, psychopathic. Dollars did not like my polyphonies. Bank accounts would not grow on my clefs. No discs of solid gold shone around the heads of my singers. Well! I was pioneering, if one can pioneer in the restoration of something. The art of choral singing had been in process of deterioration for a long time, when I felt the urge to raise it to its former level. And so I began that long expedition to Mount Parnassus with the clothes on my back and a few coppers rattling in my pocket. Probably the need of struggling always was an asset. A well-known New York musician once told me that he thought the real reason of the success of the Choristers to be their lack of funds. He spoke of the difference, financially, between his position and mine. He was a rich man personally, heir to a fortune, and had been organist and choirmaster only in churches which could afford a large annual budget. I had neither patrimony nor an adequate budget. It was always necessary to devise schemes for putting on major performances with minor resources. Underpaying the men. Eliminating necessary instruments from the orchestra. Giving soprano boys twenty-five cent pieces on occasions when only soft money would have been appropriate. This rich musician contended that poverty kept our wits alert, while his opulence induced easy-going methods. I dare say that he was right up to a point, but it would have been interesting to have had at one time or another sufficient money to oversee the musical development of the moment without the distracting anxiety of inadequate funds.

Before the Medievalists went to the Poor House, they shared a program at Carnegie Hall, New York, with the Choristers. I have already written that my mother quietly disapproved of my conducting women. But many others muttered, croaked and grunted. Having become associated with boys' singing before the public, I should confine myself to boys. I had no right to step out beyond the circumference of the boys' circle—no matter how contracted that circle!—in spite of the fact that a choral conductor could never know his trade from alpha to omega until he had trained and conducted all types of singing units!

Many in the audience at Carnegie Hall were *almost* polite in acknowledging the offerings of the ladies and gentlemen. But the applause for the Choristers was long and loud. Both units drew upon all their artistic resources, giving performances of notable merit. I caught the audience (the part unsympathetic to the alleged intrusion of the daughters of Eve) neatly a few times when both units sang together. Neither the sympathetic nor the vexed listeners could identify the contributions of either ensemble. It was a blended, homogeneous, but many colored, tonal panorama. The alto line, composed of countertenors, the alto voice distinctive of the Choristers, and mezzo-sopranos and contraltos (these the voices of women), was probably the most convincing alto line I have ever heard. The countertenor voice is the conserved treble-staff quality, resembling the soprano voice in some aspects, but denser and therefore heavier. This strange quality, merged with the timbres of sparkling mezzo-sopranos and the deep throatiness of contraltos, suggests to me the ideal combination for the alto line in a symphony orchestra. This line in the instrumental ensemble is the thinnest of the orchestral lines, so thin as to be altogether inadequate if the orchestration is full or above mezzo forte. The combined voices of Choristers and Medievalists suggested vocally the instrumental effect possible to an orchestra, if the alto line were to be assigned to violas, English Horns (the instruments considered distinctively alto by composers and conductors), some second violins, a French horn, a tenor bassoon and an alto saxophone. This latter instrument is not yet welcome in the symphonic ensemble, for many regard it as too closely associated with "swing" performances. But there is no doubt that the alto line is not well taken care of in symphony orchestras, and only the saxophone can supply the timbres which correspond to the quality of the combined Paulist Choristers' countertenor and the profoundness of the female contralto. The other instruments suggested provide the varied hues of the mezzo-soprano.

The main technical point at issue, in this combined concert of different types of units, was whether or not a group of female singers could be trained down to the simplicity of the utterances of boys. Could the consciousness of personal reactions to the emotive power of music be so reduced as to fit women for singing the impersonal music of the sixteenth century and later centuries as well. I have already written of the music sung by the Medievalists which the audience understood to be sung by the Choristers, because the singers were concealed from view. But I determined to throw the two groups together in great Carnegie Hall and see what happened. The audience was puzzled, except the vexed members. It was quite generally admitted that there was amazing similarity between the two groups when singing independently of each other, and that when they sang together, one could not distinguish between them, except for the enriching contributions of the female mezzo-sopranos and contraltos.

The English Singers gave a remarkable demonstration of the simplicity of utterance possible to women in impersonal music. They sang many motets in the polyphonic style, and I failed to hear a single note that was wistful, eager, passionate or fervid. More lately the Von Trappes, a family of Austrian ladies and gentlemen, have been proving the same point, viz., that women can be trained to exclude all gusto and personal glow from their intonations when the structure and mood of the music are better served without these.

As I have written elsewhere, women can be lyricized to sing as boys, but boys cannot be dramatized to sing as women. Dramatic sopranos cannot be so easily lyricized, for the dramatic soprano has a larger larynx. Her tones surge up from a glandular development that is proper to a sturdy adult female.

Probably many who remember the delightful programs of the Medievalists on the Catholic Hour are pleased to read these items about them. My first serious work with female singers was, as I have written, in Toronto during the spring of 1915. But I have had many choruses since, employing women on the soprano and alto lines. I shall tell more about these before the end of this book.

During the period between 1920 and 1940, when I retired from the direction of the Choristers, we sang many weddings. In 1922, we provided the music for the Mackay-O'Brien nuptials. Rarely was there a notable wedding in the vicinity of New York, either between two Catholics or between a Catholic and non-Catholic in which we did not participate. Another Mackay wedding. Consuelo Vanderbilt's. Two weddings in the McCann family (Woolworth ladies). Ewen. Ogden. Schuyler Warren. Anderson. I fail to remember all of them. The young ladies wanted us chiefly for the wedding march with which we brought the bridesmaids and the bride up the middle aisle. One of our men, Mr. James Duffy, a solo boy in the Chicago days, became an expert master of ceremonies for such affairs. We were accustomed to sing the tuneful chorus from Cowen's "Rose Maiden Cantata," "Tis thy wedding morning." (After the noon hour we would chant about her wedding evening.")

Many of the brides-elect fought for the old *Lohengrin* March which is forbidden in almost all European and American dioceses, on account of its definitely pagan text. The girls gave me a bad time on that score. Many intimated that they would not think themselves legally wed if they failed to walk to the Altar to the strains of "Here Comes The Bride." Cardinal Hayes asked me personally to accept engagements for mixed-marriage music, since he wished to make the ceremony as solemn as feasible. Once later, I was rebuked, however, by a prelate for having furnished the music. But once out of a few score does not signify.

One of the most unusual and ill-advised public performances which I ever undertook was a "pageant" at Carnegie Hall. It was in effect an opera. What I didn't know about opera would have filled many tomes. Opera is, of course, music plus. To conduct an opera with authority requires practically complete knowledge of the theatrical crafts as these affect an actor. I knew nothing about timing musical phrases properly for entrances and exits. I used to marvel at the skill of operatic conductors adjusting their tempos so as to synchronize the departure of Tosca from the stage with the final phrases of the music, after she had finished consigning Baron Scarpia to the place where bad Barons go. I was altogether unfamiliar with the resources, means and even tricks which a maestro conducting the *Ring* might be expected to use quickly and intuitively when anything went wrong with the progress of the mythological drama or a fuse blew out at Valhalla. Loudness and softness from the orchestra in the pit, with the singers of course on the stage, was a matter about which I could only conjecture. (There are some highly acclaimed conductors of opera now who do a bit of wrong guessing about the same point.) Generally, I did not know anything about conducting an opera.

Well! this pageant was an opera. A greatly gifted priest, Father Peter Moran, wrote the text and what is now termed, I suppose, the scenario. It was entitled *The Prince of Peace*. I was urged to write the music. I began writing the vocal score in October. The performance was to be during the Christmas holidays. Therefore, I could not write all the music. I slipped into the score a few compositions of others. Several things went wrong right from the start. We had planned to produce the pageant at the Paulist Fathers' Church, using the great symphonic organ there instead of an orchestra. This plan, if carried out, would have relieved me of the burden of writing an orchestral score. But Cardinal Hayes objected to the performance in the church. And so it was incumbent upon me to prepare the orchestration for a thoroughly theatrical performance at Carnegie Hall.

There is no pit for the orchestra in the Hall. Therefore, we were obliged to arrange one extreme side of the stage for the orchestra. This would and did entail many of the players sitting in places from which they could not see the conductor. No stage manager was provided. The rehearsals were hit and miss, mostly miss. Nothing definite had been agreed upon for stage business. What happened upstage at last night's rehearsal would be transferred downstage tonight. Quick entrances at one rehearsal would be slow at another.

Many of the props were homemade. Oh, so homemade! A torch for one of the soldiers of Herod's palace developed from a battered old thurible, long lost in a sacristan's closet. Much bantering appeared in one of the New York papers concerning the undertaking. Some pieces of scenery were good, notably the triptych which was the background for the performance. Some of the costumes would have been funny if not so misshapen. Extra lights were required to be hung from the ceiling over the stage.

At the dress rehearsal, I knew very little more about what I was to do in certain scenes, than I knew at the first rehearsal. I did not know the answers to any questions. I suppose that I had decided to steer by the gyroscope of instinct and concert experience. But I couldn't find a gyroscope at the dress rehearsal or at the performance. It is probably true to say that this rehearsal and the performance were not related intimately. At rehearsal, the Angel, Edward Hayes, a solo boy with an unusually beautiful voice, appeared out of the darkness on the left side of the stage where I could see him and give him his entrance beat, to announce to the Shepherds that the Christ Child would be born that night. At the performance, he was sent out of the *right* side. I signaled the orchestra to play *tremolato* until I could ascertain what he was going to do about his aria. Somehow, we finished together, although we did not begin together and the Shepherds were started on their journey to Bethlehem at least four bars too soon. King Herod flashed a sword for an extra page of orchestration. The Magi Kings were seated incorrectly, and the nervous singer who depended upon me for his beat, failing to see me, answered the questions of another Magi before they were asked. Also, he sang his phrases at least a fifth off pitch.

I should have declined to undertake the production. But I must have felt that in the Fifty-ninth Street Church, playing the organ myself, I could make allowances for uncertain stage business and irregular entrances and exits. At the organ, the experience would not be much different from playing a ritualistic service. At Carnegie Hall, it was a modified and mortified form of grand opera. At rehearsal, the concert-master sustained an injury to the forefinger of his left hand. Therefore, he would not undertake to play the performance. I had been depending upon him to help pull the performance through, for he knew the score as well as I did, and he had several expedients for keeping an orchestra going. Since many of the players could not see me, I needed his expedients for relaying the beats to the far-distant flutist, oboist, etc. Altogether the performance was a thoroughly bad show. I felt that the Fountain Pens would be justified in piercing me to death with their sharp criticism. Clearly I had invited them to strike.

But the reviews in the New York press were most commendatory, some even enthusiastic, predicting the development of modern mystery plays in the operatic form. All the Choristers were surprised at the praise bestowed, for every boy and man knew that there was hardly one redeeming feature in the whole performance. Thus it is with Fountain Pens! Perhaps both audience and critics suspected that we were singing modernistic music, and that what would have impressed as wrong notes, irregular rhythms and distortion of harmony, in the neo-classic style, was merely characteristic of the cacophony of the new music.

We escaped ridicule and disaster only by chance.

Chapter XXV *The Ground Bass Tries to Sing from the Lecture Platform*

AFTER the Paulist Choristers had been well established in their routine of Chicago and New York concerts and concert tours, there was a noticeable increase of interest among musicians in the various aspects of the choral art. I don't mean to imply that a minority of those charged with the task of training and conducting choruses had not been interested before. But the majority, and a not inconsiderable percentage of the minority, had been, consciously or unconsciously, thinking of the chorus as the thick, bulky, unwieldy instrumentality of musical expression. Volume and technical precision had seemed to constitute the excellences which would make concerted singing passably acceptable. Little thought had been directed to those nuances of color, dynamics or tempo which transform the product of a chorus, an orchestra or even a piano or organ, into a medium of magical properties.

One could travel far without coming upon a conductor who evinced any interest in balancing a diminuendo of the sopranos with a crescendo of the basses. It would be a longer journey to a concert hall or church where the altos and tenors were mutually so well adjusted (and adjusted to the whole) as to convey any right concept of the alleged counterpoints in progress. Women sopranos howled and yoicked in choral societies. Boy sopranos gave utterance to noises that have yet escaped proper definition. Alto choruses, except when encumbered sopranos caroled on the alto line, were murky, dense and altogether as intimidating as thumps on kettledrums out-of-tune. Tenors stretched their necks and, with Adam's Apples moving violently up and down, fought like Richard Coeur de Lion to lance notes far beyond their shooting. Basses growled with mighty fortitude. When a fugue (generally the choruses felt expert in singing fugues) was in progress, the Art of Music was assailed more terrifyingly than the Bastille by the French revolutionists.

Of course there were exceptions to this prevailing rioting in the choral field. But there weren't many. The former glory of the chorus, as a vehicle for the communication of the most moving inspirations of composers, was forgotten. "A nice clean-cut attack, all together." "Strict attention to the value of notes and the tempo." "At the bottom of page fourteen, everybody soften a bit." "But throw yourselves into the job." "Pep it up." Or as a Notre Dame coach might tell his team playing the Army, "Get out and smash that line." Pull that fugue formation down. "Knock it out." "Touchdowns before the finale." Etc. These were the unwritten and perhaps unspoken slogans of chorophony.

When I began in Boston at the Mission Church, a fine organist but a low-rating choirmaster, said to me that "this silly business of shading and delicate effects in a chorus should be stopped immediately. A chorus is for great mass effects. Nothing else." Well! his opinion was reflected in the results of ninety per cent of the choral conductors and choir-masters throughout the country. (Europe was just a wee bit worse!)

Throughout these pages I have been reminiscing about my lifelong efforts to recreate proper appreciation for the latent potentialities of mesmeric music in choral singing. The Paulist Choristers were not or-ganized until 1904. They made progress slowly towards ideals which were becoming gradually clearer for a few seasons. In 1910, at Phila-delphia, where they won the first prize in the national competition, con-ductors and school-musicians began to ask questions about the point of view and the methods by which they were guided. After the Boston critics had approved in 1911, and especially after the European tour of 1912, the demand for public explanation of the point of view and methods became quite insistent. And so I embarked upon a teaching career.

A few preliminary attempts before indifferent students had blunted the edge of early enthusiasm for lecturing about the topics involved. As early as 1907, I had appeared on the professor's platform in Chicago and Boston. In 1912, two courses failed to elicit much interest from pro-fessor or students. Probably I felt that I had not yet thoroughly co-ordinated the material. It is likely that during those first courses, I leaped from crag to crag as an oread. But eventually, in 1918, after our arrival in New York, I was ready to expound the subject in orderly fashion. During the autumn of that season, I invited the organists and choirmasters of New York to weekly lectures on the practical points of choral technique. It was during that season's course that I learned some-thing about pedagogy. I also profited, by the questions asked by the students, in the matter of planning a curriculum which became the basis of my later and more successful courses.

The next course was at the Castle Choir School in the summer of 1921. The boys were on vacation, and we crowded students from many parts of the country into the medieval chateau. I mention the names of some of the registrants for that course because of their later achievements: Miss Natalie Davis, of Providence, Rhode Island; Miss Elizabeth Von Fleet Vosseller, the foundress of the great and unique choir school at Flemington, New Jersey; and Mr. Ralph Harris, the secretary of the American Guild of Organists, and organist and choirmaster for the St. Paul Choristers, Flatbush, Brooklyn. There were several talented young men who were intent on wresting from me the secret of the Paulist Choristers' tone quality, blend and interpretative effects. I am writing rather at length about this undertaking, for the experience, going beyond that of the 1918 choirmasters' class, gave me a clear view of the methods I should have to pursue in other professional courses.

That first formal professional course was undertaken in difficult circumstances. Only the secretary, Mr. Lloyd Rand, and myself knew how badly off we were financially. We could not pay our bills until after the summer-school students had deposited their stipends. Fearing to try to extend our already thin credit too far, Rand and I drove through the Bronx, buying necessary supplies, including coal for the kitchen range. Rand was a born shopper. He knew where we could get thirty-five cents' worth for a quarter. The afternoon before the arrival of the students was spent in searching Washington Heights for bargains.

Although, in that particular course, the subject matter concerned the physical aspects of the art of choral singing (that is, the vocal preparation of each choral line, the blending and balancing of a complete choir, and such facilities as clean attack, release, gradual crescendos and diminuendos, singing on pitch, etc.), a few of the structural points of polyphony and contrapuntal music in general were discussed. I was struggling at that time to discover the Renaissance technique for converting the wonderfully fabricated imitations and canons of the polyphonic era into the sounds probably conceived by the composers, and my knowledge extended only to textbook information as to the rules of composition which had guided the masters. But after the introductory lecture on the Palestrinesque style (this was purely academic), I was amused to overhear a youth, who had sung for a long time under my baton, advise a group of students to cut the rest of the lectures on the subject. "That's all there is to it. I know. I've been singing that stuff for years." Fortunately, the students so advised paid no heed to the suggestion.

I continued the lectures, laying much stress on technical points of structure which now I recognize to be of no significance in rendering the polyphony into sounds. I talked about the mode in which the motet was written, gave rules for ascertaining the mode. I discoursed of the various obsolete rhythmical signs, which, of course, except to research specialists, have no import today, since scholarly editors have translated the former rhythmical symbols into modern time values. But I went through the theoretical content of the polyphonic style, perhaps hoping that one of the students might find the needle in the haystack, the hidden needle being of course the feasible means of making sound right what looked so brilliantly right.

Some of the students of that class have accomplished good results. None, to my knowledge, ever came upon the secret of polyphonic interpretation. A few of those Castle students became mixed up later, or perhaps were just satisfied that they had acquired all there was to know about the art, for I have listened to their choral efforts in various places, and regret to record that some have missed the mark. In the beginning of this book, I commented upon the necessity of a candidate artist-conductor making the long and arduous trip to Mount Parnassus. My successful students have made at least part of the journey. Those who thought the expedition to be unnecessary are gracing the slough of mediocrity, and in some cases trespassing upon opportunity. However, this in passing.

But the importance of choral and orchestral conductors meditating upon such matters as tone quality, balance, indirect attack, tempo and quantitative levels and variations cannot be emphasized too strongly. As I have written in other books, technique alone will never produce music. It is extremely difficult to convince students of this fact. During the years in which I have been conducting classes in chorophony, I have striven to make clear the need of *prehearing in one's own mind the kind of tonal effects one aims to produce from a chorus*. With some few exceptions, my striving has been in vain.

Once, after having stressed this point very vigorously, a man with quite a nice Irish brogue, spoke up: "Sure and we've had enough of that. Get on to the next precept." There is, however, one class of musicians—the Sisters, about whom I shall write later—which appreciates the value of such meditating.

During the ensuing years, it was my privilege to lecture and give demonstrations, as well as to give public performances, with choruses made up of the students, in many parts of the country. Many summer and winter courses in New York, one for the New York University. At Chicago Musical College, under the presidency of Herbert Witherspoon, three summer courses, 1929–31. In Boston, two full courses. A full course meant sixty hours, and frequently, for me, these were compressed into ten days. Six hours a day, sometimes in equatorial heat! Chalk dust from the blackboard mixing up with the perspiration around a wilted Roman collar. The Sisters, in one great college, urged me to discard the Roman collar, and willingly agreeing, I found myself furnished with an extraordinary variety of sport shirts. Sometimes, at an afternoon session,

I would glide onto the stage, looking not altogether unlike Ronald Coleman in his Hollywood garden. I did flats and sharps and naturals in blue, red, sepia, tan and white silk. The *arbiter elegantiarum* of the treble, alto, tenor and bass clefs! And from the Sisters—!

From June to September often. Days off for railroad travel. Los Angeles, many times; Milwaukee; Rosary College, Illinois; Buffalo twice under the auspices of that great musician, De Witt Garretson, dean of the Buffalo Chapter of the American Guild of Organists; Camp General Grant in the high Sierras, twice; San Francisco, twice, and lectures later for the American Guild of Organists, and Father Boyle's Guild of Catholic Organists; Spokane; Detroit; Jacksonville; University of Michigan at Ann Arbor; Cleveland; Washington; Portland; Oregon; Burlington, and Rutland, Vermont.

Without prejudice to the Middle West or the East, I must record that I found the greatest interest in the subject in the Far West. The superintendents of music in the schools (a valiant corps struggling to inculcate standards of higher culture in our teen-agers) came in large numbers, especially at Los Angeles for several consecutive years. As I wrote already, only a small percentage of students came from the Catholic fraternity of organists, except in San Francisco, where the well-known and able organist of St. Dominic's Church, Miss Frances Murphy, turned out quite a representative group of Catholics. Always (except at Ann Arbor and Jacksonville, on account of the inconvenient hours for classes) we had a large number of Sisters in attendance. My secretary took no cognizance of the Sisters in estimating the percentage of Catholics and non-Catholics registered. As far as professional Catholic musicians were concerned, I was working mainly for the non-Catholic branch of the profession. Baptists, Methodists, Episcopalians, Congregationalists, Unitarians, etc., were eager to ascertain, from the spoken word, the ideals, approaches and technics developed by the monks and levites of the Catholic Church. Curious about the Catholic musicians! No? But yes!

Two important features of the academic curriculum of these courses were the Question Box and the demonstrations with untrained singers. In many instances, the interest and enthusiasm of the students were heightened by the preparation of broadcasts and concerts in public auditoriums.

The Question Box had proved itself of immeasurable value on the non-Catholic missions of the Paulist Fathers. Questions deposited anonymously were answered fully and politely. And so I employed this relatively new device of pedagogy in my choral classes. A little timidity during the first few days kept the total of questions low, but before the end, a full hour each day was needed to answer the queries. If I had failed to make a point clear, there would be a request to go over the matter again simply. All sorts of questions. Some irrelevant to any phase of music, some pertinent to phases of the art to which we were not adverting, such as guitar-playing, and the management of the new chromatic kettledrums. Some were social rather than musical, such as: "What would you do if you had in the choir a soprano soloist who had been the soloist for thirty years. Voice gone now, but rector and vestry want her maintained in the position?" I never could give a satisfactory answer to that one. It came often. Sometimes old goose-neck tenors would be ruining the ensemble, but being relatives of the treasurer or senior warden, their sighs from the mausoleum of deceased chanters would have to continue to make Handel's "Hallelujah" a melancholy dirge.

One day, after a lecture about the changing voice and the counter-tenor, having recommended a vocalization for certain purposes on the sound *per*, a nice little Sister slipped a question into the box. I saw her in the act, and hers was the sole question deposited. It asked: "If you want them to sing *per*, why don't you spell it *purr*."

"I made the very unprofessional answer: "That's all right, even if it is a bit catty." I mention this just to indicate that I had abandoned the pompous, smug, irritably obnoxious attitude and manner of many professors. We had a lot of fun in the classes. Being Irish, I could not permit Palestrina, Bach, Beethoven or Brahms to lock up my sense of humor for long. I could not laugh or smile as I could before the Canada-California tour, but a group of Sisters can always raise my spirits.

I think that I employed, almost unwittingly, half the tricks of the radio and Hollywood comedians. When the subject matter was particularly heavy and difficult to lighten, I would be a Fred Allen, a Fibber McGee, a Jimmy Durante. If there was something subtle to be conveyed, George Arliss might appear. It was easy to arch eyebrows in the John Barrymore style whenever a blunder of dimensions was made by the singing group. Occasionally, I am sure, some of the less Irish members of the groups were fearful lest I might carry the histrionics to the public stage, and give an old-fashioned James Maffit pantomime.

The students worked hard. It was hard, indeed, to be seated for six hours a day, listening intently to one voice intoning the dull if important truths of chorophony. The Question Box period was usually the most interesting. *A*: "Why does my choir sing true to pitch on F (fifth line) in one anthem, and flat in the next?" *B*: "Why does the soprano chorus seem to be satisfactory in rehearsal, but very stringy and strident when singing with the organ or orchestra?" Such questions gave opportunities for underlining facts already discussed and for subject matter which might not otherwise have been introduced.

Here, I shall give answers to the two questions quoted above merely to indicate the value of the Question Box in such courses. To the question *A,* I should probably have answered: "Your choir sang the F accurately in the first anthem first, because their vocalism was free, which means that the breath control was good; because they sang over the note to alight upon it (that is, they thought above the note), thus not bringing weight up from lower notes; second, because the associated notes in the harmony (such as an alto C, and a unison tenor and bass A) stimulated a sense of the perfect pitch for the soprano F; because the tempo was right (not sluggish), and because the key of the piece was right for the acoustics of the hall. Probably the prevailing harmony was in the major mode. As to the choir failing to sing the F true to pitch in the other anthem, either their vocalism had become careless, with insufficient breath, upward progressions not sufficiently distanced or downward progressions too greatly distanced, and thinking *up* to the F; or because the tempo was too slow or the key (maybe the structure of the second piece showed minor harmony) too low for the hall; or there was an excess of quantity in the alto or bass section. In such cases, first of all, look to the breathing and the freedom of the vocalism. Then attend to tempo, etc. If there are minor thirds abounding in the tenor-bass region, keep them soft. If the piece is accompanied, have the accompanist play the part an octave higher than written. If the organ is in use, signal for a high string or reed stop (not very loud) for the flattening part."

Naturally there would be some discussion of the answer, and I would invariably proceed to illustrate my comments with the student chorus. Such a question would give me opportunity for insisting that the choirmaster must be on the alert for symptoms, in preceding measures, which would warn of the impending flattening.

To question *B* I should reply: "If your sopranos did sound well by all honest criteria of vocalism, in the rehearsal hall with piano accompaniment, then the difficulty later is due to the wrong registration of the organist or to the lack of understanding with which the conductor managed the orchestra. I am not referring to boy choirs at the moment, but to choirs of women sopranos. The great majority of the latter must be classified in the string-reed category of timbres. Therefore, an organist employing a dominantly string or reed registration piles Ossa upon Pelion. He adds more of which there is already too much, and the result is excessive stridency. With string sopranos, the organist should use flute or stopped diapason registers to bevel off the already edgy tones of the lassies. With trained boys, it's the other way round; the boys are too fluty and need pointing up by strings and light reeds.

"In the situation with an orchestra, usually a glance at the score reveals that the string section of the orchestra either duplicates the soprano vocal line, or plays figures so close to it as to overemphasize the string quality. Obviously, the conductor must reduce the quantitative contribution of both violins and sopranos, and give prominence to an inner part. If English horns or bassoons are playing, it is safe to let them take the lead. A good example of this situation is the Double Fugue of the Mozart Requiem, which is usually knocked all the way out of the realm of eternal rest by sopranos and violins."

Then, by way of illustration, I had the custom of assembling a group of string sopranos, and if an organ were available, I would have them sing a phrase or two with string registration, and then with flute stops. The question was thus answered theoretically and the answer corroborated by examples and illustrations.

Once in a while, a questioner would deposit another communication, saying that he or she disagreed with my opinion. This gave me opportunity for stressing a point which invariably I tried to make clear from the outset, viz., that I was not endeavoring to superimpose my opinions upon the students, but only to share with them the results of many years of research and experience; that it was good to stimulate thought about the subject; that I would be pleased if I had merely opened up a new vista for them.

And the practical demonstrations with untrained material! Many who were doubting Thomases the first few days became ardent converts after the demonstrations. The first demonstration was at the Chicago Musical College in 1929. Mr. Herbert Witherspoon, President of the College, and the manager, Mr. Carl Kinsey, suggested that I prove the validity of the principles and precepts which I had been propounding. They hinted that some members of the faculty were disturbed because these principles and precepts challenged and decried the methods which they, in common with most vocal teachers in the world (except in England), had been following. The intimation was that I was considered a quack by some of them. Both Mr. Witherspoon and Mr. Kinsey had looked in on some classes, and, although not sympathetic with what they considered my revolutionary ideas, knew that charlatanism had no place in my class room. Therefore, they urged me to give a public demonstration of the physiological and musical orthodoxy of the mooted tenets. I agreed, although I had never attempted such a demonstration before.

Taking a day or two to think over the situation, I finally decided to make the demonstration an acid test. I would write the simple procedure on a blackboard. Steps one, two, three. I would sum up, before the faculty and students and critics of the press, the subject matter which had bent some professional noses. Then I would call onto the stage a group of about forty boys, whom one of the Sisters volunteered to assemble. These boys were altogether untrained. Their vocalism was encumbered by the construction of every muscle and cartilage employed in the utterance of sounds. They were picked at random from the streets of a suburb where din and clamor reigned as the township's gods. I would give myself twenty minutes to transform the ugly noises which these lads habitually made in their throats into an adumbration of real soprano tone with acoustically and physiologically correct intonations. I would increase the upper compass of their voices by at least four notes. And I would employ no technics which had not been discussed and which were not written in orderly sequence on the blackboard.

If these principles and precepts could effect such a transformation in the voices of street Arabs, whose vocal cords were in a dire state of attrition with the surrounding tissues most likely swollen and abraded in spots, certainly it would be reasonable to conclude that less abused voices would respond more quickly and completely to the therapy, and further that the procedure was sound theoretically and practically.

And so I started my first demonstration of that kind. The theater of the college was crowded. Gray-bearded professors of many years' popularity were there. Bald-headed, thin men, who looked as though they might have weapons concealed under their coats. Severe-visaged women, with a defying dare in their eyes. Young men and women, all the students of the college. Piano players, violinists, cellists and the rest. Messrs. Witherspoon and Kinsey stood at the rear of the theater, giving the impression that in case a rumpus developed, a nearby exit would be desirable.

As I summed up the subject matter, my students paid respectful attention. Many of the others conversed audibly and moved about the auditorium. All this amused me, for I was certain of the validity of the principles and of the efficacy of the precepts. I had not invented them. They derived from the facts of the physics of sound and physiology. I was not even the first modern chorusmaster to discover them. John Spencer Curwen, of Tonic-Sol-Fa fame, had long before published a book on the boy-voice in which he stressed the agreement of the leading English choirmasters, who were the first musicians in our epoch to aim at restoring choral virtuosity, that the principles in question alone could guarantee the proper development of voices, especially voices that had suffered damage by misuse or abuse. Dr. Holbrook Curtis, the eminent throat specialist (also a vocal teacher) who cared for the larynges of the De Reskes, Emma Eames, Caruso, Pol Plancon, etc., had written a treatise on the subject, in which he, as a laryngeal specialist as well as vocal teacher, corroborated the views of Curwen's choirmasters. But I didn't know of the Curtis book at the time of the first demonstration.

Some friends of mine sat timidly and fearfully towards the rear of the theater, probably equipped with first-aid materials. Everybody, except my regular students, expected me to collapse in the first round. I was going to give myself the one, two, three, number three being a haymaker from the floor of the stage to my unguarded chin.

Well! we started off without mishap, except for the impoliteness of the gabbing and gadding audience. The boys filed on the stage. They averaged about twelve years of age. I had asked that no boys with changing voices or tone-deaf lads be included. They were nice boys, but quite clearly of the rougher type. Some were Catholics, some non-Catholics. Instinctively they felt that I was on a spot. They didn't know, of course, what kind of a spot. But they were on my side! I smiled at them and they smiled at me. I asked them to be kind and just do the things I asked them, even if these seemed silly.

First they tried to sing the national anthem. What a savage outburst of tones! The world's worst and therefore the best for the acid test. They began to suffer (and the listeners, too) in the ascending phrase, "And the rockets' red glare." Their throats were so stiffly ribbed with steel cartileges that no one of the lads could have been strangled by a giant. Then I asked them to sing an ordinary scale in the key of D. From B upwards, their throats refused to function, while their faces were contorted and their general discomfiture very plain. They showed a compass of about six notes which they could deliver with ear-splitting effectiveness. Then I asked a group of young ladies with lyric soprano voices to sing both the national anthem and the scale of D. I asked the audience if the timbre of the ladies or that of the boys were what is generally accepted as soprano tone? Even the grumpiest of the unsympathetic audience admitted that the tone of the ladies was the true soprano timbre.

Then I proceeded to apply the principles and precepts, in the order in which they appeared on the blackboard. Presently, by downward humming from E fourth space, transferring the hum on high sustained tones to an *oo* sound, and singing the downward scale pianissimo on *poo,* I had disencumbered the lads' throats temporarily. Long enough to show the trustworthiness of the principles. In a few moments, after this procedure had loosened their larynges, they were singing *poo* on A flat above the staff. Then I had the ladies and boys alternate on similar simple vocalises. Acoustically, there was little difference, what difference there was being due to the habitude of the ladies to intone properly and the custom of the boys to howl from the bottom up. Ladies and boys joined in a unison vocalization.

I asked a few ladies (surreptitiously) to drop a minor third below the boys at the start of a scale. Upon demanding from the audience whether boys or ladies were singing the second part, there was much confusion of opinion. But there was no confusion of opinion about the validity of the principles which had been so spectacularly tested. Even the most unsympathetic members of the audience applauded the boys heartily. Some of the lads left the stage at the end, looking as if an attempt had been made to turn them into sissies. Down the street they ran, howling in their accustomed manner. Eight months of the training which I had indicated would have inured those suburban urchins to proper use of their voices. Messrs. Witherspoon and Kinsey, the entire faculty and my own students were very kind in expressing appreciation of the demonstration. My friends with the first-aid kit invited me to tea at the old Auditorium Hotel.

I wrote in detail about that first demonstration, because it indicated the necessity of proving or at least illustrating theoretical subject matter. I have never failed to give such a demonstration in ensuing courses, except in one university, where the students seemed to be more interested (perhaps solely interested) in receiving the credits for the course than in acquiring information. It is a humiliating experience for a specialist to travel a long distance, intent upon giving his best to a class, only to find them interested in the credits, picnics and canoe parties. So I never accepted a second invitation from that university. Most of the time, however, the students were agog. Not only the youngsters, but the old boys and girls as well. It was charming, sometimes, to observe a well preserved group of post-Spanish War sopranos, in the student chorus, blushing and coyly fidgeting when the group would try to apply certain principles of madrigal singing to "Kill then and bliss me, but first come kiss me." The enthusiasm was not, as you can observe, just cold intellectual *élan,* but included a bit of the emotive force that makes flowers exude a lovely scent. At any rate, zeal worked its way into the veteran ladies' intonations—and attitudes.

Every phase of the subject of chorophony interested the students. My secretary once compiled a list of the single topics to be covered in a complete course in the art of choral training and conducting. The first compilation showed a total of about seven hundred and fifty topics, but this yielded to a later list of one thousand. The day has passed when a solo singer possessing fair facility in reading music can boldly and with impunity assume the multiple duties of a choral conductor.

I remember observing alleged choral conductors essaying to conduct a choral society through a standard oratorio with the accompaniment of a visiting symphony orchestra. Frequently, the only sure means for the unfortunate man on the podium to keep in time with the chorus and orchestra was to sing the top-line melodies to himself, and count on his left fingers the measures in which the orchestra was engaged alone. Also, it is very clear in my memory that many superintendents of music in the public schools proved that they knew as little of the fundamentals of music and chorophony as a seventh grader knows of differential calculus. I lectured and gave demonstrations at many of the school musicians' conventions. Years ago, the academic and artistic level of many of these meetings was low. Now the level is much higher, and presently the standards by which superintendents are judged worthy of their responsibilities will be raised still higher.

A miscellany of irrelevant subjects formerly constituted the agenda of such conventions. Now there seems to be a simple, practical and worthwhile plan proposed for the meetings. I participated in many of these conventions at New York, Detroit, Grand Rapids, Chicago, Philadelphia, San Jose, California, etc. Always I made an effort to convey a basic truth with conviction. Often I failed to gain attention.

At Grand Rapids in 1916, I was entrusted with the first public concert proposed for the chorus of supervisors. It was a huge chorus. I remember the occasion well, for I conducted with one hand clutching my abdomen, a series of pains similar to those of appendicitis having attacked me. It was not easy to focus attention on tone quality, blend and the niceties of interpretation, while the duodenum, pancreas and spleen were singing a trio loudly off key. But the concert, as usual, came through. No one in the chorus or audience knew that, during a specially disembodied ethereal effect or during the ascent to a great climax, I was debating whether to take the old-fashioned anaesthetic or try the new spinal injection which was coming into vogue. The basses of the chorus obeyed my signals with meticulous care. That was good. A few preliminary outbursts from the deep-throated gentlemen had violently agitated the painful peristalsis that was grieving the inner man.

The concerts, which the choruses made up of summer students gave in various cities, were frequently of superior quality. Especially those at Los Angeles. In 1933 I had been engaged to conduct the Verdi Requiem at the Hollywood Bowl. After I had signed the agreement, Frederic

Stock, of the Chicago Symphony Orchestra, told me that I was facing a real hazard. He had tried to work with the Hollywood Bowl chorus the preceding year. He foretold failure, if I were to undertake the great Requiem with that organization. However, I was committed to it, and having prepared the vocal and orchestral score with patient diligence, I knew that the application of the fundamental principles of chorophony would condition the chorus quickly, and that interpretatively I could fire the imaginations of the singers ardently enough to make the great textual and tonal scenes dramatically convincing.

Listening to the first rehearsal, under the baton of an assistant, I realized that I had undertaken a big man's job, that maybe Stock was right, that perhaps the valor of common sense would persuade me to fade out of Hollywood as fast as possible. But I stuck. The first night was hard going. Next day I asked about a hundred of my Los Angeles students to join the Bowl chorus, and to concentrate upon applying the tenets which I had been expounding to them. Then the rehearsals began to show results. After six hours of lecturing, I would go each evening for three or four weeks to the Hollywood High School Auditorium to rehearse sections of the unit or the entire ensemble. We rehearsed pianissimo on vowel sounds preceded by labial consonants. I deferred introducing the text until the dramatic moment when, being fit vocally, they could concentrate on the meaning of the Latin text and on the proper enunciation of syllables. The chorus totaled over five hundred. My summer students unquestionably made the task of inculcating a sense of good choral intonation much less of a burden than it would otherwise have been. At my first rehearsal the chorus would sing not only with lamentably inferior tone quality, but would sag a key or more every few measures. But the fundamental principles of choral technique, which had made the Paulist Choristers into a singing unit of distinction, soon remedied both tone quality and flattening.

The performance amazed me. I had not hoped to raise the chorus from its lowly estate to the plane of artistry it attained. Andres de Segurola, celebrated baritone of many opera houses, was in the audience. He told me privately and the radio audience publicly as well that he had never heard the Requiem done so convincingly or with such excellence of tone. The critics agreed that it was a fine performance.

When I read Oscar Levant's book *A Smattering of Ignorance,* I was reminded of my first rehearsal with the Bowl orchestra for the Requiem. Levant tells of the habit of orchestral players to send guest conductors over the hurdles at the first rehearsal in order to take their measure as conductors, and to ascertain if they really can manage an orchestra. My first rehearsal with the Bowl players (actually the Los Angeles Philharmonic Orchestra) was on a Sunday evening after they had rehearsed in the morning and played a matinee under a modernistic conductor who, attempting the classics, could give no clear indications of rhythm or classical phrasing. They were nervous, tired and disgruntled that a rehearsal was called after so strenuous a day. The lighting was poor. The orchestra at the performance was to play outside the shell, the shell being reserved for the chorus and soloists, so it was determined to have the rehearsals in the positions to be occupied at the performance. We couldn't find the chief electrician who might have been able to improve the lighting. And so, as an orchestra of an earlier era might have played in semidarkness (candles and coal-oil lamps providing what we moderns would judge to be as a murky twilight), we started to play the Verdi score. I knew every note of the score by memory. I had planned special orchestral effects. I was eager to bring to the surface, from the inner parts, much music that Verdi must have felt deeply, but that is frequently left inaudible. Two players had been under my baton before. They nodded pleasantly as I mounted the podium. The others looked me over with appraising and skeptical eyes. It was something like the experience of 1909 with the Victor Herbert Orchestra at Carnegie Hall, New York. Who is this chap from New York? Isn't he supposed to be an a cappella conductor? Do you suppose he knows the difference between a clarinet and an English horn? That sort of querying darted from the eyes of a hundred players.

I gave the violas a special signal almost at the start. It was ignored. Presently a flute came trilling in about twenty bars before its proper entrance. A trombone raised a mighty brass cry in a movement where no trombones were to be used from start to finish. The kettledrums rolled and beat tatoos, with no indication in the score that their muffled thudding should be active. I let it all happen. Gradually the players began to shrug their shoulders and make grimaces to one another, indicating that at last they'd caught a quack baton-wielder who had no notion of what the score meant.

After about sixty-four bars, during which practically every instrument made a wrong entrance and played wrong notes, I tapped on the stand for silence. "Thank you, gentlemen, for your extraordinary rewriting of the score of Giuseppe Verdi. Possibly he would have rearranged it, if he had had opportunity of hearing your alterations. But since we have been engaged to play the score as he wrote it, let us go back to the beginning and adhere to the written notation. I let you go for sixty-four bars, so that your feeling for re-creation would have full opportunity." Then the orchestra set to and followed every nuance indicated, with enthusiasm. The Los Angeles Philharmonic Orchestra became, as a unit and in its individual members, one of my best musical friends.

Mr. Philip Khagan, at that time first violist of the orchestra, now of the Paramount studios and personnel manager of the Stokowski ensembles in Los Angeles, was accustomed to taking moving pictures of the conductors at rehearsal. At another practice period for the Requiem, he "shot" me while I was working vigorously to balance some sections of the orchestra. A year later, I sat with Isabel Morse Jones, the distinguished music critic of the *Los Angeles Times,* while the movie of several conductors, including myself, was shown. Many orchestral players were in the audience (it was a private showing), and these would exclaim occasionally: "See! Look at his beat? Can you tell where the first beat is, by watching him? What meaningless gyrations! That's what we players have to put up with at rehearsals and at performances!" I admit that the postures, gestures and facial expression of several very expensive conductors, who had been photographed by Mr. Khagan, were not far from being grotesque. As far as indicating, unmistakably, the beats of a Beethoven measure was concerned, several distinguished conductors seemed to be describing only fantastic arabesques with their batons. I couldn't follow any of the conductors mentally.

When my picture came along, I admitted to Mrs. Jones that I couldn't follow even myself. What I was doing with long apelike swinging of the arms, and facial distortions that would make good exemplars for a circus clown, I could not tell. On the podium, I have always seemed to have an authoritative downbeat and a clear diagram for other beats. But, watching myself in the cinema, I couldn't distinguish horizontals from verticals, angles from circles, or any signals for change of tempo or dynamic strength. It was a splendid lesson. As the slang phrase has it, it's easy to kid oneself. And so, for some months, I practiced conducting before a mirror and have recommended such practice to students. See if you can interpret your own gestures and signals in the mirror before you try them on orchestral players. Mrs. Jones said to me: "You were pretty bad, but not half so bad as that ———." Of course, Mrs. Jones is a charming lady, and she did not want me to react too unhappily to the acrobatic performance I had been giving on the screen.

And I've improved. The cinema and the mirror have been helpful. You see, the difficulty is this: you start a measure with a clear downbeat, become suddenly interested in balancing an oboe crescendo against a string diminuendo, and inadvertently cease indicating the temporal pulsations. Or perhaps the chorus demands your entire attention, and you must leave the bassoons and cellos to take care of themselves, even in a contrapuntal rhythm, in order to avert a feud between sopranos and basses. Or the entire string section seems on the point of becoming unmanageable, and you immediately concentrate upon setting this in order. Probably Mr. Khagan photographed each conductor at his most unusual worst. That would make a better picture for fun, than showing the conductor serenely indicating time beats and that sort of thing.

During the years following the Hollywood Bowl performance of the Verdi Requiem, I gave many broadcasts and concerts in Hollywood with the students' chorus, sometimes with orchestra and several times a cappella or with piano accompaniment. The Sisters of St. Joseph of Carondolet, maintaining an excellent academy and a college in the Los Angeles area, had a bowl constructed at Brentwood Heights, which I had the privilege of dedicating with a students' chorus and a professional orchestra. Another season my students' chorus sang at the Brentwood Bowl, sharing the program with Mr. Albert Coates, the well known semi-English, semi-Russian conductor. A very clever piano accompanist, Mr. Raymond Hill, at one time professor of counterpoint in Shanghai, made a grand piano sound like a symphony orchestra for one of our Hollywood broadcasts.

In many other places, news of the Hollywood students' chorus concerts and broadcasts having reached the ears of the sponsors, I was requested to add this feature to the courses. In the high Sierras, at the Sequoia National Park, I conducted a concert in most unusual surroundings. A good orchestra and chorus were performing. The technical demands upon me were few, and so I could allow myself to be influenced by thoughts extraneous to the musical score. Most of these had to do with the impressive fact that the great tree under which we were performing was five thousand years old. It had been growing three thousand years and more before the birth of Christ. I began to feel like a speck of dust on one of the leaves of the old tree. Through what developments in the arts and sciences that enormous bole and its towering branches had lived! Long before Pythagoras had discovered the basis of the true modern musical scale, the tree had grown to its full height and probably looked about the same as it did to me that summer evening in 1938! As I have written in my book *"The Conductor Raises His Baton,"* * the experience was so stirring that I was obliged to let the tempos and dynamic nuances adjust themselves by some eternal law of propriety to the natural phenomena present, and their important historical and psychological implications. I know definitely that both chorus and orchestra sensed early in the program that I was not proceeding in the fashion established at rehearsals.

* (New York: Harper and Bros., 1944) pp. 60 ff.

Another great concert with students was in the Hill Auditorium at the University of Michigan. Bach, Brahms, Franck for the later styles; Palestrina, Vittoria, Sweelinck for the earlier styles. The first few days of the course at that university were discouraging, for a few professional male musicians were trying to rib me in the large ampitheatre in which the classes were conducted. But presently, by some stroke of luck, I was able to throw the ribbers into the equivalent of the second stage of hypnosis, in which the hypnotist freely superimposes upon the hypnotized what he plans for them to do. All I wanted was that a few husky chaps in the upper back rows, who looked as though they had been centers, guards or fullbacks twenty years earlier, would keep quiet. After the sedative of Svengali had been administered, the class proceeded normally, not only to cover the subject matter but to prepare the difficult program for the Hill Auditorium concert as well.

An incident occurred during the Ann Arbor course which deserves recording. One of the professors invited me for dinner at his home. He, his gracious wife and delightful twelve-year-old daughter were most cordial in welcoming me. There were other guests. The little twelve-year-old lady sat next to me. She was a real girl, in most ways not a day beyond her years, but in some things at least a half a generation ahead of her time. She conversed fluently and with excellent vocabulary about many subjects. We were not talking music.

As we were leaving the dining room, however, she drew me aside and told me that she was loath to attend my Sunday night concert at the Auditorium. Being the professor's daughter she was bound by the conventions of propriety to be present. It seems that she had been attending concerts by this traditional necessity ever since she crawled out of the nursery. She said that the concerts bored her "frightfully": that visiting symphony orchestras, choruses and recitalists added nothing to her intellectual or emotional appreciation. As for the summer students' concert—well! there wasn't handy just the right word to describe its banality, dire mediocrity and meaninglessness. I volunteered to try to persuade papa to excuse her from my concert, but with the cold insistence of a mid-Victorian lassie, she said: "No; I'm the professor's daughter, and in evidence I must be."

"Why have you told me this?" I queried.

"Oh! I rather liked you as a dinner companion, and I didn't want you to be under any illusions as to my interest in your professional activities at the University." Quite a series of rhythmical mouthsful from a miss of a dozen years!

The concert at the Hill Auditorium went off extraordinarily well. The big fellows, whom I had put to sleep in the amphitheatre, emerged from their trances with their dispositions admirably furbished and intent upon exemplifying the points of view which I had been underlining to the class. I don't remember the program in detail, but a broad Bach number and the lovely fourth chorus from the German Requiem of Brahms were highlights.

At the end of the concert, hurrying from the dressing room to catch a train for another summer course, my candid but very sweet little old lady of twelve was waiting at the stage entrance. Handing me a folded sheet, evidently taken from her program book, she said: "Take this and read it on the train." And I did read it. It was one of the most spontaneous and complete tributes to the principles of choral technique and interpretation, which I had been so long stressing, that ever came to my attention. The young miss wanted to know just what I had done with the chorus to create an atmosphere which she said was quite novel at the Hill Auditorium. I replied to the young lady's communication, assuring her that all I did was to make live again the points of view and the standards which had been responsible for the development of music through the Middle Ages and the Renaissance.

Once in a while, the singing qualities of the students' class, or more properly, the absence of these qualities, would tend to dissuade me from attempting a public performance. In one city, it seemed from the start that a concert would be a foolhardy undertaking. The voices of the men and women were old, dry and minus the natural endowment which is needed for a musical product. But the men and women were insistent. I could not graciously explain that they did not have good enough voices for a public performance. And so I agreed to make them into a concert choir. For me, this was to be another acid test. Perhaps the effects of the proper application of the basic tenets of chorophony would extend far enough to re-create the intonations of these old people, whose thyroid and cricoid as well as arytenoid vocal prowess had long since become very much weakened. The grandmas and grandpas, great aunts and great uncles threw themselves into the preparation of the program with a zeal and concentration that was amazing. They followed every precept of vocalization which I indicated. It was unnecessary to keep repeating suggestions. They were determined to excel the Hollywood broadcasts and students' concerts. Why, I don't know, except that old people sometimes are fired with enthusiasm to surpass achievements of their juniors. The dear veterans should have gone home to bed after listening to six hours' lecturing, but promptly after dinner each evening they returned to the hall to rehearse for two or three hours.

After two days I was surprised to observe the renascence of youthful tone qualities in the wearied throats. Before a week was finished, the veteran outfit began to sing beautifully. The sponsors of the course were so surprised that they engaged a large auditorium for the public performance. The music selected for the program was not easy. The veterans declined to be restricted to simple pieces. The Fountain Pens were invited. One of these usually scribbled most sarcastic and caustic comments about musical events in the district. The only fear that harassed the sponsors or singers was of the review which that particular Pen would contribute to the local press.

Beauty parlors and barber shops must have been extra busy that day, for my aged *cantatrices* and reminiscent tenors and basses filed onto the stage before a large audience, the ladies looking as seductive as a bevy of Misses America and the men as mesmerically menacing as a phalanx of Casanovas. Probably those in the audience who had grandparents in the chorus had difficulty in identifying them. I remember that when I stood on the podium to set the concert in motion, the group looked unfamiliar. I had become accustomed, during rehearsals, to be on guard against sudden and dreadful outbursts from certain members. Now I wasn't quite sure of who was who.

We went into a cappella polyphony. The notes rippled down the contrapuntal ramps as clear rivulets run merrily down a mountain side. When ascending passages were to be negotiated, the generation of long-ago singers soared lightly to the higher registers. The concert was a prodigy of rejuvenation. We made real music. The feared Pen wrote poetically and approvingly of the event in the morrow's paper. But I left the stage with an extra score of years on brows and shoulders. Someone had to assume the discarded decades! I think that that concert was the nearest thing to a musical miracle I ever conducted myself, or heard about.

The technical point which held my attention in later years in connection with that concert by contemporaries of the G.A.R. is that even with persons well beyond their singing prime, the proper principles of vocalism can induce the withered glands to function and assist the vocal cords in producing not only agreeable but even captivating sounds—temporarily, for a last telling moment, perhaps. However, I am not recommending choirmasters to specialize in the Art of Reanimating the Musical Communicability of the Superannuated.

Once a student class chorus thought well of its qualities. I rated them much lower than they rated themselves. They were keen to sing an all polyphonic program. They voted among themselves for the motets to be sung. The Lotti six-part "Crucifixus" was chosen almost unanimously as the *pièce de résistance*. But they could not sing the *etiam* figures fluently. (Most choruses attempting this motet are handicapped by the same disability.) The women were disinclined to follow the necessary precepts for lyricizing their intonations. After several days of futile efforts, I announced that there would not be a concert. If they elected not to be guided by the proper principles, I elected not to stand on a podium before them and bring ridicule upon the art of choral singing. When I finished the course some days later, the women forgot to say adieu to me. They simply walked out, with my signature on certificates attesting the fact that they had been in the lecture room a sufficient number of hours for the college credits.

But generally the student class concerts were of high quality. It was in connection with the Los Angeles concerts of students that the plan of using an orchestra made up only of ancient viols was suggested. The tone quality and general excellence of the Los Angeles singers persuaded an excellent specialist in the "chest of viols" that the more delicate timbres of the older and now obsolete instruments would furnish a more suitable background for the voices than the modern developments of the viols. I agree that probably a less piquant violin tone would be more suitable to the intonations of a volatile soprano timbre than the brilliant qualities of the modern violin which have been developed chiefly for symphonic and concerto effect. I am not so sure about the viola d'amore being a better alto string instrument than the present viola, which is weak enough at its best for alto delineation, or the viola da gamba in place of the modern cello for the tenor and baritone lines. Also I question the relative effectiveness of the older bass viol and the modern string bass. Circumstances did not permit an experiment.

Perhaps one day, before the trumpet call comes from the Archangel (I hope He will use a mute on His instrument, unless this is voiced according to standards no longer prevailing on this noisy planet), I shall have opportunity of truing the value of the old chest of viols as an accompanying instrumentality for aesthetico-spiritual singing. If opportunity does present itself, I promise not to write a long book about the subject, but merely to add an appendix to a book which I must finish as soon as the pages of this album have gone off to my publishers. This next book treats of organ registration and orchestration correlated with voices. Many organists and conductors underline the wrong timbres both in the organ and orchestra. I have already referred to the disruptive influence of marcato string choirs of orchestras on the tonal structure of Mozart's Requiem, when stringy female sopranos dominate the chorus. Well! I'll put an appendix about the chest of viols into this new book when and if I shall have had a chance to experiment with the delicate old instruments.

The classes for professional student-conductors revealed two needs:

first, the need of frequently repeating, with different examples and with different vocabulary, the fundamental principles and the precepts which would assure the application of these; second, the need of illustrating, with practical demonstrations, the validity of these principles and precepts in actual use. One gifted student registered at three consecutive summer courses in California. He told me that only after the third course was he able to comprehend the significance of the basic tenets. Upon my apologizing for having been as clear as New Jersey mud during the first two courses, he was kind enough to insist that my pedagogy had not been at fault, but that the points of view offered were so different from those accepted and followed generally by alleged masters of the choral art that considerable time was required to adjust oneself to the unfamiliar orientation.

I have continued to conduct the courses. Nowadays I assemble all the subjects, except tempo, under one major caption: *Quantity controls the art of concerted singing and orchestral playing.* This means, obviously, that an understanding and control of loud and soft determines the degree of effectiveness tonally that may be achieved, and the rhythmical and interpretative phases of chorophony.

It has been a joy to note the progress towards better standards that has been indicated over the past two decades. How much or little I personally contributed to this progress, I have no sure means of gauging. I do know that in southern California, the superintendents of music in the public schools credited my courses with the marked improvement of the school music. However, my personal contribution to the forward march of choral standards in this country is of little moment. But the fact that a large number of professional music practitioners have begun to think correctly about the art is important enough to emphasize. As I have already written, it is lamentable that the Catholic musicians have on the whole taken much less interest in the renascence of the old monastic standards of choral singing than the non-Catholic fraternity. With very few exceptions, one can hear the standards of the golden era of choral music exemplified only in Protestant churches or Jewish synagogues. Generally, one must seek a Presbyterian or Episcopalian church, where a good choir is maintained, to hear the great Catholic motets and Masses of Palestrina well sung.

Presently, perchance, the good Sisters will come to the rescue and restore their own heritage to the Catholics.

After some years of teaching, I collated the important material in book form. The two principal books which I have published on the subject are *The Art of the Choral Conductor,* published by C. C. Birch-

ard of Boston, and *"The Conductor Raises His Baton,"* published by
Harper and Brothers, New York. These two books were long in the
making. So little had been written about chorophony in any language
that the division of the subject into its component parts in orderly
fashion was a major problem. The first of these two books was in the
making a leisurely full score of years. Five years of intensive writing,
rewriting, eliminating and editing were required for the second book.
This latter is a "headache" book, especially in the later chapters, for I
compressed into its pages all the essentials I had learned by study and
experience that bear upon the correct interpretation of polyphony and
other involved forms.

A fact quite worthy of note here is that orchestral units need as much
training in the basic technics of interpretation as the choruses. The
average symphony orchestra will play a four-four time pattern as a two-
four with the same unawareness as the average choir shows in turning
the "Adeste Fideles" into a two-four distortion. Even with the Sisters
it has required much patience to inculcate a sense of the undulating flow
of rhythmical stresses and slacks. Our century has grown away from
both the surface refinements and the latencies of music. The Ground
Bass insists that these patent and latent elements be made audible, lest
the art fail to move the minds and hearts of men with its full emotive
power.

And so we come back to the need of a Ground Bass. What influence
is paramount in the average musician's consciousness when he under-
takes to make music? Is it an ambition to excel in technics? Is it a sort
of vague appreciation of the structure of a Bach fugue or a Mozart
chorus? Is it a cold measuring of the distinction possibly to be gained by
a conductor who can impress an audience even with the futile gestures of
crass ignorance? Just what urges men (and some women) onto the conductor's podium? During my earlier years, it was anyone's guess. More
latterly, one sees indications that the Ground Bass has been coming
through. May it emerge more clearly! May the silly sticks of silly conductors be replanted in richer soil, so that after the dew of many mornings and the sunshine of many noons they may resprout, this time as
the magic wands of great artistry!

Chapter XXVI *The Ground Bass Resounds in the Convent*

OVER the years, both in summer and winter courses there was a large registration of the Sisters, in Southern California especially. From all communities they came, except the cloistered and hospital Orders. They were alert students; making much and intelligent use of the Question Box. They had no reluctance in asking directly for a better explanation of a point than the one already offered. I knew that there were a few Sisters who were intent on "telling me off" if I sponsored points of view more liberal than those inculcated in their novitiate. For instance, whenever I referred to the place of modern music in the scheme of the Church's use of the fine arts, some pious little Sister would become nervous, fearing that I might give a wrong impression to the non-Catholic students. When I mentioned the name of Gounod, I am sure that the most conservative of the holy ladies would begin to tell their beads. Gounod's name was anathema among the rigorists, chiefly because he wrote that naughty opera *Faust*. Many who remember *Faust* forget that he wrote a very prayerful "Ave Verum," a highly spiritual oratorio, *The Redemption,* the beautiful and moving Mass of the Sacred Heart, and many other works quite worthy of association with public worship.

But my ultraconservative monitors in the convents disliked my giving the moderns much of a chance, and would insistently demand, during recreation periods, that I underline the more serious, which they interpreted of course to be the more ancient, styles of music, especially Gregorian chant. It used to plague the more sensitive of the monitor-nuns to hear me discourse about the minstrels and troubadors who sang love songs to the old Gregorian melodies, and always used the same scale forms in their ditties as the Church did in Her antiphons, etc. One Sister was afraid that I was "giving scandal" by intimating that the medieval church musicians believed the devil to be actually hovering about when a tritone (F-B natural), forbidden by the ecclesiastical music censors, was accidentally intoned. The old Latin verse

Mi contra *Fa,*
Diabolus est in Musica,
(If *Fa's* against *Mi,*
Ye faithful, flee,)

was interpreted so literally by composers, and even by the great Gla-
reanus who reattached Grecian titles to the modes in the sixteenth
century, that no trifling was done. One of the earthly homes of the Satan
of Melody was between the first space and the third line of the treble
clef. Musicians exorcised this area with a B flat as an Irishman blesses
himself skirting a cemetery at night. The Sister who was worried because
of my references to the state of mind of medieval musicians about the
Demon of the Scale told me that I was tamping into the minds of the
non-Catholic students the conviction that all medieval and Renaissance
Catholics were cowed by superstitions.

But only a few in many hundreds, perhaps thousands of Sisters, with
whom I had the pleasure of sharing information about chorophony, were
long-faced or puritanical. The very great majority was light-hearted,
very catholic and Catholic in understanding, and quick to sift the chaff
from the wheat in repertoire as well as in methods of concerted singing.
How the Sisters could laugh! They didn't merely giggle. They gave out
peals of hearty but politely rendered cachinnation. Sometimes my attention would be caught as readily by the quality of their expressed merriment as by the beauty and sheer spirituality of their vocalism.

After having had the experience of dealing with large numbers of
Sisters who formed blocks in the professional students' classes, I began
to specialize in courses for the Religious. During the season 1942–43 in
Chicago, I gave Saturday morning and afternoon courses to large classes.
During that season, I confined myself to academic lecturing and practical
demonstrations. One of the demonstrations was amusing. Since the tone
quality of the parochial school boys who lived in the neighborhood of
the convent auditorium where the classes were held was highly refined
due to the splendid teaching of Miss Mary Anderson, who had been long
the gifted accompanist of the Paulist Choristers, we were obliged to
apply to a public school for raw material. The principal kindly sent a
small group of boys under the chaperonage of one of the teachers.

This dignified prefect strode down the middle aisle followed by her
ten charges. "Are you the Reverend Finn?" she queried from mid-
auditorium.

"Yes."

"Well here are the boys from school! There are no Catholics among
them! Two are Jews and the rest Protestants!"

When the boys came on stage, they tried to hide one behind another. The strange garbs, especially headgear, of Sisters of many different Orders seemed to affect the non-Catholic lads strangely. Maybe they were panicky lest by abacadabra or some Latin formula I would transform them from good little Jews and Protestants into little Catholics who would have to go to church every Sunday and tell their sins to a priest. I may have appeared to them as a hospital surgeon preparing to carve up their young bodies, and the Sisters as nurses waiting for them to come out of the anaesthetic before taking their dying messages to the parents. At any rate those lads, except the two Jewish boys, were terrified.

I asked for volunteers to step out into a space which I designated as the first row. The two Jewish lads immediately stepped forward. The younger Sisters smiled rather obviously. Of course, the older Sisters maintained a rigorous decorum! After the demonstration, the boys having gone, I found opportunity to discuss with the younger Sisters the reason for their smiling. The alacrity with which the young Jews had stepped forward was, I pointed out to the young Sisters, a manifestation of the ambition which is urging the members of their race to the very top of the professions. The great musicians, lawyers and doctors of our era are Jews. They not only refuse to allow opportunity to pass unnoticed, as do so many of the non-Jews, but create opportunity where none seems to exist. And so a very amusing little episode turned out to be subject matter for serious thought.

Early in the season 1943–44, I organized the Chicago Sisters' class into a formal choral unit. Immediately, we began to prepare for a broadcast which I knew could be easily arranged. Rehearsals, only once a week for a while, lasted all afternoon each Saturday. The Sisters of twenty-two Religious Orders gathered at the celebrated St. Xavier's College conducted by the Sisters of Mercy. These latter were gracious hostesses to the visiting Orders. Sister Mary Albertine, who probably could have had a brilliant career as a concert singer if she had not entered the convent, became the efficient secretary.

We applied in vocalization and actual singing all the tenets which I had brought to their attention the previous season. Progress was rapid. There were two substantial handicaps to be overcome. First, an inferiority complex which manifested itself upon the introduction of the first polyphonic composition. Second, the lack of low, real contralto voices.

The first handicap was never disposed of as far as that original polyphonic piece was concerned. The Sisters simply could not sing it. They probably felt that they should be afraid of polyphony, since the mistaken idea that this style is difficult for modern singers is prevalent. Although very simple in structure, there was an inhibition in the subconscious mind of the unit which hindered and frustrated every carefully made effort to keep that first motet in rhythmical balance. Soon the Sisters began to feel perfectly at ease in the rendering of involved compositions in the polyphonic style, but that original piece always escaped their control. I tried various bits of unit psychoanalysis upon the chorus, but the trio of Freud, Adler and Jung could not have brought the sopranos and those singing on the alto line beyond a few bars before the motet would break into fragments.

The handicap offered by the lack of true contralto or even true mezzo-soprano voices was an interesting challenge to one who had so long explored the field of chorophony. The Sisters, who, upon entering the convent, might have possessed true contralto or mezzo-soprano voices, had lost their naturally deep timbres by singing in the soft, high tessitura which is customary in convent chanting. A year or two in a convent and Schumann-Heink would have lost her low notes. And it would not be possible, in the circumstances, to restore the lost timbres to the Sisters' voices. But I gave them vocalizations which would tend to reanimate some of the forfeited qualities, raised the pitch of unaccompanied compositions so that least the Sisters on the lowest voice line could make the notes audible, and undertook so to arrange the orchestration of pieces which would be accompanied by a symphonic ensemble as to reinforce the alto vocal line with a synthetic tone from such instruments as violas, English horns, second clarinets, cellos and bassoons.

The majority of the very young Sisters sang on the first soprano line. These had a lovely, smooth, flexible and haunting quality, but they were prone to sing under the notes in ascending passages and to overaccent a high note which would suddenly emerge from a prevailing low rilievo. I think that two seasons were required to remedy these defects.

Our first broadcast was over a coast-to-coast net work and consisted chiefly of Christmas carols. St. Philip Neri's choir of boys and men contributed some numbers, for the repertoire of the Sisters was at that time limited. One of my settings of the *Benedictus* became the theme song of the Sisters. They paid me the compliment of singing this with extra care. They even seemed to like the setting!

The first broadcast was so great a success that we were invited to give a Lenten program. For this we prepared the naïve setting of the "Stabat Mater" by Giovanni Pergolesi in the early eighteenth century. This composer, in spite of the few years God allowed him on earth, wrote many admirable operas and cantatas, but the work by which the modern world knows him best is this "Stabat Mater." If this young composer was gifted with foreknowledge, it could be reasonably alleged that he had the Chicago Sisters' Choir in mind when he wrote the opus which is a combination of the strictest and lightest forms of the era. Only a choir that makes beautiful sounds without trying to do so, that is to say, so well-trained in all the essential aspects of choral singing that its vocalism is habitually and uniformly aesthetic and vital, may reasonably hope to interpret the score of this cameo setting of the great Jacopone da Todi sequence, so as to convey the artless art of the young Italian composer. The rigorous requirements of dissonance, fugal form and counterpoint in general abound throughout the pages. And then there is the charming atmosphere which the young Italian created by sensing that the Blessed Virgin Mary was happy to be suffering at the foot of the Cross because She, alone of all human beings, understood just what was transpiring! I have in mind two stanzas, in particular, where an appreciation of Pergolesi's impression in this connection is required for adequate communication by a chorus. The "Quae Moerebat" and the "Fac Ut Ardeat" degenerate into lilting, secular and almost unspiritual tunes and counterpoints if not safeguarded by the paradox of Mary's simultaneous joy and sadness.

The Chicago Sisters' Choir, as they became familiar with the forms and contents of this Pergolesi work, revealed at each rehearsal an increased understanding of the paradox involved. They lifted the lovely seemingly self-contradictory ideas from under the written notes, the stern stanzas emphasing sorrow being tinted with delicate silver, and the blithe measures shaded with the precise hue of darksomeness needed to keep the paradox intact and convincing. We broadcast this composition on a country-wide network, receiving many letters of commendation for the technical and tonal facilities of the Sisters, as well as for the authoritative interpretation they accorded the composition. I made special orchestrations for all the movements in order to conserve to the Sisters' tone quality the spiritual traits which were its outstanding characteristics. No trumpets, trombones, tubas, piccolos or tympani! Having observed, over the years, the deleterious effects upon vocalism wrought by the use of the instruments named, I decided to "clear the cirrus clouds," to make unobstructed pathway to Heaven for the voices, by marking those instruments *tacet*. And how the volatile quality did soar! Nothing held it down to earth to make it "of the earth earthy." The orchestra was sympathetic and gave excellent support. Not once did a first violin or a flute cry out too poignantly in the upper register.

But the following season was to be the gala season for the Chicago Sisters' Choir. It provided several opportunities to stress several important facts. That is to say, important in the field of choral music, with and without orchestral accompaniment. First there was another broadcast of

Christmas carols, with the St. Philip Neri's choir again participating. In this latter choir were many of the former members of the Paulist Choristers who, upon the removal of the organization to New York, had made up the personnel of the unit which Miss Mary Anderson established to keep alive in Chicago the standards and ideals of the choir which had pioneered for so many years. One of the features of this broadcast was a macaronic setting of "Mater Ora Filium," an extraordinarily impressive composition by William H. Bell of Capetown, South Africa. The term "macaronic" is used here in its better sense, indicating the use of both Latin and English in the text. I think that the Sisters found every hidden musical gem in that beautiful score. Their enunciation was crystal clear. The phonation of vowel sounds and the articulation of consonants, the latter being perhaps the more important in speaking and singing English words, were as nearly perfect as choral enunciation can be. Of course, the top sopranos were not so successful with the utterance of syllables on high notes. The rapid pitch vibrations of high treble sounds interferes with the clarity of pronunciation and the acoustical difference in the pitches of the vowel sounds and the actual notes sung tends to make expression murky. Every vowel sound has its own fundamental pitch, if properly projected. When this is at variance with the piquant pitches of high notes, it is obvious that good enunciation is effectively hindered.

My first soprano Sisters worked earnestly to apply the precepts which I had worked out for lessening the ill effects of the feud between the fundamentals of the vowels and the notes sung. The singers on the second soprano and alto lines profited much from a study of the rules of enunciation which I had culled from Thornfield's *Lip and Tongue Training,** a book which I have recommended to thousands of students.

The success of this broadcast was such as to induce me to undertake a unique plan with the Sisters' Choir. Music had been born and bred and led to maturity in medieval and Renaissance convents and monasteries. The art had been swinging (no pun!) towards pagan and merely sensuous purposes for several recent generations. The spirituality had been fast seeping out of the great art. Symphonic performances of the works of immortal composers had forfeited the aesthetico-supersensible aura with which the spiritual perspicacity and genius of the composers had invested them. Neopaganism was ruling the art of music. Acoustics and timbres had for a long time usurped the place of psychic quality. Bows drawn across the stringed instruments produced sounds calculated to reach only the outer ear. The latencies of the art had been disregarded as inconsequential features. Musicians were intent upon pleasing the immediate

* New York: Schuberth and Co., 1915.

hearing of listeners. Choruses roared with great resonance at audiences to impress them with the magnitude of their prowess. The lovely things of concerted music had been fading in the glare of worldly bombast and noise.

I determined to give a concert with the Sisters' Choir which would bring to life again some forgotten standards in a concert hall where the pagan criteria were regularly stressed. And so my friend and collaborator, Father Joseph O'Donnell, a distinguished Pastor in the archdiocese of Chicago, arranged to have the Sisters sing with a section of the Chicago Symphony Orchestra. Permission to proceed with so novel a venture was secured from the Archbishop and the Superiors of the Religious Orders. Several gentlemen, under the honorary leadership of His Honor, Mayor Kelley, and under the active leadership of Mr. Irwin Walker, distinguished attorney, financed the undertaking. Thus, we were able to dispense with the sale of tickets, and to surround the event with the dignity which attaches to an invitation concert. The entire capacity of Orchestra Hall was disposed of to the clergy, the Sisters, educators, musicians, and dilletanti of the Chicago district. We had two rehearsals with the orchestra, which from the outset was most co-operative. The professional players were enthusiastic about the vocal effectiveness of the Sisters. The program consisted of Gregorian chant, polyphonic numbers and modern music, including the eighteenth-century setting of the "Stabat Mater" by Pergolesi.

In order to avoid the monotony unavoidable in a lengthy program by a chorus of women, I devised certain orchestral effects to make possible the offering of numbers requiring, usually, tenor and bass voices. The chief of these orchestral effects was the assigning of tenor and bass vocal lines to French horns. Thus, the "Salve Regina" of Waddington, which I had first heard in England in 1908, resounded through the Hall with even greater aesthetic enrichment than if the tenor and bass lines were sung by the average male vocalists. The French horn choir of the orchestra contributed a beautifully balanced substratum for the higher voices, and the fact that there was no text uttered on these voice lines did not subtract from the convincingness with which the Sisters propelled the great text of the medieval prayer out to the audience.

We took opportunity at that concert to indicate the aesthetic worth and feasibility of presenting Renaissance motets and madrigals, written originally for S.A.T.B. choruses, with the string orchestra taking over the lower parts. Thus "O Bone Jesu" by Palestrina and "The Silver Swan" by Orlando Gibbons arrested the attention and caught the fancy of the huge audience. Plenty of viola and cello tone in the low alto and regular tenor compass plus the sturdy tones of string basses playing in the octave where vocal basses are effective instead of in the low area in which string basses are generally heard, set off the first and second soprano voice lines to great advantage. Many of the Elizabethan composers had published compositions which could be sung by voices alone, or with a single top line or two upper lines rendered vocally while strings supplied the lower parts. And so I was justified in so arranging some numbers in this latter fashion. This was a service to the music teachers in the audience, who, having string orchestras at their disposal in most of the high schools and academies but no tenors or basses, were probably induced to add numbers from that rich repertoire to the rather banal lists of music usually scheduled.

It was a delight to be conducting such a perfect combination as the Sisters' Choir and the Chicago Symphony Orchestra on the stage where, so many years before, I had started the Paulist Choristers on their unique concert career. The Sisters were in gay mood. I had told them about a charming experience I had had during the preceding summer when I conducted a great orchestra at the Hollywood Canteen, under the management of the cinema actress, Bette Davis. The story which I had retailed to the Sisters had to do with a young miss about fifteen years of age. She was the regular tympani player for the Leopold Stokowski Symphony Orchestra in Los Angeles. The maestro had said that she was a most accomplished performer, knowing not only what she was required to contribute personally to the ensemble, but also the principal entrances and figures of all the orchestral instruments. Her mother invited me to write in the girl's autograph album. I wrote a little phrase for chromatic kettledrums.

At the performance, the charming lass, dressed, if I remember correctly, in pure unrelieved white, and standing on the top tier at the back of the orchestra, raised her album book, looked out from under it at me, from over it, and from both right and left sides. Then she smiled with such unsophisticated naïveté that of course I smiled in return. I think that I was obliged to lower the baton with a signal to the orchestra not to begin. Presently, we got under way. At every signal to my young tympanist, Nancy Moyer, she smiled. I smiled. The first flutist, over whose head I waved my signals to Nancy, smiled. The concertmaster, finally becoming aware that there was more in progress than the performance of the score, began to add his broad smiles. It was a merry concert. Even the Renaissance compositions, which do not ordinarily call for much temperamental effervescence, took on a bit of gaiety. The Sisters, enjoying the telling of the story, remembered it, and carried the memory onto the stage at Orchestra Hall. I mean, of course, the younger Sisters! The postgraduate novices!

There was a group of these in the first soprano section, standing high on my left side toward the rear of the stage. Every once in a while, when I gave them a signal, they would pull a "Nancy" on me. The audience couldn't detect the slight shrugging of shoulders or the sly raising of eyebrows. But I could and did.

Also, during rehearsals it was my custom, as it had been even in public performance with the Paulist Choristers, to blow over the top of the baton when a composition had been particularly well rendered. And some of these holy vixens, during the Orchestra Hall concert, would remind me by slight gestures to blow my approbation to them. It was a serious undertaking and most carefully and successfully completed. But there was a lot of fun connected with the rehearsals and performance.

The audience was under a spell. Even the symphony players seemed to be listening to the lovely sounds that they knew to originate in the chorus bank but that did not seem to be coming physically from any particular place. They were just happening.

The "Ave Maria" of Jacques Arcadelt, one of the best known simple polyphonic motets, was an adventure in listening. This familiar setting of the Archangel Gabriel's announcement to the Blessed Virgin that She would be Mother of the Saviour is generally given a stiff, slow and altogether unsuitable interpretation. I had asked the Sisters at rehearsal to think of the opening phrases as the rustle of the Archangel's wings as He descended from Heaven to bring His message to Mary. I candidly admit that I was probably reading into the notes the sort of impressionism which of course was not established as a genre of music until Debussy's day. But I have often suspected that with some of the polyphonists, especially Antonio Lotti of the late seventeenth century, there was a subconscious urge to delineate scenes with a few notes, as Manet and Monet, the painters, later did with a few strokes of the brush, a shadow here or a lighter tint there.

At any rate, the Chicago Sisters immediately sensed the spiritually poetic idea and, at both rehearsals and at the performance the faint sound of angelic wings revealed itself if not to the ears at least to the consciousness of the listeners. I am sure that I did not conduct the number in the ordinary sense of the word. Having indicated the tempo in advance, I let the Sisters take over. I became one of the audience. So too was each player in the orchestra who, the piece being unaccompanied, could advert without distraction to the disembodied effects taking mysterious form in the chorus banks. With the possible exception of the few moments required by the Paulist Choristers to create the extraordinarily unworldly atmosphere at Carnegie Hall, New York in 1918, while singing Gretchaninov's "Cherubic Hymn in D," I have never elsewhere observed an audience so rapt in the mystic elements of music as the large audience that fell under the spell of the Sisters' singing of the Arcadelt motet.

Apropos of this unique concert with the Sisters, it is interesting to note that the newspapers of Chicago practically ignored the undertaking. Although the publicity was carefully prepared and sent to the editors as directed by a well-known newspaper man who served on the publicity committee along with a representative of the Mayor's office, one of the most unusual concerts ever given in the long history of music was denied the public annoucements and the reviews which so notable event deserved and demanded. I was told later that if I wished to ascertain the reason for the boycott by the press, the information was at hand. But I declined to know too much about the matter. We were given the necessary permissions by ecclesiastical superiors; we had financed the concert without the sale of tickets; we gave a program of the worthiest types of sacred music; we received letters from many bishops commending the undertaking; and finally, we received an Apostolic Blessing from His Holiness Pope Pius XII, with a letter which rejoiced the Sisters.

But the Chicago newspapers gave hardly a courteous nod. A fortnight after the concert, a flippant article in a weekly magazine referred to the concert in quite a lengthy article as a program given by "Finn's Jennies." The Sisters were shocked and saddened by the lampoon. We had set out to deal a blow to paganism in music and to unauthentic interpretations of polyphony, and I dare say that the devotees of both softpedaled the enterprise.

Upon the death of President Franklin D. Roosevelt, the Sisters sang two memorial services, one for the Blue Network with a small orchestra, and the other for the National Broadcasting Company on the Catholic Hour with the orchestra oᶜ the Chicago Civic Opera Company.

The following autumn found me stationed again in New York. I had departed from the great metropolis in October, 1940, leaving the destiny of the Paulist Choristers in other hands. Thirty-six years devoted to turning small wriggling boys into agencies of artistic communication were an abundant enough, especially when the financial and general circumstances of continuing the grind indicated that it was time to toss my baton to another. Just what the musical future of the Paulist Choristers will be, I have no right to conjecture. More than one choral unit bears the name and uses the publicity of the original chorus. Perhaps there will be other similar units. In New York, the talented and hardworking young Father Foley, with his associate Mr. Herbert Becker, is giving increasing evidence of understanding the history of the Paulist Choristers. His soprano-boys sing with a hauntingly lovely tone.

When I returned to New York in 1945, I arranged to lecture for the Sisters of that metropolitan center. It seems, as the day declines towards the west, that my activities will be mostly directed to the training of Sisters in the fundamentals of choral music. The Sisters constitute one of the most influential agencies for the dissemination of ideals and aesthetic, as well as spiritual, standards in the world. They are consecrated to sublime purpose. Once they sense that an instructor is sincerely and devotedly anxious to share information with them, they become his most eager and sensitive students.

I could not fancy a more advantageous position from which to watch the sun of one's life approach the final horizon than from the peaceful surroundings of a convent rehearsal room. Boy sopranos and sopranos in the Sisters' Choirs—what lovely intimations they can give of the blessedness of eternity, about which Brahms wrote so radiantly in his German Requiem! The Ground Bass sends its basic theme up to such soprano tone qualities with unmistakable authority. Sometimes, while rehearsing the Sisters, I have felt that perhaps my trip to Thessaly brought me farther up the slopes of Mount Parnassus than I suspected. If Orpheus and Euterpe were not the creations of mythology, I could write with fluency about the enchanting musical phrases which they directed into the assembly hall where the Sisters practiced. Down the slopes from Mount Olympus finally came the echo of the perfection of concerted singing which I had determined to hear. Maybe not precisely perfection, but as near perfection as my natural resources would permit me to evoke. The top of the mountain of the Muses is very high up. The ascent is sheer. There are not many trees or roots or shrubs to cling to when one is fairly near the peak. One is almost sure to slip down some hundreds of feet!

In 1944 I published a brochure of *Ten Letters About Child-Voice Training** for the Sisters. This was an effort to provide them with a little handbook of basic principles and the sure means of developing choral virtuosity with the ordinary talent which most of their pupils display. As I wrote, equivalently, at the end of this brochure: some day soon I hope to soar above the clouds and listen to the harmonies of the choirs of cherubim and seraphim.

If I made a lot of bad guesses about music, you, dear Sisters, will know that at any rate I tried very earnestly to guess correctly. Perhaps the celestial Choirmaster will set me right. So there!

* (Chicago: H. T. Fitzsimons.)

Chapter XXVII   *The Ground Bass Makes a Final Inspection of the Vocal Lines*

FIVE decades! Quite a spell of time. This reminds me of a review of a concert which the Choristers gave many years ago in Decatur, Illinois. The typesetter had mispelled a word. The reviewer was commenting upon the amount of patient work required to produce the choral effects which we had offered on the preceding evening. The reviewer termed me "An *indeafatiguable* worker." A Chicago wag among the pressmen later wrote that this was "some spell of work."

Well! the five decades of toil were worth the energy, the anxiety, and what one might reasonably call the final dissatisfaction involved. Probably even the extra vowels of the Decatur reviewer vindicated their use! First of all, there was the inspiring satisfaction of working to make a fine art contribute its best to the Liturgy of the Church. Then, too, there was the gratification accruing from habitual thinking about the more refined and perhaps mysterious phases of the fine art. The blunders, gropings, failures, handicaps and untoward circumstances of certain days and periods could not delete from my mind and heart the gladness that came with the toil. The loyalty of boys and men, of lay women and of Sisters over the fifty years softened what would often have been hard moments. The necessity of closing the choir school in New York was the greatest grief of my career in the musical arena. At the funeral of my hopes and plans on the grounds of the Castle, I felt as though the cosmic laws had gone awry; that the impossibility of financing the choir school was a bit of irony which I would never understand.

But during the ensuing years, I have come to understand, at least in part. If the good Lord was as much interested in the perpetuation of the school and the ideals of the choral art as I had once imagined Him to be, He would have provided me with an efficient manager, an impresario who would have kept the coffers well enough filled to carry on. As I wrote many pages back, I never wept with tears that fall from the eyes, but I admit quite candidly that I lost much of my earlier spontaniety. I had a task to keep on doing, and so I set myself to its fulfillment, doggedly but with a more prosaic approach than had marked the days of my optimism.

My relations with the professional musicians generally were cordial and pleasant. I knew many of the opera singers intimately, and many of the great conductors. They were uniformly kind and encouraging, although once in a while, I would come upon a near-great who liked to loose satires. I profited by much constructive criticism of my methods. After the first few years, there was a minimum of destructive criticism. The early press notices which rebuked me for shortcomings were invaluable in urging me to zealous study of every aspect of my specialty. My tactlessness with orchestral players in the beginning days as well as with some professional Fountain Pens, gradually taught me, by the influence of the difficulties such gaucherie created, at least some of the major principles of diplomacy.

Among the outstanding conductors who were among my students, I have pleasure in mentioning the names of William Ripley-Dorr of Long Beach, California, Mr. Norman McCulloch of New York, and Mr. James Welch who last season made his debut with an excellent choral group in New York, winning much commendation from the Fountain Pens. These men have been serious students. They think, they read, and they talk the art of choral conducting when among musicians. Their success is a necessary consequent to their uninterrupted application and industry. The books must never be closed and put up on the shelves if a conductor expects to mature in his art. The shortcomings of most conductors who have been standing in front of choral or orchestral units for years, attaining no true musical success, are probably due to their lack of postgraduate study. It is easy for the many to feel smugly satisfied if they have acquired a few tricks with the baton, but such smug satisfaction means that their highest achievement will not pass beyond drab mediocrity.

One who would be a master of any of the sciences or arts must be a lifelong student not only of the topics, phenomena and problems immediately relevant to his specialty, but of all subjects which may bear remotely upon this. Religion, history, philosophy, aesthetics, physiology, psychology, acoustics—all these and other fields of inquiry must attract a musician's daily interest. Otherwise he cannot be a master of his subject, either in theory or practice. An organist once told me that when he had finished his formal schooling under preceptors, he considered himself fully qualified for his life's work. The insufficiency of his knowledge and the year-by-year increasingly inferior craftsmanship attested his folly. His attempts to present great compositions were almost as much misrepresentations as a Beethoven's Ninth would be misrepresented by a concertina and a Sunday-school choir!

It was my good fortune to meet, know and observe in action some of the outstanding specialists in other fields—concert organists, concert pianists, singers, violinists, cellists, doctors, surgeons, lawyers, mathematicians, astronomers, playwrights, composers, masters of prose and verse, architects, financiers, merchants and industrial tycoons, and bona fide orators and preachers. They all shared one quality in common: assiduity and ardor in the pursuit of knowledge. They were zealots who never closed their books or minds. On the other hand, the host of unsuccessful practitioners of the sciences and arts which it has been my misfortune to encounter was content to wade in the shallow water of inert ignorance.

After these many years of activity and observation in my special field, I am convinced that what concerted music needs, with dire necessity, in both the choral and orchestral theaters, is highly trained postgraduate conductors.

There are not many genuine geniuses in any fields of endeavor. There are talented men and women. Some of these hide their talents (not through modesty or humility, but generally through laziness or self-deception) in the dark. Others develop them, bringing them out into the full light, and, glorifying God Who gave them their gifts, influence for better the lives—spiritual, cultural and physical—of all whom they serve.

In concerted music, many fundamental truths must be learned by the majority of modern conductors. The unrecognized facts of rhythm. The implications of fast and slow paces. The psychological influence of varying degrees of loudness and softness. The elements of tone quality which raise it above the estate of mere acoustical sounding. The effect of latent features upon the surface notes. Technical virtuosity has for a long time usurped the seemingly undistracted attention of men and women who, by study, could learn that superficial brilliance is not a substitute for the musicianship that reveals the validity of the Ground Bass over which these reminiscences have been written.

From top to bottom, the vocal and orchestral parts need realignment. The draftmanship of tonal figures is crooked, capricious, often grotesque. The communicability of each vocal and instrumental line is impeded by lack of understanding of its special traits. The truth of the Ground Bass must be as clear in the treble as in the bass and vice versa. The vitality of the resources hidden in the alto and tenor parts must not continue to be forgotten. Probably, if these latter were properly employed, the top and bottom parts would improve almost automatically, as it were, by a tonal transfusion.

As I have already written, there has been progress of a kind during the years which I spent physically on the podium and mentally on my expedition to Mount Parnassus. But choirs still sing badly. Orchestras, with large annual budgets, continue to try to disprove the contention of the

Ground Bass. Violin, reed, brass and vocal sirens scream on high; growling trombones, tubas and vocal basses make threatening noises below. The family of the synthetic orchestral inner parts and the alto-tenor lines of the chorus are as little children "who should be seen but not heard."

Many of the choirs of men in seminaries, colleges and monasteries concur to hinder progress. One of the most trying experiences is to listen to such choirs struggling with Gregorian chant. The torture of their high notes and the murkey meaninglessness of their low grunts! The Church through Her local hierarchies must ostracize from the directorship of such choirs, especially the seminarians' choirs, such leaders as fail to give unmistakable evidence of proper qualifications for directorship. Just because a man has a pleasing voice himself and can read the notation of the Gregorian chant is not sufficient reason to appoint him to give false notions to the seminarians, who presently will be the pastors of churches, and permit their organists and choirmasters to foist on the people the same false notions. Prelates are careful that such subjects as theology, Scripture, philosophy and notably canon law, are taught by thoroughly trained preceptors. But music—oh! that! How about the young man who sang the "Last Rose of Summer" at the entertainment on the patronal Feast Day? Won't he do? Splendid! That's taken care of! And it is taken care of! Music is given another fatal ride. In the "Last Rose of Summer," there was one flower left blooming. In many a seminary choir only weeds grow, and these even become frightened presently and wither away.

In this connection, it is required, to be fair to facts, to point out that some leaders in the seminaries and monasteries are approaching their tasks with understanding, and therefore are accomplishing good results. Father Zeyen at Milwaukee and Father Selner at Baltimore are blazing a trail which perhaps others will follow.

The influence of radio programs and cinema music on the public is generally bad. There are some excellent radio programs, certainly, notably those of the leading symphony orchestras. But the style of music purveyed is for the most part poor and wretchedly performed. The argument of the sponsors is that they are providing what the people in majority want. The sponsors aim to sell goods. The largest possible radio audience must be attracted. And so inane lyrics and unworthy music, interpreted by alleged singers and players, are listed regularly. The only feature more regularly worse than the music on the so-called popular shows, is the travesty of wit and humor offered by the raucous voices of burlesque comedians.

Perhaps the unsettled state of the world, the desire of the common people to escape from the cares and frustrations of the era and an eagerness to find refuge in silly things, predispose the race to applaud the parodies which are served up for their amusement. If the low level of popular entertainment, which is noted today, prevails over a long period of time, then the radio and cinema will justly be obliged to accept blame for debasing the cultural sensibilities of the people.

We are in a transient period. Composers are confused. The classical styles are judged to be worn out. The styles of harmony and orchestration which had long been accepted as agencies of real art are now condemned as outmoded. Cacophony has taken the honored place of consonance. Weird sounds emerge from instruments forced to play out beyond their musical properties. Probably some measure of good eventually will have accrued to the art of music from all the painful experiments which are now in progress. The history of the art shows that in other epochs there were moments when the more refined people suffered, the while a new form or an unfamilar use of harmony was being developed.

During my five decades with the sharps and flats, I have observed the exit of old forms and the advent of new. Rules of harmony which were rigorously enforced during my youth have long since been abandoned. Today, in the radio studios, some of the most musical of all the orchestral instruments are being slighted in favor of noisier and therefore less emotive instruments. The viola and cello, with the latencies of deep poetry ready to leap into hearing with the drawing of a bow, are regarded as superfluous instruments by the producers of many popular programs. The trumpet and saxophone (and ever-present clarinet) are the sine qua nons of many broadcasts. And, according to some well-informed and experienced production managers, involved music, such as the medieval polyphony and more modern contrapuntal types, are taboo. A sturdy melodic line which trumpets and shrill violins can delineate unmistakably, with opportunities for swing figures, every so many measures by the clarinet, is the sure-fire style of composition to broadcast.

A few good choruses sing regularly on the air waves. Fred Waring and Robert Shaw have done much to improve the choral standards of the radio. But, by and large, the radio's current criteria of acceptability could not descend much lower. They stroll along the nadir now. An atomic bomb may one day scatter these low ideals to the winds. Maybe Alfred Einstein, himself a violin player, will invent an agency by which to accomplish this.

With the average person a process of disillusioning is in effect as the years pass. Impressions that seemed valuable and trustworthy in one's youth often disclose their apocryphal nature in the mature years. As an average person, I experienced this gradual disenchantment. Many stinging realities taught me early not to be caught up in the spider's web of flimsy fancies. But once I had sensed the validity and urgent truth of the Ground Bass which has been persistently singing through these pages, I never let it go. It has been in the hearing of my mind and soul always. Through seeming successes and real failures, its mighty theme has continued to resound. I thank God and the many friends whose co-operation in my varied undertakings has made possible the occasional manifestation of the truth that : *Music* (after religion and racial prepossessions) *is the most powerful spiritual instrumentality by which human beings can be moved.*

INDEX

Abington, my first "road" concert, 44 ff, 72

A cappella
  needs variety in tone colors, 93 ff
  Paulist Choristers tire of it, 207 ff
  Tenebrae, 92 ff
  Washington, 80 ff
  Yale, 272
Acid test for validity of tonal principles, 294 ff
Acoustics
  create tonal impressions, 11
  "finder," 274
  influence on tone at St. Peter's, Rome, 115
  modify timbres, 11
Adams, Maude, serenade at Duluth, 170
Advertising, ill advised, 44
Albertine, Sister M., 311
Albuquerque: romance lures tenor, 214
Alla breve, causes trouble in New York, 131 ff
"Alla Trinita Beata," popular motet, 57
"All We Like Sheep," satire, 86 ff
Alto, adult male, at Washington, 79 ff
Alto line, 182 ff
  choir school, 232 ff
  chorus and orchestra, 38 ff
  contraltinos, 115
  development of technique during voice change, 137 ff
  falsetto, 181
  "purring," 292
  saxophone, 283
  viola, English horn, bassoon suggest countertenor, 250
Altos and sopranos, grandmothers' choir, 17 ff
Altos: Are there boy altos?, 38 ff
Alto-tenor axis, 49 ff
Alverno Music School, Milwaukee, 266
Ambrosian Rite, Milan, 118
Ambrosius, Robert, 247
Anderson, Horace, 181
Anderson, Mary, 170, 310, 314
Anerio, Sistine Choir, 158
Angelo, Abbot of Santa Maria de Rivaldis, 157

"Anxious, Miss," nickname for satirist, 86 ff
Apollo and Euterpe
  hear grandmothers' choir, 18
  move to Chicago, 84
  sing a dirge with the Ground Bass, 260
  sometimes kind, often unkind, xi
Apostolic Mission House, course at, 78
Approval of Europe helps American success, 162
Arabic, S.S., my first Atlantic crossing, 106 ff
Arcadelt, Jacques: "Ave Maria" by Chicago Sisters' Choir, 317
Archangelsky, 138
Archbishop of Toronto (1915), 185 ff
Archbishop Williams of Boston, instruction to organists, 5
Arensky, 138
Armitage, Miss Teresa, 89
Arpeggios, a few pizzicato, 135 ff
Art of the Choral Conductor, Birchard, 137
Artistry, requirements for, 321
Atempause, 65
Attire
  for concerts, 137
  my dress on stage, 90
Aunt Massie, 6
Aura
  emanation from latencies of music, 10 ff
  missing from average English choral efforts, 12
Auxentia, Sister M., prefect of Mission Church Choir, Boston, 44
"Ave Maria," love songs masquerading as, 60
"Ave Maris Stella," Grieg, 151
Axis, choral, 49 ff, 138

Bach
  calculations of, 4
  Passacaglia in C Minor, ix
Baer, Arthur "Bugs," satirizes New York, 222 ff
Baini, Abbé, Sistine Choir, 158